END THE BIGGEST

EDUCATIONAL AND INTELLECTUAL

BLUNDER IN HISTORY

A $100,000 Challenge to Our Top
Educational Leaders

Norman W. Edmund

Scientific Method Publishing Company
Fort Lauderdale, Florida

End the Biggest Educational and Intellectual Blunder in History

Published by:
Scientific Method Publishing Co.
407 NE 3rd Avenue
Fort Lauderdale, FL 33301

ISBN 0-9632866-6-8

Library of Congress Cataloging-in-Publication Data

Edmund, Norman W., 1916-
End the biggest educational and intellectual blunder in history: a $100,000 challenge to our top educational leaders / Norman W. Edmund.--1st ed.
p. cm.
Includes index.
ISBN 0-9632866-6-8
1. Thought and thinking. 2. Science--Methodology--Study and teaching. 3. Education--United States--Philosophy. 4. Educational leadership--United States. I. Title
LB1590.3.E34 2005
371.1'001--dc22
2005002601

1st edition 2005

10 9 8 7 6 5 4 3 2 1

Printed in the United States of America

Contents

Introduction

This Book Is Independently Published

This is being done for these important reasons:

- to speed its availability to you
- to provide recommendations and suggested solutions to current educational problems of timely importance
- to stop as soon as possible the waste of billions and billions of dollars a year in educational funds and other negative effects of *the* **BLUNDER**

It is difficult for a first-time author to get a book published. The time involved in the process of finding an agent and the agent finding a publisher and getting on the publisher's schedule is usually 1 to 2 years. After considering a long list of pros and cons, I decided that time and the public interest were so important that I would publish the book independently through the Scientific Method Publishing Co.

Fast publication is essential, especially since education in general is now under review after the 2004 presidential election. In addition, many educators at all levels are dissatisfied with the No Child Left Behind Act. This book contains solutions to its faults. Independent publication places a greater burden on me in terms of money and time because I will have to manage a broad marketing campaign. But *the* **BLUNDER** must be corrected as soon as possible for your good and that of society.

Editors and reviewers often will not review independently published books. I hope that exceptions will be made. This is warranted by the evidence-based claims in this book, my $100,000 challenge, 15 years of specialized research on the scientific method, and my 35 years of experience during my business career in abstracting basic principles in my product evaluation work. Above all, I point out to all editors and reviewers that your readers need to know about *the* **BLUNDER**. My exposé of *the* **BLUNDER** is so important that it also warrants articles in your news sections.

The Value of Science and Its Method

What science accomplished for society was most eloquently stated by Vannevar Bush, Dean of the MIT School of Engineering from 1932 to 1938. Bush was appointed by President Franklin Roosevelt to be the first director of the Office of Scientific Research and Development in 1941. In *Endless Horizons* (1946), Bush states:

> Advances in science when put to practical use mean more jobs, higher wages, shorter hours, more abundant crops, more leisure for recreation, for study, for learning how to live without the deadening drudgery which has been the burden of the common man for ages past. Advances in science will also bring higher standards of living, will lead to the prevention or cure of diseases, will promote conservation of our limited national resources, and will assure means of defense against aggression. But to achieve these objectives—to secure a high level of employment, to maintain a position of world leadership—the flow of new scientific knowledge must be both continuous and substantial.

The flow of new knowledge (and its benefits) comes from use of the scientific method. Among the many names given to the scientific method is:

The Idea That Most Changed the World for the Better

Acknowledgments

My main contribution to research on the scientific method and education has been abstracting the ideas of the thousands of others who went before us and did the original deep and creative thinking that has allowed the presentation of this summary. My thanks to all the authors whose ideas I have used. Some I quote directly in this book, but they represent only a fraction of those whose ideas I present.

As this book is about a public matter of "supreme importance" (Conant), I have extensively employed the fair use provision of the copyright law.

Professor Lastrucci and Professor Feibleman wrote the best 20th century books specifically on the scientific method. Both remarked that they owed a debt to so many authors it was not possible to acknowledge them all. I, too, share this sentiment.

Thus, this book is dedicated to all the authors who aided my research, with special thanks to Professor Kenneth B.M. Crooks, whose paper "Suggestions for Teaching the Scientific Method" was presented at the National Association of Biology Teachers annual meeting with the American Association for the Advancement of Science in December 1958 and published in *American Biology Teacher* in 1961. It was this paper that excited my interest in the scientific method.

Preface

Why Are Our Top Educational Leaders Blundering So Badly?

Surveys show that the public is very dissatisfied with education. The record indicates that insufficient progress has been made in solving the ills of education. While our teachers and bad schools are often blamed, my many years of specialized research show that it is our top educators who have blundered badly. We currently have a national program to hold teachers, schools, and students accountable. After you read in this book about all the disasters that have resulted from poor leadership at the top levels of education, I believe you will agree with me that fairness requires that we also hold our top educators accountable! Otherwise, the ills of education will not really improve.

When I claim without fear or favor that, in my opinion, our top public educators have **blundered** badly and have influenced others to do so, it is a serious matter. These people are intelligent and often dedicate their lives to education. So some unusual, strange, weird reason or carelessness must be responsible. I don't want to be labeled a crank, so I have done my homework well and will provide plenty of evidence.

This blunder I have termed

The Biggest Educational and Intellectual Blunder in History

The blunder, simply stated, arose from a false claim:

The scientific method does not exist

This does not sound very important until you understand that the scientific method is actually

The greatest quality control method ever recognized

I shall explain that this false claim caused immense harm in all areas of our lives. I will cover many of these, but this book is concerned mainly with education and with showing the origination of the blunder, the basic reasons it occurred, the harm to education, various suggestions for study, and, last but not least, two practical recommendations to end the blunder and improve education.

An outline of the blunder appears on the next page. Please review it for an extraordinary tale of woeful blundering. Then read on.

The Biggest Educational and Intellectual Blunder in History

The false claim of non-existence of the scientific method by the Harvard/Conant group and misguided followers (or whoever they are) is extremely significant because it started the biggest intellectual and educational blunder in history, which has resulted in many of the ills of education.

The Biggest	◆ Billions of people affected from 1946 to the present as the blunder spread across the world. ◆ In amount of money, trillions of dollars (or equivalent currency) have been wasted worldwide.
Educational	Because of its disastrous effects on education.
and intellectual	For these reasons: ◆ Intelligence is based more on mental activity than just memory of knowledge. ◆ The scientific method concerns the stages of mental activity leading to reliable knowledge.
Blunder	Because the preponderance of evidence shows ◆ The scientific method <u>is</u> the method of science and is responsible for the great advances in scientific knowledge. ◆ The method, while largely developed by scientists, is also the complete method of creative problem solving and decision making for all fields. ◆ It is the basic method and guide by which we originate, refine, extend, and apply knowledge; thus, it is the method of knowledge. ◆ Experience has shown that it is the best method ever recognized for obtaining reliable knowledge. Thus, it is the best quality control method for research and planning in the natural sciences, education, and all other domains.
In History	Never before has something so well established, important, and documented been claimed by such a prestigious person, group, and followers not to exist. Then this false concept was accepted by so many important people and for such a long time, with huge financial consequences.

Almost no one will claim today that education does not have many ills and big problems. In recent years hundreds of thousands of articles and thousands of books have been written about them. We have had the progressive education wars, the Dewey wars, and, in more recent years, the reading wars, the math wars, the science wars, the standards wars, the school choice-voucher wars, the testing wars, and accountability wars.

In addition to education's ills being frequently blamed on our teachers and bad schools, they are often being blamed on the "education establishment," but one professor defined it as "the five million 'professionals,' from classroom teachers to state education commissioners, who...control our public schools"—without any mention of those above this level.

Educational ills are also blamed on a wide variety of other things, including social and behavioral sciences, unions, bureaucracies, social and demographic changes, and those who cling to the status quo.

I claim—and support in this book with valid evidence—the real, basic, fundamental causes of most of our educational ills.

These educational ills are the fault of our top educators. It is they who have blundered badly.

Since everything revolves around the scientific method, let's take a few minutes and consider its essence.

Originally science was called natural philosophy. Around the middle of the 19th century, science and philosophy separated into different domains, and the way in which "scientists" (a word first used around 1841) conduct their pursuit of knowledge began to be called by a variety of names. Originally, the most popular name was "the experimental method." Gradually refined over the years, the method came to be known most commonly as The Scientific Method or Scientific Method.

The word science comes from the Latin word *scientia*, a form of *scire*, which means "to know." How do you know? Use the scientific method for reliable knowledge.

The many other names (or variations of them) for the scientific method are listed on the next page.

NAMES FOR THE SCIENTIFIC METHOD

Original names:

Experimental method	Method of men of science
Method of science	Heuristic method

and then most commonly called

The Scientific Method or Scientific Method

Over the centuries, numerous names have been used for what is basically The Scientific Method. It is not just for scientists, but a general creative problem-solving and decision-making method for all fields. These are just some of the names it, or a variation of it, has been called:

Method of discovery	Method of knowledge
Process of inquiry	Operation research
Pattern of scientific investigation	Method of inquiry
Scientific research	Way of knowing
Method of study	Reflective inquiry
General pattern of research	Process of search
Scientific mode of thought	Scientific investigation
Key processes of scientific method	Processes of science
Processes of discovery	Scientific procedure
Art of experimental research	Pattern of investigation
Complete method of explanation	Experimental inquiry
Procedures of scientific inquiry	Scholarly investigation
Patterns of thought	Method of reason
Genesis of scientific method	Art of investigation
Scientific research method	Scientific approach
Ways of a scientist	Method of invention
Technique of scientific method	Creative problem solving
Scientific method of inquiry	Tool of inquiry
The scientific pattern of thought	Research methodology
General approach for gathering information	Method of study
	Research method
The greatest idea of all time	Method of thought
Complete act of thought	Research process
Method of multiple hypotheses	Method of hypothesis
The method of development	Method of rational inquiry
Hypothetico-deductive method	Method of intelligence
The complete method of problem solving and decision making	Greatest discovery in science

For Better Education, End *the* BLUNDER

Until *the* **BLUNDER** is corrected, it is not possible to have the long-term basic continuous improvement in education that you and the public want.

Since education is our largest industry, it is amazing that, as I claim in this book, no one knows the big picture of education. We have no organization that devotes its attention to this objective. Certainly, it is not an easy task, but it can be done, even if there are controversies. In this book I try point out the need to see the big picture of education. This is essential for successful reforms.

Wow! Imagine claiming to have discovered or recognized the biggest educational and intellectual blunder in history and many of its disastrous consequences!

I'm a crank, a genius, lucky, or it was accidental (sometimes also called a "surprise"), like so many great scientific discoveries.

I analyzed myself and again claim that I'm not a crank, for I present in this book an evidenced-based logical story that does not ignore contrary claims. My wife, family, and associates will gladly testify that I'm not a genius. As a sideline, I invested in oil well drilling from 1956 to 1995, and in 40 years, I never got a really lucky break, just minor wells and a load of dry holes, not like those lucky guys on make-believe television soap operas. That leaves only an accident or surprise—and that's what it was. I started out to spend only a few months in 1989 to write a little booklet for students on the scientific method, and I was surprised at what I found!

But the real story that provoked the internal motivation that has kept me going all these years is the harmful effects *the* **BLUNDER** has had and continues to have on you, your children, grandchildren, schools, and society in general. The real story also includes the details of why I have been forced to write this book to acquaint you with *the* **BLUNDER** and seek your help in ending it.

In Chapter 1 you are asked to be curious and skeptical about your author. I provide my qualifications. I detail how I came to write this book and explain a little about my unsuccessful efforts to get many of our educators to study the misunderstandings about the scientific method.

While I have written the book mainly for the general public, I have also kept in mind our important intellectual community, for I feel that a large number of its members have been innocently misled by *the* **BLUNDER**.

Having made the startling claim of recognizing the greatest educational and intellectual blunder in history, and that the ills of education are mainly the fault of our top educators, it is my duty to substantiate these claims with details and evidence.

There is an old saying, "put up or shut up." In the spirit of this and to help ensure that this book is not ignored like my previous efforts, I make the $100,000 challenge described on the next page.

The **BLUNDER** is a fascinating story because of its importance, yet it is a tragic one because of its consequences to society. Read on!

My $100,000 Challenge

On the next page I explain the terms of my challenge. Here are the 17 organizations I have previously challenged. They are eligible to accept the challenge.

Harvard University
American Association for the Advancement of Science (AAAS)
U.S. Department of Education
National Academy of Sciences (NAS)
National Science Foundation (NSF)
National Science Teachers Association (NSTA)
Association for Supervision and Curriculum Development (ASCD)
U.S. Department of Labor
Educational Testing Service
Carnegie Corporation
History of Science Society
National Association for Research in Science Teaching (NARST)
Sigma Xi Scientific Honor Society
National Association of Scholars
American Psychological Society
American Psychological Association
Cognitive Science Society

Terms of My $100,000 Challenge to Our Top Educational Leaders

Acceptance

In this book and on the preceding page, I mention the 17 organizations to which I previously issued challenges that were not accepted. Any of these, or a combination of them, is eligible. If there is any dispute among those volunteering, I may select one or more willing ones to be official accepter of the challenge. In the event they do not accept by December 31, 2006, I may or may not consider offers of other organizations that volunteer.

One value of this challenge is that it provides an official study group. It is hard for any one individual or organization to take a position in favor of my claims for fear of offending those perpetuating *the* BLUNDER.

Study Panel of the Accepter

The official accepter is to appoint three individuals to form the study panel that shall devote full time to the project. *I have no say in who these individuals are.*

My Requirements of the Study Panel

- The members of the panel will swear or state to uphold the honor of science in their work.
- They will spend part of their time in my office, as my library and files, accumulated over 15 years, will greatly speed their work.

Possible Payment of $100,000 Challenge

If two or more members of the official panel state unconditionally, when publicly publishing their findings, that a big educational and intellectual blunder has not occurred about the scientific method, I will contribute to the official accepting organization or organizations one payment of $100,000 without argument or protest. In the event I lose, I may publish a scholarly rebuttal. I have used the term "big blunder" rather than "biggest in history" to make it easier to arrive at a determination that a blunder has occurred.

Expiration of Challenge

The challenge will expire on December 31, 2007. In the event of my death before that date, the challenge will be an obligation of the trust I set up. On the acceptance of the challenge, to ensure possible payment, $100,000 will be placed in trust. Any disputes about this challenge shall be settled by arbitration, with my liability limited to $100,000.

I recommend at this time that you either read or skim my publication *The Scientific Method Today*. From it you will get an idea of what the method is all about. It will benefit your personal life and career if you study this material. It appears in Appendix A. The topics covered in the booklet are

       The Basic Principles of the Scientific Method
       The 11 Stages of the SM-14 Formula and Famous Examples
       The Three Supporting Ingredients of the SM-14 Formula
       Everyday Problems and Decisions and Explanation of
       Methods and Method
       Helpful Information on Creativity
       Decision Making, Invention, and Scientific Management
       Guide and Worksheet for Applying SM-14

The Style of This Book

This book presents so many valuable ideas, insights, and basic principles that I felt it was necessary to use a style that would aid the reader in understanding and absorbing what was being presented. I hope that you will find this more helpful than continuous lines of type.

You May Want to Skip-Read

It may be unusual for an author to tell his readers to skip-read his work. This book has been written to cover a wide range of subjects and inform a wide range of people. If a page does not interest you, simply skip-read until you come to a more interesting page. My style of writing makes this easy to do.

Short Name

For my writing and for historical writing by others, the term The Biggest Educational and Intellectual Blunder in History is too long. So in this book I use the abbreviated version

the BLUNDER

What term the public and historians will give it remains to be seen.

Introduction to Part 1

Your Author and Problem Solving

This book is primarily about problem solving. I had the really big problem of how to write a book for you about the misunderstandings concerning the scientific method.

Do we have experts who know how an unusual book crusading to end the biggest educational and intellectual blunder in history should be written? I did not think so. Thus, I had to decide myself how to write the book and did it on my own. If I made it too short, I could not cover the whole story. If I made it too long, fewer people might buy it. *The* **BLUNDER** is so important that I had to make the book rather long. I hope that, rather than consider less important features, readers will focus on whether or not a big blunder has occurred and whether I have supplied enough evidence for the public to understand the problem.

Many will find it very difficult to believe that the biggest educational and intellectual blunder in history has been going on without people calling attention to it! Am I a kook? Am I making a mountain out of a mole hill? Before you read my book, you should know something about me, my research, and the history and importance of problem solving. This part is devoted to telling this story so you can evaluate more accurately the book that tells a story that has vitally affected your life.

Chapter 1

Be Curious, Be Skeptical about Your Author

In the Preface I made some unusual claims—so extraordinary that they should arouse your curiosity and your skepticism. Here I share with you the record of how I really dug into the scientific method and education. I discovered *the* **BLUNDER** and its many harmful effects. Now, with your help, we can end it for the benefit of you, your children, grandchildren, and society.

You certainly have a right to be skeptical about my statement that I know the main cause of the ills and problems of education. There have been hundreds of thousands of articles on the problems of education. In August 2004, Barnes and Noble listed 6,455 books on education reform. So, be skeptical, but keep an open mind.

My Life before the Scientific Method

This book is not intended to be an autobiography, so I will only cover a few details of my life that helped prepare me for the project of improving education. While I have only a partial college education because of a serious illness in 1939, you might recall that others with only a partial college education—Bill Gates of Microsoft, Edwin Land of Polaroid, Steve Jobs of Apple Computers, and many others—have accomplished great things. When I started my research in 1989, I was 73 years old, so I began my research into the scientific method with a lifetime of practical experience, an open mind, and the motivation to make the world a better place to live.

"What's in It for You?"

Shortly after I issued my first booklets, I received a telephone call from an individual who was disturbed by my challenge of existing teaching about the scientific method. He wanted to know why I was doing it and what was in it for me? About this time my attorney advised that I start a foundation and also obtain funds other than my own to support the project. I declined because I thought that I could sell enough booklets to finance the project. At that time I was naive and didn't realize how institutionalized and politicized the opposition to the scientific method had become.

Thus, from 1989 to the end of 2004 I spent more than $1,000,000 of my personal funds on the project. Assuming that my time is worth at least $130,000 per year, or $1,560,000, a total of more than $2,560,000 was spent on the research that went into this book. This should assure you that if my only objective was to make a profit, I would have given up long ago.

The Origin of My Interest in the Scientific Method

In 1942 I founded a mail order business selling lenses, which eventually became Edmund Scientific Company, and I remained its head until 1975. In those years, it was my habit to read, skip, and skim through (eventually) 200 magazines a month, looking for new products, progressive developments, and ideas, and for self-evaluation. I ran across Dr. Kenneth Crooks' article "Suggestions for Teaching the Scientific Method" in the March 1961 issue of *American Biology Teacher*. A flash of inspiration told me that I should write an easy-to-read, illustrated booklet based on his article for my customers. I started a file and an idea notebook but did nothing more. I goofed! I didn't fully realize the urgent need for this booklet.

By 1975, the Edmund Scientific plant had grown to a 68,000-square-foot building. I retired to Florida after turning what had become a family business over to my son to operate and expand. He changed the product mix over the years and the name to Edmund Optics Inc. in 1999.

I had good intentions to work on the booklet and other projects, but my passion for fishing and boating distracted me. In May 1989, at the age of 73, I decided to begin work on "The Scientific Method" booklet to have it ready to include a free copy with each order during Edmund Scientific's 50th anniversary year in 1992. I quickly discovered the subject to be far more important and complex than I had ever envisioned, and I adopted it as a personal retirement project. Our Fort Lauderdale home's dining room table and garage were soon overflowing with books, so my wife and I purchased a small office. I gave up boating and fishing and devoted my full attention to the project. I began my new career as an educational researcher.

Being an "Outsider" Has Been Helpful

Before starting my research in 1989, I had almost no knowledge of the scientific method other than what I had read in Dr. Crooks' article in 1961.

In the course of operating Edmund Scientific Company from 1942 to 1975, I realized I was fulfilling a vital public service, as well as making a profit, by making available for the first time a wide variety of inexpensive optical and scientific items to experimenters, research laboratories, and schools. So rather than participate in many organizations, I participated only in the local Tuberculosis Association and the local Boy Scouts Council. I made no friends in the science or education fields or in the associations that I had joined.

Thus, I started this project with no set ideas, biases, or friends or associates I might offend. Since I was retired and financially independent, I had no fear of losing my job, promotions, honors, etc. I had no professional reputation to lose. Therefore, I have been free to do a job with an open mind and unfettered by anyone or anything.

The Big Factor—Over 15 Years of Specialized, Valid Research of the Scientific Method

In this age of complexity, the path to more reliable knowledge is the application of the scientific method to a special problem. In order to be valid and more reliable, research should follow a formula such as SM-14. So, as I researched the scientific method, I also learned how to apply it to the problem of what the scientific method really consists of and its application and uses.

In effect, I was working on the science of science, for it is well established in the reliable literature that science is its method. However, as human activities are involved, the science of science falls in the inexact sciences and not in the exact or natural sciences. In the social or inexact sciences, problems can sometimes be harder to define properly or accurately and it is harder to reach reliable conclusions. Nevertheless, much can be done.

The Last 15 Years

I Devoted Full Time to This Project. I've lost time during working hours to do necessary errands (trips to the doctor, etc.), but I have a passion for the project and usually work at home in the evenings and many hours on weekends.

I Built a Specialized Library on the Scientific Method, Education, and Related Subjects. I visited more than 70 used book stores from Buffalo, New York, to Miami, Florida, and in Ohio and Louisiana. I perused numerous new book catalogs and visited many libraries. My library now consists of approximately 3,000 volumes. I have spent from 5 minutes to many hours on most of them, depending on their value to my project.

I Have Read or Skip Read Periodicals. I have subscribed to *Education Week*, the *Chronicle of Higher Education*, National Science Teachers Association magazines, *Science*, *Educational Leadership*, *Issues in Science and Technology*, *The Sciences*, *Skeptical Inquirer*, local newspapers, the *Wall Street Journal*, the Sunday *New York Times*, the *American School Board Journal*, *American Biology Teacher*, *Journal of Research in Science Teaching*, *Scientist*, *Science News*, *Scientific American*, *Phi Delta Kappan*, *Technology Review*, various foundation bulletins, and others, including various newsletters, etc. Thus, I have kept up with developments in education and science.

I Have Built up My Files. During the past 15 years, I have loaded about 16 four-drawer file cabinets with data and information that greatly facilitate my work.

I Have Not Ignored Opposing Views. I have not ignored claims contrary to my hypothesis that the scientific method exists. I have included in my files information concerning the various claims about the scientific method, both what I consider good and what I consider false. I have also been careful to analyze those that appear false in order to confirm or disprove my evaluations.

Intellectuals—Creativity—Accidental Discovery

As my skills in math, music, drawing, and public speaking are so limited, I appreciate all-around intellectuals, of whom America has many, and their great value to the country. Fortunately, I have been blessed with a better-than-average imagination, and I seem to be more creative than most people. Creative people are sometimes said to thrive on complexity. What the scientific method is and the mixed-up situation into which it has fallen are complex issues; it has been a real challenge to sort ideas, abstract principles, and concepts.

The ability to evaluate and abstract basic principles has been largely responsible for my having compiled "The Scientific Method Today." Note that I make no claims to the numerous concepts in it, as these were mostly the work of numerous famous and little-known people over the last four centuries.

Accidental discovery is consistently mentioned in the science literature. I started out just to write a little pamphlet based on Dr. Crooks' article, then accidentally discovered the misunderstandings and false claims about the scientific method. I finally concluded that this has resulted in the biggest educational and intellectual blunder in history.

My Attitude, Dilemma, Challenges, and "the Crass Confrontation"

On the mailing envelope for the first edition (1992) of Edmund's Idea and Research Report, I indicated that the scientific method was a skeleton in the school closet.

Instead of titling my booklets The Scientific Method, I used The General Pattern of the Scientific Method because I thought this would give those who object to the use of the term "scientific method" a way out by saying "yes, there is no rigid method, but there is a general pattern to the method of science." In addition, to help end the misunderstandings and disputes, in my large pamphlet I appointed myself as an outside referee and suggested six compromises.

I sent thousands of copies of my booklets to the leaders of the educational and scientific communities, but they were ignored. I eventually started to use simply "the scientific method," leaving out "the general pattern," as this is much easier and has been used historically.

In 1994, I published a revised edition of Edmund's Idea and Research Report on the General Pattern of the Scientific Method. My family thought that I was too critical in the first edition, so I dropped many pages and devoted most of the pages in the new edition to information about and the advantages of using the general pattern of the scientific method.

I also issued a friendly public challenge to eight important organizations to appoint panels to study my research report. When time had passed and the challenges were ignored, I realized that I would have to become a real crusader for the scientific method.

In an article entitled "New Ideas in Science" (*Journal of Scientific Exploration*, vol. 1, no. 2), Professor Thomas Gold (1920–2004) states:

> Once a herd has been established in a subject, it can only by broken by the most *crass* confrontation with opposing evidence. There is no gentle way that I have ever seen in the history of science where a herd once established has been broken up.

So I have been forced to go for "crass confrontation with opposing evidence" to try to improve education and end ***the* BLUNDER**.

Summary

I have been lucky to live to be 89, and in my second career acquired a crusading spirit for the scientific method that has inspired me to spend 15 years trying to get the scientific method properly understood. At first, the research was pure joy, but the period since 1992, when I began to try to get our top educators to study the matter, has been stressful. However, the only way our children's education is going to substantially improve, and the only way you and your children will enjoy all the benefits of the scientific method, is to end *the* **BLUNDER**. Be skeptical, but I assure you that there will be plenty of logical thinking and evidence to support my claims.

As a boy I was a freckle-faced redhead and not very handsome. In my old age, I am even less so. I always like to be able to visualize an author when reading a book, so, for your convenience (and not vanity), I include my picture here.

Chapter 2

A Brief History of Problem Solving and Its Importance Today

Some of our top leaders frequently talk about the basic "core curriculum," but they don't seem to know about the very basic of the basics: problem solving and decision making.

What did humans learn first? Was it reading? Writing? Arithmetic? No, it was problem solving and decision making that humans first had to learn. We know this from simple reasoning and research that points to the fact that humans had to learn how to survive first. In order to survive, one must be able to make crucial decisions, to experiment, to use trial and error, and to solve problems such as what to eat, where to sleep, etc.

Eventually, humans' problem-solving abilities helped them create tools and develop languages. Later, reading, writing, and arithmetic were developed. For millennia, people looked to the elders, medicine men, religious leaders, scholars, wealthy individuals, political leaders, philosophers, etc. for knowledge, but this reliance did not consistently yield reliable knowledge.

However, people also learned from trial and error, accidental discovery, practical experiences of craftsmen and others, and the thinking and experimenting of various people, thus building and accumulating what eventually became a body of knowledge. But real progress was slow because a method for producing reliable knowledge was not recognized, developed, and communicated.

In *A Guide to the History of Science* (1952), George Sarton describes the reason why progress was so slow:

> The discovery of the sexuality of higher plants by Camerarius in 1694 could have been made two thousand years earlier, if the experimental method [the scientific method] had been applied to it. It was retarded

9

by non-experimental thinking and by prejudices, and after its publication it was rejected and its general acceptance was delayed for half a century because of the same prejudices. Similar remarks could be offered with regard to almost every fundamental discovery of modern science down to the theory of evolution (1859). Each discovery was delayed by a kind of intellectual inertia, and when it was finally made, its acceptance was delayed by the same inertia, the refusal to experiment (or even to observe) and to abide by the experimental results.

Some authors trace the "beginning of the scientific method" back to the ancient artisans, Arabs, Greeks, Spaniards, and others. But in our western culture, Galileo (1564–1642) is generally credited with being the father of the method.

Just as it took a long time to recognize that there was a method of obtaining more reliable knowledge, once recognized, the method was slow to be fully known and developed. But through debates, discussions, meetings, and publications (with both accurate and false information), humans gradually added much information about the method to our existing body of knowledge. Considering man's long history of development, isn't it amazing that the basic method of originating, refining, extending, and applying knowledge was not really recognized until the 16th century? The Renaissance is described as a period marked by great strides in knowledge and progress, much of which occurred because of the recognition and application of the scientific method.

This brief history is important to those interested in education. One frequently hears people clamoring for "back to basics," but failing to include the very basic of basics—problem solving and decision making and the associated thinking skills.

I can't stress enough that, in addition to the many names for the scientific method, the scientific method is also the complete method of creative problem solving and decision making. Think about it. What do you do most of the day? Don't you solve problems and make decisions? While most of the daily problems and decisions you face are relatively simple ones (what to wear, what to eat, how to take care of your family), some are more complex, and at times there may be highly complex problems or decisions that you must resolve. Since the scientific method is the complete method of creative problem solving and decision making, you should make every effort to learn the correct method in order to help solve the problems and make decisions life presents to you, your family, and your associates.

In school we are taught "reading, writing, and arithmetic," among other subjects, to provide us with a foundation of knowledge. We also gain knowledge from practical, everyday activities that help prepare us for a life of solving problems and making decisions. In both school and daily life, we learn to some extent how to think, to reason, and to imagine, which also helps our problem-solving and decision-making skills. However, since we must be able to solve complex problems and make good decisions in order to survive (and to be successful), do you think you were adequately taught these skills? Were you taught the full formula for the basic stages of the complete method of creative problem solving and decision making? The method by which we originate, refine, extend, and apply knowledge? Were you adequately taught the scientific method?

More important than what you were taught in the past is the present. Are we currently adequately teaching this valuable method for problem solving and decision making? The answer is no, and in the reason for this lies the biggest blunder in the history of education.

In recent years Nobel Laureate Herbert Simon (1916–2000), often called the Father of Artificial Intelligence (AI), wrote some excellent books on problem solving and decision making. The following is from *Research Briefings* (1986) published by the National Academy of Sciences.

> The work of managers, of scientists, of engineers, of lawyers—the work that steers the course of society and its economic and governmental organizations—is largely work of making decisions and solving problems. It is work of choosing issues that require attention, setting goals, finding or designating suitable courses of action, and evaluating and choosing among alternative actions. The first three of these activities—fixing agendas, setting goals, and designing actions—are usually called problem solving; the last, evaluating and choosing, is usually called decision making. Nothing is more important for the well-being of society than that this work be performed effectively, that we address successfully the many problems requiring attention at the national level (the budget

and trade deficits, AIDS, national security, the mitigation of earthquake damage), at the level of business organizations (product improvement, efficiency of production, choice of investments), and at the level of our individual lives (choosing a career or a school, buying a house).

Professor Simon gives this condensed formula for the activities of the stages of problem solving and decision making:

- Choosing issues that require attention
- Setting goals
- Finding or designating suitable courses of action
- Evaluating

The recognition that these are stages, phases, etc. of problem solving is of great importance to understanding the blunder that has occurred and, unfortunately, continues today.

Problem Solving Leads to Knowledge

To further impress you with the value and need for problem solving, I would like to explain its close relationship to knowledge.

Curiosity leads to the discovery of problems. Problem solution and challenge of solution leads to knowledge—reliable to various degrees.

What Is Knowledge?

Philosophers and others have been debating a definition of knowledge for ages. My humble attempt here is only for a practical explanation that shows the relationship of knowledge to the source of reliable knowledge—the scientific method.

In my research, I accumulated hundreds of definitions of the scientific method but only very few definitions of knowledge. For comparison, I checked seven dictionary definitions of knowledge. They refer mostly to:

facts, information, body of facts, principles accumulated by mankind, general truths, enlightenment, wisdom, and others.

There were no references to reliable knowledge being a product of the scientific method.

How Important Is Knowledge?

◆ Knowledge is said to be our greatest industry.

◆ Our schools, colleges, and industries spend $1 trillion *a year* on education and training.

◆ Business and industry leaders talk proudly about their companies' knowledge capital, intellectual capital, and human capital.

◆ Estimated number of years it took for knowledge to double since 1750:

1750–1900	150 years
1900–1950	50 years
1950–1960	10 years
1960–1992	5 years

Projection: Knowledge will double every 73 days by the year 2020.

These estimates and the projection were reported by a presenter at the June 1992 Conference Teach America: Teacher Preparation for the New American School. The accuracy of this projection remains to be seen. How much will be just data, and how much will be reliable knowledge?

◆ There is little doubt about it—knowledge and the knowledge of knowledge are of ever-increasing importance.

The dictionary definitions of knowledge don't really give us an adequate picture of knowledge, so I searched my files and offer these descriptions.

From *Process Education* (1972) by Henry P. Cole:

> Many have assumed that knowledge is something other than process. But knowledge is in no way static. It is a collection of ever-changing and expanding information about the meaning individuals and societies have constructed from their singular and collective experiences. It always has ill-defined boundaries, no limits on its extension, and exists only in a continual state of flux.

From *The Meaning of It All* (1998) by Richard Feynman:

If we were not able or did not desire to look in any new direction, if we did not have a doubt or recognize ignorance, we
would not get any new ideas. There would be nothing worth
checking, because we would know what is true. So what we
call scientific knowledge today is a body of statements of
varying degrees of certainty. Some of them are most unsure;
some of them are nearly sure; but none is absolutely certain.
Scientists are used to this.

From "On Scientific Method" by D.R. Newth in *Science and Its
Context* (1964), edited by John Brierley:

Science is the process by which men create knowledge in
which they can place a high, and often measurable, degree of
confidence

Summary

As Nobel Laureate Professor Simon stated:

Nothing is more important for the welfare of society than
that the work of problem solving and decision making be
performed effectively.

The scientific method is also the complete method of creative problem solving and decision making and thus helps you perform effectively.

Way back in 1905, in his lecture "Scientific Method as Applied to
History," published in *Lectures on the Method of Science* (1906), the
Very Reverend T.B. Strong stated:

All science, we may say, consists in strengthening, solidify-
ing, and rendering conscious and coherent the ordinary
processes of knowledge. The scientific man makes no claim
to an absolutely separate method of acquiring information,
as if he had some exceptional gift of inspiration.

Because our body of knowledge is increasing so quickly, we must use
the scientific method extensively to recognize and improve reliability
in all fields. It is not possible to memorize even a fraction of this
knowledge or often even to find what we need, so we must teach the
method of knowledge—the scientific method.

Introduction to Part 2

The Story of *the* BLUNDER

Investigating the past is usually not easy to do. However, in Part 2 I give my opinion of how *the* **BLUNDER** started. Historians will have to check the accuracy of my work. I believe that they will find it correct.

It is easy after years of investigation to give you the correct picture of the scientific method. But remember that in past years no one was clearly presenting this easy to understand definition. Thus, the ambiguity of the word method led directly to *the* **BLUNDER**.

"Method" as used in the scientific method refers to the stages of mental activity used in originating, refining, extending, and applying knowledge. Thus, the scientific method will not solve problems. It is simply a guide.

However, we then have the creative, non-logical, logical, and technical methods—better called techniques. Although they are often called scientific methods, many of these—not just one—are actually applied at the various stages to help solve problems. I often call these action methods or techniques to distinguish them from the mental stages.

This distinction will help you understand how the confusion about the meaning of the word method resulted in *the* **BLUNDER**.

The importance of *the* **BLUNDER** springs from the scientific method being the greatest quality control method ever recognized and developed, so I explain it in Chapter 5.

Chapter 3

The BLUNDER Begins

This is the story of the beginning of one of the strangest, weirdest, most unbelievable, most overlooked, and most harmful blunders ever to occur in the history of education, knowledge, and science. It began in the middle of the 20th century and is still seriously affecting you, education, and all other fields at the beginning of the 21st century.

Before I describe in detail the origin of *the* **BLUNDER**, I would like to give a few reasons why it is important to discuss its background:

♦ We should learn from our mistakes. Since a huge, expensive, and harmful blunder is involved, the reasons for it should be widely known for corrective, preventative, and historical purposes.

♦ The Harvard/Conant group and misguided followers (or whoever they are) are still, even in the year 2004, perpetuating erroneous claims that the scientific method doesn't exist and that there is no one method, and they are repeating other erroneous claims about it. They are preventing the teaching of the scientific method in most educational reform programs. They need to be educated about the origin of *the* **BLUNDER** and why my research reveals that these claims are erroneous.

♦ Revealing the origination and perpetuation of *the* **BLUNDER** should be a warning to prestigious organizations and great men and women, including Nobel Laureates, to be careful about making false claims, especially in areas outside their fields of expertise.

♦ The general public has never been informed to any extent about what has been done to prevent the adequate teaching of the scientific method. *Most are surprised to learn there is a problem.*

♦ As Albert Einstein said (and as is inscribed on his statue at the National Academy of Sciences), "One must not conceal any part of what one has recognized to be true." So I must convey what I have recognized and discovered.

The First Half of the 20th Century

Looking back to the first half of the 20th century, before *the* **BLUNDER**, John Dewey, a professor at Columbia University and one of America's greatest educator-philosophers, wrote *How We Think* in 1910. Dewey and others in the Progressive Education Movement approved of teaching the scientific method in all our schools. Keep in mind that schools in the first half of the century taught the so-called "basics" of reading, writing, and arithmetic and were not as well attended or as developed as they are today.

Karl Pearson wrote his famous book *The Grammar of Science* in 1892, and it gained a considerable audience in the United States in the first part of the 20th century. Pearson was a great believer in the scientific method, and, according to Ernest Nagel, "argued vigorously that the scope of scientific method is not limited to the natural sciences."

Dr. Harold G. Moulton, President of the Brookings Institution, made the following claim in the March 1936 issue of *Science* in an article titled "Scientific Method in the Investigation of Economic Problems."

> I begin by saying that there is no such thing as *the* scientific method. There are as many different scientific methods as there are different fields of knowledge; in fact, various types of methods may be used within any given field or even in a single investigation. Being scientific is a matter of *spirit* and not of *method*. This spirit is not the exclusive possession of the scholars in any particular realm of inquiry.

This, of course, is a partially erroneous statement based on the ambiguity of the word "method." It is true that there is no one action method, but there is *the* scientific method or guide, as I explain throughout this book. By spirit, Moulton probably means the Procedural Principles and Theories (Ingredient 13; see *The Scientific Method Today* in the Appendix). Moulton was not quoted to any extent. I do not know whether he influenced Dr. Conant.

Dr. Vannevar Bush is famous for marshaling civilian science to support the military effort in World War II. With Conant's assistance, he was instrumental in the establishment of the National Science Foundation. At the beginning of this book I quote Vannevar Bush on the importance of science. In a speech at the George Washington Education Foundation Forum, May 16, 1946, he made these remarks:

> I am decidedly not one of those who speak of the scientific method as a firm and clearly defined concept and who regard it as a mystical panacea immediately applicable to any trouble and immediately productive of complete cure. Of course,

there is a system of approach to specific problems which we know as the scientific method—an orderly sequence of hypothesis and analysis which, by a series of approximations and tests, culminates in a practicable theory of operation. But to give this name of "scientific method" to mental operations involving no more than the use of common sense, or indeed to operations which are no more than rigorous logical thinking, is a mistake. I therefore wish not to be taken as joining those who facilely argue that all we need to do to settle any difficulty is apply the scientific method to it.

He Was Right—The scientific method is not a mystical panacea immediately applicable to any trouble and immediately productive of complete cure. In the first half of the 20th century, exaggerated claims were made for the scientific method. In addition, there were no really clear and well-researched formulas for the stages of the scientific method, such as SM-14. However, Bush admits its existence.

He Was Wrong—That the scientific method is not a general method. The research literature on the scientific method from 1863 to the present indicates that it is essentially a general problem-solving method for all domains.

Was Bush, in 1946, echoing Professor Bridgman of Harvard? Bush said, *"I am decidedly not one of those who speak* of the scientific method as a firm and clearly defined concept" (emphasis mine). Nobel Laureate Percy Bridgman of Harvard stated (in 1945): *"I am not one of those who hold* that there is a scientific method as such" (emphasis mine).

Professor Harold Rugg of Columbia University devoted 86 pages of his book *Foundations of American Education* (1947) to "Fifty Years of Scientific Method in Education: What Have We Learned?" This was from the favorable standpoint of using the scientific method in the design of educational programs and educational research.

Clouds on the Horizon

Dr. James B. Conant was President of Harvard University from 1933 to 1953. In his books written between 1947 and 1966, he expressed some extraordinary ideas about the non-existence of the scientific method. In order to understand the far-reaching influence of Dr. Conant, both at that time and today, consider first just a few of his accomplishments:

◆ President of Harvard University from 1933 to 1953 and often called one of the great teachers and scientists of our age

◆ A central figure in organizing the United States for World War II, including the development of the atomic bomb

◆ A founder and first chairman of the board of the National Science Foundation and a founder of the Education Commission of States

◆ A leader in the post-war era in the study of education, "Inspector General of the nation's schools"

◆ Served one term as President of the American Association for the Advancement of Science; twice declined nomination for the presidency of the National Academy of Sciences

◆ Winner of numerous awards and honors and a member of influential organizations such as the Royal Society of London

James Hershberg, in his biography of Dr. Conant (*James B. Conant*, 1993), says:

> By mid-century, at the age of fifty-seven, Conant outwardly seemed to be at the crest of national esteem and prominence, repeatedly in the headlines for his pronouncements on education, science, and national security. Despite his persistent disclaimers of any interest in electoral politics, he heard himself repeatedly touted as a dark horse presidential candidate, and in late 1951 a Gallup poll rated him fifth behind Eisenhower for the GOP nomination. He was showered by honorary degrees, awards, and attention, from the Presidential Medal for Merit with Oak Leaf Clusters for his atomic-bomb work, to the Freedom House award for his championing of the defense of Europe; in September 1952 *Newsweek* published a cover story on "U.S. Education's No. 1 Man."

The cover copy of Dr. Conant's 1947 book *On Understanding Science* states that he "is one of the country's most eminent scientists as well as one of its most notable practitioners of education." In the book, Dr. Conant expressed his concern about "... how we can in our colleges give a better understanding of science to those of our graduates who are to be lawyers, writers, teachers, politicians, public servants and businessmen." He had a solution to the problem:

Let me now be specific as to my proposal for the reform of the science education of the layman. What I propose is the establishment of one or more courses at the college level on the Tactics and Strategy of Science. The objective would be to give a greater degree of understanding of science by the close study of a relatively few historical examples of the development of science. . .I also draw confidence from the knowledge of how the case method in law schools and a somewhat similar method in the Harvard Business School have demonstrated the value of this type of pedagogic device.

My Challenge of Conant's Views

Time and experience have shown that the historical case study method of teaching science is not practical as the primary way of teaching students or laymen. It does, however, have a minor value when used as a supplement.

Some schools, including Harvard, tried Dr. Conant's idea. Dr. Conant, with the aid of Thomas Kuhn, Fletcher Watson, I.B. Cohen, and Leonard Nash, taught his case history course for a few years. However, the course was dropped because the approach was a failure at Harvard and elsewhere as the principal way to teach science. That it is not used as the principal way today can be confirmed by examining various college and high school science textbooks.

Dr. Conant claimed that the scientific method didn't exist to support his concept of teaching science by Harvard's case history method. This method was not successful, and in spite of this:

His associates and followers have perpetuated the false concept that the scientific method doesn't exist.

For example, to support his concept, Dr. Conant made this claim in *On Understanding Science* (1947):

Only an occasional brave man will be found nowadays to claim that the so-called scientific method is applicable to the solution of almost all the problems of daily life in the modern world. Yet some proponents of this doctrine have at times gone even further and maintained that only by a widespread application of the scientific method to the problems of society at every level can we hope for peace and sanity.

My Challenge of Conant's Views

Authors such as Thomas Huxley, John Dewey, Albert Einstein, and Herbert Simon, say that the scientific method is a general method and thus is applicable to almost all problems in any field.

In subsequent books, Dr. Conant continued to attack the existence of the scientific method. In *Education in a Divided World* (1948), he made this statement:

> At the risk of being redundant, I shall pursue my analysis of the so-called scientific method still further. There is no doubt about it, this phrase is still in favor; almost every program of general education includes it. Indeed, in the last twenty-five years, indoctrination in the scientific method has been put forward with more and more insistence as one of the primary aims of modern education.

My Challenge of Conant's Views

In the statements quoted above, Dr. Conant admitted that the primary aim of almost every program of general education included teaching the scientific method and had done so for the last 25 years. Yet without research and submitting valid evidence, he took an extraordinary position.

In *Science and Common Sense* (1951), Dr. Conant said:

> To be sure, it is relatively easy to deride any definition of scientific activity as being oversimplified, and it is relatively hard to find a better substitute. But on one point I believe almost all modern historians of the natural sciences would agree and be in opposition to Karl Pearson. [1] there is no such thing as *the* scientific method. If there were, surely an examination of the history of physics, chemistry, and biology would reveal it. For as I have already pointed out, few would deny that it is the progress in physics, chemistry, and experimental biology which gives everyone confidence in the procedures of the scientist. [2] yet, a careful examination of these subjects fails to reveal any *one* method by means of which the masters in these fields broke new ground.

My Challenge of Conant's Views

[1] The foremost reason why the scientific method must exist is that thousands of books and papers—written by researchers and famous

figures in all fields—have claimed or cited the existence of "the scientific method." [2] Dr. Conant's interpretation of the word "method" to mean that one method could discover and solve all problems is erroneous. In my research, I found only one claim of no one method prior to his (that of Dr. Moulton), but many since Conant made his false claims.

The correct interpretation of "method" as used in "the scientific method" is that it is a guide consisting of a number of stages, ingredients, phases, thought processes, etc. Under these, in a flexible manner, one applies thinking skills to use creative, non-logical, logical, and technical methods or techniques to actually accomplish results.

In *Modern Science and Modern Man* (1952), Dr. Conant made this strange claim:

> The usual descriptions of "the scientific method" are descriptions actually of the very limited procedure by which a person can improve a particular practical art.

My Challenge of Conant's Views

For centuries our greatest scientist, philosophers, and others had been offering descriptions and formulas for the scientific method, based on their extensive studies. Then Dr. Conant made one of the strangest false claims imaginable! The statement above is another example of Dr. Conant not really researching the scientific method and of his carelessness in going to extremes in advancing his idea of teaching science via the case history method.

A Knock-Out Blow in 1952

In 1952, Dr. Conant, the most prestigious educator and scientist of that era, made this inhibiting statement in *Modern Science and Modern Man*, sending a clear message to all those who might have wanted to research or challenge his claims:

> It would be my thesis that those historians of science, and I might add philosophers as well, who emphasize that there is no such thing as "the scientific method" are doing a public service.

The record shows that a great many people accepted his thesis rather challenge such a prestigious man.

My Challenge of Conant's Views

Dr. Conant knew very well that a basic principle of science is free and open discussion. Even so, with this statement, because of his prestige, he not only stopped most historians and philosophers of science from researching his claims and the scientific method, but he also inferred that *anyone* doing so is performing a public *disservice* by promoting the method.

It is almost unbelievable that such a great and well-regarded scientist would make this kind of statement, especially in view of the basic principle that extraordinary claims require extraordinary evidence—evidence Dr. Conant certainly did not provide.

In *On Understanding Science*, Dr. Conant described the work and role of a scientist:

> The traditions he inherits, his instruments, the high degree of specialization, the crowd of witnesses that surrounds him, so to speak (if he publishes his results)—these all exert pressures that make impartiality on matters of his science almost automatic. Let him deviate from the rigorous role of impartial experimenter or observer at his peril; he knows all too well what a fool So-and-so made of himself by blindly sticking to a set of observations or a theory now clearly recognized to be in error.

On another occasion, Dr. Conant stated that "without free inquiry, universities cannot flourish" (Hershberg, 1993). These statements about the researcher and his work clearly show that Dr. Conant understood the importance of free inquiry and of trying to remain impartial despite outside pressures. Nevertheless, in his position as top educator and scientist, he still exerted that pressure on others not to perform "free inquiry" into his false claims about the scientific method.

Despite the failure of his case history approach to teaching science and Dr. Easley's essay challenging his position, Dr. Conant was still denying the existence of the scientific method as late as 1966 in his Eddington Memorial Lecture at Princeton University, published in 1967 as *Scientific Principles and Moral Conduct*. I have considered the reasons why such a highly intelligent and well-regarded man would insist on maintaining such an extreme position without adequately researching it. Dr. Conant did have a reputation for being opinionated. Hershberg reports in *James B. Conant* (1993):

In October 1950, facing a welter of science-policy dilemmas, Truman deputized the Wall Street investment William T. Golden to make sense of the muddle and report back. Golden, a close associate of Lewis Strauss, for the next few months talked to scores of leading figures in science, academia, government, and the armed forces. Not surprisingly, Conant's name soon emerged as a candidate for a top post— Carroll Wilson suggested him for presidential science adviser, Stewart and Rabi considered him a logical NSF chairman—but Golden also heard reports that the old OSRD leadership had made some enemies. Several sources told him that Conant was *"too opinionated"* [emphasis mine] and "not sufficiently well-liked," and mentioned the revolt at the National Academy. Better Conant should remain an "elder statesman," Golden was told, than be put in a formal position where he would alienate key scientists.

There is another possible reason. Feinberg writes in an article entitled "Why Smart People Do Dumb Things" in *The Wall Street Journal* (December 21, 1992):

> Recklessness: There is something inside the super brain that keeps announcing "Now for my next trick. . ." spurred on by a feeling of omniscience, brilliant people can develop into risk junkies. "Smart guys get used to knowing more than anyone else," says Brendan Sexton, vice president, the Rockefeller Group. "It's all too short a step from knowing more than anybody else to thinking that you know everything." When things come too easily, the mind looks for bigger challenges. Boredom combined with brilliance make an explosive and self-destructive mixture.

In Defense of Conant

I found that, at Harvard, Dr. Conant did not have a supporting organization behind him fully familiar with or very much interested in the scientific method. So conditions at Harvard were favorable to his misunderstandings and erroneous concepts.

◆ Dr. Conant cited both Harvard Law School and Harvard Business School as the basis for his confidence in proposing teaching science by the case history method. Even though law involves investigations, problem definitions, disputes, solutions, and challenges of solutions, no formula for the complete method of creative problem solving is taught. The same situation exists in the Harvard Business School. Although there is extensive discussion of case problems, no formula for problem solving is taught. This indicates an amazing lack of knowledge of the scientific method and certainly contributed to misleading Dr. Conant.

◆ In 1945 Nobel Laureate Professor Percy Bridgman made his famous (but inaccurate) statement about the scientific method, and Dr. Conant used it in *On Understanding Science* to support his position.

◆ Professor George Sarton, head of Harvard's History of Science Department from 1921 to 1951, was famous in his field and wrote extensively about the history of science. However, he stressed subject matter and made only a very few references to the part method had played—an astonishing viewpoint, since science is its method.

◆ In 1945 the "Red Book"—"General Education in a Free Society," a report of the Harvard Committee (with an introduction by Dr. Conant)—was issued. It mentioned "scientific method of thought" but gave no formula. The committee later endorsed Dr. Conant's proposal to teach science courses based on case studies.

◆ In 1893, President Charles W. Eliot headed a committee of NEA "that argued that the primary task of secondary education should be to develop and discipline students' minds through the teaching of academic subject matter" (*In the Name of Excellence*, by Thomas Toch, 1991). It may be that the concept that one teaches a person to think by teaching subject matter became a tradition at Harvard. Only a few professors ever showed an interest in the scientific method with a formula. (My research shows that, in addition to subject matter, one must teach the scientific method and associated thinking skills to properly prepare students for their careers and personal lives.)

◆ In the first part of the 20th century, some people in the social sciences became overenthusiastic about the power of the scientific method and made exaggerated claims as to what it would accomplish in the social sciences. This concerned Dr. Conant.

The BLUNDER began, was perpetuated by various Harvard professors, falling in line, following the boss, and being "team players." Unfortunately, Dr. Conant's associates and friends did not follow the peer review procedure and challenge his claims to any extent.

Thus, another lesson to be learned from this blunder is that even the "team," associates, friends, and fellow practitioners of a prestigious man should not fail to follow the scientific method and challenge him for the sake of his reputation and society's well-being. Long ago, John Dewey called attention to this type of situation in *The Sources of a Science of Education* (1929):

> The existence of scientific method protects us also from a danger that attends the operations of men of unusual power; dangers of slavish imitation partisanship, and such jealous devotion to them and their work as to get in the way of further progress. Anybody can notice today that the effect of an original and powerful teacher is not all to the good. Those influenced by him often show a one-sided interest; they tend to form schools, and to become impervious to other problems and truths; they incline to swear by the words of their master and to go on repeating his thought after him, and often without the spirit and insight that originally made them significant. Observation also shows that these results happen oftenest [sic] in those subjects in which scientific method is least developed.

Although I am a critic of Dr. Conant's views of the scientific method, I am also an admirer of his technical knowledge, his contributions to World Wars I and II, and his improvements to Harvard.

For more information about James Conant, please read his autobiography, *My Several Lives* (1970), and James Hershberg's biography, *James B. Conant* (1993).

Name for the Group That May Have Originated and Perpetuated *the* BLUNDER

The BLUNDER did not, as I have explained, develop on its own. It was originated and perpetuated by people.

As *the* BLUNDER is a matter of "supreme importance" (Conant), I needed a name for the group that I thought originated and perpetuated it. The term "old boys network" is often used, but I felt that this was not definite enough. I finally settled on *the Harvard/Conant group and misguided followers (or whoever they are)*.

In Chapter 26, Contribution of Harvard to *the* BLUNDER, I explain in greater detail my justification for this name. Here I give only a brief explanation of this name.

Harvard—Conant was president of this great institution when he first made his false claims. He made use of the "bully pulpit" of Harvard.

Conant—Conant's great reputation as the most prestigious leader of the education and scientific communities made it possible for him to start *the* **BLUNDER**.

Group—No Harvard professors stepped forward and disputed Conant's claims until Easley in 1958. He was ignored. The record shows that some Harvard professors endorsed Conant's claim in their books. Conant's friends and associates did not challenge him.

Misguided followers—While the age of authority has passed, from a practical standpoint people have to depend on authoritative people such as the Conant group for guidance. This whole situation is so complex and the word "method" has so many meanings that it is no reflection on those I term "misguided" that the misunderstandings have occurred. This group also includes those who might have contrary views but, because of the power of those perpetuating *the* **BLUNDER**, have to keep quiet and follow along.

Or whoever they are—As a user of the scientific method, I must keep an open mind. So little has been explored about *the* **BLUNDER** that I have to acknowledge that there may be omissions in my research and that my opinions and/or my assumptions may be incorrect.

History will settle the matter. I forecast that in the future historians will thoroughly investigate *the* **BLUNDER**, with thousands of books being written. They will probably have the final say on who was responsible for *the* **BLUNDER** and its perpetuation.

Summary of Dr. Conant's Key Statements

In *On Understanding Science* (1947):
> There is no such thing as "the scientific method."

In *Modern Science and Modern Man* (1952):
> "so-called scientific method"

In *Science and Common Sense* (1951):
> "There is no *the* scientific method."

Chapter 4

Challenges to Conant's Concept

Even though Dr. Conant's claim that the scientific method does not exist was contrary to the prevailing consensus and of supreme importance to education, very few people challenged him.

Why did so few people challenge Dr. Conant? Look what happened recently when other extraordinary claims required extraordinary investigation and evidence. In March 1989 the University of Utah held a press conference and announced that two chemists had discovered "cold fusion." Based on what was known about nuclear fusion, this was an extraordinary claim, and it came from relatively unknown scientists. The scientific community responded immediately with theoretical denials and big discussions, and, even better, numerous tests were launched. A few scientists claimed that they had duplicated "cold fusion," but most were not able to verify it. The media and scientific journals followed the story for many months, and there are still occasional articles.

Contrast this with Dr. Conant's story. He stated in 1947 in *On Understanding Science* that the question "Is there such a thing as a scientific method of wide applicability in the solution of human problems?" is "of supreme importance to the future of the free people." Unfortunately, there were very few who dared to challenge him on this matter of "supreme importance," even though his claim was contrary to centuries of development and use of the scientific method. In addition, as quoted in Chapter 3, Dr. Conant called attention to the fact that it was the modern objective of education to teach the scientific method.

I hunted but found surprisingly little rebuttal or criticism of Dr. Conant's views. Here, however, are two of them.

Rudolf Flesch (1911–1986) was not afraid to challenge top educational leaders in his books *Why Johnny Can't Read* (1955) and *Why Johnny Still Can't Read* (1981). In addition, he was not afraid to challenge Conant. In his famous book *The Art of Clear Thinking* (1951) he states:

> In other words, President Conant thinks there *isn't any* sci-
> entific method. That surely is extreme. Even if there is no
> clearly definable scientific method, there's a way in which
> scientists work, and it's certainly worth knowing about.
> Let's look at a careful description by Dr. W.I.B. Beveridge, a
> British biologist. . .

He goes on to quote Dr. Beveridge's common sequence in an investigation of a medical or biological problem, which is quite similar to the
general pattern of the scientific method.

Here I report on the one I found who made a real challenge to Conant's
false claims.

As his doctoral thesis at Harvard University, Professor Jack Easley
(1922–1994) wrote a scholarly 30-page essay *Is the Teaching of
Scientific Method a Significant Educational Objective?* He challenged
Conant's views and contrasted Dewey's, Schwab's, Conant's, and his
own views on scientific method. Easley's doctoral advisor, Professor
Israel Scheffler, included Easley's essay in *Philosophy and Education:
Modern Readings* (1958). The article was subsequently published in
Philosophical Essays on Teaching (1969, edited by Bandman and
Guttchen). Dr. Easley's paper is the only one I have found that exten-
sively challenged Conant's statements about the scientific method.
Easley courageously showed the defects of a great and influential
man's claims. The essay is a well-crafted challenge to Conant's
claims. It should have provoked extensive citing and debate about
teaching the scientific method. But he was ignored.

Many of the tremendous disasters that have occurred in education and
harms in other domains can be traced to not listening to and investigating Easley's report.

The following material is taken from a section of Easley's doctoral
thesis.

> The other point pertaining to the analysis of scientific method
> is Conant's claim that there is no one method by means of
> which the masters in the different sciences broke new ground.
> If this claim were acceptable, it would require revision of
> claims of teaching scientific method, and apparently it was
> made with the intent of calling a halt to such interests.
> However, there are two peculiarities of this claim which, at the
> very least, call for a postponement of judgment.

First, the claim does not follow from the reason that Conant gives for it. Conant argues that, "There is no such thing as *the* scientific method. If there were, surely an examination of the history of physics, chemistry and biology would reveal it. . .careful examination of these subjects fails to reveal any *one* method. . ." Taken as it stands, this is a claim that something does not exist because it has been searched for and not found. This is a *non sequitur* of a well known form. It is well known that claims to non-existence cannot be proven, since no search can be exhaustive and since every search is also selective in terms of the abstract idea of the thing searched for. Conant's argument would be like a claim by Tycho Brahe that the earth does not move based on the argument that if it did surely the evidence of astronomy would have shown it.

Thus, in summary, we find that Conant raises valid objections to a common misconception of scientific method but refuses to apply the term "scientific method" to his own formulation of principles of scientific inquiry, preferring, for whatever reason, to call them "tactics and strategy of science."

In Chapter 50, A Few of the People Who Should Have Been Listened to Since the Start of *the* **BLUNDER**, I review some of the work of other people who should have been listened to who spoke out after Conant's books were published. Thus, the failure of the intellectual community to properly challenge a great intellectual leader has permitted *the* **BLUNDER** to develop and continue into the 21st century.

Chapter 5

The Scientific Method Is Also the Greatest Quality Control Method of All Time

---

The self-correction features and completeness of the scientific method earn it the honor of being the best quality control method of all time. Over the centuries all other methods of obtaining or originating knowledge have been tried, and none has been found to be as reliable as the scientific method.

I asked you to be skeptical of me in Chapter 1, so I have to provide you with plenty to think about and plenty of evidence. Here is more evidence before we go on with the amazing story of the mystery of why so many people and prestigious, authoritative organizations are perpetuating *the* **BLUNDER** and ignoring my efforts to end it.

In Chapter 2 I pointed out that the scary but prestigious name "the scientific method" was nothing but another name for what is, basically, the complete method of creative problem solving and decision making. Here I explain to you that it is also

THE GREATEST QUALITY CONTROL METHOD OF ALL TIME

I'll explain the importance of this to education in later chapters. Here I want to explain why the scientific method merits this title. Please refer to *The Scientific Method Today* in the Appendix.

Quality Characteristic #1—The Scientific Method Is a Complete Act of Thought

The scientific method is a guide requiring all the mental activity stages comprised in a complete act of thought. However, these stages can be followed in a flexible manner. This guide prevents aimless wandering and keeps you on the right path, preventing mistakes and errors of direction. For example, the problem must be properly defined. Stage 4—Search, Explore, and Gather the Evidence—must be complete, with no evidence ignored. Seeing only what you want to see is at the very least unethical and will lead to poor-quality work.

Quality Characteristic #2—The Self-Correcting Nature of the Scientific Method Makes It Superior to All Other Methods

Evidence from two famous authors:

In *An Introduction to Logic and Scientific Method* (1934), Morris Raphael Cohen and Ernest Nagel say:

> The other methods discussed are all inflexible, that is, none of them can admit that it will lead us into error. Hence none of them can make provision for correcting its own results. What is called *scientific method* differs radically from these by encouraging and developing the utmost possible doubt, so that what is left after such doubt is always supported by the best available evidence. As new evidence or new doubts arise it is the essence of scientific method to incorporate them—to make them an integral part of the body of knowledge so far attained. Its method, then, makes science progressive because it is never too certain about its results.

This self-correction feature of the scientific method is mentioned time after time in the literature. Quality comes from "what is left after such doubt is always supported by the best available evidence."

Quality Characteristic #3 — Suspend Judgment, Keep an Open Mind

Unbiased high quality of thought, reasoning, and testing are often hard to achieve, so the method requires one to keep an open mind at every stage. In addition, when a conclusion is reached at Stage 10 of the SM-14 formula, the principles require that no claim of absolute truth or "it is a fact" be made. Rather, it should be stated:

> On the evidence available today the balance of probability favors the view. . .

Thus, the conclusion, theory, decision, etc. remains open to correction by anyone—a top leader, a teacher, or someone outside the field of endeavor. There is no place in a science for arrogance.

As Professor Hans Selye said in *From Dream to Discovery* (1964),

> The question is not "Who is right?" but "What is right?"

Quality Characteristic #4—Use It Also on Sub-Problems

Complex problems usually must be broken down into sub-problems, sub-sub-problems, etc. On those of sufficient importance, you must again use the scientific method or guide to ensure the quality of your work on the basic problem.

Quality Characteristic #5—Self-Challenge of Your Working Hypothesis

The principle of keeping an open mind is further included in the SM-14 formula of stages at Stage 8—Challenge the Hypothesis. You must be skeptical of even your best thoughts. Not only must you try to support them, but you must also try to falsify them. A whole body of theories has developed in falsification, some good and some doubtful.

In *The Grammar of Science* (1911 edition), Karl Pearson reports

> No less an authority than Faraday writes:—
> "The world little knows how many of the thoughts and theories which have passed through the mind of a scientific investigator have been crushed in silence and secrecy by his own severe criticism and adverse examination; that in the most successful instances not a tenth of the suggestions, the hopes, the wishes, the preliminary conclusions have been realised."

Quality Characteristic #6—The Use of the Scientific Method Requires Using Supporting Ingredients at All Stages

The Supporting Ingredients in the SM-14 formula are:
(12) Creative, Non-Logical, Logical, and Technical Methods
(13) Procedural Principles and Theories
(14) Personal Attributes and Thinking Skills

In following the scientific method guide through its stages, scientists and others through the centuries have devised the above supporting ingredients of the scientific method to help ensure that the results produced by the method are as near to the "truth" as humanly possible. Those action methods that actually solve problems are the creative, non-logical, logical, and technical ones. Many of these have been intensively developed into a little science of their own. Proper use of these methods helps ensure the quality of the results achieved. The correct use of personal attributes and thinking skills further adds to the quality of results.

Many of the procedural principles and theories, including ethics, are tacit and unwritten, but in recent years many have been put into writing and have been included in government regulations.

Information on responsibility and the conduct of research (including an endorsement of the scientific method) can be found in the National Academy of Sciences' *Responsible Science: Ensuring the Integrity of the Research Process*, Volumes I and II (1992), published by the National Academy Press.

Quality Characteristic #7—Action Stage (#11 in the SM-14 Formula)

The action stage (Stage 11 in the SM-14 formula) calls for an individual or team's conclusion or theory to be submitted to the peer review process. Theoretically, while importance, time, and money factors must be considered, the peer reviewers should also follow the stages and standards of the scientific method in reaching their conclusions.

Often action is taken in problem solving without the availability of or the need for peer review. In these cases, and often after peer review, it is especially important to "look back" to be sure the theory is proving itself when reduced to practice.

Quality Characteristic #8—Accumulation of Reliable Quality Knowledge

Some other words that are used in place of "accumulated" include:

communicated	evaluated	conserved
interpreted	systematic	fragmented
arbitrary collection	clarified	organized
ever-changing	expanding	public
temporary and defensible	probabilistic	

To engage in any activity in a quality way, it is essential to have a background of reliable knowledge on which to base your actions. It is through the scientific method that this base is built up.

Quality Characteristic #9—The Value of Method

The Sherlock Holmes stories illustrate the value of using the general pattern of scientific research in investigative work compared to the bungling work of the investigator who "just does his thing."

In *Scientific Knowledge and Its Social Problems* (1971), J.R. Ravetz elaborates:

> There is no doubt that without an appropriate "method," in some sense of the term, scientific work is impossible. A trained scientist can instantly identify the traces of the bungling amateur, or the crank, by the absence of "method" revealed in a report of his work.

The Advantages of Method

I searched the literature on the value of method. Various authors stress that method

organizes our thoughts
clarifies our thoughts
ends aimless wandering
helps ideas gather shape
doesn't have to be reinvented
guide to new knowledge
increases self-confidence
provides a system
provides an organized approach
uses human potential
is a repeatable procedure
is a remembered procedure
aids in transfers of learning

aids specific transfer of learning
keeps us in the right direction
avoids relying only on intuition
aids learning to learn
gives direction on future
     problems
trains for change and innovation
encourages conceptual thinking
model of mental processes
helps extend principles
overcomes laxity of thought
generates greater profits
teams follow same method

The Opposite of Method Is Chance

When you do not use methods in the problem-solving process, the results may often be:

haphazard guesses
superficial analyses
wasted time
no solutions
"pig in a poke"
decreased earnings
mistakes and errors
carelessness
misdirection
confusion
trial and error

quick fixes
chaos
uneducated guesses
poor productivity
loss of lives and health
stewing and fretting
overlooked opportunities
wandering aimlessly
wasted energy
seat of pants management
losses instead of profits

Quality Characteristic #10—Use in the Application of Knowledge

Remember that the scientific method is used to originate, refine, extend, and apply knowledge. To be of the greatest value, knowledge must be properly applied. Thus, especially in complex situations, the cycle of using the scientific method begins again. In the field of invention the term "reduce to practice" is often used. The method of invention, the method of engineering, and the method of technology are essentially the scientific method.

Quality Characteristic #11—Unity of Science

To have unity of thought and practice, people in each individual science must be using the same system. It is especially necessary for team work to be done efficiently.

Quality Characteristic #12—Promotes Creative Thinking

The method requires not only logical thinking but also the use of imagination to arrive at creative solutions.

Summary

All these things contribute to the remarkable quality record of the scientific method in the natural sciences. While acknowledged to be imperfect because of the human factor, it still has been phenomenally successful quality-wise overall in the natural sciences and in other domains when properly used. From this description and by reading *The Scientific Method Today* (Appendix A), you can see that, properly used, the scientific method is the greatest quality control method of all time.

? ?

The Mystery

When will the opponents of the scientific method wake up to the value of the greatest method ever recognized and developed?

? ?

Introduction to Part 3

The Blunder as It Affects Education

In Part 3 I confirm the widespread belief that education reform has been a continual disaster. I claim that the basic reasons for this are as simple as A B C.

The reasons for the failure of most school reform programs and other controllable ills of education are numerous, complex, and little understood. However, I have, in my research, applied the scientific method to the situation. This reveals that the **very basic reasons** are as simple as the ABCs below.

A   Killed —
     The widespread teaching of the scientific method

B   Killed —
     The proper use of the scientific method by top education leaders, educational researchers, and others in the education field

C   Killed —
     The development of the science of education

Chapter 6

Reasons for Educational Ills and the Failure of Most Educational Reform Programs

This chapter will make history in the battle over the biggest intellectual and educational blunder in history.

**For here I present to the public
in clear A B C form
the three basic reasons
for many of the ills of education
and
the failure of most education reform programs**

Our top educational leaders ignored Easley in 1958, and they have ignored me for 15 years. Read carefully—if you don't, you'll just get "more of the same," that is, educational disasters that have hurt you, our students, and the public.

The public has long been dissatisfied with our education efforts—and rightfully so. Political analyses and polls usually show that it is a major concern.

An indication of the ills of education and the failure of most reform efforts is that each year new books on educational reform are published. In August 2004, Barnes and Noble's web site listed 6,454 books after a search on the keyword "education reform." Here is what happens, even though many cover important issues:

♦ They are read by only a small number of people (although occasionally one becomes a bestseller).

♦ Our top educational leaders and researchers pay little attention to them.

These books cover hundreds of specific situations that need improvement and deserve study and evaluation. None that I read stressed the blunder about the scientific method. It was through accidental discovery and more than 15 years of specialized research that I have been able to get to the very basic A B C reasons I present here for the many ills of education and the failure of most educational reform programs.

Read on for the details about the basic A B Cs.

Basic Reason A for the Ills of Education and the Failure of Most Educational Reform Programs

A	Killed— The widespread teaching of the scientific method

Tragic but "true"!

Regardless of all that had been written and said about the scientific method, Conant's claim that it did not exist started a movement and acceptance of his false claims. This acceptance was not complete or instant, but over the years it

Killed the widespread teaching of the scientific method

I have covered some of this subject in previous chapters; here is a brief review.

In Chapter 2, I gave a brief history of problem solving and discussed why it is important today. There is little doubt that it should be taught across the curriculum. Please be sure to read *The Scientific Method Today* (Appendix A) to become familiar with the method.

In Chapter 3, I quote Dr. James Conant's 1948 admission that "in the last twenty-five years, indoctrination in the scientific method has been put forward with more and more insistence as one of the primary aims of modern education." I also quote Dr. Conant's statement that "it would be my thesis that those historians of science, and I might add philosophers as well, who emphasize that there is no such thing as 'the scientific method' are doing a public service."

In Chapter 4, I quote Dr. Easley about how Dr. Conant apparently made his claims of no one method with the intent to call a halt to the teaching of scientific method.

This killing of the widespread teaching of the scientific method affects and harms all domains year after year. Each domain's harm is a story in itself. Unfortunately, many of these harms spill over and affect education. In later chapters, I will tell you of the educational disasters and harm **the BLUNDER** has caused in every phase of your life.

It directly affects our "professional educators" and supporting people.

◆ They themselves are not adequately taught the scientific method.

◆ They in turn do not promote and aid in teaching the scientific method. Nor do they include it in national educational reform programs. Thus, they perpetuate **the BLUNDER**.

◆ While the scientific method has been included (in just a few pages) in about 65% of science textbooks, this is far from adequate. Today the groups pushing for improvements in science textbooks are those who do not acknowledge the existence of the scientific method. Thus, it may be forced out of the new science textbooks.

◆ The No Child Left Behind Act requires that students be tested in science beginning in the 2007-08 school year. Since the 1996 National Science Standards disclaim the scientific method, even the present tiny bit of teaching we have now may decrease unless **the BLUNDER** is corrected.

I will give you the details here and in subsequent chapters. You'll be amazed to learn what famous, prestigious organizations are involved!

To prevent misunderstandings, remember that the scientific method is taught to a limited extent in many science classes. As I have mentioned, 65% of the science textbooks cover it in the first chapter. I am continually pleased when I explain my crusade to people and have them contradict me and say, "But I was taught the scientific method." It develops that they were not taught a proper formula for it or very many other principles of the method. Nor were they given the oppoturnity to actually practice its use. They usually have no memory of the method being taught in subject classes other than science. This condition exists in spite of the scientific method being

The idea that most changed the world for the better
The complete method of creative problem solving and decision making for all fields
The greatest quality control method ever recognized

Basic Reason B for Educational Ills and the Failure of Most Educational Reform Programs

B	Killed— The proper use of the scientific method by top education leaders, educational researchers, and others in the field of education

These are the factors most responsible for the above not adequately using the scientific method.

◆ Conant claimed that it does not exist and perpetuated the claim. The above could claim that they did not have to use something that does not exist!

◆ As explained in Chapter 33, Kuhn became famous for his paradigms. Those in the field of education claimed that they were operating under paradigms rather than being required to use the scientific method.

◆ Erroneous claims were made that the social sciences and education "were different" and therefore did not have to follow the natural sciences (see Chapter 27).

◆ Sir Karl Popper and other philosophers of science and many historians of science claimed that there was no scientific method, ignored it, or claimed that it started with the hypothesis. These claims will be explained later.

◆ Natural scientists performing under government research contracts must use prudent judgment and conform to a government-wide definition of what constitutes misconduct in science, such as fabrication, falsification, and plagiarism. For some strange reason, educational researchers can ignore contrary evidence without anyone pointing out that this represents falsification in the resulting research.

The net result of all these claims has been that the scientific method has not been required to be used in the field of education. This has resulted in the many educational disasters mentioned in this book.

These two quotes illustrate the sad state of our educational research.

In his book *Educational Research — The Art and Science of Investigation*, Professor J. Mouly describes the condition of educational research in the 1970s.

> Perhaps more fundamental as the reason for the lack of progress in the development of, say, education as a science has been the persistent lack of scientific orientation on the part of educational personnel, who presumably have become discouraged over the complexity and the precarious nature of educational research. Borg and Gall (1971), for example, see even today an uncritical acceptance of authority and an overdependence on personal experience as predominant techniques in the solution of problems in education in a fashion reminiscent of the uncritical acceptance of the wisdom of Aristotle and Plato that retarded the growth of knowledge for centuries prior to the Renaissance. Not only has this "Dark Ages" orientation led to many blunders in education, but it has also led to disenchantment and disillusionment on the part of teachers and laymen alike.

As you can see, things have not changed since Dr. Moulys 1978 book. In 2000, in *An Elusive Science—The Troubled History of Educational Research*, Professor Ellen C. Lagemann states:

> Neither singular in focus nor uniform in methods of investigation, education research grew out of various combinations of philosophy, psychology, and the social sciences, including statistics. The variety that has characterized educational scholarship from the first, combined with the field's failure to develop a strong, self-regulating professional community, has meant that the field has never developed a high degree of internal coherence. For that reason, much that I will treat would not fit within strict conceptions of either science or research, which is why I shall use the terms "educational scholarship" and "educational study" interchangeably with "education research."

Basic Reason C for the Ills of Education and the Failure of Most Educational Reform Programs

C	Killed— The development of a science of education

Reasons A, B, and C are intertwined. When leading "authoritative" people claim that the scientific method does not exist, it is not taught. If professional educators do not use it, then there cannot be a science of education. Great harms, blunders, and disasters result.

If there is no science of education

♦ No one can determine the Big Picture of Education.

♦ There is no systematic program of accumulating reliable educational knowledge. A science builds on reliable knowledge and expands.

♦ No fair code of ethics is enforced.

♦ There is no development of a group that merits the name "professionals."

In Chapter 55 I go into great detail about what it takes for a domain to be a science. All the ills and disasters of education are clear evidence that there is no science of education.

Here I will tell you briefly what it takes to be a science and how the development of education into a science was killed by *the* **BLUNDER**.

What Is a Science?

Science is best described by what has been developed over the centuries and what exists in the natural sciences today. This is not an easy job, and many people will challenge my description. It would help the teaching of science if we had an official description. Many point out that this is difficult because science is an ever-changing discipline.

Feature 1—A community of specialized practitioners exists.

This community exists in our top educational leaders, education researchers, professors, teachers, and allied professional people. However, there is no adequate self-regulation.

Feature 2—The practitioners follow the scientific method and its code of ethics and culture in their research, planning, etc. There may be a licensing organization for the profession.

This definitely does not exist to a sufficient degree.

There are undoubtedly many educational researchers who have faithfully followed their version of the scientific method and produced reliable knowledge. The problem is discovering who they are and how to identify them.

Feature 3—There are professional organizations that represent the profession and require the use of the scientific method.

There are plenty of professional organizations in the field of education, but I know of none that requires the use of the scientific method.

Feature 4—Papers describing the results of research based on the scientific method are presented for peer review and publication.

Papers are prepared, but it is questionable which ones followed the scientific method. In addition, it is questionable whether the "peers" use the scientific method in their review. Both the older literature and the most recent literature call attention to the unreliability of educational research and programs.

Feature 5—There is rivalry and competition to be first to find "the truth" (actually, as always, as close to the truth as can be determined).

In education, there is more likely to be rivalry to promote some new, untested fad rather than to find "the truth."

Feature 6—There is an accumulated body of reliable knowledge in the area of specialization.

In education, there are specialized groups with their journals, books, and internet sites. There are groups of "experts," but which ones follow the scientific method is unknown. It appears that not many do.

Thus, there is a great deal of data, but no system to evaluate the research and organize it into an available body of accumulated reliable knowledge.

Summary

Close your eyes. Visualize and remember this if you want to stop the ills of education and end the failure of educational reform programs. Because our very top educational leaders perpetuate the false claims that the scientific method does not exist, they

A   Killed —
     The widespread teaching of the scientific method

B   Killed —
     The proper use of the scientific method by top
     education leaders, educational researchers,
     and others in the education field

C   Killed —
     The development of the science of education

This all results in ...

DISASTERS AT THE SCHOOLHOUSE
FROM THE GREATEST INTELLECTUAL AND EDUCATION
BLUNDER IN HISTORY

Chapter 7

Analysis of Misunderstandings That Resulted in False Claims about the Scientific Method

After 15 years of specialized research on the scientific method, my concluding hypothesis remains that the scientific method exists, despite many claims to the contrary. In accordance with the procedural principles of the scientific method, I sought out and studied claims for and against it in the literature.

In a matter that, according to Conant, is of "supreme importance," many misunderstandings that resulted in false claims about the scientific method have been allowed to go unchallenged by our top educational leaders. Professor Easley's 1958 essay was the only educator's challenge of real significance. Even my extensive efforts were ignored. Here, and at many other places in this book, I analyze and refute the various false claims and misstatements I found about the scientific method.

Remember that, in addition to its use in the sciences, the scientific method is also the complete method of creative problem solving and decision making for all fields. Therefore, the false claims about it have harmed society in general, science teaching, and the basic teaching of problem solving and decision making across the curriculum.

"Thou Shalt Not Ignore Contrary Evidence"

The heading above states a sacred and basic procedural principle of the scientific method.

There have been plenty of discoveries made because people have disobeyed this principle at times, but for everyday research and problem solving, it should be followed.

One of the biggest errors that perpetrators of the false claims against the scientific method make is that they *consistently ignore contrary evidence* presented to them by others or available by searching the literature or by testing or experience.

The Main Pattern of False Claims about the Scientific Method

A definite pattern can be found as to why the false claims against the scientific method are erroneous. The basic reason is illustrated by

Claude Bernard in *An Introduction to the Study of Experimental Medicine* (1865):

> The art of investigation is the cornerstone of all the experimental sciences. If the facts used as a basis for reasoning are ill-established or erroneous, everything will crumble or be falsified; and it is thus that errors in scientific theories most often originate in errors of fact.

Thus, when the "facts" used are erroneous, the conclusions drawn are false. This is the pattern I found—false conclusions because of erroneous "facts."

In the material that follows, I summarize many of the false claims. People reach their conclusions after misinterpreting and wrongly defining what the scientific method actually is.

This chapter is of special importance to educators. The U.S. Supreme Court acknowledged the existence of the scientific method in its 1993 *Daubert* decision. Thus, anyone holding a government contract or appropriation should not rely on these false claims as their reason for not including the scientific method in their educational programs.

For better understanding of the claims against the scientific method, I break them down into types.

Type: Nonexistence of the Scientific Method

These false claims are the same or variations of Conant's claims made from 1946 to 1967:

so-called method	no universal method
no such thing	no single method
alleged method	no one method

Explanation and Falsification

A mass of supporting evidence indicates that the scientific method does exist. There have been thousands of books and papers—written by distinguished and famous figures in the fields of education, science, research, psychology, and philosophy—claiming or citing the existence of the scientific method. Many called it by another name (e.g., method of discovery, method of inquiry, method of invention, method of research), but they were all referring to the same basic method or guide. A review of more than 1,000 books mentioning the subject produced more than 100 slightly different formulas for the steps or stages of the scientific method. It all adds up to a substantial body of knowledge supporting its existence.

"No one method" or "no single method." These claims are a clear case of getting the "facts" wrong by misinterpreting the meaning of the word "method" as used in "the scientific method." Method, as used in "the scientific method," is not meant to be a technique which, if applied, will actually help solve a problem. Instead, it is a collective term for the types of mental activity that define the stages of the scientific method.

At these stages, you use creative, non-logical, logical, and technical methods or techniques. No one of these techniques will solve all problems if used alone.

There is a flexible general pattern to the stages of the research process. Where the techniques are applied, the stages are often called "steps," but referring to them as "stages" prevents misunderstandings and false claims of rigidity.

In the event anyone using the above claims means that there is "no one guide" to reliable knowledge, then this does not hold up either. There may be "no one guide," but the vast amount of experimenting and debate in the literature clearly points to the scientific method being superior to all other methods or guides.

There is a usual pattern to the method of how we originate, refine, extend, and apply knowledge in all fields. Human thought is not a random operation. Thus, in almost any complex human activity that is repeated over and over, you can safely assume that there will be patterns to the activity.

Problem solving and decision making. Many people, including some authors, do not realize that problem solving and decision making formulas are derived from the scientific method. Even some of those claiming that the scientific method does not exist will offer formulas for problem solving and decision making. This situation is due largely to the lack of adequate research, development, discussion, and publicity about the scientific method that has occurred since Dr. Conant and Sir Karl Popper expressed their negative views. To confirm the relationship of discovery, problem solving, and decision making, read the works of Nobel Laureate Herbert Simon, often called the father of artificial intelligence.

Type: It Is Not a General Method

The false claim is made that the scientific method is only for scientists, that it is not a method suitable for all domains, that it is not a general problem-solving method.

Explanation and Falsification

These claims have hurt the understanding and acceptance of the scientific method. Throughout this book I show that it is a general method. Please see page 6 of *The Scientific Method Today* (Appendix A) for additional information.

Type: Lack of Flexibility

Claims are made that the scientific method consists of a "set of rules," "mindless adherence to a rigid series of steps," or that it's "a fixed set of steps," a cookbook recipe, "a rigid approach to scientific inquiry," and that "traditional discussions of scientific method have sought a set of rules that would permit any *individual* who followed them to produce sound knowledge."

Explanation and Falsification

While some authors use "stages," "phases," "ingredients," and "elements" to describe the stages of the scientific method, it became customary to use the word "steps." Only an occasional author said that the "steps" had to be followed one after another. The Harvard/Conant group and misguided followers (or whoever they are) used this misinterpretation of the word "steps" to infer a rigid process. In actual use, there is a general pattern to the method that allows one to backtrack, loop, skip, stop, detour to sub-problems, coil, interplay, etc. This false claim that the scientific method is rigid is yet another red herring used to discredit the scientific method.

Type: Only Logic Is Involved

False claims are made that "it's only a rational method" or "one set of logical rules."

Explanation and Falsification

Karl Pearson in *Grammar of Science* (1892) and John Dewey in *How We Think* (1910), among others, explained long ago that imagination and creativity are essential ingredients of the scientific method.

The famous mathematician Henri Poincaré (1854–1912) stated: "It is by logic we prove—it is by intuition we invent."

Type: It Is Only a Textbook Method

Textbooks are often criticized for including the scientific method. The descriptions of the method are also criticized.

Here are some of the false claims made about textbook descriptions of the scientific method:

◆ so abstract that it's not vital
◆ interlocking, succinct cookbook-type steps
◆ "laws" of scientific method
◆ cookbook sequence of truism
◆ consists of three steps, each following logically and mechanically after the other
◆ such a formal and highly structured description is unrealistic

Explanation and Falsification

The Harvard/Conant group and misguided followers (or whoever they are) have been very successful at keeping the teaching of the scientific method out of all national education reform programs for over 40 years, including the 1995 *National Science Education Standards*. They are now trying to use the *Standards* to drive the scientific method out of textbooks in favor of "science as inquiry," even though they present no *method* for inquiry!

Usually, formulas for the scientific method in textbooks are condensed ones, although some are fairly good. The need is not to criticize them but to promote a good standard formula, such as SM-14, for authors of textbooks to use.

Type: Philosophical Grounds

There are philosophers, scientists, and others who have not favored the scientific method or claimed that it does not exist as it has been described and formulated over the years, largely on philosophical grounds. I cover these claims in various chapters, especially Chapter 33, Contribution of the Philosophy Domain to **the BLUNDER**. Remember that grade school students cannot be expected to understand deep philosophical reasoning like the big dispute in the field of philosophy about induction and deduction.

Type: Giving False Attributes to the Scientific Method and Then Claiming That It Does Not Exist

Claims are made that the scientific method is a myth, "fallacy," "artificial method," or "mystical way in which scientists get answers."

Explanation and Falsification

Garbage in, garbage out. People making these claims follow the usual misinterpretation of and false claims against the method. Based on these incorrect "facts," they claim that the scientific method is a "myth," etc. It is like the computer industry's old saying: "garbage in, garbage out."

Type: Based on the Nature of Science

In *Scientific Research in Education* (2002; National Research Council of the National Academy of Sciences) the following appears under the heading "Nature of Science":

> Advances in scientific knowledge are achieved by the self-regulating norms of the scientific community over time, not, as sometimes believed, by the mechanistic application of a particular scientific method to a static set of questions.

Here they come up with a poor and limited definition of the "nature of science" and make it worse by misrepresenting the scientific method.

Baloney Detection

In a two-part article in *Scientific American* (November and December 2001), Michael Shermer, the founding publisher of *Skeptic* magazine, mentions a term coined by the famous astronomer Carl Sagan—"Baloney Detection Kit"—to detect baloney, that is, to help discriminate between science and pseudoscience.

Baloney detection is a very descriptive term for identifying the false claims that the scientific method does not exist and should not be taught.

Shermer suggests 10 questions to ask for baloney detection when encountering any claim. Here I present these questions and give my baloney detection answers regarding the false claims that the scientific method does not exist.

1. How reliable is the source of the claim?

Many of those at the source of the claims are very well-known "authoritative" people. However, since they have never fully researched and then explained their claims in peer-reviewed journals or published a full, accurate evaluation of them anywhere else, you cannot rely on their claims. They make red herring-type claims such as "no one method," "rigid method," "textbook method," etc.

2. Does the source often make similar claims?

No, on the whole they are very intelligent people dedicated to science and education. However, because they do not follow the scientific method when working on education programs, many have been associated with untested fads foisted on our teachers and schools over the last 50 years.

3. Have the claims been verified by another source?

Many have echoed the false claims about the scientific method, including a number of Harvard professors, but there has been no scientific verification of the claims in peer-reviewed professional journals. Thus, the claims have never been fully evaluated. In general, the matter has been a deep, dark secret, so most people do not know about the dispute.

4. How does the claim fit with what we know about how the world works?

It does not fit. From Bacon and Galileo in the 16th century to the present, there have been discussions, debates, analyses, etc. about the method of science, the experimental method, now most commonly called the scientific method. The preponderance of evidence favors the scientific method (SM-14) as reflecting the stages and supporting ingredients of what we should teach about how scientists work.

5. Has anyone gone out of the way to disprove the claim, or has only supportive evidence been sought?

In 1958 Professor Jack Easley published his doctoral thesis falsifying Conant's claims. From 1989 to the present, I myself have researched claims for and against the scientific method. I have shown and falsified all the claims I found against it. I have also explained the many features of it in my various publications and in this book.

6. Does the preponderance of evidence point to the claimant's conclusion or to a different one?

The preponderance of evidence points to the existence of the scientific method, contrary to the conclusions of the claimant and his followers. This is easily verified by conducting a search of the literature. Much material about the scientific method can also be found on the Internet by entering the search term "scientific method" into a search engine like Google.

7. Is the claimant employing the accepted rules of reason and tools of research, or have these been abandoned in favor of others that lead to the desired conclusion?

There is no logic to his conclusion of claiming that something does not exist. Conant never really researched the literature about the scientific method. He used the red herring of misinterpreting the word method to justify his conclusion.

8. Is the claimant providing an explanation for the observed phenomena or merely denying the existing explanation?

Conant's explanation of the observed phenomena is based on misinterpreting the word method and false claims of no one method. In addition, he based his claims on others' misstatements about method.

9. If the claimant proffers a new explanation, does it account for as many phenomena as the old explanation did?

No, his explanation disregards all the historical evidence of the universal nature of the scientific method.

10. Do the claimant's personal beliefs and biases drive the conclusions, or vice versa?

Conant was very biased in favor of teaching via Harvard's historical case history method. He never really researched the scientific method, so he was simply expressing his personal opinions.

In this book I have not used the term "common sense." Conant called one of his books belittling the scientific method *Science and Common Sense*. However, as Borg and Gall state in *Educational Research: An Introduction* (1971), "History is filled with instances in which common sense has been proven wrong by science."

Summary

As I explained at the beginning of this chapter, when researchers get their "facts" wrong everything will crumble or be falsified.

All these false claims have caused the tragedy that the practical method of teaching science as its method—the scientific method—has been greatly retarded. No other practical method of teaching science has been developed. Thus, each year billions of taxpayers' dollars are spent on "new" ways to teach science.

The Greatest Educational and Intellectual Blunder in History

Conant claimed that the question of the existence of the scientific method was of "supreme importance," and I show the same. These factors contributed to *the* BLUNDER:

- the inaccuracy of our top leaders about the scientific method
- the lack of adequate skepticism and challenge of these claims for more than 50 years, creating a climate for perpetuation
- the confusion and ambiguity over the word "method"
- the acceptance of authoritative opinions without proper skepticism

Introduction to Part 4

Perpetuation of *the* BLUNDER

Contrast — The Difference

This: The literature on the whole supports the existence of and the great importance of the scientific method.

Against: There is a group that is perpetuating misunderstandings that the scientific method does not exist.

As a result: It is not included in any national educational reform program.
It is seldom used in the social sciences, including education.
It is not widely used in business and industry.
There are misunderstandings about the scientific method in our intellectual community.

A surprise: There is no debate, discussion, or study of this great difference. It has been, in effect, a deep, dark secret. The public has not been informed of the great harms that result.

My Objectives Reviewed

♦ Inform the public and those misguided about the scientific method so that they ask for its study and correction of *the* BLUNDER.

♦ Try to convince the group intentionally and unintentionally perpetuating the misunderstandings to study the situation.

Here in part 4 I give a preview of the perpetuation of *the* BLUNDER so that you can better understand all the educational disasters that I describe in Part 5. Later, in Part 6, I report in detail on some of the many contributions to *the* BLUNDER.

The Splintered Control of Education in the United States
(No chart of top-to-bottom responsibility is possible)

The American People

The Federal Government

The President   Congress   Federal Courts

U.S. Dept of Education	National Science Foundation
and	National Academy of Sciences
Presidential Commissions,	National Institutes of Health
Panels, and Advisors	Congressional Commissions,
	Committees, Panels, and Advisors

Other government agencies with educational appropriations or control of safety, buildings, transportation, etc.

Schools of the U.S. Armed Forces

State Government

State Depts and Boards	Governors	State Courts
of Education	State Education	State Colleges
State Panels and Advisors	Commissioners	
Education Commission of the States		

Local Government

Local School Boards	District Superintendents	Principals
and their departments	Teachers	
and specialists	Local courts	

Non-Government

Universities	Foundations	Special Interest
Teachers Colleges	Educational Testing	Groups
Alumni Groups	Service	Religious Orgs.
Teachers Unions	Textbook Publishers	Professional
Teachers Orgs.	Media	Regulatory and
Educational	Business and Industry	Licensing Orgs.
publications	For-profit private schools	Lobbyists
College Board	Non-profit private schools	Think tanks
	For-profit public schools	

Chapter 8

Our Top Educational Leaders Perpetuate *the* BLUNDER

Even though control of education is splintered, some of our top educational leaders have been in enough effective control to perpetuate the greatest educational and intellectual blunder in history, thus preventing the adequate teaching and required use of the scientific method in education.

Our top leaders are people devoted to education and science. To avoid embarrassing any living individuals, to avoid libel suits, and to avoid getting into name calling rather than the correction of *the* BLUNDER, I have made it a policy to try not to name living individuals. However, I do name organizations. Sometimes I name an individual because I wrote to him or her, or for some other reason.

I readily admit that our top leaders are honest, hard-working people who have dedicated their careers to education and to work in other domains, such as science. In the domain of business, financial dishonesty often occurs. In education, financial dishonesty occurs infrequently. In fact, the desire to do a public service misled many of our top leaders into *the* BLUNDER.

Who Is Really Doing a "Public Service"?

Dr. Conant, a famous and prestigious leader and then-President of Harvard University, stated that "historians of science and philosophers [and thus, by inference, everyone]. . .who emphasize that there is no such thing as 'the scientific method' are doing a public service."

Now I claim that Conant started and our top educational leaders, by not challenging him and by perpetuating his false claims, have made the greatest educational and intellectual blunder in history. Thus, they have done the opposite of Conant's statement—a public disservice of historical importance.

Who Are Our Top Leaders?

What do I mean by "top leaders"? Because education is so decentralized and because not all "top leaders" are involved, it is hard to define. In general, I mean people in top positions of authority, decision making, policy setting, and advising. This can include professional organizations, officers, boards, some professors, college officials, government officials, industry and business leaders taking part in reforming education, and foundations. *Of course, I don't mean all our top leaders, just as people don't mean all teachers when they blame teachers for bad schools, etc.*

Historically, control of our schools was local; gradually state governments also assumed responsibilities. In the second half of the 20th century, the federal government began to join the fray in various ways. However, there is no one person or body in direct control top to bottom.

My purpose is not to say whether our control system is good or bad. However, I do want to show how many of our top educational leaders have been effectively able for more than 40 years to prevent the adequate teaching of the scientific method at the bottom level.

I assure you that I would not make this claim if I had not investigated and researched the scientific method situation thoroughly. It is a strange, tragic, and history-making situation.

The Big Picture (and It's Not Pretty) of How Our Top Educators Perpetuated *the* BLUNDER

◆ I have already given many details about the beginning of the blunder and its importance.

◆ Here I give a list so that you can visualize how many famous and important people are involved.

◆ You have every right to be shocked and doubtful that all these people are involved, so I give references to chapters presenting details and evidence to help you understand what happened.

◆ I also present a partial list of the means these people used to perpetuate *the* **BLUNDER**.

◆ Remember, many of our top leaders have been misguided and simply became caught up in a movement that took on a strange life of its own. Many do not even know what has happened. Also remember that there has been no well-publicized debate about whether the scientific method exists based on Conant's claims. If there had been debate, many people would not have perpetuated *the* **BLUNDER**.

The **BLUNDER** Started at the Top

As explained in Chapter 2, *the* **BLUNDER** started when the very top leader of our very top university claimed that *the* scientific method does not exist. It was an extraordinary claim; it was in direct contradiction to the prevailing thought. Conant provided no extraordinary evidence. Instead, he used the ambiguity of the word "method" to claim that "there was no one method." He never submitted articles with his claims to peer-reviewed periodicals.

Other Top Leaders at Harvard

The conditions were favorable for no opposition to develop (see Chapter 3). Instead of contradicting Conant, many top professors supported his position with similar claims.

Many of the Top Leaders of These Professions, Groups, and Organizations Have Perpetuated *the* BLUNDER

National Academy of Sciences (Chapter 28)
American Association for the Advancement of Science (Chapter 29)
National Science Foundation (Chapter 32)
Educational Testing Service (SAT) (Chapter 41)
Other testing organizations (ACT, etc.) (Chapter 41)
National science education reform groups (Chapters 29, 32, 41)
Foundations "aiding" education (Chapters 35 and 40)
Philosophers and their societies (Chapters 33 and 41)
Think tanks (Chapter 41)
Honor societies and education fraternities (Chapters 36 and 41)
National Science Teachers Association (Chapter 31)
Business and industry leaders attempting to help education
    (Chapter 39)
Officials of college and universities (Chapter 41)
U.S. Department of Education and its predecessor the Bureau of
    Education (Chapter 30)
Other government agencies (Chapter 41)
Professional societies and their journals (Chapter 41)
Historians of science (Chapter 36)
Psychologists and their societies (Chapter 34)
and many others

How Did They Do It?

♦ In Chapter 7 I discuss the false claims that were put forward—usually innocently—to mislead people about the scientific method.

◆ They gave no grants for the study of the scientific method.

◆ They ignored evidence in numerous books on science concerning the scientific method (see Chapter 4).

◆ They ignored and gave no publicity to Easley, me, and others who tried to promote the scientific method (see Chapter 50).

◆ They used their power and influence over

appropriations	honors	jobs
awards	grants	promotions
appointments	awards	publications
special subsidies	delay or acceleration	
citations of work	of research	

◆ They did it through their control of some (not most) textbooks.

◆ They control most teacher organizations.

◆ Although only about 7% of education funds come from federal dollars, they have used control of these funds to prevent the study of the scientific method.

◆ They have avoided publicity about the real question of the existence of the scientific method. They have kept the dispute a deep, dark secret.

◆ They have kept the scientific method out of all national education reform programs, including the 1995 National Science Education Standards.

◆ There are other ways that I will explain in the intriguing chapters to come.

The Trouble Is at the Top—It Has Not Been the Teachers' Fault

In thousands of articles, our grade school teachers are being labeled "bad." However, *the* **BLUNDER** is not their fault. It is the fault of the "bad" top educators, who are seldom criticized. The scientific method is mentioned in a few pages in about 65% of science textbooks. Thus, many teachers and professors have taught it a little. I discuss this in more detail in Chapter 11.

Motives

It is a mystery to me why so many people and organizations are involved in *the* **BLUNDER**. I discuss this in Part 6. Although I discuss Harvard in greater detail in Chapter 26, here I give a preview of what I believe is a major motive for what happened.

To challenge *the* **BLUNDER** also means to challenge Harvard. The institution originated it, has perpetuated it, and has refused to study the situation. Harvard graduates are everywhere, and a great many are in positions of power and influence.

In his biography entitled *James B. Conant* (1993), James Hershberg states:

> Though he had voted for Nixon in 1960, Conant easily adjusted to the presence in the White House of John F. Kennedy, who, after all, as a Harvard undergraduate had broken with his father in 1940 when he publicly commended Conant's vigorous interventionism. Kennedy had, moreover, vigorously revived the Washington-Harvard connection initiated by FDR at the outset of the New Deal: so-called action-intellectuals with Harvard ties, especially economists and military strategists, streamed down from Cambridge to stock the new administration, some, like McGeorge Bundy and Arthur Schlesinger, Jr., taking senior positions on the White House staff, and they admired their pre-Pusey leader.

Since Harvard attracts our brightest (not necessarily our most creative) students, it should be to its credit that under FDR and John Kennedy they streamed to Washington. But that its graduates have been educated in false ideas of the scientific method and carried them to Washington is a disaster that has greatly aided the perpetuation of *the* **BLUNDER**.

In *Scientific Autobiography and Other Papers* (1949), Max Planck said:

> A new scientific truth does not triumph by convincing its opponents and making them see the light, but rather because its opponents eventually die, and a new generation grows up that is familiar with it.

Even though Conant and many of the original perpetrators have died, *the* **BLUNDER** goes on, for it seems that it has become a tradition at

Harvard that the scientific method doesn't exist. Harvard continues to send out many graduates who have false ideas or inadequate knowledge about the scientific method and a formula for it.

Thus, out of respect for Harvard's reputation as a center of reliable knowledge and fear of the consequences of challenging powerful Harvard professors, officials, and graduates, *the* **BLUNDER** was more easily and quickly perpetuated. To tell the story, I had to be frank about Harvard. As a man close to the end of life, I don't have to fear what younger people do.

Summary of the Perpetuation of *the* BLUNDER

- It was first started and perpetuated by top leaders at our top university.

- The misunderstanding and *the* **BLUNDER** are based on Conant's claims that, as Easley stated, "something does not exist because it has been searched for and not found. This is a *non sequitur* of a well-known form. It is well known that claims to non-existence cannot be proven, since no search can be exhaustive and since every search is also selective in terms of the abstract idea of the thing searched for." So something illogical is being perpetrated.

- Top leaders and top organizations have perpetuated it.

- Efforts to publicize it and have it studied and corrected have failed.

- It is the biggest educational and intellectual blunder in history. To that you must add that it is also the most expensive educational and intellectual blunder in history.

A big point is, what explanation should be given to students concerning the nature of science, problem solving, and inquiry? Those who may continue to oppose the existence of the scientific method as represented by SM-14 must present a practical teaching alternative.

Coming Next—Disasters!

There cannot be a giant blunder without disasters. Before discussing the contributors and the perpetuators, I want to discuss the disasters produced by *the* **BLUNDER** and why the public has been so dissatisfied with education.

You'll get "more of the same" unless you read on and see the need for action more clearly.

After the serious business of picking on our top educational leaders and threatening more disasters

A Little Humor

[Adapted from the comments of J. Mark Iwry, former Treasury benefit tax counsel, at a farewell banquet, as reported in the *Wall Street Journal* (July 11, 2001), about those who want to run the world and those who want to save it.]

There are two types: those who want to run education and those who want to save education.

After working together for a short while, those who want to save education generally find that they want to save it from those who want to run it.

I want to save education by having the scientific method taught and used in educational reforms and research. Rather than wanting to save education from those who want to run it, I want them to use the scientific method to help them really run it—instead of producing a mess of disasters.

A number of people have remarked that a carrot approach accomplishes more than a stick. So why do I criticize our top leaders so harshly? I tried a gentler approach early in my efforts, and I was ignored. *The* **BLUNDER** continued to cost the nation untold billions, even trillions, of dollars.

20th Century School Movements and Fads–
Ranging from Potentially Good to Bad

progressive education
bilingual education
teach subject matter
whole language vs. phonics
core knowledge
new math
new new math
whole math
self-esteem movement
hands-on
constructivism/discovery learning
performance-based testing
multiple intelligences
restructuring school
Bloom's taxonomy
competency-based education
outcome-based education
open classroom
moral education
direct instruction
character education
brain-based curricula
testing—standards-based
school choice
no homework, more homework
vouchers
first—big schools better than
    small
now—small schools better than
    big
right brain-left brain
low order-higher order thinking
critical thinking
1995 National Educational
    Standards
local authority
computers in every classroom
every child can learn
less is more
life adjustment education
mastery learning
efficacy training

adopt-a-school
site-based management
test the teachers
hire noncertified teachers
uniforms for students
performance contracting
implement total quality management
instructional grouping
single-sex schools and classes
rewards programs
Piaget's theories
Montessori schools
process education
social promotion
minimum competency movement
school to work movement
school-wide improvement program
mastery learning
competency-based education
team teaching
block scheduling
year-round school
charter schools
schools without walls
privatization of education
alternative teacher certification
school operating companies
block scheduling
structural reform
multiple pathways
citizenship education
and others

System Overload of Untested Programs

Education's problem has been that our top educators have overloaded the system with numerous untested programs on top of others.

Introduction to Part 5

Educational Disasters

This section covers many of the major educational disasters that have occurred in the last 50 years. Most of them could have been prevented or greatly diminished if our top leaders had
- used the scientific method
- required all educational researchers to use it
- developed a science of education
- established permanent specialized SM-14 type national research centers

---

Education in the United States Today

Education in the United States is a very complex situation—so broad and so complex that no one person understands it and sees "the big picture." Remember the constant statement, "You can't change schools"? Well, just examine my list of movements and fads (see the preceding page) thrown at our teachers in the 20th century. We have no permanent organizations set up to study education properly. In Chapter 58 I make a recommendation about this.

We do have thousands of people and organizations claiming to know what is wrong in whole or in part. I am, of course, one of them. Although I have tried to see "the big picture" through an extensive search of the literature, I make no claim that I see it completely. However, I do claim that no one can accurately see and present a big picture of education to the public if that person is not thoroughly familiar with the scientific method (SM-14 type).

The Cause of the Disasters

Because I have spent more than 15 years researching the scientific method, I believe that my conclusion that the lack of its use is the basic cause of all the disasters is correct. Therefore, I wanted to present the disasters and show that they were caused by non-use of the scientific method. Many of them have harmed you personally, and these descriptions will help you understand why.

Chapter 9

The Absurd Disaster in the Teaching of Reading

- It's a Matter of Degree

- The History of the Teaching of Reading in the United States

- At Last

- Publishers—Good and Bad

- The Absurd Cost of Reading Studies

- If Only It Had Been Done!

- Tremendous Part of *the* **BLUNDER** Given No Recognition

- We Still Have a Problem: What Are We To Do Now That Phonics Has Been Declared the Way To Teach Reading?

- The Overall Problem of Teaching Reading

- Many New Programs To Improve Reading

- Mystery

- An Apology to All Our Teachers of Reading

It has long been recognized that the first duty of public schools is to teach students to read. The ability to read, write, and spell will, to a great extent, influence a student's development and learning of other subject matter. I am not a reading expert, but my study of the scientific method, its relationship to education, and the writing of this book led me into the history of the teaching of reading.

As a member of the public and an avid reader of newspapers and magazines, I have read article after article about our "bad schools" and demands by many that the teachers, principals, etc. be forced to change by the competition of vouchers, takeover, closing of the bad

71

schools, etc. In reading, as in the non-teaching of the scientific method, I found an absurd situation of blundering on the part of our top educational leaders. I share with you here some history of the teaching of reading.

Two basic methods of teaching reading (with variations and combinations of each) are phonics and whole language.

Phonics (also called intensive phonics, systematic phonics, decoding, and code emphasis) is described in the *Report of the National Reading Panel* (2000) as follows:

> Phonics instruction is a way of teaching reading that stresses the acquisition of letter-sound correspondences and their use in reading and spelling. The primary focus of phonics instruction is to help beginning readers understand how letters are linked to sounds (phonemes) to form letter-sound correspondences and spelling patterns and to help them learn how to apply this knowledge in their reading. Phonics instruction may be provided systematically or incidentally. The hallmark of a systematic phonics approach or program is that a sequential set of phonics elements is delineated and these elements are taught along a dimension of explicitness depending on the type of phonics method employed. Conversely, with incidental phonics instruction, the teacher does not follow a planned sequence of phonics elements to guide instruction but highlights particular elements opportunistically when they appear in text.

Whole language, while more inclusive, was previously referred to as look-say, word method, whole word, and sight reading. In a continuation of absurdities, the *Report of the National Reading Panel* fails to even mention whole language or any of these. Whole language theory holds that learning to read and write English is analogous to learning to speak it—a natural, unconscious process best fostered by unstructured immersion. Children learning to read English essentially memorize words in much the same way that Chinese children memorize their ideograms.

It's a Matter of Degree

Professor Rudolf Flesch used the term "phonics first," which has not been picked up by many other reading researchers. In teaching reading, it's not all black and white. The use of the phonics method also requires some look-say, as students must also learn what a word stands for. Many who teach with whole language also include some phonics but stress memorization to a greater extent than those using phonics first.

The History of the Teaching of Reading in the United States

Up to 1830, phonics methods were predominantly used.

In 1830 (approximately), Thomas H. Gallaudet introduced the look-say method, and others published similar primers.

In 1843, Horace Mann passionately recommended the use of the look-say method to the Massachusetts Board of Education. However, a few years later, 31 Boston school masters protested that it didn't work well, and its use diminished.

From 1881 to 1955, there was a tremendous increase in teaching the look-say or word method. By 1955, there were very few schools teaching phonics. Teachers colleges were indoctrinating future teachers into the look-say, whole word method and eventually whole language.

In 1951, before writing several books on reading, Dr. Rudolf Flesch wrote *The Art of Clear Thinking*. His reasoning and breadth of knowledge about research and thinking impressed me. Therefore, I paid special attention to his other books. *The Art of Clear Thinking* is excellent and still makes good reading. Flesch was far more alert and analytical than others. In Chapter 15, "The More or Less Scientific Method," he remarks about Dr. Conant's claim that the scientific method doesn't exist, "That surely is extreme." He then quotes Dr. W.I.B. Beveridge's excellent sequence on scientific investigation. He realized that Dr. Conant was wrong and had the guts to publicly challenge him. In his later books, Dr. Flesch was not afraid to challenge our top educators about reading education.

In 1955, Dr. Flesch published his first book about reading, *Why Johnny Can't Read*. It took the nation by storm, became a bestseller, and remained one for 30 weeks. The reading situation is best explained by a few excerpts from this book.

The following is from the fly leaf of *Why Johnny Can't Read* (1955):

> *Why Johnny Can't Read* is an angry book by an aroused parent. It is addressed to the thousands of bewildered parents

whose normally intelligent youngsters can't read well enough to do their school work. Dr. Flesch has visited classrooms, talked to students, teachers and parents, worked his way though a mountain of books and articles, and examined study materials. Johnny can't read, Dr. Flesch concludes, "for the simple reason that nobody ever showed him how."

The American system of teaching children to read is no longer the traditional alphabetic-phonetic method. Since 1925 most pupils have been forced to memorize entire words one after another, like Chinese characters—a process which ends in disorderly guesswork. Failing to learn how to sound out words letter by letter, the child never masters the mechanics of reading. Dr. Flesch provides a cure in this book.

Dr. Flesch says this in *Why Johnny Can't Read*:

> I said in the last chapter that whenever the results of phonics and of the word method were compared by tests and experiments, phonics came out on top. Let me repeat that statement and amplify it: In every single research study ever made phonics was shown to be superior to the word method; conversely, there is not a single research study that shows the word method superior to phonics.
>
> A few weeks ago I spent two days in the library of Teachers College, Columbia University, tracking down every single reference to a study of "phonics vs. no phonics." I carefully read each one of those papers and monographs. Naturally, it is possible that some item or items in the bibliography have escaped me; but I honestly don't think so. I covered the ground as diligently as I possibly could, looking for scientific evidence *in favor* of the word method.
>
> There was none.
>
> In the books and pamphlets by the "experts" there are plenty of statements referring to those research studies. Usually the findings are called "contradictory." Sometimes a few stray statistics are quoted out of context; sometimes the actual findings are boldly misrepresented. The result is always the same: the preconceived notions are endlessly repeated, the true facts are concealed.

In *Why Johnny Can't Read*, Flesch urges teachers to rebel against the reading "experts" as follows:

> You are a grade-school teacher. I know that you are doing a conscientious job, that you work overtime for very little pay, that you love children and are proud of your profession. Aren't you getting tired of being attacked and criticized all the time? Every second mother who comes in to talk to you tells you that she is dissatisfied, that her child doesn't seem to learn anything, that you should do your job in a different way, that you don't know your business. Why should you be the scapegoat? The educators in their teachers' colleges and publishing offices think up all those fancy ideas, and you are on the firing line and have to take the consequences. Have another look at the system you are defending with so much effort. I know you are an intelligent young woman. You belong on the other side.
>
> Mind you, I am not accusing the reading "experts" of wickedness or malice. I am not one of those people who call them un-American or left-wingers or Communist fellow travelers. All I am saying is that their theories are wrong and that the application of those theories has done untold harm to our younger generation.

Unfortunately, teachers didn't rebel to any extent.

In 1967, Dr. Jeanne S. Chall of the Graduate School of Education at Harvard University wrote *Learning to Read: The Great Debate*. Revisions were published in 1983 and 1996. This is a very scholarly report, well presented and well researched by a respected member of the academic community. Dr. Chall says:

> Since the middle 1950s, however, one after another of these principles has been vehemently challenged, largely as a result of the popular success of Flesch's *Why Johnny Can't Read*. Out of these challenges have come new reading programs, some resembling rather closely the older programs long ago discarded in favor of the "modern" programs of the 1930s. As in the past, most current innovators claim that theirs is the "new," "natural," "true," "logical," or "most scientific" way to begin.

In her conclusions and recommendations, Dr. Chall recommends phonics.

Although our top leaders and the educational press ignored Flesch, it surprises me that so little action was taken after a Harvard professor's scholarly works and recommendations were published. Marilyn Adams, a reading expert whose book *Beginning to Read* (1990) confirmed Dr. Chall's findings, has said, "Jeanne also exhibited great strength, as she was loudly and brutally maligned for her work."

In 1981, Flesch's second book about reading, *Why Johnny Still Can't Read*, was published. By that time, about 15 percent of schools were teaching phonics, but 85 percent were still sticking to the old, discredited look-say method. Here is an excerpt from the book's fly leaf:

> This book deals with a national scandal that in lasting effects dwarfs Watergate—the fifty-year destruction of the American educational system. For five decades the vast majority of American school children have been taught to read by the look-and-say method rather than by traditional phonics. Look-and-say, as Dr. Flesch proves with overwhelming evidence in this book, is a fraudulent, pernicious gimmick. Because of this method, the statistical majority of today's American adults are handicapped readers, and one-quarter of them are wholly illiterate. The U.S. literacy rate has already dropped to the level of Burma and Albania and is approaching that of Zambia.
>
> Based on painstaking and wide-ranging research, the book shows how the majority of American educators abandoned phonics fifty years ago and how they conducted a fifty-year coverup in the face of hundreds of scientific studies unanimously proving the ineffectiveness of look-and-say. One chapter lists educator's ten favorite alibis, and the next ten chapters show with a wealth of research data, anecdotes, and case histories how phony those alibis are. The educators tell the public that Americans read better than ever, that the prevailing textbooks do teach phonics, that inner-city children are incapable of learning to read, and so on ad nauseam. Dr. Flesch quotes chapter and verse to prove that many educators, in their journals and among themselves, tell each other how to keep their knowledge of letter-sound relations to a minimum and how to diagnose the victims of look-and-say as learning-disabled from birth.

Note that Flesch died in 1986, ending his fight for reading improvement. Many efforts were made to discredit him.

In 1961 the Reading Reform Foundation was organized to promote the teaching of phonics. Eventually it changed its name to the Phonics Institute. In his excellent book, *Preventing Reading Failure* (1987, still in print), Professor Patrick Groff of San Diego State University states:

> While it is clear that the RRF [Reading Reform Foundation] has and is making a significant impact on the way information about phonics teaching is disseminated, notice of its existence has been effectively suppressed. Never has the organization been acknowledged in any way by the International Reading Association or the National Council of Teachers of English. Its name has never appeared in any well-known text on the teaching of reading.

And look! In this 1987 book, he beats me to the cause of the reading disaster! But only in one paragraph, while I shout it from the rooftops with a whole book! Groff says:

> Broad and Wade's denunciation of scientists in this regard applies well to the reading experts who espouse *the scientific method* and yet at present defend the myths of reading instruction: "Many scientific communities do not behave in the way they are supposed to. Science is not self-policing. Scholars do not always read the scientific literature carefully. Science is not a perfectly objective process. Dogma and prejudice, when suitably garbed, creep into science just as easily as into any other human enterprise" (p. 210). [emphasis mine]

Reading experts are social scientists. As I point out in Chapter 27, the social sciences have largely abandoned use of the scientific method. Dr. Groff deserves credit for telling us in 1987 the basic cause of the reading disaster: non-use of the scientific method by our top reading experts!

In 1995, Congress provided directives in the Health Research Extension Act for a research program on reading to be conducted by the National Institute of Child Health and Human Development (NICHD).

In 1997, Senator Thad Cochran, based on a discussion of the report of the NICHD with Director Duane Alexander, introduced a bill in Congress to establish a National Panel to Review Reading Research and Implement New Reading Programs. The bill became law. Wow! After all the years of the "reading wars," at last an official body calls for an assessment of various approaches to teaching children to read.

> **Consider well the absurdity that, in spite of the importance of reading, it took this long for an official panel to be assembled.**

AT LAST

In April 2000, the National Reading Panel issued its report in favor of phonics and comprehension skills. The Panel stated that before 1966 about 15,000 research studies about reading had appeared, and since 1966 approximately 100,000 research reports on reading have been published.

In May 2000, Senators Paul Coverdell and Bill Goodling introduced legislation that would require participating states to use phonics-based instruction.

In October 2000, the Fordham Foundation, in its program of publishing interesting reports, issued a booklet "Whole Language Lives On" by Louisa Cook Moats, Project Director of the NICHD. Ms. Moats received a doctorate in reading from Harvard University and studied under Dr. Chall. She warns about embracing "balanced reading instruction" claims, this being a way for people to take no stand on phonics vs. whole language. She goes on to explain what is wrong with whole language.

The Elementary and Secondary Education Act of 2001 (signed by President Bush in January 2002) includes Reading First, a provision that reading be taught in a way indicated by scientifically based research. According to the U.S. Department of Education, grants will be available to state and local programs in which students are systematically and explicitly taught five key early reading skills: phonemic awareness, phonics, fluency, vocabulary, and comprehension (www.ed.gov).

> In this chapter I have tried to give you a full picture of the reading disaster. After the Reading Panel's report, almost everyone was silent about the disaster that had occurred!

Publishers—Good and Bad

In *Why Johnny Still Can't Read* (1981), Rudolf Flesch lists five publishers who offer textbooks on phonics and then the "dismal dozen" who push the look-say method. In *Learning to Read: The Great Debate* (1967), Jeanne Chall describes some good deeds of publishers and some bad ones. Some authors severely criticize some of the publishing companies for their contribution to the reading disaster. Overall, I would say publishers have contributed to the reading disaster rather than making a contribution to the settlement of the dispute.

The Absurd Cost of Reading Studies

The National Reading Panel reported that since 1966 approximately 100,000 research studies have been done. What did these research reports on reading cost? Each one might have cost from a few thousand dollars to millions. Let's say the average was $20,000 (which may be low).

$$100,000 \text{ reports} \times \$20,000 = \$2,000,000,000$$

This $2 billion is a wild guess, but probably low. What about the teachers' salaries that were wasted teaching reading the wrong way? The effect on the economy of students defective in English and spelling? The human misery of students and parents? My guess here is billions to trillions were wasted!

It has been a terrible and absurd situation. I claim that it shouldn't under any circumstances have occurred, but it did! **It would not have if educational research had been required to follow the scientific method.**

If Only It Had Been Done!

In 1955 Flesch's book provided enough evidence that the teaching of reading was a mess that action should have been taken then. By action, I do not mean one of the usual temporary panels, which are inefficient at problem solving.

There should have been established a

permanent specialized SM-14 type national research center
on reading

If such a center had been established, it would long ago have gone on to develop the best ways in total to teach reading. Just imagine the progress that could have been made, and the money and human misery that could have been saved since 1965!

Tremendous Part of *the* BLUNDER Given No Recognition

In a letter to the editor (*Education Week*, July 9, 2003), Charles M. Richardson of The Literacy Council points out:

> The reason black students benefit from moving to non-public schools is largely that the reading programs of the latter are more heavily phonics-based. You published a letter of mine in February 1998 on the research showing that African-Americans suffer more damage from whole language instruction than do other ethnic groups and, therefore, benefit more from a switch to phonics.

> Besides the new research, the late Albert Shanker, in a *New York Times* column of Aug. 20, 1995, reported a "Baltimore Success Story" in which the Barclay Elementary School switched its curriculum to that of the Calvert School, with a phonics-based reading program. In four years, Barclay's inner-city test scores rose by 30 to 50 percentile points, and its referrals for special education went *down* by a factor of four. Similar data exist for the schools described online at www.noexcuses.org/pdf/noexcuses.pdf, at which reading programs emphasize phonics early and African-Americans are high achievers.

> I have tested 200 students on Long Island, N.Y., and the data are very consistent that black kids suffer twice as severely as whites from nonphonics teaching of reading.

This tragic result of the reading disaster has been given very little publicity. Yet it is so important for understanding the low achievement of all those students currently in grade 3 and higher, in urban and other schools, who were taught reading mainly by whole language.

While he was Superintendent of the Houston Independent School District, Rod Paige, now Secretary of Education, initiated (in 1996) the teaching of reading by phonics. However, many urban schools elsewhere did not start using phonics until very recently.

The National Right to Read Foundation stated in 1993 that this group "picked up the phonics torch and is carrying the message to the nation, that direct, systematic phonics is an essential first step in teaching reading." Their report by Robert W. Sweet, Jr., *Illiteracy: An Incurable Disease or Education Malpractice?* (1996), is similar to mine on the history of teaching reading. The organization has many chapters around the country.

We Still Have a Big Problem: What Are We To Do Now That Phonics Has Been Declared the Way To Teach Reading?

Since the Reading Panel issued its report, we have this condition:

Numerous articles and a few books have appeared challenging their findings.

The Overall Problem of Teaching Reading

In 2002, the National Council of Teachers of English passed a resolution asking Congress to critique the research base of the National Reading Panel and others. If we had a permanent specialized SM-14 type national research center on reading, it would examine these and report on them to settle the questions raised. While the reading war is greatly diminished, there is no peace!

Remember that phonics versus look-say or whole language is only part of the overall problem of teaching reading. There are many additional problems, such as:

> children with various learning disabilities (e.g., dyslexia)
> deaf children
> children with attention deficit disorder
> illiterate parents
> special problems of urban and rural schools
> children whose first language is not English
> comprehension programs for those never taught phonics
> brain research related to reading
> which commercial reading programs are good
> summer reading programs
> which reading toys are most helpful
> older immigrant students
> preschool and prekindergarten programs
> bilingual education
> and many others

The December 2003–January 2004 issue of *Reading Today* contained a survey entitled "What's Hot, What's Not for 2004" on reading research and practice.

There are two things I point out:

- It is a disaster that all these things were not studied soon after Professor Rudolf Flesch's book appeared in 1955.

- We still need one or more permanent specialized SM-14 type national research centers on reading to tackle the problems.

Many New Programs To Improve Reading

While teachers are still not being given enough reliable guidance on how to teach reading, here are some programs I have read about:

- In 2001 the U.S. Department of Education and the U.S. Department of Health and Human Services set up a joint task force to identify practical programs for young people.

- From the *American School Board Journal* (January 2001):

  A coalition of 12 national education associations has issued a new guide telling teachers and policymakers exactly what they have to do to improve reading instruction.

  It is called *Every Child Reading: A Professional Development Guide*, issued by the Washington, D.C.-based Learning First Alliance.

- The Haan Foundation for Children is financing a study (begun in 2003) to compare six published reading intervention strategies.

- On January 7, 2004, the U.S. Department of Education announced the award to RMC Research Corporation of Denver, Colorado, of a 5-year contract to run a National Center for Reading First Technical Assistance, which will include three regional centers to be operated by Florida State University, the University of Texas at Austin, and the University of Oregon.

It is great that much attention is being given to improving the teaching of reading. However, temporary centers are not as good as permanent specialized SM-14 type national research centers on reading.

? ?

The Mystery

How long will it take us to really solve the problem of how to teach reading in a practical manner?

? ?

Since our top leaders have not done it, I make

An Apology to All Our Teachers of Reading
(When the National Reading Panel issued its report in favor of phonics in April 2000, this apology should have been made.)

Before the 1920s, the phonics method was used. Then a new method called look-say, then whole language, was proposed by some leaders. After a fair trial period, research into which method or combination of methods was best should have been conducted. Instead, endless debate ensued at top levels, with the result that the wrong method—look-say, whole language, etc.— became the dominant method that was taught in teachers colleges and thus taught in most schools.

Therefore, the majority of you were sent to teach after being indoctrinated in the wrong method. Thus, the majority of students presently in school were taught reading by the less efficient method. Logically, a permanent specialized SM-14 type national research center on reading should have been established long ago to properly research all the details of teaching and learning reading. We have instead financed some 100,000 research reports, with no practical way for you and your local leaders to separate the good from the bad.

This absurd situation has been a terrible burden for you over the years, and even today the many detailed problems of how to teach reading remain unresolved. The National Reading Panel lists numerous questions remaining for future research and puts a heavy burden on you in terms of responsibility, but it provides no recommendations concerning how questions will be answered in the future without the disasters of the past.

We hear constant charges of "bad schools," and about teachers and principals who had better improve or there will be vouchers. You have been and continue to be blamed unfairly for things that are largely not your fault.

Others have also suffered, including our professors, who have to try to teach many students deficient in reading, writing, and spelling. Employers too have suffered and too often blame our "bad schools."

For all this, we extend our sympathy and apology.

Chapter 10

The Absurd Disaster in the Teaching of Mathematics

Before proceeding, I must state that I am not very experienced with the subject of mathematics. It is easy to just criticize. My investigation of what has happened in math teaching is only for the purpose of fair comment on a matter of public concern and showing basic causes and a way out of the disasters that continue to occur.

In this chapter:

- ◆ The Importance of Math

- ◆ The National Council of Teachers of Mathematics (NCTM)

- ◆ "Arrogance Run Amok"

- ◆ "The Malevolent Tyranny of Algebra"

- ◆ Comments about an Article on the Issues

- ◆ Teaching Toys Are Ignored

- ◆ The Problem of How To Teach Math Continues

- ◆ Summary and Suggestions

- ◆ An Apology to Our Teachers of Mathematics

The Importance of Math

Mathematics is another of the first fundamental education subjects (second only to reading) we have always tried to teach early. As tests and professor and employer complaints show, our students fare badly in math. Again our "bad" schools and our teachers are frequently blamed. I will show that this is unfair. There have been continual "math wars." Also involved is whether we try to teach higher-order math to some students who would be better helped by another subject and thus not as likely to be high school dropouts.

In fairness to everyone, we must recognize that in recent years, with an increased number of immigrants for whom English is a second language, with many students from poverty areas, with math being difficult to learn and not a popular subject, and with increasingly high standards, the problem of the proper teaching of math has not been easy to solve. However, with application of the scientific method and a permanent specialized SM-14 type national research center, the situation can be solved or greatly improved.

Therein lie the absurdities that have occurred. Instead of solving the problems, we have done so many wrong things that we have made many new problems and disasters.

These disasters result in a very serious situation. Other authors have written many good books and articles about the math problem that have been largely ignored. My job here is to stress the very basic reasons that the disaster continues.

Also:

♦ Teachers' creative and different ideas have been and are still being ignored, fought, and not properly evaluated. Often a teacher or other educator will design a more creative way to teach math. It is then offered as a commercial program to schools. Our top leaders usually ignore these programs, no matter how good they are. The designers then have a hard job in trying to get schools interested.

♦ The question of learning the multiplication tables is still not completely settled, with uniform guidance to teachers.

We begin our brief recent history of the teaching of math with the National Council of Teachers of Mathematics, one of many organizations that have attempted to improve math teaching.

The National Council of Teachers of Mathematics (NCTM)

This organization has been the most influential in recommendations on the teaching of math. It has made a long and sincere effort to improve the teaching of math. For example, in May 2000 the Council of Scientific Society Presidents commended NCTM, saying that their work is "a significant and high-quality contribution toward the improvement of mathematics education for all students." The National Research Council found ". . . the process established by NCTM to solicit comments from the field to be commendable and the process established by them to analyze those comments to be exemplary." These were authoritative endorsements.

Who Really Controls NCTM

Please keep in mind that most grade school teachers of math belong to NCTM, but membership also includes professors of math in our colleges and universities and, in addition, people in government, foundations, industry, consulting, etc.

I reviewed the membership of their Board of Directors in 2002. There were

- Three K-12 teachers
- Eight teachers from universities
- Three in other types of higher education positions

I think that this shows that the organization is dominated by some of our top leaders rather than our K-12 teachers. There may be nothing wrong with this, but don't blame or credit to any extent our K-12 teachers for these leaders' actions, good or bad.

The NCTM "New Math" of the 1960s

I know little about this except that it seems to be regarded as a "disaster" by a great many people, including a large number of parents.

The 1989 NCTM Curricula and Evaluation Standards for School Mathematics

For a number of years this received a great deal of praise. Even in 1995, it was still being talked about favorably in some quarters. But, over time, NCTM started to receive criticism. It is too big a job for me to go into detail on all the points that have caused discontent. I understand that the main complaints have been:

Basic skills such as learning the multiplication tables have been de-emphasized.

Students are allowed to use calculators too early and too often.

Estimates instead of accurate answers are allowed, and too much emphasis is placed on group activities, especially if group estimating is employed.

There are objections to the theory of pupil-led discovery, or constructivism.

> The claim that under the NCTM standards, students grasp mathematical concepts, which has resulted in increases in achievement, is not valid. If basic skills are not learned, students are deprived of the computational basics.

Charles J. Sykes, in *Dumbing Down Our Kids* (1995), in a chapter called "Why Johnny Can't Add, Subtract, Multiply, or Divide (But Still Feels Good About Himself)," says

> Historically, of course, mathematics has not gone unscathed by the periodic fads that sweep across the nation's schools. The disaster of the New Math in the 1960s is still a fresh memory for many parents. But most Americans have a very clear idea of what kind of math they think the schools should teach their children. For most Americans, the teaching of arithmetic is a basic test of common sense. There is a nearly universal sense that 4 x 8 = 32—and that this is something that children ought to learn, even if some of them think it is hard or irrelevant, or insensitive to the needs of their inner selves.

> But there is perhaps no other issue in the nation's schools where the gap between the public's expectations and the reigning ideology of the educationists is wider or more profound.

> An overwhelming 86 percent of Americans think students should learn to do arithmetic "by hand," including memorizing the multiplication tables, before they start using calculators. The nonpartisan Public Agenda found that "the inability of some students to do simple arithmetic without a calculator was frequently offered as foolproof evidence of educational failure."

> But an equally overwhelming majority of "math educators" disagrees.

"Arrogance Run Amok"

Those who challenge our top educational leaders must often resort to paid advertising. "Arrogance Run Amok" was the title of a paid public service announcement in the advertising space of *Education Week*, December 6, 1995, by John Saxon, founder of Saxon Publishers. Another in the April 1966 issue of *Teachers Magazine* was titled

"Time to Consider the Unthinkable: The NCTM Math Standards Are a Very Bad Joke."

Unfortunately, Mr. Saxon died in October 1996. He had been an Air Force lieutenant colonel, then a college math instructor. He became frustrated with students who were not retaining basic math skills. He started publishing math textbooks and then books on phonics for teaching reading. He had to fight the math establishment continually in an effort to get his program used. Nevertheless, these books became popular with private schools and in states where public schools select books locally.

Here are some selected comments from Saxon's public messages:

> The disaster in mathematics education in America is a direct result of the refusal of the leaders of the National Council of Teachers of Mathematics (NCTM) to test their theories in massive tests in schools all over the country before they are forced on American students.

> Instead of using the process Dr. Bloom describes, you and your NCTM buddies have come up with a pedagogy that you call the **constructivist method**. This method used to be called the **discovery method**, and many critics call it **touchy-feely** mathematics. The use of this method has been forced on publishers by the NCTM and has caused a national uproar. Because the NCTM demands that publishers produce books that contain this nonsense, taxpayers are demanding charter schools so that their children can learn enough to survive in our technological society. They know their children can think and discover. That is why parenting is difficult. They want their children to be taught the fundamentals of mathematics and to get practice in applying fundamentals.

> The NCTM used its regional and state organizations to force the "new math" into schools all over the nation. The teachers objected to being forced to switch their emphasis away from fundamentals, but teachers wanted to do what was right, so they went along. Anyone who objected was considered unpatriotic. Parents were bewildered and some students cried a lot. But, the teachers still sneaked in the topics and concepts they knew were important, so the scores of students did not decline precipitously at the outset.

We have overwhelming proof that a turnaround in math education is possible by switching from *touchy-feely* books to books that use a much improved method of *direct instruction*. The direct instruction methods in the past have had great flaws. Direct instruction will work well when used properly. The NCTM's basic philosophy for thirty years has been terribly flawed. We have followed the lead of "experts" who have been unable to produce even small gains in any school anywhere. Can you imagine the national celebration the NCTM would be having if they produced even one of the gains that I report in this article? There have been no measurable gains in any school in America for over thirty years as a result of using the NCTM's recommendations, yet this organization has announced plans to put out another set of wild guesses!!! American parents want out.

The disaster in math education is a direct result of poor leadership from the top. It is one thing to make statements such as I have made, and it is another thing to prove it. My associates and I have written math books that have caused great gains at all grade levels and for students at all ability levels. Almost every high school that has used our books has been able to double the number of seniors who take academic math courses, to triple calculus enrollment, and to raise college board scores from 20 percent in schools whose scores are average to over 40 percent in schools whose scores are low. Best of all, these schools have been able to reduce, by over 50 percent, the number of students taking "dum-dum," slow-track courses such as basic math and consumer math.

I agree with Saxon that "the disaster in math is a direct result of poor leadership from the top." Saxon's announcements posed quite a challenge, but our top educators did not accept them. It is interesting to know that in January 2001 California approved the use of Saxon's math books, a belated victory for him in that state. John Saxon had a passion for correcting the math disaster, but unfortunately he died in 1996 at the age of 72. With my passion for the teaching of the scientific method, I am fortunate to still be fighting for it at age 89 in 2005, but without any victories so far. I hope that with your help this book will bring some victories for the scientific method—the idea that has most changed the world for the better.

In 1995, the NCTM, as its part in the standards movement, issued *Assessment Standards for School Mathematics*.

Gradually a storm of protest started to build up. In December 1997, after much fighting, the California State Board of Education decided to adopt K-12 math standards that "emphasize computational skills over problem-solving, and precise answers instead of estimated ones." In January 2001 the California State School Board approved a slate of mathematics textbooks that heavily favor a skills-based approach.

There was an incident of major importance described in various articles. In 1994 Congress directed that the U.S. Department of Education establish "panels of appropriate qualified experts and practitioners" to evaluate educational programs and recommend which of them should be designated as exemplary or promising. An Expert Panel on Mathematics and Science Education was established. In 1998, the panel reviewed mathematics programs. It issued its report, "Exemplary and Promising Mathematics Programs," in October 1999.

On November 18, 1999, an advertisement urging the Department of Education to withdraw its endorsement of the 10 new mathematics texts recommended by the Panel (Saxon's program was not included in the Department's recommended 10 texts) appeared in the *Washington Post*. It was signed by a group of 200 prominent mathematicians and scientists. They argued that the programs were damaging to children because they omit instruction in basic mathematics skills.

In April 2000, the NCTM issued final Principles and Standards for School Mathematics, containing revisions of the 1995 standards.

Prior to this, in October 1998, the NCTM mailed 30,000 copies of a Discussion Draft on Principles and Standards for School Mathematics. I had originally written to the NCTM in 1993 about including the scientific method, and I received a nice letter in reply. In November 1998 I wrote to many of those working on the Standards 2000 Project. However, the final version, which appeared in April 2000, had no mention of the scientific method, even though mathematics is often called the language of physics and math is used in all sorts of complex problem solving.

The Expert Panel on Math and Science Education mandated by Congress and appointed by Secretary Riley is another example of the failure of the "big panel" method of arriving at the "truth."

My specific complaint is that the panel had two members I could easily recognize as opposed to the teaching of the scientific method.

"The Malevolent Tyranny of Algebra"

In reading about the problems of urban schools, minorities, immigrants, "bad schools," and dropout rates over the years, I began to wonder about the value of algebra. I'm also biased—I had only 6 weeks of blackboard teaching of it in junior high. I did not like or understand it, and I never experienced any need for it in my career.

Thus, I was impressed to read an article with the above title in *Education Week* (October 25, 2000). The article was written by Gerald Bracey, a research psychologist and author of *Put to the Test: An Educator's Guide to Standardized Testing* (1998, Phi Delta Kappa).

Here are a few paragraphs from the article.

> Although algebra is all about finding values in equations, it has no value for most people. Its actual uselessness in most people's lives was wonderfully revealed in a *Washington Post* article from several years back. The story described how parents in Fairfax County, Va., were rushing home from work, bolting down dinner, and going to school to learn. . . algebra. "They came not for their benefit," the reporter wrote. "They had learned algebra years ago and most of them had no use for X's and Y's in their current lives.". . . Yet, they are inflicting those useless X's and Y's on themselves for the second time. This time, they're doing it so they can help their *kids* get through algebra.

> Why has algebra taken on such dimensions lately?. . .

> Why? Because virtually the whole nation has been algebra-scammed. Said Mr. Weast: "No algebra means no SAT test. No SAT test means limited college choice" (never mind that even the most selective colleges admit a wide range of SAT scores, and never mind that, in terms of later earnings, it doesn't *matter* what college you go to). Even the reporter fell for it and wrote: "Algebra is the gateway to college and higher-paying careers in a new technical world."

My opinion is that this is a subject for continual careful study by a permanent specialized SM-14 type national research center on mathematics or algebra itself. Settling this dispute could go a long way toward ending the problem of so many high school dropouts if it is determined that is not necessary for everyone to study algebra.

Comments about an Article on the Issues

An article that interested me greatly was published in the February 1999 issue of *Phi Delta Kappan* magazine. The article, written by Michael T. Battista, Professor of Mathematics Education at Kent State University, is titled "The Mathematical Miseducation of American Youth." It covers the issues better than any other I have found. The article can be found at www.pdkintl.org.

Professor Battista identifies the issues in improving mathematics learning:

> Because opponents of reform have sensationalized the mathematics education debate and turned it into a naive "basics and tradition are good—reform is bad" dichotomy, their attacks have obscured the genuine issues that require careful analysis. I now briefly outline several of these issues.

He went on and covered lack of knowledge and disregard of science. He also discussed the bad situation in math testing and other dilutions and distortions.

My Comment

There is no doubt that we members of the public have confused views of mathematics and a lack of knowledge of its complexity. The inability to identify the science of math teaching is the heart of the problem. Until we have a permanent specialized SM-14 type national research center on math teaching, this confusion will continue.

Professor Battista's article really raises and outlines basic issues of great national importance. Yet apparently little happens. The February 2005 issue of *Phi Delta Kappan* contains an aptly titled article "Endless Ping-Pong Over Math Education."

Teaching Toys Are Ignored

The situation in math is the same as in reading. Our toy industry produces all sorts of wonderful teaching and learning aids, but our top educators largely ignore these, even though well-to-do parents use them extensively, as do many preschool groups. The technological advances in recent years and the decrease in the price of components have made some amazing teaching aides available.

The Problem of How To Teach Math Continues

Here are some recent developments.

RAND

From *NSTA Reports* (May/June 2003):

> Mathematics instruction is hindered by a lack of research, reports a study released April 21 by RAND, a broad-based policy research and development think-tank. The RAND committee that authored the report, entitled *Mathematical Proficiency for All Students: Toward a Strategic Research and Development Program in Mathematics Education*, was composed of math educators, mathematicians, psychologists, policymakers, and teachers whose experiences have shown that current math instruction efforts are incomplete and misdirected...
>
> The first step toward change should include the creation of a standing committee of researchers and education, business, and nonprofit leaders to gauge "what has been learned through research and evaluation and propose future directions," according to a summary of the report.

Here they support what I have been calling a disaster by saying "that current math instruction efforts are incomplete and misdirected."

National Research Council

A new study and report *Adding It Up: Helping Children Learn Mathematics* was issued in the spring of 2003 (*NSTA Reports*, May/June 2003).

National Council of Teachers of Mathematics

From an article entitled "Adding It All Up," which appeared in *Education Week* (February 19, 2003):

> In the 14 years since the National Council of Teachers of Mathematics issued its standards for teaching the subject, a debate has raged over whether schools should follow its recommendations and emphasize conceptual understanding as well as performance skills.

U.S. Department of Education

From an article that appeared in *Education Week* (February 12, 2003):

> The Department of Education wants to spend $120 million on research into mathematics education as the first step in its five-year effort to improve the quality of math and science instruction and raise student achievement in those subjects.

Conclusion about Current Efforts

It is great that all the effort is being made. However, everyone has been trying to improve math teaching at the federal level for many years, but, as you can see, things are still in a mess. RAND's suggestion of a standing committee should instead be directed toward the formation of a permanent specialized SM-14 type national research center on mathematics teaching.

Under the No Child Left Behind Act, we have high-stakes testing on math. However, as I have shown, it has been a disaster for years, and we still don't have agreement on reliable programs. This situation is not fair to students and is costing taxpayers billions of dollars. Programs of independents such as Saxon and others continue to be ignored.

Summary and Suggestions

I believe that we have done so much research on how to teach math that if a good analysis and abstraction were done, we could come up with practical programs to test or more authoritatively identify present ones.

Therefore, my suggestions are:

- All those engaged in mathematical planning and research should be educated in the scientific method (SM-14 type) and be required to use it.

- Immediately establish a permanent specialized SM-14 type national research center on the teaching of math in K-12. To gain the confidence of all factions for national programs, we must have one and be sure that it is properly operated. There is a science of teaching math, and we must abstract it and start to test programs based on it.

An Apology to Our Teachers of Mathematics

While mathematics can be a fascinating subject and many people love it, unfortunately the majority of students find it uninteresting and even scary. Many of you teachers individually have devised ways to make it more interesting and easier to teach. But usually these methods are not utilized by those designing programs and standards.

On top of your difficulties of an increased diversity of students from other countries and poverty areas, the difficult behavior problems facing teachers today, etc., you have been faced with change, change, change. First came the New Math, then the 1995 Math Standards, then the open letter of November 18, 1999, in which 200 scientists and mathematicians advised your school district to exercise caution in choosing math programs until a review of Secretary Riley's Expert Panel's recommendations of Exemplary and Promising Mathematics Programs could be made. Then in 2000 the NCTM Revised Standards were issued, followed by complaints that these still are not satisfactory in many respects. How in the world you as a teacher can even begin to absorb all the instructions, specifications, standards, and recommendations in this 402-page volume, let alone have any faith in them, is beyond belief!

The National Council of Teachers of Mathematics is a teachers organization, but it is run by professors and education "officials." These people have caused much of the confusion. The basic cause of what has happened can be traced to their lack of training in the scientific method and the lack of a requirement that those working on government contracts concerning education use this quality control method.

There has been little sympathy for your problems, but plenty of threats about what will happen if your pupils' test scores are low.

The absurd things that have occurred could largely have been prevented.

Even now there is no permanent specialized SM-14 type national research center on math teaching that is properly run to try to put an end to the absurd situations you have had to endure, even though billions are spent on "improving the teaching of mathematics."

For all this, we extend our sympathy and apology. I hope my readers will do something about it.

Chapter 11

The Science Teaching Disaster

I believe that the Harvard/Conant group and misguided followers (or whoever they are) have avoided discussion and debate about the controversy over whether the scientific method exists and whether it should be taught widely.

This disaster of the teaching of science, unlike the teaching of reading and math, has not been widely discussed. It has been a deep, dark, well-kept secret, so the public and many in the educational field are not aware of it. They have heard a great deal about the public's and students' lack of science literacy, but nothing about their lack of knowledge of the scientific method.

- ◆ Science Education Paradox

- ◆ Injustices to Our Science Teachers

- ◆ *The* **BLUNDER** Continues at High Leadership Levels

- ◆ Summary and Suggestion

- ◆ Mystery

- ◆ An Apology to Our Teachers of Science for Past, Present, and Future Injustices

---

Science Education Paradox

The following opening paragraph was part of an interesting article of the above title that appeared in *Technology Review* (September 2001).

> The United States by any conceivable measure has the finest scientists in the world. But the rest of the population, by any rational standard, is abysmally ignorant of science, mathematics and all things technical. That is the paradox of scientific elites and scientific illiterates: how can the same system of education that produced all those brilliant scientists also have produced all that ignorance?

I am not criticizing the author. He is among hundreds I have read in my 15 years of researching the scientific method lamenting our lack of scientific literacy but never calling attention to the lack of teaching the scientific method. *The* **BLUNDER** has been so widespread that these authors, not having been adequately taught the scientific method or a formula such as SM-14, are not familiar with the "deep, dark secret" I refer to on the previous page.

It is quite correct that we have a huge problem concerning what to do about the public's and students' lack of knowledge of science and technology.

Science is its method, and the method has not been adequately taught. Thus, the very essence and heart of science are still not being adequately taught to students and properly explained to the public. A first-class disaster! This blunder is still wasting billions of dollars of taxpayers' money each year.

In this chapter I will not go into great detail about this. Many organizations are involved in science teaching, and I cover the matter in coming chapters. Please see the chapters or pages on the contribution of the following organizations to *the* **BLUNDER**: U.S. Department of Education, National Science Teachers Association, National Science Foundation, National Academy of Sciences, American Association for the Advancement of Science, National Association for Research in Science Teaching, and Biological Science Curriculum Study.

Injustices to Our Science Teachers

National programs in grade schools and colleges have taught teachers an incorrect definition of science. For more than 40 years, all the numerous national educational reform programs for grade schools and teacher training programs have not included the scientific method, although students taught from many science textbooks often received a tiny bit of instruction in the scientific method.

A major reason for limited textbook coverage is that the Educational Testing Service (ETS), which owes its existence to Dr. Conant, has always followed the concept that the scientific method doesn't exist. Although a few pages about the scientific method are included in many science textbooks, it has never been included in ETS testing. I believe other testing organizations have followed its example. Since teachers are under pressure to "teach to the test," this has retarded the inclusion of more material in textbooks and in the classroom.

Teachers were subjected to special training and extra demands to learn new, but erroneous programs. For more than 40 years, teachers have often attended numerous workshops, weekend or summer institutes, day training sessions, in-service programs, staff development programs, home study programs, academic year institutes, and other special training sessions. Much of this training was wasted because these programs did not properly present science and what really should have been taught along with science subject matter—the scientific method. The National Science Foundation alone has spent over $5 billion to "improve science and math teaching." A large part of these funds and those of the U.S. Department of Education spent on improving science teaching were wasted.

The erroneous national "improvement" programs include:

Physical Science Study Committee	Elementary School Science Project
Harvard Project Physics	School Science Curriculum Project
Biological Sciences Curriculum Study	Cooperative College School Science
Engineering Concept Curriculum Project	Science Curriculum Improvement
Chemical Education Materials Study	Secondary School Science Project
Chemical Board Approach Project	Introductory Physical Science

ISIS   SAAWOK   TSM   ESCP   SCIS   SMSG

American Association for the Advancement of Science: Science—A Process Approach

More Recent Programs

National Academy of Sciences (in cooperation with The Smithsonian Institution): National Science Resource Center Programs
U.S. Department of Education: Dwight D. Eisenhower Mathematics and Science Education Program

American Association for the Advancement of Science: Science for All Americans—Project 2061

National Science Teachers Association: Theory into Action and Scope: Sequence and Coordination

National Science Foundation: Statewide Systemic Initiatives Program

The Newest and Biggest Blunder

1995 National Science Education Standards (National Academy of Sciences held the contract to compile and recommend)

Teachers are required or encouraged to teach discovery, hands-on inquiry in an incomplete manner. National programs requiring these methods do not include the scientific method. As a result, students obtain little or no transfer of learning, despite extra effort required of teachers for this type of activity.

Teachers are set impossible goals. In 1994, Goals 2000 set an unrealistic short-term goal: "By the year 2000, United States students will be the first in the world in mathematics and science achievement." Of course, this goal was not reached.

Organizations representing teachers ignore the scientific method problem. I sent a special report to the officials of the National Science Teachers Association and my regular reports to the National Education Association and the American Federation of Teachers. No one is making any attempt to study these injustices imposed on teachers. Because there are no publicity and no debate about the scientific method situation, most teachers are unaware of the harm and injustices done to them by those who perpetuate a failure to teach the scientific method. But they *are* aware of the change, change, change.

Teachers were incorrectly guided from 1957 to 1995 and are again being incorrectly guided by the National Science Education Standards of 1995. The Standards present science as inquiry, with no method of science—the scientific method. Since 1995, when the National Research Council of the National Academy of Sciences compiled and recommended these "standards," billions of dollars and millions of teacher hours have been wasted on incorrect standards. I sent the National Academy of Sciences a detailed special report in 1995 and other communications which, had they not been ignored, would have prevented this additional disaster and blunder. I explain this in greater detail in Chapter 28, Contribution of the National Academies to *the* **BLUNDER**, and Chapter 31, Contribution of the National Science Teachers Association to *the* **BLUNDER**.

Science Teacher Magazines

As these come into my office each month, I notice that there are numerous articles on teaching "science as inquiry" but no reference in them to the fact that inquiry leads to process and the process of science is the scientific method. I am surprised that occasionally one of these publications will run an article on the scientific method. Sometimes the article is fairly good, but some of them are poor. They may want to pacify teachers who believe in the scientific method.

Science and Technology

Since the reform efforts to improve the teaching of science began in 1957, there has been a huge increase in technology—the application of science. Today the aim should be the teaching of science and technology. However, our top educational leaders are largely ignoring this new situation. The 1995 Science Education Standards do not stress technology. In 2000, *National Educational Technology Standards for Teachers* was issued, but it hasn't gotten much attention.

Professor Paul Hurd of Stanford University was, until his recent death, a crusader for improvement in science education. In an article "Modernizing Science Education" in the *International Journal of Research in Science* (January 2002), he stated:

> A new framework is required for a general education in science, one that is student centered and up-to-date on the nature of science technology. As stated in the Science Bulletin (2000), "Science and technology have become the driving force for mankind's quest for a better society" (p. 1). The new science curriculum also should be focused on the utilization of science technology for public welfare and human benefit...
>
> No organization in science education has as yet emerged that specializes in the theory or philosophy of a science education for all students. Consequently, efforts to reform science education have been limited to the facts and principles of traditional disciplines and to presumed modes of inquiry ("thinking like a scientist"). The current call for a *reinvention*, rather than an updating, of science education compels a different perception of what a general education in science should mean. Simply updating the traditional principles and generalizations of science disciplines and labeling them standards can no longer be considered a reform of science education.

Professor Hurd points out that our current standards, which call for modes of inquiry, are inadequate. We need his "reinvention" of teaching science and his call for "what knowledge is of most worth." We need a permanent specialized SM-14 type national research center, not a big name panel, to examine the nature of science and technology teaching for today's requirements. At present there are a wide variety of science research centers, but none is doing the big picture job.

The BLUNDER Continues at High Leadership Levels

The Glenn Commission

I describe the 1999 National Commission on Mathematics and Science Teaching in Chapter 30, Contribution of the U.S. Department of Education to *the* **BLUNDER**. The report of the commission, *Before It Is Too Late*, which cost $800,000, was issued in 2000 and soon forgotten.

The Center for Curriculum Materials in Science

I describe Project 2061 in Chapter 29, The Contribution of the American Association for the Advancement of Science to *the* **BLUNDER**. The Summer 2003 issue of the Project 2061 newsletter describes the Center for Curriculum Materials in Science, which is funded by a $9.9 million 5-year grant from the National Science Foundation. The newsletter states:

> The Center for Curriculum Materials in Science allows Project 2061 to play a major role in the future of science curriculum development and, as a result, to help all students gain essential science knowledge and skills. The work is carried out in collaboration with the University of Michigan, Northwestern University, and Michigan State University, along with school districts in Detroit, Chicago, and Lansing.

It is another example of the endless spending of taxpayers' money on so-called research and improvement in the teaching of science. You can be sure that they will continue to ignore teaching the scientific method and a formula for its stages.

The Secretary's Mathematics and Science Initiative

On February 6, 2003, Ron Paige, Secretary of Education, announced that the department was launching a major 5-year Mathematics and Science Initiative to improve mathematics and science achievement. He said, "The U.S. Department of Education, National Science Foundation, National Institutes of Health, and National Aeronautics and Space Administration, as well as other federal departments and mission agencies involved in education and workforce development, will work together to develop the particulars of this initiative and to assure its success."

The three goals they set are worthy ones. However, I believe this will just be another of the many movements to improve math and science teaching that have come and gone without a great deal of success.

The BLUNDER Keeps Expanding

I have called your attention to the billions of dollars that have been spent in the past on the improvement of science teaching without the inclusion of the scientific method. This blunder keeps rolling along.

U.S. Department of Education Mathematics and Science Partnership

Education Week (March 12, 2003) reports that this partnership will receive a 708 percent increase this year—from $12.5 million in fiscal year 2002 to $101 million in fiscal year 2003. This money will go to all the states to advance math and science. The disaster is that the teaching of the scientific method will not be included in these efforts.

First Summit on Science, March 16, 2004

This meeting was held by the U.S. Department of Education as part of the No Child Left Behind bipartisan education reform. More than 700 educators, researchers, scientists, and business leaders attended. Their news release makes no mention of teaching the scientific method.

Federal Testing Deadline on Science Coming

Education Week (January 4, 2004) points out that the No Child Left Behind Act will require students to be tested on science in three grade spans—3–5, 6–9, and 10–12—at least once a year beginning with the 2007–2008 school year. **Unless *the* BLUNDER is corrected quickly, there will be nothing in these tests on the lifeblood of science—the scientific method.**

NSTA Reports (January/February 2005) reports that "The National Assessment Governing Board (NAGB) has awarded a $1.3 million contract to WestEd and the Council of Chief State School Officers (CCSSO) to develop a new framework and specifications for the National Assessment of Educational Progress (NAEP) science assessment." The National Science Teachers Association and the American Association for the Advancement of Science will collaborate on the project. All these organizations have participated in perpetuating *the* BLUNDER. Unless this book is successful in ending *the* BLUNDER, the scientific method probably will not be included in their work. It is of great importance that students be properly tested in science. The public should contribute to efforts to have the scientific method included on tests.

NSTA Reports (January/February 2005) also reports that the U.S. Department of Education hosted a conference for university presidents at which the presidents were challenged to improve science teacher education. Here again I doubt that they were given any guidance to include the scientific method. *The* **BLUNDER** will continue at schools of education unless this guidance is given.

Summary

In the last 40 years or so, billions of dollars have been spent on how to teach science. Numerous important organizations have been involved. None of this "research" has produced a report that the scientific method and a formula for its stages should be taught. The reason, of course, is the power and prestige of the Harvard/Conant group

and misguided followers (or whoever they are). Because I cover this situation elsewhere I will not go into further detail here.

Suggestion

Throughout this book I recommend that we have a permanent specialized SM-14 type national research center on the scientific method. Here I suggest that we need such a center on the teaching of science in general. It is not logical to continue the endless spending of millions and billions of dollars on how to teach science without ever coming up with a successful program that includes the scientific method.

? ?

The Mystery

Look at the rate of growth in science textbooks:
In the 1930s, general science textbooks had about 150 pages.
In the 1970s, they had about 300 pages.
In the year 2000, many were about 1,000 pages.
Given the rate of knowledge explosion and the rate of expansion of textbooks, textbooks could be more than 3,000 pages in 2020.

Students can't really learn all this "knowledge." Why can't our top leaders understand that method—the scientific method—must be taught?

? ?

An Apology to Our Teachers of Science for Past, Present, and Future Injustices

Those of you who have been teaching science for years know that you have seen nothing but change, change, change in how you were instructed to teach science. The programs listed in this chapter are just the national ones; there are probably state and local programs or variations of the national ones. No one has ever publicly apologized to you for all the mistakes and errors to which you have been subjected. Some misdirection is normal, but not the amount with which you have been plagued.

Science is known as "the exact science" and the social sciences as "the inexact sciences." While education is an inexact science, how an exact science came to be taught so inexactly is a sorry tale of blundering, all because of the complete lack of use of the method of science—the scientific method. *Since others have not, I apologize for the past injustices you have endured.*

Before the 1995 National Science Education Standards, most of you taught the scientific method a little because few pages about it have been included in most science textbooks.

In Chapter 28, I describe a little about the setting of the 1995 Standards, which were supposed to be the consensus of more than 1800 individuals and 250 groups, although at the last minute drastic changes were made. The Standards include this statement: "Individuals from all of the these groups were involved in the development of the *National Science Education Standards*, and now all must act together in the national interest." Not only were you asked to join in teaching the Standards—which present "science as inquiry" but not its method—but your nose will soon be held to the grindstone with test results that must measure up or else . . . *I apologize for the present injustices you are enduring.*

So now look at the pickle you are in again since our top educators have blundered again and worse than ever on the 1995 Standards!

Before very long they are going to have to ask you to do what they should have done more than 40 years ago—teach that science is far more than inquiry. Inquiry leads to process, and the process of science is the scientific method.

So here is an advance apology from me for all your troubles to come. It is to be hoped that those at fault will apologize to you, too.

Chapter 12

The Disaster of Our Curriculum

The introduction of *The Great Curriculum Debate* (Tom Loveless, editor, 2001) opens with this statement:

> For the American school curriculum, the twentieth century ended like it began, with an intense debate over what schools should teach and how they should teach it.

Therein is the disaster of our curriculum! For a century, we have had much debate, with little closure of the debate, and little reliable knowledge available to our policy makers, teachers, and schools. Or, more likely, it is a question of how much of the great amount of information we have is reliable.

Section 1
Our General Curriculum

- Our General Curriculum
- Summary of Our General Curriculum

Section 2
The Disaster of the Subject Matter
Only Curriculum versus the Subject Matter
and Problem-Solving Curriculum

- An Early Wrong Decision on Subject Matter
- We Blundered Badly on Method
- What Our Modern Objective Should Be
- Summary
- Mysteries

SECTION 1
OUR GENERAL CURRICULUM

I have described the disasters in the teaching of reading, math, and science. Yet to come are many of the disasters concerning teaching in general. I haven't researched other subject areas. However, the literature is full of disputes about teaching art, music, history, geography, and other subjects. How important they are, what knowledge should be taught, how and when, are all points constantly being argued. The

107

matter of curriculum is another very complex one. I limit myself to only a few comments.

Association for Supervision and Curriculum Development

This organization impressed me as being very progressive when I began my research on the scientific method. However, when I issued my challenge in a Special 1995 Report, it was ignored. The group has done a lot of work on our curriculum and issues numerous reports and books. My observation has been that, even though they are a group of more than 110,000 education professionals, our top educational leaders do not pay much attention to them. I don't know why.

Failure To Teach Students Properly

According to the *The Achiever* (February 1, 2004):

> Forty-two percent of entering freshmen at public two-year colleges and about one out of five (20 percent) entering freshmen at four-year public institutions enrolled in at least one remedial course in fall 2000.

This certainly indicates the results of our general curriculum and the other disasters I describe in this book.

Summary of Our General Curriculum

Permanent Specialized SM-14 Type National Research Center

While we need many of these centers in specific subject matter areas, I believe that we need one on curriculum as a whole. There is only so much that can be squeezed into the school day, so we need someone to specialize in this, especially since things change so fast now. It will be extremely difficult to achieve consensus on what our curriculum should be, but the work of this group and its recommendations would be far better than using the authoritative opinions of those presently guiding our curriculum.

SECTION 2
THE DISASTER OF THE SUBJECT MATTER ONLY CURRICULUM VERSUS THE SUBJECT MATTER AND PROBLEM-SOLVING CURRICULUM

On the previous page, I discuss the curriculum in general, but the above disaster in our curriculum has been the key element in the biggest intellectual and educational disaster in history. Therefore, I discuss it here in greater detail.

Our basic educational effort has been to teach subject matter. This overemphasizes the value of memory rather than thinking ability. With the knowledge explosion, this objective must be reviewed. Our modern objective must again become to teach subject matter and the scientific method with its supporting ingredients.

An Early Wrong Decision on Subject Matter

In 1893, Charles W. Eliot, President of Harvard University, headed a Committee of Ten of the National Education Association (before it became a teachers union) that "argued that the primary task of secondary education should be to develop and discipline students' minds through the teaching of academic subject matter" (according to Thomas Toch in *In the Name of Excellence*, 1991). This greatly helped to perpetuate the idea that students learned to think as a by-product of learning subject matter.

We Blundered Badly on Method

History of Teaching Thinking Skills

I am no expert on the history of teaching thinking, but in my opinion real progress on teaching thinking started with Bacon in the early 17th century and grew slowly as the scientific method was recognized and developed. The 18th century even earned the title of the Age of Enlightenment. In the 19th century, the first edition of Karl Pearson's famous book *The Grammar of Science* (1892) for students and the public made a substantial contribution, along with subsequent editions, to teaching thinking and the method of science. He clearly recognized the relationship of thinking and method with this statement (from *The Grammar of Science*):

> Personally I have no recollection of at least 90 percent of the facts that were taught to me at school, but the notions of method which I derived from my instructor in Greek grammar (the contents of which I have long since forgotten) remain in my mind as the really valuable part of my school equipment for life.

This principle is of great basic importance: A large part of subject matter is forgotten, but method, because it is used over and over, is

remembered. Therefore, how to use method properly should be taught.

In Chapter 3 and throughout this book, I explain how Dr. Conant's false claims, starting in 1947, that the scientific method does not exist greatly restricted the teaching of the scientific method. This was extended to retarding the teaching of complex problem solving, as they are one and the same.

Good Features of the Progressive Education Movement Were Not Utilized

The decline of the progressive education movement in the early 1950s further retarded the teaching of problem solving and resulted in a big return to teaching just subject matter.

Another reason the objective of teaching the scientific method and problem solving in the period 1900 to 1957 was never achieved to any extent was the lack of summarized knowledge of the subject in an easy-to-use form and the lack of good teaching material.

Which of all of the various objectives of the progressive education movement were correct or wrong is a point that is still debated. However, the objective of teaching the scientific method and problem solving should have survived the decline of the progressive education movement. It did not because, as mentioned in Chapter 3, the "greatest educator of the time" declared that the method did not exist.

In *Problem Solving: Toward a More Humanizing Curriculum* (1975), Professor Otto Hollaway says this about what happened to our education system:

> Many leading educators endeavored to launch reforms after World War II aimed at making education more responsive to the needs of students and a democratic society. A large number of outstanding experimental programs were moving effectively forward but were challenged by critics of life-centered, problem-centered education like Bestor, Conant, Hutchins and Rickover. These critics and many others became more vocal following the launching of Sputnik in 1957. Such events created doubt in the minds of many Americans concerning the quality of American education and its leadership. Pressures demanded a return to the uniform college preparatory, subject-centered curriculum.

What Our Modern Objective Should Be

In order to have a modern curriculum, we should have one with:

The scientific method and its supporting ingredients being taught across the curriculum in all grades. Special classes should be available in some schools and at the college level. All grades above grade 12 granting certificates or degrees should require special, more detailed, courses in the scientific method. The higher the degree, the more complex should be the courses required.

My estimate is that fewer than 5% of our students (an exception being our scientists, who are taught the scientific method by the apprentice method) are receiving an adequate education in the scientific method. A few are receiving some of it under the term "the scientific method," others under problem solving, guided design, engineering method, creative problem solving, etc.

The following is from the article "It's Not What You Know, But How You Use It," by Professor Robert J. Sternberg (*Chronicle of Higher Education*, June 28, 2003):

> What is to be done? Although I do not claim to have any solution to the problems of hate and foolishness, I do believe that we need to rethink our goals in education. Increased academic skills may be necessary for many kinds of success, but they are not sufficient. Students need something more. In my work and that of my colleagues at Yale University's Center for the Psychology of Abilities, Competencies, and Expertise, we are seeking a solution—teaching students from roughly age 10 or so to think wisely. Underlying this program is the view that we need to teach students not only knowledge but also how to use that knowledge well.

The method of using knowledge well is the scientific method. To teach for wisdom, you must also teach it. Because of *the* **BLUNDER**, this is not being adequately done.

Evidence of the Disaster of Students Not Trained in Problem Solving

How much do college students know about problem solving when they arrive in college? Professor Donald R. Woods of the Chemical Engineering Department, McMasters University, who has spent many years teaching problem solving, issued a newsletter on the subject. He has also written several excellent manuals. In the article, "What Is the

Problem in Teaching Problem Solving?," in *The Teaching of Elementary Problem Solving in Engineering and Related Fields* (1980), edited by James L. Lubkin, Dr. Woods and his co-authors presents some of their observations, including the following:

> Students do not have an organized method of defining or thinking about problem solving. They just "do their thing". To many this meant starting to solve a problem with whatever came into their head first. To others this meant that they tried to locate a worked example problem. Still others found they just did not have confidence to do anything; getting started on solving any problem was just a traumatic experience. When they got "stuck" on solving a problem, few could describe where they were, what was causing the difficulty and what obstacle they were trying to overcome. In trying to develop plans for solving problems, too many students try to solve problems by "playing around with the given symbols and data" until they find an equation that "uses up all the given information". Such a dependence means that the students cannot function when they are given problems where too much or insufficient data are given.
>
> In summary "doing their own thing" did not provide satisfaction to most of the problem solvers and much of what they were doing was reinforcing what we would identify as bad habits. Our observations were confirmed by the correspondence of Doyle (19), Fuller (15) and Van Wie (20). Counterbalancing this, when we gave students specific assistance in improving their problem solving skills these are their comments: "this experience opened my mind", "now I have a new awareness of how to look at a problem" and "the best thing I gained from this experience was confidence; I no longer panic, when I see a new problem I just patiently start to apply the problem solving strategy". These illustrate the deficiencies as perceived by the students.

Summary of the Disaster of Subject Matter-Only Curriculum versus Subject Matter and Problem-Solving Curriculum

I claim that the experiences we have had in the teaching of critical thinking skills and problem solving, and the relative ease with which this knowledge can be abstracted from the literature, great progress can easily be made.

That we are not abstracting this vital knowledge about thinking and problem solving is a

major disaster and a major contributor to the biggest intellectual and educational blunder in history.

?????? ???????????????????????????????????

The Mystery

"To Teach All Things to All Men"

Modern education is said to have begun with John Amos Comenius (1592–1670). The following is from Comenius' *The Great Didactic* (translated by M.W. Keatinge), reprinted in *The Teacher and the Taught* (1963), edited by Ronald Gross.

> Hitherto the schools have not taught their pupils to develop their minds like young trees from their own roots, but rather to deck themselves with branches plucked from other trees, and like Aesop's crow, to adorn themselves with the feathers of other birds; they have taken no trouble to open the fountain of knowledge that is hidden in the scholars, but instead have watered them with water from other sources. That is to say, they have not shown them the objective world as it exists in itself, but only what this, that, or the other author has written or thought about this or that object, so that he is considered the most learned who best knows the contradictory opinions which many men have held about many things. The result is that most men possess no information but the quotations, sentences, and opinions that they have collected by rummaging about in various authors, and thus piece their knowledge together like a patchwork quilt.

Why, in our subject-oriented curriculum, are we still failing to a large extent to teach students to "develop their minds like young trees from their own roots, but rather to deck themselves with branches plucked from other trees"?

???

Chapter 13

The Disaster of the Charter School, Voucher, and School Choice Movement

This Disaster Is Growing Every Day

We have numerous reports, articles, speeches, and books for and against charter schools, vouchers, and school choice. It is a complex subject involving billions of dollars of taxpayers' money.

Here I show that its proponents are not applying the scientific method to the subject.

- ◆ A Diversion of Effort and Funds to Improve All Schools Results from the Charter School, Voucher, and School Choice Movement

- ◆ The Public and Our Policymakers Are Misled on Charter Schools, Vouchers, and School Choice

- ◆ A Double Blow to Public Schools

- ◆ The Competition Argument Is Tragically Wrong

- ◆ Competition among Our Top Leaders Is Needed to Find Alternatives to Charter Schools

- ◆ Need for Special Purpose Charter Schools

- ◆ Ivory Tower Theory of School Choice

- ◆ Conclusion: Two Views of Charter Schools

A Diversion of Effort and Funds to Improve All Schools Results from the Charter School, Voucher, and School Choice Movement

There is a small place in our educational system for charter schools, vouchers, and school choice, but the real need is to improve all schools. Here is the statement of Professor Seymour Sarason in *Questions You Should Ask About Charter Schools and Vouchers* (2002):

> After all, in the post-World War II era billions upon billions upon billions have been expended to improve schools with little to show for it.

Since some of our top leaders are advocating and influencing others for charter schools, vouchers, and school choice, let's review the reasons why the billions of taxpayers' dollars spent by the federal government have been wasted to a great extent:

- The money has been spent by our top educational leaders on unreliable research that did not follow the scientific method.

- Researchers have been writing for each other rather than for productive results that would really help the schools.

- This unreliable research produced fad after fad, including unsuccessful ways of teaching reading, math, and science.

- Schools of education did a poor job year after year of training our teachers despite the importance of teachers for improving schools.

- The many real needs of our schools and teachers have not been substantially met, contributing to the lack of improvement. Our urban and rural schools have especially suffered.

- Because their real needs were not met, other problems arose, contributing to the overall problem.

Therefore, large numbers of charter schools, vouchers, and school choice will not correct these problems and may even take operating funds away from public schools and worsen the situation.

Thus, the main fault for failure belongs at the top level. The logical thing for our top leaders and others to do is get busy and investigate why they have failed so badly! They should stop misleading people in favor of widespread charter schools, vouchers, and school choice.

The Public and Our Policymakers Are Misled about Charter Schools, Vouchers, and School Choice

We have known for more than 50 years that we have "bad" schools or rather low-achieving ones. The logical way to improve them is to thoroughly study all the reasons I have listed in Chapter 24, in an unbiased way, that they are not meeting our standards. This would involve, of course, applying the scientific method to the problem and establishing a permanent specialized SM-14 type national research center on low-achieving schools.

But that is not what has been or is being done.

Instead, we have a movement that is not based on "scientifically based research." We have advocates for charter schools, vouchers, and school choice making all sorts of claims, ranging from practical to wild. When some organizations try to produce unbiased reports, they are ignored to a great extent. Yet demands that government units spend millions and millions of dollars on a poorly researched movement go on and on, and often succeed.

The Very Bad Part of This

Our policymakers and government officials are misled or pressured into spending taxpayers' money on yet another fad. *The appropriate place for charter schools, vouchers, and school choice is lost in the clamor for extensive, unsound proposals of proponents.*

Reports on Charter Schools, Vouchers, and School Choice

The Center for Educational Policy (CEP). I have found this organization to be more reliable than many others. Its report, *School Vouchers* (June 2002), which gathered information from groups for and against vouchers, states: ". . . inconclusive evidence for vouchers."

Rand Corporation. In 2001 the Rand Corporation published its study *Rhetoric vs. Reality: What We Know and What We Need to Know About Vouchers and Charter Schools* in book form. The report states:

> Our review of the evidence leaves us without a crisp, bottom-line judgment of the wisdom of voucher and charter programs. A program of vigorous research and experimentation is called for, but not one confined to choice programs. Better information on the performance of conventional public schools and alternative reform models is needed as well. In the meantime, political decisions will undoubtedly be made, for and against vouchers and charter schools. They will be informed by good evidence, one hopes, but they will not be fully justified by it for many years to come.

Brookings Institution. This organization received a $1 million grant from the Gates Foundation to finance *A Report from the National Working Commission on Choice in K-12 Education*, issued in November 2003. While it is an excellent report, "the Commission was not created as an advocate for choice or to make judgments about whether choice is desirable or undesirable."

> At its worst, the choice debate is partisan, shedding more heat than light on the subject. Pitting ideologues on both sides of the question against each other, it is more reminiscent of a political campaign. . .than a discussion of education policy.

Thus, the report doesn't do much to settle the basic question of whether the school choice movement is a disaster, as I and many others claim. This dispute is an example of my claim that disputes in the educational field go on for years, preventing progress and adding to the ills of education.

Professor Seymour Sarason's Book *Questions You Should Ask About Charter Schools and Vouchers* (2002). Sarason is a professor emeritus at Yale University. He is also the author of *The Predictable Failure of Educational Reform*, a 1990 book that accurately predicted the failed outcomes of our educational reforms. He points out concerning charter schools and vouchers:

◆ It's a very complicated issue that is being oversimplified, with proponents and opponents publicizing their positions in brief, simplistic ways.

◆ Neither side can yet say that its claims are justified.

◆ Educational reform is more complicated than most people realize.

***Charter Schools in Action—Renewing Public Education* (2000) by Chester Finn, Jr. et al.** They ask the question "Can charter schools save education?" and offer illumination. The authors are on record as supporting charter schools. For balance, they offer a 10-count indictment against charter schools, but do not include the big picture that the charter movement detracts from our main goal of improving all schools. Their description of a "new concept of education" is inaccurate in describing our present system. In their epilogue, they state:

> It's a bet we are making, though, not a firm conclusion that we are drawing.

My comment is that it is a huge bet on which to waste taxpayers' money. These funds would be better spent on solving educational problems that our top leaders have failed to solve because they do not use the scientific method and on establishing permanent specialized SM-14 type national research centers.

Center for Education Reform. In my opinion, this organization is an advocacy group for charter schools, vouchers, and school choice, and not a scientific research organization.

American Federation of Teachers. *Education Week* (August 7, 2002) reports on AFT's critical report about charter schools, *Do Charter Schools Measure Up?* What caught my eye was a comment by AFT's director of educational issues: "Charter schools are a distraction from what we need to be doing." I agree! It's an expensive one, too!

Double Blow to Public Schools

I am all for pressure. However, too much pressure can be very discouraging, confuses issues, and actually prevents real improvement. Schools have been heavily bombarded with the threat of charter schools, vouchers, and school choice. Now look at their latest intense and legal pressure.

The No Child Left Behind Act of 2001

From *Education Week* (July 10, 2002):

> Under the "No Child Left Behind" Act of 2001, if a school fails for two years in a row to meet a state-set bar for "adequate" academic progress, the district must allow some form of public school choice and use a portion of its federal Title I dollars to pay transportation costs.
>
> If the school fails to make adequate progress for three years running, the district must also use a portion of its federal aid to provide supplemental education services, such as tutoring for its students. Parents will be able to select from a list of state-approved providers, including for-profit providers, non-profit organizations, or even the district itself.

Wow! This is real pressure! Why then do schools need the double whammy of the threat of competition from charter schools being set up now and often at their expense?

The Competition Argument—Tragically Wrong

I'm all for fair competition. It is the lifeblood of our nation. I suppose that if I hadn't researched the scientific method and the disasters that have befallen education, I would have believed the claims of many of our top leaders who push for charter schools.

We have famous economists, influential top business leaders, top educators, top political leaders, and others claiming that charter schools, vouchers, and school choice will provide competition for "bad schools," "bad teachers," and other local personnel and make schools improve or go out of business. I have pointed out elsewhere that all these leaders have not been educated in the scientific method. It certainly shows up when they make the erroneous claim that competition is *the way* to make schools improve rather than improve the work of our top leaders, especially those clamoring for charter schools.

The Argument of Competition as the Way to Force Low Achieving Schools to Improve Is Badly Flawed for These Reasons

In Chapter 24, The Disaster of Our Urban Schools, I cover the large number of unfavorable conditions with which urban schools must contend. Remember that there are not just a few; I describe 35 of them. Please keep these in mind when reading this chapter.

◆ Dr. Conant pointed out the important problem of urban schools in his 1961 book *Slums and Suburbs*. Yet our leaders never adequately analyzed and took practical steps to correct the situation, but instead produced all the disasters I cover in this book.

◆ The theory of competition is a simplistic solution. All the alternatives to really improving low-achieving schools have not been previously compiled, thoroughly studied, and tested.

◆ Until we give urban schools adequate guidance, preschool assistance, and greater financial help, they cannot overcome their problems merely by the threat of competition.

◆ The improvements that are possible to make from increased pressure, attention, and threats still may not be enough to meet expectations or possible to accomplish in the time allowed.

◆ Competition requires fairness. There are numerous features in these movements that are not fair to low-achieving schools.

◆ Through charter schools, vouchers, or school choice, separate entities with special privileges or fewer restrictions are set up. This is usually unfair competition.

♦ The big problems of discipline, student motivation, and varied student mix are not helped by taking funds and better students away. In addition, a poor solution to one problem creates new problems.

♦ I am sympathetic to the idea of giving parents choice, but is this fair? We give teachers *no choice* in competing, but require them to follow the usually defective programs of our top educators. We give them no choice but to teach to incorrect standards and to the tests about which there is such controversy.

♦ In fair competition, deceptive advertising is prohibited. What is happening in the reports promoting vouchers?

♦ The federal government has antitrust laws for fair business competition. It has laws and regulations requiring prudent judgment on government educational contracts that are not enforced. Therefore, so-called educational research is "antitrust," that is, it cannot be trusted.

In summary, you do not have fair market forces prevailing. Therefore, claims that competition should prevail are based on incorrect "facts."

Competition between schools of education in our colleges and universities hasn't worked!

We have always had school choice for those desiring to enter the teaching profession. Public, non-profit, and for-profit schools have competed to train teachers and train them in the ways the schools thought best.

Yet today it is generally acknowledged that, despite its great importance, teachers have not been properly trained, and society has suffered. *Here competition has failed*—the scientific method was not applied, and a permanent specialized SM-14 type national research center on teacher training was not used.

Competition among Our Top Leaders Is Needed to Find Alternatives to Charter Schools

Many of our top leaders in industry, economics, government, and education are pushing charter schools, vouchers, and school choice, and some are claiming that they will provide competition that will improve schools. It is obvious that they have not applied the scientific method to the problem.

I believe in fair competition. So I would like to see these people compete in searching for the best ways to correct the problem that federal school reform efforts have largely been a failure since 1957. Now that would be *productive competition*! It is easy to jump on a simplistic solution like charter schools, vouchers, and school choice, but it requires hard work and creative thinking to analyze what is wrong.

To help them, I offer this book, plus the following list of alternatives to improving schools. These alternatives have a much greater chance of success in helping all students rather than just a few students.

Alternatives

1. Find out why educational reform has been such a failure. It is generally agreed that educational reform has mostly been a big failure. Why? To what extent am I correct in claiming it is the

- fault of our top educators and for the reasons I present
- fault of the nonteaching and nonuse of the scientific method
- lack of permanent specialized SM-14 type national research centers

My estimate is that this is costing us more than $50 billion per year— a far more important topic than charter schools, vouchers, and school choice.

2. Study urban and rural schools. These schools are a continual problem, with "bad schools" and "bad teachers" often blamed. Study these schools scientifically. Establish permanent specialized SM-14 type national research centers on urban schools and rural schools.

3. Study how to change schools. In *The Predictable Failure of Educational Reform* (1990) and his other books, Seymour Sarason explained how our top leaders have not understood how to change schools. Study his books. He has largely been ignored. For years, other authors and teachers have been suggesting good ideas that our top educators have ignored, just as they have ignored me.

4. Establish a system of permanent specialized SM-14 type national research centers. Study the advantages of discontinuing most educational research grants in favor of these centers. I have reported on how unreliable educational research has been and how little is really used.

5. Really teach what "scientifically based research" actually is. The No Child Left Behind Act calls for "scientifically based research." All official efforts to identify what it really is have been poor, and state officials are puzzled. Establish a permanent specialized SM-14 type national research center on the scientific method.

6. Student motivation and discipline. Establish a permanent specialized SM-14 type national research center on student motivation and one on discipline. Change curricula in accordance with its findings, so we do not waste so much of our educational effort.

7. Properly educate, train, and induct our teachers. Report after report stresses the importance of our teachers. Way back in 1983, *A Nation at Risk* told us that we were not properly training our teachers. While some improvements are being made, we still do not have a permanent specialized SM-14 type national research center on how to educate and train teachers.

8. Loss of teachers from the profession. Stop the loss of a large number of teachers, who leave the profession disgusted by the difficulties of the task they are expected to perform.

9. Do a complete and continual study of successful urban schools. A small number are succeeding. These schools should be more thoroughly studied and their methods communicated in a way that is easy to understand and possibly duplicate or adapt.

10. Study Professor Laurence Steinberg's book *Beyond the Classroom* (1996). He claims that parent disengagement, student peer culture, and a heavy student activity schedule are the biggest educational problems.

11. Study Jack E. Bowsher's book *Fix Schools First* (2001). This is another good book of many books on school reform that our top leaders ignore.

In summary, the huge amount of time, debate, and money spent on charter schools, vouchers, and school choice would be far better spent on some of these alternatives to improve our schools for all students.

Need for Special Purpose Charter Schools

I have challenged the value of having numerous charter schools for the purpose of competing with public schools. However, there are practical reasons to have some for special purposes. Some practical uses currently being suggested are:

- for exceptional children
- for gifted, creative, or advanced students
- for students in large school districts who are disciplinary problems
- for vocational subjects, science, art, etc.
- for reclaiming dropouts
- for experimental or test design purposes

The Ivory Tower Theory of School Choice

Economist and Nobel Laureate Milton Friedman takes credit for suggesting the revolutionary idea of applying free market principles to our nation's educational system nearly 50 years ago. He also states that the quality of schooling is far worse today than it was in 1955. His theory involves a radical reconstruction of our educational system, which already has major problems.

One of the results of *the* **BLUNDER** is that the economics departments of our universities have not taught the scientific method to any extent. Thus, no science of economics has developed. Therefore, ivory tower economic theories can prevail without sufficient challenge and consideration of alternatives.

I recently received in the mail a solicitation to contribute to the Milton and Rose D. Friedman Foundation to help school choice and to help each state enact a voucher system. Friedman's letter says:

> No one can predict in advance the direction that a truly free-market educational system would take.

This is true. In scientific or even simple, basic logic, you do not take the huge and radical step of changing a current nationwide system without testing. Why don't those in favor of school choice do this:

Controlled Test in One State

Controlled experimenting, testing, and experience is the lifeblood of the scientific method. Our country is conveniently divided into states. Why haven't the proponents of charter schools, vouchers, and school choice tried to get a well-planned and studied test in one state that is typical as far as its mix of urban, rural, and suburban school districts? This would also be a test of whether the public is ready for such a drastic change. That this has not been done is an example of theorists and advocates not being properly trained in the scientific method, but starting and promoting another untested fad nationwide.

School choice is an ideal to work toward, and it does have some fair uses. But until we better correct our educational system, its time has not come for all. It is an extraordinarily complex matter for our system to adjust to, and it does not have the capacity to do so on a large scale with all its other unsolved problems.

Free Markets and Poverty

America's capitalist system has resulted in even those at the lowest economic level being far better provided for than in many other countries. It is still not a perfect system because we haven't been able to end poverty. We also have fair competition regulations. Any fair competition has to take into consideration the many unfavorable factors that urban schools face in poverty areas. We capitalists usually go where it is easiest to make the most money, and that sure isn't in poverty-area schools! The scientific method system is the greatest idea of all time, but it is not perfect—and neither is the capitalist system, even though it has proven its worth!

My Guilty Conscience

Continually pointing out that the major cause of "bad schools" and the ills of education are mainly the fault of our top educational leaders—our "experts"—makes me feel bad, for the great majority are hard-working, well-intentioned, dedicated people, but misguided or failing to use the scientific method. This results in teachers and principals being unfairly blamed. In *The Predictable Failure of Educational Reform* (1990) Professor Sarason expresses a similar view. He states: "The educational researcher tends to use the practitioner as a scapegoat."

Conclusion

I hope that the public will continue to largely reject charter schools, vouchers, and school choice, except when they are truly practical.

Suggestion

We need a permanent specialized SM-14 type national research center on charter schools, vouchers, and school choice.

Chapter 14

The Disaster of Standards, Testing, and Accountability

Standards, testing, and accountability became the law of our country with the enactment of the No Child Left Behind Act of 2001.

◆ The public is dissatisfied with education, and rightly so. Beginning around 1989, some of our top educators, business and industry leaders, and others began advocating education goals, school choice, model schools, national content standards, and national tests. These eventually evolved into today's standards, testing, and accountability movement. These have been largely based on authoritative opinions, with no use of the scientific method or study by a permanent specialized SM-14 type national research center.

◆ Our political leaders listened and were misguided into sponsoring major programs such as

> President George Bush—America 2000
> President Bill Clinton—Goals 2000
> President George W. Bush—No Child Left Behind Act

- ◆ The Complexity of Educational Reform
- ◆ National Educational Standards of 1995
- ◆ High-Stakes Testing
- ◆ Will the No Child Left Behind Act of 2001 Be a Success?
- ◆ Summary, Suggestions, and Mystery

The Complexity of Educational Reform

In the 1990s we had the national goals programs of President George Bush and President Bill Clinton on which billions of dollars were spent following the advice of our top educational leaders.

The January 13, 1999 edition of *Education Week* contained the following:

> Almost 10 years ago, President George Bush and the state governors set goals aimed at preparing all the nation's chil-

dren to improve their achievement in core subjects and outpace the world in at least math and science by 2000.

With one year remaining, the prospects of reaching those goals—and most of the other four set soon after the chief executives' 1989 summit in Charlottesville, Va., and two others added in 1994—appear practically nil.

Student scores have risen in mathematics but stayed about the same in reading, according to the panel charged with tracking progress toward the goals. And the results from international assessments given in 1996 suggest the United States is far from dominating the world in math and science.

Because of the money and effort put into the educational goals during the administrations of Bush and Clinton, and because student achievement did not even approach the goals set, these can be classified as disasters.

From the same article quoted above:

"The goals are written from the school perspective, and they lay all the responsibility on the school," said Dorothy Rich, the president of the Home and School Institute, a Washington nonprofit that trains school officials on how to encourage parents to be actively involved in their children's learning. "It tends to be a top-down or school-out perspective."

Please note "lay all the responsibility on the schools." In reality, the ills of education are mainly the fault of our top educators.

In a nation that spends up to $1 trillion per year on education and training, we should by now be able to plan, design, and implement successful programs. As polls in recent years have shown, the public is very dissatisfied with education. It would be expected that our top educational leaders would respond with more successful programs.

We now have the No Child Left Behind Act of 2001. It is early to judge its success or failure to improve education as a whole rather than just raise test scores. This program, too, suffers from not being planned and based on the use of the scientific method. This is unfortunate because standards and testing are very complex subjects.

In this chapter, I attempt to provide some information on these complex matters.

National Education Standards of 1995

In the early 1990s, some of our top educators, business leaders, governors, and others urged the federal government to finance the setting of national education standards. These were to be voluntary standards offered to the states.

The major subject matter domains were given contracts to set the guidelines. Various temporary groups were set up to arrive at a consensus on what these should be.

In Chapter 11, The Science Teaching Disaster, I explain how the National Academy of Sciences and the National Research Council blundered in setting the National Science Education Standards by not including the scientific method. In the 1994 edition of my booklet, *Edmund's Idea and Research Report on the General Pattern of the Scientific Method SM-14*, I called attention to an *Education Week* article that said that each domain will be asking that more subject matter be taught than the school day will allow.

In *Educational Leadership* magazine (September 2001), Marge Scherer reported on an interview with Robert J. Marzano, a Senior Fellow at the Mid-continent Research for Education and Learning (McREL) Institute. Here is one of her questions and his answer:

> What conditions are necessary to implement standards effectively?

> Cut the number of standards and the content within standards dramatically. If you look at all the national and state documents that McREL has organized on its Web site (www.mcrel.org), you'll find approximately 130 across some 14 different subject areas. The knowledge and skills that these documents describe represent about 3,500 benchmarks. To cover all this content, you would have to change schooling from K-12 to K-22. Even if you look at a specific state document and start calculating how much time it would take to cover all the content it contains, there's just not enough time to do it. So step one toward implementing standards is to cut the amount of content addressed within standards. By my reckoning, we would have to cut content

by about two-thirds. The sheer number of standards is the biggest impediment to implementing standards.

The original national groups that set the 1995 standards for their domains were never required to go back and shorten them. The states have had to do that themselves, or set their own standards. Thus, we have a confusion of "standards" varying from state to state.

Standards Good and Bad

Standardization. In this book, I advocate standardizing by agreeing on a single formula to use in teaching the scientific method, such as SM-14. In the educational field, money and effort could often be saved by very selectively standardizing some things.

Standards for Subject Matter—A Different Matter. Several subject matter standards efforts at the federal level have been disastrous. The idea was that they should be set by consensus. They were often designed by people working only during the summer vacation period.

The only way to do this is to have a permanent specialized SM-14 type national research center for each domain. It is a very difficult job. Knowledge is increasing so fast that there must be permanent centers to provide guidance.

Education Week (January 12, 2000) reported on a gathering of Harvard colleagues to honor former Education Commissioner "Doc" Howe, then 81 years old. He said:

> On standards and assessment:
> "[The standards movement] is a strategy which uses kids as burnable matter in the process of improving things. . .The whole spirit of the present standards-and-test game is the spirit of top down 'We know what to do, here it is, you guys do it, and we'll give you a test.'. . .And it really hurts when the kids haven't had a chance to learn what's coming."

I could also quote hundreds of people in favor of subject matter standards and many more against standards. Since the standards advocates are currently in control, it is important to have an impartial continuing evaluation of the effects of subject matter standards on education. In addition, the accuracy of testing, the loss of the opportunity to teach creativity, and the lack of teaching the scientific method should be evaluated.

High-Stakes Testing

We have always had testing in schools, but now, with the standards, testing, and accountability movement, we have what is termed "high-stakes testing." The states all have their own testing programs. In each state, one test is used to grade a school as "failing" or to determine whether a student graduates or is promoted. There has been an outcry by many against this type of testing. It is required in accordance with the accountability burden placed on the states by the No Child Left Behind Act.

In my research, I have found that there is no permanent specialized SM-14 type national research center on testing. Again, we have a disaster because we don't know what is correct or reliable about testing.

W. James Popham, who has a lifetime of experience with testing, wrote *The Truth About Testing—An Educator's Call to Action* (2001). It was published by the Association for Supervision and Curriculum Development. Here are a few excerpts from the book:

> U.S. educators have been thrown into a score-boosting game they cannot win. More accurately, the score-boosting game cannot be won without doing educational damage to the children in our public schools. The negative consequences flowing from a national enshrinement of increased test scores are both widespread and serious. . .

> All this would be sensible, and our children would benefit, *if* the testing instruments used in large-scale assessment programs actually indicated how effectively a school's staff performed. Unfortunately, that's not what these tests do. And with that realization, the entire high-stakes assessment bubble bursts.

The literature is rife with reports that the No Child Left Behind Act is causing almost all teachers to "teach to the test." Popham says:

> In the previous chapter, I described teachers who relentlessly drill students on actual items lifted from an existing high-stakes test. Can you see how such test-preparation activities completely negate the validity of any score-based inference about what a student knows? The student's score on the high-stakes test sample might soar because of the student's total familiarity with those particular items. Yet, if you were

to give the student a test containing different items measuring the identical cognitive skill, the student's apparent mastery would evaporate.

Here is a quote from *Put to the Test* (2002) by professor and independent researcher Gerald W. Bracey:

> I have spent a fair amount of time over the last 25 years being astonished by the growing role of testing in American education. Just when I would think, "things cannot get any crazier," they always have. Testing was once a tool. Now it's a juggernaut, a weapon to be used for political and social control. . .

> We've gone test mad.

> As an exercise in perspective-building, I suggest you read and think about the following qualities that tests *don't* measure:

Creativity	Civic mindedness
Critical thinking	Self-awareness
Resilience	Self-discipline
Motivation	Empathy
Persistence	Leadership
Humor	Compassion
Reliability	Curiosity
Enthusiasm	

> After the events of September 11, 2001, I added two more:

Courage	Cowardice

Here is what Bracey said in an article entitled "International Comparisons: An Excuse to Avoid Meaningful Education Reform" (*Education Week*, January 23, 2002):

> Advocates of high standards and high-stakes testing have described them as engines for social justice. They are instead infernal machines of social destruction, exacerbating the achievement gap between rich and poor.

Many researchers point out that many good students are poor test takers, especially under pressure. So here, too, high-stakes tests are impractical.

Testing of Students Graduating in June 2005 and the Next Few Years

Students in suburban schools are usually able to master high-stakes tests. Recent reports say that, even in these schools, teachers, to be safe, are "teaching to the test" and neglecting more creative parts of the curriculum. But let's look at those raised in poverty. They have a big problem:

Students' Fault They Fail the Test

◆ Some students have simply muddled along.

◆ Some students are not motivated to really study and achieve for a variety of reasons.

System's Fault

◆ Because of the "one mind at a time" and "multiple intelligence" factors, etc., some students who should have been in vocational, technical, art, music, etc. courses took a regular high school curriculum that was not suitable for their minds and background. Thus, they have not been motivated or able to achieve.

◆ Seventeen-year-olds were 3 years old in 1986. At that time, only a small number had Head Start or any early childhood program available to them. The available programs probably did not include literacy. The importance of this is discussed in Chapter 23.

◆ These students probably attended urban schools that were subject to the unfavorable conditions explained in Chapter 24, The Disaster of Urban Schools.

◆ These students were probably taught reading by the whole language method, rather than phonics. See Chapter 9, The Disaster of the Teaching of Reading.

◆ Their math teaching was influenced by the 1989 whole math program. See Chapter 10, The Disaster of the Teaching of Math.

◆ These students were subjected to the many effects of the other disasters I describe in Part 5.

While I understand that the high-stakes graduating tests have been "dumbed down" and should not be too difficult to pass, the question remains: how much was the student's fault, how much was the test's fault, and how much was the fault of the broken education system?

The ESEA, Better Known as the No Child Left Behind Act of 2001

The standards, testing, and accountability movement of the 1990s culminated in Congress passing (in 2001) and President Bush signing (in 2002) the No Child Left Behind Act. This is a tough, harsh, high-pressure, very complex measure. It puts responsibility on our schools and teachers. It does, however, for the first time, require "scientifically based research." It does not include any requirement for improvement of our top educators. The funding level is probably not adequate for all the goals it includes.

Remember: The act should not have been necessary. It would never have had to be passed if, over the years, our top educators had not created all the fads and disasters I describe in this book. The act resulted not from our "bad" teachers and "bad" schools, but from our "bad" top educators. This is another example of the harm done by the Harvard/Conant group and misguided followers (or whoever they are) in preventing the teaching and use of the scientific method.

Remember: Although it is not publicly stated, the NCLB Act of 2001 is aimed mainly at urban schools.

In business and industry, when a unit, department, etc. is failing, it is easy to institute an accountability program for that unit without disrupting other units.

In the area of public schools, however, it is not now politically possible to be selective. It has been mainly rural and, more noticeably, urban schools that have been low achieving and turning out the graduates to which business and industry object. Our suburban schools have a small percentage of poverty students. Because of this and all the educational disasters I have described, they have not done a really good job. However, it was the low-achieving schools and constant complaints that they would not change that enabled Congress to pass the drastic No Child Left Behind Act. Imagine the uproar if the act applied only to rural and urban schools!

When the big picture is studied, I believe it will show that we need a separate improvement and accountability plan for suburban, rural, and urban schools.

Political Maneuvering To Pass the NCLB Act of 2001

The November 2001 edition of *Washington Monthly* contained an article by Thomas Toch, a guest scholar at the Brooking Institution's Brown Center on Education Policy. The article described some of the political maneuvering, errors in the proposed bill, etc. It was shocking to read of the last-minute efforts to correct errors and change the proposed act. The shock is that our political leaders and their educational advisors have such unreliable information on which to base billion-dollar educational decisions. Again, this is caused by the lack of permanent specialized SM-14 type national research centers and not using the scientific method.

Dropout Rate

The reports in the literature are that students are being encouraged to drop out or are being forced out of high school by high-stakes testing and accountability. To counteract this trend, we should be offering more vocational and technical courses and insisting less on algebra for some students. However, we will always have some dropouts. If they do drop out without a complete high school education, they should at least have been taught the complete method of creative problem solving and decision making for all fields, the scientific method.

Complexity of the NCLB Act of 2001

This quote from an advertisement placed by the National Association of Secondary School Principals (*Education Week*, November 20, 2002) calls attention to the complexity of the act:

> The law is so complicated that a small industry is popping up to work on it. Law firms are specializing in it. Large school districts are adding employees to coordinate NCLB compliance. PR firms are approaching states with offers to help write report cards and craft language that parents can easily understand. Testing companies are getting ready to do a lot more business. Textbook companies are gearing up to sell reading books that pass the "scientifically based research" requirement. Websites are describing and defining the law and offering online training for educators. Workshops, seminars, and professional development programs are trying to address many aspects of NCLB. And every education reporter in the nation has written about it and will continue to do so for years.

Programs in the NCLB Act That Should Be Studied by a Permanent Specialized SM-14 Type National Research Center

The act sets up a number of well-intended programs that are on the right path. However, the research for these should be done by a permanent specialized SM-14 type national research center. Examples are the Early Childhood Educator Professional Development Program, the Reading First Program, the Office of Innovation and Improvement, and the Teacher Quality Initiative.

Certain Aspects of Accountability Need Clarification

Polls Show That 80% of Americans Support High School Graduation Testing. This poll is often quoted by accountability fad promoters as justification for their work. Consider these facts about those polled:

- Graduation testing sounds like a solution.
- They have been misled as to who is responsible for the majority of the ills of education—our top educational leaders, not "bad" teachers and "bad" schools.
- They have not been informed about all the bad features of the accountability fad and that it has no basic reliable research by the scientific method behind it.
- In plain words, they have been misled about accountability.

But those who report on the poll often do not mention that the poll shows that "63% of voters did not agree that a student's progress for one school year can be accurately summarized by a single standardized test."

"Ultimately, the Choice Is between an Imperfect System and None at All." In a guest editorial entitled "Resist the Urge to 'Refine' Graduation Testing" (*Education Gadfly*, June 12, 2003, published by the Fordham Foundation), a resident scholar at the American Enterprise Institute made the statement above.

Yes, accountability is an imperfect system. The literature has been filled with numerous articles about its imperfections.

It should be remembered by the public and realized by members of the Harvard/Conant group and misguided followers (or whoever they are) that if they do not use the greatest quality control method ever recognized and developed—the scientific method—we will have a much more imperfect world.

The phrase "none at all" in this guest editorial also shows the lack of use of the scientific method. Part of the system we need to study and that can be implemented I cover in my suggestions and recommendations in this book.

A Public Agenda poll showed that 75 percent of teachers feel they are scapegoats. The many imperfections of accountability are adding to the teachers' feeling that they are the scapegoats of the ills of education. These ills are largely the fault of our top leaders. In 1990, Professor Seymour B. Sarason wrote in *The Predictable Failure of Education Reform*:

> Far from seeing his kinship with the practitioner, the educational researcher tended to use the practitioner as a scapegoat. And all the while, both researcher and practitioner knew in their hearts that they were seeking their ways through a forest of ignorance that seemed to grow trees faster than they could be cut down.

Will the No Child Left Behind Act of 2001 Be a Success?

For me to make a complete analysis at this early stage would take too much time. I simply forecast:

◆ The act will, with the pressure and money being spent, raise test scores to some extent. Based on this, its proponents will claim it is a success.

◆ It does have provisions that will help education in the long run if they are properly interpreted and applied.

◆ Its provisions that force teachers to "teach to the test" will harm education overall.

◆ It puts great pressure on our low-achieving schools without enough help and consideration for the 35 unfavorable conditions faced by urban schools. Therefore, the gap between low-achieving students and higher-achieving ones will actually widen.

◆ It puts new and needed requirements on our educational researchers but none on our top educational leaders. Therefore, the disasters they create and sponsor will continue. It is remarkable how seldom those at the top are asked to improve.

Critics of the No Child Left Behind Act

The *PEN Weekly NewsBlast* (April 18, 2003, published by the Public Education Network) included a comment on a position statement by the National Center for Fair and Open Testing:

> Why "No Child Left Behind" Will Fail Our Children
> A new position statement from the National Center for Fair & Open Testing (FairTest) claims that the No Child Left Behind Act will exacerbate, not solve, the real problems that cause many children to be left behind. FairTest cites unrealistic demands, punitive sanctions, inadequate funding, and an over reliance on standardized tests. FairTest calls for a reduction in the amount of required testing and the removal of "draconian penalties."

Critics of the Results of Student Achievement Efforts

The September 5, 2001, issue of *Education Week* contained an excellent article "Student Achievement: What Is the Problem?" by Donald B. Gratz. This is the type of article our top policy makers should be paying attention to (but they don't). I quote two paragraphs:

> To solve the country's educational problems, we need to employ a basic problem-solving framework: Identify the symptoms, seek their underlying causes, develop strategies that directly address these causes, monitor progress, and modify our strategies if the symptoms don't improve or others appear. This may sound fundamental, but current practice is to lump a range of symptoms into a single "problem," and to address this problem with one main improvement strategy—high standards and rigorous testing. As results have disappointed, state and national leaders have been unwilling to re-examine the symptoms or review their methods. Instead, when rigorous testing has not led to higher scores, teachers and students are accused of not taking the test seriously. And the most often proposed solution is more rigorous testing. Little attention is paid to the possibility that our strategies may not address the real issues. Perhaps this explains why so much effort and money have yielded so few improvements.
>
> If we truly want to solve our "student-achievement problem," we will have to clearly articulate our goals and identi-

fy problems related to these goals. I fully support education-al accountability, and have seen how thoughtfully implemented standards can help both high- and low-performing schools. But without a clear definition of its educational problems, and the willingness to change course if its strategies aren't working, the country's call to "leave no child behind" while it raises the bar further from their reach is hypocritical—as likely to harm some students as to help others.

In addition to the above, there have been numerous other people, organizations, and books critical of the act to various extents. The February 2005 issue of *Phi Delta Kappan* contains an excellent article aptly titled "NCLB Dreams and Nightmares."

Summary

What our national education improvement plan should be is a very complex matter. Our past efforts have been largely disasters, and our present one is of doubtful value. All this despite the expenditure of billions and even trillions of dollars and millions of lives affected. Our top educators, business and industry leaders, and others continue to mislead our political leaders into programs that will not correct the major ills of education.

Our current No Child Left Behind Act has good features, inadequate features, and bad features. It does not get to the heart of the ills of education. Thus, it is not likely to be really successful in improving education overall.

The act does have a breakthrough feature—it calls for "scientifically based research." As I explain in Chapter 55, Big Change!, so far our top educators have misled everyone about the real meaning of the term—that it requires the use of the scientific method.

The Big Picture of Education

While I am continually trying to give you an idea of the big picture of education, it is beyond the ability of one person to present a complete reliable big picture. That requires a permanent specialized SM-14 type national research center devoted to the topic to do a proper job. My recognition of complexity and suggestions of alternatives are in sharp contrast to our top educational leaders, who think they know what is wrong. They place the blame on our schools and teachers and design programs that require impossible accomplishments by our schools and our teachers.

Suggestions

♦ I first suggest that we follow my recommendation #1, the scientific method should be taught, learned, and applied, and #2, establish permanent specialized SM-14 type national research centers on education, in Chapters 57 and 58, respectively.

♦ I suggest that an impartial, full-time, nonpolitical study group (not a big name panel) be established to monitor and report to the public and political leaders on the successes and failures of the NCLB Act. Stage #10 of SM-14 calls for "suspend judgment." Any complex program as expensive as this one should be reviewed often. In the past, when teachers were presented with disastrous fads and untested programs, they were often able to brush them off or cooperate until they faded away. This time, the NCLB act has drastic penalties in it. Thus, fairness to teachers requires the establishment of this study group.

♦ I suggest that alternative programs to standards, testing, and accountability be studied. It appears to me that, rather than one program to fit all, we may need a reform program for

  rural areas   urban areas   suburban areas

♦ Special attention should be paid to my suggestions on
  ♦ the need for Head Start and preschooling for all or most children raised in poverty (Chapter 23, The Disaster of Head Start)
  ♦ the list of 35 unfavorable conditions faced by urban schools (Chapter 24, The Disaster of Urban Schools)

? ?

The Mystery

Why, with the past failures of our top educators in designing and implementing programs such as America 2000 and Goals 2000, does a nation as great as the United States continue to initiate untested programs following the authoritarian opinions of our top educators?

? ?

Chapter 15

The Disaster of Identification of All Students' Mental Abilities and Skills and How We Handle Our Advanced, Gifted, and Talented Children

Section 1
Identification of All Students' Mental Abilities and Skills

- The Overall Problem
- J.P. Guilford—The Structure of Intellect
- Robert J. Sternberg—Triarchic Intelligences
- Howard Gardner—Multiple Intelligences
- Arnold Skromme—7 Ability Plan
- Mel Levine—*A Mind at a Time*
- Exceptional Children
- Summary

Section 2
Advanced, Gifted, and Talented Children

- The Overall Problem
- The Social Problem in Educating the Gifted and Talented
- Ability Grouping
- Identification of the "Gifted"
- The Problem Is Really Complex
- Suggestions

SECTION 1 IDENTIFICATION OF MENTAL ABILITIES AND SKILLS

The Overall Problem

Teachers have a huge problem when presented with a large class of children of all mental abilities, talents, and attributes. Parents, too, need guidance in understanding their own children. They have simply not received enough reliable guidance from our top educational leaders in the past and even today.

While I cannot say that what I present is the complete big picture of the problem, I do present some of the parts of it that I have encountered in my research on the scientific method and education.

J.P. Guilford (1897–1987)—Structure of Intellect

The following is from an obituary that appeared in the December 1988 issue of *American Psychologist*.

> Early in his career as a psychologist, Guilford became convinced that intelligence was a composite of different abilities, and ordinary intelligence tests were insufficient. He eventually turned to studying individual differences. In the early 1950s he developed the first version of his famous structure of intellect (SOI) with 90 abilities, which he later enlarged to 180.

Although I have found no references to the scientific method in Guilford's works, in *Way Beyond the I.Q.* (1977) he does call attention, as I have, to the problem-solving formulas of Dewey, Graham Wallas, and Joseph Rossman.

Robert J. Sternberg—Triarchic Intelligences

Sternberg is a professor of psychology and education at Yale University. In 1985 he published *Beyond IQ*, with his triarchic theory of mental abilities. It has received considerable publicity. Sternberg's theories are being researched at Yale. The theory consists of three parts:

♦ analytical intelligence, which is used, among other purposes, for analyzing, judging, and comparing

♦ creative intelligence, involving imagining, discovering, and inventing

♦ practical intelligence, or "street smarts," used for putting ideas into action

Howard Gardner—Multiple Intelligences

Gardner is a professor of education and director of Project Zero at Harvard University. In 1983 he published *Frames of Mind* and in 1993 *Multiple Intelligences: Theory and Practice*. These books have received a tremendous amount of publicity. Gardner describes seven intelligences: linguistic, logical-mathematical, spatial, musical, bodily-kinesthetic, interpersonal, and intrapersonal. There are many seminars and numerous books on his theories. A number of teachers are using Gardner's concepts. Like Dewey, he complains that some misapply his ideas. He also has a number of critics who question whether he is really describing intelligences.

Arnold Skromme—7 Ability Plan

Skromme is a professional engineer. In 1989 he published his *7-Ability Plan*. The seven abilities are

- academic
- creativity
- dexterity
- empathy
- judgment
- motivation
- personality

Skromme's book has received almost no publicity and very little consideration in the educational field. He heavily stresses creativity, which I like, whereas Gardner does not refer to it specifically. Skromme also offers good, practical advice.

Mel Levine—*A Mind at a Time*

Dr. Levine is a professor of pediatrics at the University of North Carolina Medical School and Director of the Clinical Center for the Study of Development and Learning. In 2002 he published *A Mind at a Time*. It hit the *New York Times* bestseller list and remained there for many weeks. This is an indication of the public's interest in the subject and a thirst for knowledge about "important mind functions that play a leading role in school performance (and in career success)." Levine stresses eight categories of the systems of a mind:

- attention control system
- memory control system
- language control system
- spatial order system
- sequential ordering system
- motor ordering system
- higher thinking system
- social thinking system

While Levine does not mention the scientific method, he does give a formula for problem solving. He has this to say about problem solving thinking (expressing the basic concept I am trying to convey in this book in support of the scientific method):

> Problem solving is not an ability you can measure with confidence on an IQ or end-of-grade achievement test, yet it may be so much more relevant in life than a standardized score in spelling accuracy or an intelligence test component that requires a child to repeat numbers in the correct order. Effective problem solving is a systematic, logical, well-paced, and planned step-by-step process. It is the direct opposite of doing the first thing that comes to mind. Instead it represents excellent judgment, well-founded decision making, and the use of logical thought processes. In school and in everyday life we can be sharing and modeling meticulous problem solving in nurturing the developing minds of kids. I think parents and schools should be preparing students for those many critical moments in life when they will need to shift into a sophisticated and systematic problem-solving mode.

Levine's book contains many interesting, short case histories from his extensive experience that will help parents, teachers, and others better understand his descriptions of mental functions.

Exceptional Children

I am ashamed to say that I did not allot much time in my research to children with major deficiencies or handicaps. I have the impression, however, that, in this very emotional and complex area, the situation has been a disaster because of the lack of a permanent specialized SM-14 type national research center on the subject.

Summary of Section 1

The disasters here are

♦ Following the publication of Guilford's research on the 180 abilities, there should have been extensive refinement, extension, and development of his concepts.

♦ The disagreement of Sternberg and Gardner on the mental abilities and skills versus intelligences should have been settled long ago, and the relationship to the big picture should have been researched.

◆ Levine's introduction states:

> As such, this book might well be read by all parents and educators committed to the earliest possible detection of breakdowns in learning as well as the prompt identification of a child's assets.

Parents are reading it, but, based on past history, educators will do little about it or will misapply it.

◆ Because of the lack of use of the scientific method, nondevelopment of a science of education, and no permanent specialized SM-14 type national research center for the accumulation of reliable knowledge, we continue to fail to understand students.

◆ Remember all the comments about "bad" schools and "bad" teachers? How about "bad" top educators who can't abstract reliable basic principles from billions of dollars of research to guide those "bad" teachers?

SECTION 2 ADVANCED, GIFTED, AND TALENTED CHILDREN

The Overall Problem

A disaster again—this one is how we identify and educate our advanced, gifted, and talented students. "One size doesn't fit all" is especially important here. The public and educators do not have a good description of the big picture of the problem of educating our advanced, gifted, and talented students available on which to base decisions, so the disaster continues.

It is a big, complex problem, not easily solved—especially in an environment in which we have many disastrous situations. Nevertheless, we have top leaders for the purpose of guiding us in the solution of complex problems. If they had applied the scientific method, this complex problem would not be the disaster it is today.

The Social Problem in the Education of the Gifted and Talented

In *Human Intelligence* (1976), Jack Fincher, a science journalist, has a very interesting chapter on "The Gifted Child." Since this book was written, we have made much progress in the education of the gifted, but basically it is still a disaster. Fincher's comments give you a historical view of the problem. On the social problem of the gifted,

Fincher says:

> That kind of education [for the gifted], manifestly, costs
> more than we as a nation have until now been willing to
> spend—for the gifted or any child, in faith and understanding
> as well as money and energy. Schools, after all, it can be
> legitimately argued, have enough trouble educating the great
> mass in the middle or raising up the disadvantaged at the
> bottom in the manner we have always employed. To divert
> a school's limited resources or further fragment a teacher's
> energies, especially to the heady requirements of those who
> by definition are already the most fortunate, seems unthink-
> able to many. But ducking the issue is at best a copout, at
> worst a recipe for disaster.

Disaster it is! We are still really "ducking" the issue. An example is
the 2001 federal government's requirements for "standards and tests."
This is pushing the time and interest in educating the gifted to extinc-
tion in some cases or a lower level in others without our top national
leaders calling attention to what is happening. It remains for a few
teachers and other leaders to do so, but little attention is paid to their
warnings.

Ability Grouping

I have not researched all the pros and cons of ability grouping. I read
opinions that it should not be done, but I also read many remarks of
more gifted students about how bored they are in ordinary classes.
My unresearched insight is that, while ability grouping creates some
injustices, lack of ability grouping creates other injustices. Applying
creative forward insight, many people point out that if we do not properly develop our more gifted children, in the long run it will create
great harm for the less gifted.

It also makes a teacher's job still more difficulty, having the responsibility for teaching students with a wide range of abilities. Less time
can be spent on lower-ability children who need more help.

Loss of self-esteem is often stressed as one reason for not grouping by
ability, but some recent research has indicated that this is not as big a
problem as had been claimed. While ability grouping is hotly debated,
what is often forgotten in this type of debate is

Correcting one injustice produces another injustice.

Involved in the debate is what is really best for everyone, especially in the end. Here are two main reasons for ability grouping and special attention to the gifted.

Money for Education

Going back a number of years, the people of the United States were much less prosperous than they are today. As a result, less money was spent on education. Thus the funds available for education of the less gifted, the gifted, and immigrants who need special help to bring up to our test requirements depend on our nation's prosperity. An important factor here is international competition. If America does not maintain its competitive edge in an ever- and quickly changing world, there will be less money to educate all students.

Our Entrepreneurs, Gifted Leaders, and Intellectual Elite Produce Jobs

To a large extent, future money for schools and good jobs for the less gifted as well as the more gifted depends on the creativity, leadership, and intelligence of our top people. You can have good skilled workers, which is also a requirement for competition and prosperity, but if you do not constantly develop and have a well-developed more gifted class of students and people, everyone suffers.

Bad Conditions for Everyone

Although ability grouping may create some social injustices, correcting them by neglecting or holding back the development of some students eventually creates bad conditions for everyone. It is not a perfect world.

The *New York Times* (November 9, 2003) published an article by Fran Schumer in which Schumer describes "differentiated instruction, a method of teaching students of different abilities in a single classroom." The idea needs research and development. There is a popular book by Carol Ann Tomlinson on the subject available from the Association for Supervision and Curriculum Development.

Identification of the "Gifted"

In the past, identification of the gifted was largely based on intelligence tests. However, Sternberg, Gardner, Skromme, and Levine all challenge the accuracy of intelligence tests in identifying the gifted, talented, more intelligent, etc. Dr. E. Paul Torrance at the University of Georgia spent a lifetime developing tests for creativity. Sternberg is also working on improving existing intelligence tests. However, until the best tests are identified for teachers, the selection of the "gifted" remains a problem.

The Problem Is Really Complex

One purpose of Section 1 of this chapter is to show the complexity of the problem. The situation is a disaster not only because of the social problems, which are hard to solve, but also because the more controllable problems are not being properly solved.

The gifted will greatly benefit throughout their lives and be much more productive if they are experts in the scientific method. Therefore, encourage them to learn the SM-14 version and practice using it. Then, if they are mainstreamed or even in special classes, they can be assigned a problem. Better still, they can originate their own problem. While other students are doing regular work, the gifted can proceed through the stages of SM-14 in attempting to solve problems, thus avoiding wasting their time.

Importance to Country and Society

In *Engaging Minds* (2003), David A. Goslin reports that the late Albert Shanker, President of the American Federation of Teachers, when asked how America could be the world's preeminent democracy and economic power when our education system has all its problems and inequities, answered:

> Because. . .our top 20 percent are as good as any in the world, and that's all we have ever needed.

The Rise of the Creative Class

In the paperback edition (2004) of *The Rise of the Creative Class*, Richard Florida points out:

> Human creativity is the ultimate economic resource. The ability to come up with new ideas and better ways of doing things is ultimately what raises productivity and thus living standards.

Today we need more and more creative people and thus must be sure that our educational system produces them.

Suggestions

Establish a permanent specialized SM-14 type national research center for "the gifted." There is already a National Research Center on the Gifted and Talented. A brief review of their literature impressed me. Their research and mission statement makes no reference to the scientific method, which is essential. They probably have never been properly educated about the scientific method. Until this is corrected, the reliability of their work will be in question.

The whole subject of ability grouping and tracking needs a permanent specialized SM-14 type national research center of its own. The January 28, 2004 issue of *Education Week* contains an article by Carol Corbett Burns, "When Excellence and Equity Thrive," sharing her experience in avoiding tracking and suggestions. It is this type of article and others that a permanent specialized SM-14 type national research center would evaluate.

? ?

The Mystery

Why do we—the "world's preeminent democracy and economic power"—fail to adequately develop the minds and abilities of our students?

? ?

Prepare a Self-Development Program

[This page was included in the first two editions of my student booklet, *The General Pattern of the Scientific Method.*]

1. <u>You must motivate yourself to improve and develop—student or adult.</u>
   It is a frightening (but challenging) economic forecast! Because of world competition, you will have to work smarter and become more innovative and creative than your parents were in order to be equal to or to exceed their economic status. Allocate your time wisely. Lead a balanced life using all resources. Don't devote **excessive** time to:

TV watching	*Idle music listening*	*Competitive sports activities*
"Hanging out"	*Spectator sports*	*Sleeping*

   Respect your parents and teachers. Maintain good communication with them. Look to your parents for religious guidance. Utilize your school counselor. Remember, self-improvement is **your** responsibility.

2. <u>Have an educational and personal learning program.</u>
   Be sure that you have a good base of reading, writing, speech, and math.

3. <u>Build your intuitive base and learn how to learn.</u>
   These are essential in this age of fast changes and knowledge explosion.

4. <u>Develop your thinking skills and other intelligences.</u>
   Learn methods and processes. Study and practice SM-14. Join others in problem projects.

5. <u>Learn to be a better innovator and to become more creative.</u>
   Innovation and creativity can pay off!

Take courses	*Practice curious observation*	*Be a SEA GEE*
Keep idea book	*Apply ideas at home*	*Develop courage*

6. <u>Keep up with how to retrieve information—learn systems and technologies.</u>
   Knowledge sources and the technology of retrieving information are developing faster, less expensive, more prolific, and universally available.

   Become computer-friendly at school, home, etc.—expand your computer knowledge. In schools, offices, retail stores, warehouses, factories, farms, and restaurants—in fact, practically everywhere, you will be exposed to the use of a computer and new systems. Learn how to type!

7. <u>Improve and develop desirable attributes.</u>
   Develop your overall personality. Think about these attributes often. Do things that will help you.

Join an organization (e.g., Scouts)	*Get part-time jobs for experience*
Read self-improvement books	*Read, skip, and skim periodicals*
Learn to be a good team member	*Engage in helpful hobbies*
Practice tolerance of others	*Enter science & engineering fairs*

   Take part in school, company, religious, and civic activities
   Learn to work quickly and effectively—improve your personal efficiency!

8. <u>Career.</u> Prepare a career plan or a career investigation plan.

9. <u>Personal health program.</u>

Say NO to drugs!	*Develop proper eating and exercise habits*
Maintain emotional stability	*Have regular physical exams*

   Don't abuse your body or take unnecessary risks

10. <u>Set goals and keep updating your self-development program.</u>

Chapter 16

The Disaster of Student Motivation

Motivation—One of the Biggest Factors That Determines Whether People Reach Goals and Achieve the Personal Success They Desire

♦ *Motivation by pressure*—We have always used tests, etc. to motivate students by pressure. In 2002, with the implementation of the No Child Left Behind Act, the pressure on students was greatly increased and in a largely untested way.

♦ *Potential of other methods of motivation neglected.* The potential in national programs for increasing students' grades and preparation for life by utilizing personal motivation is largely neglected and ignored. Each year this results in the waste of billions of dollars and increases the degree of our disasters in other areas.

- ♦ Motivation Is Essential for Efficient Classroom Learning

- ♦ Motivation by Pressure

- ♦ Common Student's Lament

- ♦ Students' Peer Culture

- ♦ Other Educational Researchers' Conclusions on Motivation

- ♦ Alternatives to the Present Disaster

Motivation Is Essential for Efficient Classroom Learning

In *Educational Psychology* (1964) James Sawrey states:

> There is some disagreement among psychologists as to what constitutes the subject matter of motivation; however, there is enough agreement as to what motivational phenomena are that some general understanding can be established. . . Some psychologists contend that all behavior is motivated. Whether or not this is true, it appears rather certain that motivation is essential for efficient classroom learning and that an understanding of motives is basic to the understanding of personality and social behavior.

Student Motivation Theories and Principles and Our Top Educational Leaders

I glanced at a list of available books on the motivation of students. There were a number on how teachers and schools can motivate students. I found none that were applicable to our top educators and how, in designing policies and reform programs, they should utilize student motivation in various ways. In addition, an Internet search turned up this statement: "The question of how to motivate students in the classroom has become a leading concern for teachers in all disciplines." Our top educators should be concerned.

Again, we have a complex problem that is national in scope and in which

◆ the burden of solving the problem is placed mainly on teachers

◆ teachers are not adequately trained in teachers colleges to solve the problem

◆ programs designed by our top educators and legislators usually make teachers' efforts to motivate students harder rather than easier

◆ there is already a large body of information on motivation, but its accumulation, evaluation, and presentation in usable form is not being accomplished.

Our Top Educators

Long ago they should have provided reliable research on student motivation for others at the top so that they could properly design national education reform programs and guide teachers colleges on what to teach in the area of motivation. They should have had a "Guide to Student Motivation Principles You Can Trust for Educational Leaders, Researchers, and Teachers."

Our Psychologists

One would think that the preparation of reliable research of this nature should have been done (maybe it was in some cases!) and accumulated in usable form by psychologists. See Chapter 34 for how the tiny bit psychologists are taught about the scientific method and how little on basic research methodology is included in their education.

Motivation by Pressure

This is what the current standards and testing movement is all about. There is nothing wrong with pressure. Students will be subjected to it all their lives. I am familiar with the problem of student suicides, but the solution to this is not to take all pressure off students. Years ago, Lynn Townsend, then president of Chrysler Corporation, stated:

> No organization can survive—let alone succeed—without an almost constant application of pressure all along the line. Nothing in the art of management is more important than the ability to apply that pressure to stimulate the desire to succeed.

But the trouble with our current standards and testing movement is that it forces teachers to "teach to the test" and students to "learn what is tested" with little or no emphasis on the overall need to learn what it takes to prepare for the real world.

I have shown in this book that the scientific method is what has most changed the world for the better, and it is what can most change an individual's life for the better. Yet we do not take advantage of the motivation of such a wonderful method to get children more interested in learning and top educators to prepare better reform programs.

I show the great need for pressure on our top educational leaders for better performance in Chapter 8; they are increasingly demanding more pressure on teachers and students. If pressure is good for one, it is good and fair for the other.

Common Student's Lament

Why should I study this? I see no connection between it and my needs in the future.

First, we know that many students are

- short-sighted, unfamiliar, or uneducated about what they may need in the future

- prone to take the easiest courses when given a choice; often, however, it is because they are under pressure to get good grades

But, second, we also know that

◆ our curriculum is a mess

◆ billions of dollars are spent every year to teach or try to teach students subjects that will never be of benefit to them or to society

◆ the time and money wasted could be far better spent on developing students' knowledge in other areas, especially problem solving and associated thinking skills abilities

◆ the problems of student motivation, the subject-centered curricula, academic course versus vocation-technical courses, etc. continue year after year, with no scientific-grade research that results in the accumulation of reliable knowledge on which to act

◆ often, pressure groups or "authoritative experts" continually prevent solutions to these problems

Motivate Students by Making School Interesting

> The founding fathers in their wisdom decided that children were an unnatural strain on their parents. So they provided jails called school, equipped with tortures called education.
> —John Updike

I am advocating more attention to motivation and have read in my day hundreds to thousands of teachers' articles on how they do it. I do not want to create the impression that students will not often have to do boring work and be drilled at times in mathematics, etc. However, while many claim that school is and will always be boring, there is plenty of evidence that just learning is interesting and fun to many. These past teachers' articles are a "gold mine" of ideas that should be reviewed, evaluated, and communicated by those at the top with teachers' advice on their practicality.

For many decades there have been disputes about *hands-on and student-centered activities*. There is a large body of evidence that these types of activities motivate students to learn. Yet, even when used, the stages, etc., of the scientific method are not also taught, wasting transfer of learning.

Students' Peer Culture

In his book *Beyond the Classroom* (1996), Professor Laurence Steinberg places very great importance on improving students' interest in their educational and career success. He states:

First and foremost, we must transform the national debate over the causes and cures of our achievement problem from one about reforming schools to one about changing students' and parents' attitudes and behaviors. It is essential that the public understand that no amount of school reform will work unless we recognize the problem as considerably more far-reaching and complicated than simply changing curricular standards or teaching methods.

It is basic that students come to better appreciate that learning takes hard work.

Other Educational Researchers' Conclusions on Motivation

In my motivation file is a page from the *Review of Educational Research* in which the researcher calls attention to motivating the unmotivated as a critical issue for the 21st century. I am sure there have been similar articles in the past. Our top educators pay little or no attention to them and go on their "merry old way" or rather the usual way of ignoring the importance of elements of the big picture.

Alternatives to the Present Disaster

A permanent specialized SM-14 type national research center on motivation. The problem, as shown in this chapter, is complex. It will always be a problem. Elements of the problem will constantly change. Therefore, we need one (and possibly more) research centers specifically devoted to it.

Top educational leaders and researchers. In Chapter 54 I propose that they be licensed as teachers are. They should be required to pass a test on student motivation as part of the licensing process.

Officers of the proposed permanent SM-14 type national research center on motivation. They should be consulted on all national education reform programs.

Motivation and Sensitivity

In my first little student booklet (1992) on the *General Pattern of the Scientific Method (SM-14)*, Ingredient #12 was Motivation and Sensitivity. When I revised the supporting ingredients in June 1997, I included these characteristics in Ingredient #14, Personal Attributes. Here is what the original page included to help you better understand motivation.

Motivation

Our actions are influenced by motivation, which is stimulated by certain needs, instincts, desires, and emotions. Some of these are:

Love	Curiosity	Social status	Goal seeking
Fear	Food & water	Self-preservation	Achieve potential
Hate	Self-esteem	Financial gain	Recognition hunger
Joy	Physical needs	Usefulness	Sensory stimulation
Comfort	Happiness	Adversity	Anxiety & anger

There are times when we must solve problems of necessity, for school, to satisfy parents, and for other special reasons. *It can be fun and is a part of the essence of life!*

Some basic motivations for problem origination and solving are the joys of:

Financial gain	Discovery	Problem solving
Feeling important	Taking risks	Being successful
Competition	Teamwork	Self-improvement
Teaching	Helping others	Fame and prestige
Intellectual achievement	Work	Competence
Satisfying curiosity	Creation	Good school grades
Contributing to humanity	Learning	Being useful
Dedication to organization and family		Being an innovator

Sort out and utilize your emotions to help you with SM-14

Sensitivity

Sensitivity to people and things, such as the following, plays a big part in problem origination and solving:

People—Awareness of:

Needs and desires	Dissatisfactions	Actions and reasoning
Emotions	Motivations	Self-image
Values and morals	Social relations	Ambitions and hopes

Things—Increased awareness of:

Need to learn	Environment	Purposes	Opportunities
Improvements	Creative endeavors	Patterns	Values/criteria
Communications	Conceptual blocks	Inquiries	Problem solving
Mental alertness	Organizational needs	Challenges	Differences
Innovations	False assumptions	Leads	Hidden points
Classifications	Community needs	Systems	New technologies

SM-14 shows you the route to solving complex problems.
Be confident—you can do it!

Chapter 17

The Disaster of the Classroom Discipline Problem

◆ The Huge Size of the Disaster

◆ The Public Is Concerned

◆ One Disaster Adds to Another Disaster

The Huge Size of the Disaster

It has been my major theme that we have bad schools because we present or create problems for teachers and do not help them enough to solve these problems. This is very apparent in the area of classroom discipline.

While the media is full of stories of violence resulting in shootings and of schoolyard bullies, I am not going to expound on these issues. They are hard to prevent and, in part, just a result of the disastrous way our top educational leaders have failed to provide enough real research and guidance to principals and teachers on classroom discipline and student behavior.

Poor classroom discipline has been the biggest reason for teachers leaving the profession. It is also the biggest reason that teachers in urban schools use their seniority to transfer to suburban schools. Teachers are inadequately trained in teachers colleges to handle the problem. I have not researched the discipline problem thoroughly, but I believe that these claims are correct. I have been amazed at how little consideration is given to this problem by our top educational leaders, considering its importance.

The Public Is Concerned

An article in the *Wall Street Journal* (April 22, 2003) reports:

> Washington—Ill-mannered pupils, demoralized teachers, uninvolved parents and bureaucracy in public schools are

greater worries for Americans than the standards and accountability that occupy policy makers, a new study says.

Teachers, parents and students said they were concerned about the rough-edged atmosphere in many high schools, according to the report released by Public Agenda, a non-profit research and policy organization in New York.

Indications are that our top educational and political leaders are not listening to the public, for they are doing so little in the area of class-room discipline.

Support for this appeared in the June 23, 2004, issue of *Education Week* in an article by Jean Johnson, Senior Vice-President of Public Agenda. She calls attention to their new study, "Teaching Interrupted," and states:

> Given these numbers, I have often wondered why educa-tion's top echelons don't invest more time and energy under-standing why discipline problems arise, which policies work best, and what schools, teachers, parents, and others need to do to improve the situation. Leaders in academia, business, government, and foundations have invested money and formed task forces to address other important topics. In fact, it's easy to lose track of the dozens of reports, evaluations, and symposia devoted to standards, teacher quality, testing, school choice, school leadership, bilingual education, special education, reading instruction, and school finance. Yet disci-pline seems to be the ugly duckling of high-level education debate.

One Disaster Adds To Another Disaster

A quick review of the Internet shows a small number of books on the subject. An excellent article by Ann Bradley in *Education Week* (January 19, 1994) reviews Cincinnati's struggle to find a solution. She states:

> Given the fact that many of the students who are discipline problems are also low achievers, the schools also have to do a better job at teaching academics. And discipline problems multiply when students are bored in school or when what they are learning seems to have no relevance to their lives.

When problem solving is taught, students easily see its relevance to their lives.

I believe that many of the other disasters described in this book have helped add to the problem of discipline that teachers face.

What Should Be Done

Many schools or school districts have tried various solutions. *Education Week* (January 1, 2000) reports on a behavior management system developed by the University of Oregon. Discipline may be a local problem, but it is so important that it requires national attention and practical help. The recent spate of shootings and the killing of students and teachers is a good indication that it is not going away, and the lack of adequate efforts in the past. Therefore, this is another area in which I believe that we need one or more

permanent specialized SM-14 type national research centers
on student violence, behavior, and motivation

Who Said Schools Will Not Change?

It is often said that schools will not change! I have shown just some of the many disastrous changes thrown at schools in the second half of the 20th century.

From an *Education Week* (February 14, 2001) article titled "It Takes Capacity to Build Capacity" and subtitled "Why the Biggest Threat to Reform May Be System Overload" by Thomas Hatch, a senior scholar at the Carnegie Foundation for the Advancement of Teaching:

> "We have too much to do and too many scattered ideas," one principal in a district in the San Francisco Bay area told me recently. "It seems like we have eight major initiatives and 25 subsets of those." From the perspective of one associate superintendent in the same district, this problem is not unique. As he put it, "Our principals are going crazy." The result, he explained, is that frustration and anger at the school level have never been higher. When attempting to garner new funds or develop new programs, over and over again he hears this from principals and teachers: "We don't want anything else. We're in over our heads."

Chapter 18

The Disaster of Our Schools of Education

In the last few years there have been numerous reports and articles by our educational leaders claiming that the most important factor in reforming education is improvement in the quality of our teachers.

Wow! If it were only that simple! What about the quality of our top educational leaders? Teachers have complained about their poor training for years. This book shows that we have had one disaster after another as a result of the poor leadership of our top educational leaders. This shows up again in the way our schools of education have been allowed to operate. Until our top leaders correct this situation properly, there will never be a continuous supply of effective teachers. While Congress and the U.S. Department of Education are finally putting pressure on our schools of education, this is not enough. We need to put pressure on our top leaders before these schools of education can reach their potential.

- ◆ The Poor Record of Our Schools of Education

- ◆ Specific Reasons from the Literature for the Disaster of Our Schools of Education

- ◆ What Is an Effective Teacher?

- ◆ Summary and Mystery

The Poor Record of Our Schools of Education

Please remember that almost all our top or near-the-top organizations in the educational field have what I would call a poor record. None has recognized, promoted, and adequately used the scientific method.

There are many acknowledgments that America's high leadership status in the world has been greatly helped by its college and university system. However, our schools of education have, *on the whole*, done a poor job, according to many reports in the literature.

For example, from the February 3, 1995 issue of the *Chronicle of Higher Education*:

Education-School Group Issues
Scathing, Self-Critical Review

A group of the nation's leading teacher educators says colleges of education need to shape up or shut down.

In a long-awaited report that was released last week, a coalition of education schools at 80 research universities presents a scathing, self-critical review of the job its members and other institutions have done in preparing teachers.

Many education professors are not prepared to train prospective teachers to deal with the problems in public schools today, says the coalition, known as the Holmes Group. It says education courses often are watered down, outdated, or unconnected with each other.

In 1998, because of our top educators' failure to adequately solve the problem of poor schools of education, Congress got into the act. In its 1998 reauthorization of the Higher Education Act, Congress required report cards from colleges that receive federal funds to train teachers on their performance on state licensing and certification exams. They were due by April 2000. This was extended to April 2001.

From the statement of Vartan Gregorian, President of the Carnegie Corporation (August 17, 2001 issue of the *Chronicle of Higher Education*):

Almost every day, we hear about the crisis in our public schools, especially the poor quality of teaching. As a nation, we blame our teachers for their professional shortcomings, their failures in the classroom. But that blame is misdirected. Higher-education institutions, in fact, must accept much of the responsibility for the dismal state of public-school teaching today.

From *What Matters Most: Teaching for America's Future* (1996), issued by the National Commission on Teaching and America's Future (a blue ribbon panel established in 1994): By the year 2006, "all teacher education programs will meet professional standards or they will be closed." From the *Teacher Quality Bulletin* (vol. 2, no. 40, October 2001):

According to Ronald Wolk, writing in Teacher Magazine, the influence of our colleges and universities on public K-12 education has been "largely negative." Mr. Wolk notes, "The most egregious example is their preparation of teachers. Studies consistently document that many soon-to-be educators leave college unprepared in either pedagogy or the subjects they teach ... College officials know this, but they continue to offer teacher-prep programs that have low standards for admissions and graduation, are rarely academically rigorous, and are often not relevant to the challenges teachers face in the classroom."

There are, in the literature, claims contrary to those I have presented. For example, from "Critics Claim Missteps on Execution of Title II" (*Education Week*, August 7, 2002):

"I have rarely seen such a high level of anger," said Arthur E. Wise, the president of the Washington-based National Council for Accreditation of Teacher Education, an organization that currently accredits 525 teacher-training institutions. "It is not true that ... colleges of education are not effective."

My opinion is
* This mixed-up disaster exists because of *the* BLUNDER.
* A great many schools of education are poor.
* While schools of education are not meeting teachers needs, the major fault lies with our top educators, who have prevented the teaching of the scientific method. Without requiring its use, we will always have a lot of confusion and disasters. You must fix things at the very top level before things will function correctly at lower levels.

Specific Reasons from the Literature for the Disaster of Our Schools of Education

Just some of the numerous reasons found in the literature for the deficiencies of our schools of education are:

* Education schools have long been looked down on by other departments in our universities. Many are not accredited.

* They are often neglected and used as profit centers.

* They are influenced by or start various educational fads.

* They do not analyze or listen to the needs of teachers.

- They push "ivory tower" theories that are not practical.

- They operate under a competitive grant system.

- Students should be required to spend a fifth year of internship.

- They do not provide classroom experience.

- There are no clear-cut national goals on what should be taught.

- They do not weed out unqualified students.

- They do not teach how to deal with pressure, stress of teaching, student discipline, new technologies, etc.

- They do not collaborate enough with K-12 schools.

- They do not concentrate enough on academic subject matter.

- Professors instruct students based on personal views rather than research.

There are others, but these are representative. These specific reasons may be important. However, in the big picture, I would like to point out that our schools of education cannot adequately train teachers if there is no well-researched and established reliable body of knowledge on what an effective teacher is. Thus, it is logical to ask "Isn't this lack of guidance a national problem and the fault of our top leaders?"

What Is an Effective Teacher?

Quality in a teacher calls for effectiveness. For schools of education, for certification, and for employment evaluation reasons, it is important that we know what an effective teacher is.

If you search the Internet and printed literature, you soon find a lot of material on what an effective teacher is—so much that it leaves you realizing that we know a lot, but it is all a mixed-up mess. It is hard to arrive at reliable conclusions.

In addition to the Internet, let me call your attention to two books:

How To Be an Effective Teacher, The First Day of School (1998) by Harry K. Wong and Rosemary T. Wong

Classroom Teachers Survival Guide (1999) by Ronald L. Partin

These books have isolated various principles and ways to be a more effective teacher. It is true that a few people have the "art" of being a good teacher without being trained; the reasons for this can be isolated in most cases. Most teachers have to learn the basic principles.

The books mentioned above are an excellent contribution to the science of teaching. Unfortunately, a science of teaching, like a science of education, has never developed. We already have a huge body of knowledge about teaching, but we have not adequately

- isolated all the reliable principles
- classified them as to their importance
- explained and presented them in easy-to-understand and teachable form
- certified them as being reliable knowledge

The need now is to sort, evaluate, communicate, refine, and extend the knowledge we already have.

Summary

To end the disaster of our schools of education, we must:

- have accountability from our very top educational leaders

- provide our schools of education with a reliable description of an effective teacher and all the problems of our teachers

- require schools of education to use the scientific method in determining how they are going to educate our future teachers

These things require that we:

- we teach and require the use of the scientific method throughout the educational field
- establish permanent specialized SM-14 type national research centers on

effective teachers
schools of education
and other subjects

? ?

The Mystery

Why Don't Our Top Leaders Take Adequate Steps To Correct This Disaster?

Way back in 1952, Harold Rugg, Professor Emeritus of Education at Teachers College, Columbia University, in his book *Teacher of Teachers: Frontiers of Theory and Practice in Teacher Education*, called attention to the inability of teachers of teachers to improve the situation—even though "enough is known." He stated:

> Enough is known. If the wealth of creative thought can be gathered and organized, teachers will command sufficient wisdom to guide the youth of the world. The School of Tomorrow can be brought to life today.

> But we, the Teachers of Teachers, stand silent, unable to organize our wisdom and command the motive power to put it to work.

? ?

Chapter 19

The Disaster of Homeschooling

The National Center for Education Statistics reported in 2001 that, in 1999, 850,000, or 1.7 percent, of school-age children were being taught primarily at home. This was up from about 360,000 children in 1994.

That so many parents are so dissatisfied with public and private schools that they go to all the trouble to teach their children at home is another result of *the* **BLUNDER**. Religion, better-educated parents, violence, and some other factors have contributed to the amazing growth in homeschooling. While religion is a big factor, a big one remains, in my opinion, the many disasters I describe in this book. Considering how many families have two parents who work, the growth rate in homeschooling is even more surprising.

However, there are those who claim that the figure of 850,000 is far too low. One recent report claimed that there are as many as 2,000,000 homeschooled children; another claimed that there are 1,100,000.

- ◆ Homeschooling Is Another Area of Inadequate Guidance By Our Top Educational Leaders

- ◆ We Need a Permanent Specialized SM-14 Type National Research Center on Homeschooling

- ◆ The Importance of Homeschooling to Developing Nations

Homeschooling Is Another Area of Inadequate Guidance by Our Top Educational Leaders

Our national educational leaders are allowing us to blunder along with inadequate policies, research, and action. Although we have local and state control of education, homeschoolers need national guidance. Many educators have resented homeschooling because it reflects on the public education they have provided.

Policies Are Needed

A *Poll of the Public's Attitudes Toward the Public Schools* by Phi Delta Kappa/Gallup published in September 2001 found that 41 percent of those polled were in favor of homeschooling, compared to 16 percent in 1985. This is due to the present greater understanding of homeschooling and the dissatisfaction with our public education situation in general.

Regardless of our personal feelings, this is the United States, where we have the liberty and laws allowing homeschooling. It is here to stay. Therefore, we need some national policies on how we can aid and how far we should go in aiding those who are homeschooling.

Research on Homeschooling

The December 9, 1999 issue of *Education Week* had a research report on homeschooling called "Unexplored Territory." The research was funded by the Spencer Foundation. Here are a few comments from the report about educational research on homeschooling.

> There are few areas of education research, though, where those troubles are as prevalent as they are in home education. . .

> Add to these quirks the claim—made by many researchers—that the interest of scholarly journals and potential funders diminishes the further a topic moves away from public education. The result is a dearth of high-quality studies on a form of education that, by most accounts, serves at least 1 million U.S. children. . .

> For now, researchers have few definitive answers. "It's dozens of isolated, one-time studies," Gregory J. Cizek, an education professor at the University of Toledo, says of the current state of research. "It's a very uncoordinated research agenda, by people who often don't know each other or who have never met each other, and it's the first or last thing they've ever done on home schooling."

Some Social Aspects of Homeschooling

Homeschooling adds to the diversity of our workers. Instead of our having just one group trained the usual public school way, we have a small group trained in a large number of ways.

Homeschooling is competition for our top educators. The better the job homeschoolers do, the better the job top educators must do if they do not want to be shown up.

Are Homeschooled Children as Well Prepared for Life?

In 2000, the ACT reported that for the third year homeschoolers achieved higher scores on the American College Test (ACT) than those who attended regular schools. However, many people worry about the social adjustment of homeschooled children. To date I know of no adverse studies on this topic.

We Need a Permanent Specialized SM-14 Type National Research Center on Homeschooling

We need some action for homeschoolers. There is already a private National Home Education Research Institute in Salem, Oregon. However, we need a public permanent specialized SM-14 type national research center with adequate financing that would act as part of a national system of permanent specialized SM-14 type research centers. A system of accumulating reliable educational knowledge is essential to improving education in the United States.

Advice to Homeschoolers

Homeschoolers should visit my web sites:

www.homeschooling-problemsolving.com
www.scientificmethod.com

They can immediately start teaching their children the complete method of creative problem solving and decision making without waiting for our top educators to wake up to the greatest idea of all time.

Here Is Another Great Opportunity

Homeschoolers are not subject to the many factors that prevent better teaching of creativity in public and even private schools.

♦ Promote a big movement to encourage homeschoolers to do even more than they are doing now in teaching and training their children in creativity.

♦ We already have a great body of knowledge about how to do it. Assemble and provide an inexpensive program to homeschoolers.

♦ Aid those providing homeschoolers with computer programs to include more creativity material in their programs.

Homeschoolers' Ideas

Those who homeschool their children, like our teachers, are coming up with ideas on how to teach children better. We have neglected to collect, evaluate, and use our public school teachers' ideas adequately over the years. I suspect that the same situation exists in home-schooling.

My proposed permanent specialized SM-14 type national research center should be the organization to collect, evaluate, and communicate valuable ideas. These should be classified into two groups:

♦ ideas suitable for use in homeschooling and in public schools

♦ ideas mainly for homeschoolers

Hybrid of Homeschooling and Public Education

Education Week (December 3, 2003) reports on Mountain Oaks School, just outside San Andreas, CA, which is a cooperative effort of home-schooling and public education.

The Importance of Homeschooling to Developing Nations

It is going to be a long time before poor countries have adequate schools. In the United States, many companies are developing home-schooling computer programs and have also designed some for students to teach themselves.

Some organizations should utilize the know-how we accumulate on homeschooling to translate materials into other languages for under-developed countries, if this is not already being done on a large scale.

? ?

The Mystery

Homeschoolers don't take away any funds from taxpayers, laws allow homeschooling, many people are determined to do it. So why don't our top and local educators act to make it more successful for those who are motivated to do it?

? ?

Chapter 20

The Disaster of the Big Name Panel Method of Solving Educational Problems

The Bad Problems Should Have Been Prevented or Solved Long Ago

While there is a need for education blue ribbon panels at times, what usually happens is a big problem exists for years and years. Finally, it becomes so bad that a blue ribbon panel is appointed to review the situation.

♦ Here Are Better Ways To Solve Education's Big Problems

♦ New Disasters Are Created and Old Ones Are Not Solved Because Big Name Panels Are Basically Flawed

♦ All Else Being Equal

♦ *A Nation at Risk* Report

The education field has consistently had and still has numerous major problems, and we will have them in the future.

The lack of a central person directly responsible for education at the state and local levels contributes to this. Nevertheless, this is no excuse. Our top educators allow these major problems to continue year after year. The scientific method is a method of problem prevention as well as a method of problem solution. It has not been properly used. Its use would help prevent, solve, or help solve the problems.

Here Are Better Ways To Solve Education's Problems

♦ Establish a system of permanent specialized SM-14 type national research centers (see Chapter 58).

♦ In 2001, Congress mandated "scientifically based research" in more than 100 places when it passed the Elementary and Secondary Education Act. This is a step in the right direction. I have shown in this book what "scientifically" consists of. Now educational researchers working on government contracts should be held to this general standard as I have shown it should be interpreted.

◆ When a big problem surfaces, if no permanent center is available, set one up. If it is not needed, use a study group instead of a big name panel. I define a study group as one consisting of qualified specialists in researching the problem who devote full time to the project and follow the scientific method (SM-14 or similar). Currently, study groups are sometimes used, but the extent to which they follow the scientific method is questionable.

New Disasters Are Created and Old Ones Are Not Solved Because Big Name Panels Are Basically Flawed

We live in an increasingly complex world. Everything is getting more specialized and complex and is constantly changing, so the superficial work that a big name panel and temporary staff does becomes increasingly unreliable. *This is no reflection on the members.* It is just not an efficient way to accomplish educational reform.

Panel members are big name, prestigious, very busy people. Often, on a matter of policy or a simple problem, an authoritative panel serves a useful purpose. However, on a complex one, where a lot of in-depth research is involved, very busy, big name people do not have the time. They may hold periodic meetings, but meetings are often not enough to reach the correct decisions. Furthermore, the panel members are often not specialists in the area of the problem, although they may or may not be specialists or generalists in some phase of education or represent Congress, business, etc.

They are "safe" people. They are often selected by the controlling group to reflect the views or results they want.

The staff. The staff members will usually also reflect the views of the controlling group. The staff is hastily appointed. Members are usually only partially or poorly qualified to really do the detailed research involved and in a limited amount of time. The panel often does little more than rubberstamp the staff's work.

"Consensus" is not always the answer. Today, in my educational research reading, I find that the need to reach a "consensus" is expressed frequently. The real need is to reach a conclusion by specialists based on the scientific method.

Too much politics involved. Some members are afraid to contradict the more powerful members. Members often conform to the views of those who appointed them (so how can we rely on their "findings" being impartial?). The staff members know they must conform to the views of the panel big shots, not what they may really find in their "research."

Panels with a teacher or two. This looks great, and claims are made that teachers are represented, but who on the panel of big shots will pay any attention to what a "lowly" teacher might say, even if the teacher has the nerve to speak out?

Reports are often unreliable. They are frequently just position papers on what "ought to be." Their unreliability is reported by Barbara Z. Presseisen in *Unlearned Lessons* (1985):

> Stedman and Smith's (1983) analysis of reform literature speaks to the problem of addressing the reports as reasoned documents. These researchers maintain that the four studies they reviewed (*A Nation at Risk, Action for Excellence, Academic Preparation for College* and *Making the Grade*) fall short mainly because 'they present a litany of charges without examining the veracity of their evidence and its sources' (p. 87). Their conclusion is the result of examining three arguments presented in the studies, and particularly brought out in *A Nation at Risk*. First, in looking at the evidence for the sad state of American education, Stedman and Smith found that, in some cases, the poor use of test data spawned unfounded conclusions. The researchers even go so far as to suggest that the authors of *A Nation at Risk* ignored the findings of their own commissioned studies in producing their report.

They can even be extremely disastrous. While they often spur a lot of publicity and discussion, if their advice or conclusions are not correct, they can do more harm than good.

Read my description in Chapter 28 of the disaster that occurred when the National Research Council of the National Academy of Sciences was given a U.S. government contract to recommend National Science Education Standards. Their assembly of smaller temporary panels and committees gave us standards that do not include the scientific method. Important complex matters are best handled by permanent specialized research centers.

All Else Being Equal

Some panels do a good job and provide needed public discussions, but my belief is that most are a waste of taxpayers' money. In *The Scientific Method—Its Function in Research and Education* (1932) Professor Kelley faulted and critically reviewed the history of the Committee of Ten headed by President Eliot of Harvard University and several others prior to 1920. In *Unlearned Lessons* (1985), Barbara Z. Presseisen reviews eight reports. An unbiased scholarly study of all recent panels would fill a need, if such a study does not already exist.

Another thing that would make these panels unnecessary is a system (outside of our usual legal system) of Courts of Education and Courts of Science.

A Nation at Risk Report

Panels—How Wrong They Can Be

Here are my comments on the famous 1983 report *A Nation at Risk* (by the National Commission on Excellence in Education) from the standpoint of the need to teach the scientific method. It states:

> Many 17-year-olds do not possess the "higher order" intellectual skills we should expect of them. Nearly 40 percent cannot draw inferences from written material; only one-fifth can write a persuasive essay; and only one-third can solve a mathematics problem requiring several steps.

All these deficiencies in our educational system are the result of not teaching the scientific method (SM-14 type). By not specifically calling for the teaching of the scientific method, it is clear that those who prepared *A Nation at Risk* contributed to *the* BLUNDER. Your children and grandchildren will continue to be at risk until the scientific method is recognized, used, and taught in the educational field.

? ?

The Mystery

Why, with the poor record of panels, do we continue to use them so frequently?

? ?

Chapter 21

The Disaster of Our Dropout Students

We have two disasters here:

♦ That we have such a high dropout rate

♦ That we don't better prepare dropouts for their lives after dropping out. There seems to be no real effort to do anything about this situation as important as it is

---

♦ Statistics That Indicate the Extent of the Disaster

♦ One of the Bad Effects of the High School Dropout Rate

♦ Why Is the Dropout Rate So High?

♦ The No Child Left Behind Act of 2001

♦ Preparation of Dropouts for Life

♦ Summary and Suggestions

Statistics That Indicate the Extent of the Disaster

In the article "Out of School and Unemployed" (*Education Week*, September 3, 2003), Richard M. Freeland, President of Northeastern University, and Joseph M. Tucci, President of EMC Corporation, report:

> What's most disturbing about this trend is how high school dropouts are faring in the contemporary economy. Other research findings by the center reveal that today, nationwide, a stunning 5.5 million young men and women between the ages of 16 and 24 are both out of school and jobless, and 2.2 million of them are high school dropouts. This translates into 15 percent of the nation's population in this age group.

The statistics on the dropout rate vary a little, but in general they indicate that the rate is from 25 to 32 percent. A goal set in 1989 was

10 percent, but our rate for actual dropouts has not diminished over the past 20 years.

One of the Bad Effects of the High School Dropout Rate

In February 2003 the Center for Labor Market Studies at Northeastern University prepared a report for the Business Roundtable entitled *The Hidden Crisis in the High School Dropout Problems of Young Adults in the U.S.: Recent Trends in Overall School Dropout Rates and Gender Differences in Dropout Behavior*. This report states:

> The survey found that 49 percent of the estimated population of prison inmates had no regular diploma or GED and that another 17 percent only had a GED; thus, two-thirds of the nation's prison inmates lacked a regular high school diploma. A 1991 Bureau of Justice Statistics survey of state prison inmates revealed that 41 percent of the inmates lacked both a diploma and a GED certificate, and it is quite likely that a majority of them lacked a regular high school diploma.

It would appear that we need to reduce the dropout rate and also better prepare those who do drop out for a more promising life.

We have a number of organizations concerned with the dropout problem, such as the National Dropout Prevention Center, Communities in Schools, Kids Count, the National Alternative Education Association, the Business Roundtable, the Gates Foundation, MDRC, and others.

Why Is the Dropout Rate So High?

From the Metlife Survey of the American Teacher (*American School Board Journal*, December 2002):

> The major reasons students consider dropping out are, "School is boring" (76 percent) and "I'm not learning enough" (42 percent).

In *The Cause and Cure of Dropouts* (1998), Arnold B. Skromme states:

> A GREAT DISCOVERY is shown: "The cause of dropouts!"
> It is not the student's born-with attitude, or their parent's lack of concern, etc. . .it is caused by the schools themselves,

who believe that our children only have ONE ability, that of IQ-Memory! This automatically places one-half of them below average! Cruel! This is one of the greatest discoveries of this century, world-wide! We cannot blame the teachers or the school boards. . .we must blame the "professors who teach-our-teachers." Our professors refuse to recognize the great discoveries beginning in 1917.

In *Fix Schools First* (2001), Jack E. Bowsher states:

> Again, successful learners do not drop out of school. Almost all drop-outs are students who are two or more grades behind and who have experienced serious academic trouble. Rather than sit in a seat feeling lost for two or three more years, they leave school. As stated previously, the General Educational Development (GED) certificate is becoming a major educational credential because of the high rate of drop-outs. It's easy for a school to identify potential drop-outs because at-risk students have low grades, low test scores, high truancy rates, and frequent negative interactions with teachers and principals. These students need remedial tutoring and counseling.

The No Child Left Behind Act of 2001

There are already many reports that the high standards of this act are forcing students out of school. If we are going to set high standards, then one end result will likely be an increase in dropouts. Although the act may eventually help to reduce dropouts, this remains to be seen. In the meantime, we need to help and guide those being forced out.

Preparation of Dropouts for Life

While some schools make an effort to prepare dropouts for life after they leave school, we have no well-prepared national program to do this. Considering that 25 to 32 percent of students end up as dropouts, this is a disaster that needs correction.

Freeland and Tucci state (*Education Week*, September 3, 2003):

> Such testing does show promise, but it comes too late for the 5.5 million disconnected young adults who are already out of school, out of work, and maybe out of luck. We need to

develop a national strategy that will enable us to reach out to these young Americans, give them a second chance to acquire basic academic skills, and provide them with the means to enter the mainstream job market. An array of research studies reveals that one of the most effective ways to accomplish this is through programs that give young trainees opportunities for hands-on work experience while also strengthening their basic literacy proficiencies and developing skills tied to specific occupations.

Summary

The reasons given by those quoted for dropouts seem reasonable. I did not do a complete search, but undoubtedly such a search would turn up a long list of reasons.

The disaster of vocational and technical education, which I cover later, is a major one. The No Child Left Behind Act is likely to increase our dropout rate. Since it is already in the 25 to 32 percent range, this is a major educational problem and disaster.

Suggestions

◆ We need the scientific method applied to all areas of education to end the many disasters that are contributing to the dropout problem. This will take time, but it must be done.

◆ We need a permanent specialized SM-14 type national research center on dropouts. These will always be a problem. We need to summarize and evaluate all the research that has been done on the problem. Our educational leaders need reliable guidance every year on the status of our dropouts and their reasons for dropping out.

Without these two improvements, the disaster will never end.

? ?

The Mystery

A great many dropouts end up in prison. This is expensive for society. Why don't we spend money more wisely by providing dropouts with better preparation for life after school?

? ?

Chapter 22

The Disaster of the Misguidance and Unfair Burden on Our Teachers

All the National Disasters Plus State and Local Disasters Add Up to a Grand Slam of Injustices to Our Teachers Resulting in Great Harm to Education

Stop—Careful

I'm not exaggerating about the harms being done to our teachers, students, and society.

Look—at Teachers

Repeatedly blamed for bad and poor schools, but
- never properly trained in schools of education
- forced to take part in one disastrous fad after another
- in the past, not furnished practical curriculum material in vital reading and math
- often must use old textbooks and buy supplies
- many quit the profession in disgust
- forced to "teach to the test"

Listen—and read here about:

———————

- Teachers Are Inspired To Teach But Are Disillusioned by Problems and Injustices

- How Many Bad Teachers Do We Have?

- Our Teachers Are Well Educated Degree-Wise

- Edmund's Partial List of Teachers' Problems

- Endless Uncoordinated Studies of Teachers and Their Problems

- Teachers' Ideas on Effective Ways To Teach Are Largely Ignored

- Conclusions, Suggestions, and Mystery

———————

Teachers Are Inspired To Teach But Are Disillusioned by Problems and Injustices

In the Public Agenda report *A Sense of Calling—Who Teaches and Why* (2000), 96% of teachers say "teaching is work they love to do."

But in *Fix Schools First* (2001), Jack E. Bowsher reports:

> Attrition is a big problem in the teaching profession. Between 25 and 30 percent of graduates from the colleges of education never take a teaching position. In his October 6, 1999, *Education Week* article, "The Teacher Shortage: Wrong Diagnosis, Phony Cures," John Merrow stated, "Simply put, we train teachers poorly, then treat them badly, so they leave in droves. The teacher shortage is a problem of retention rather than recruitment." He also reported that an estimated 30 percent of new teachers leave the teaching profession within 5 years. In some city schools, the exit rate is an astonishing 50 percent or more.

So, while they love to teach, many teachers leave the profession for less stressful and better paying jobs. It has been reported that many of those who leave are better-quality teachers.

In my chapters on the disasters of teaching reading, math, and science, my apologies to these teachers explain some of the hardships those who teach suffer. Many of the other disasters I describe have also made a teacher's life hard.

There are many accounts of teachers who go home at night and have a good cry because of the stresses of the job. But there are also accounts of those who go home with the joy of realizing that they have helped someone who was in difficulty. This is what keeps so many of them going—the love of teaching.

Often, however, they are helpless to change things, so they become hopeless. Even though many teachers do complain, and even though some of their articles are published, nothing happens. Being helpless, they then become hopeless. Many then just leave the profession.

The inspiration to teach is what attracts many talented people to the teaching profession. Thus, if we want better quality teachers to stay, it is necessary that our top leaders and others do a better job of educating, guiding, and helping them solve their problems.

How Many Bad Teachers Do We Have?

According to *Bad Teachers* (1998) by Guy Strickland,

> Best estimates indicate that 5 to 15 percent of teachers fall into the 'incompetent' category. That means that, of the one million elementary schoolteachers in the country, 50,000 to 150,000 are bad teachers.

What Have Our Top Leaders Done about This Problem?

The bad teachers problem is as old as schools. Since the 1950s, we have piled millions of dollars into educational research. Do we have a permanent specialized SM-14 type national research center devoted to researching and developing practical programs on retraining ineffective teachers? The answer is NO.

♦ Have we ever developed a practical researched and tested plan to prevent bad teachers from being certified? The answer is NO.

♦ Do we know how many teachers are labeled "bad" because of burnout caused by one fad after another, impractical government programs, classroom discipline problems, and other stresses on teachers? The answer again is NO!

♦ Every occupation has incompetent workers. Do we really know how many "bad" teachers we have and what percentage is normal, since all occupations have some "bad" workers? The answer is NO.

♦ Unions are often blamed for preventing the firing of "bad" teachers. Have we really worked out a plan that is fair to teachers with the points above taken into consideration? Again the answer is NO.

♦ Have we researched and accumulated an accepted reliable body of knowledge about how to train teachers? Again the answer is NO.

♦ Long ago we knew that our teachers colleges were not doing a very good job of training teachers. Has this been corrected in most teachers colleges? The answer is NO!

♦ There are a lot of "pie in the sky" descriptions of what an effective teacher should be or do. Have we ever developed a practical, well-researched, easily communicated, and acceptable description of the basic principles of an effective teacher? Not that I know of.

♦ Do we have "bad" or ineffective top educational leaders and researchers? The answer is YES! And because they don't use the scientific method, it is more than 5 to 15%!

Our Teachers Are Well Educated Degree-Wise

A 1999 Center for Education Policy bulletin pointed out that our teachers are well educated, that U.S. Department of Education statistics for 1993–1994 reveal that

> 52% have a bachelor's degree
> 42% have a master's degree
> 4.6% have an education specialist degree
> 0.7% have a Ph.D.
> only 0.7% have less than a bachelor's degree

It is really remarkable that about 42% of teachers have more than a bachelor's degree. Currently, it is probably more than 50%.

With this "well-educated" group of teachers, why then do we hear all the claims of bad teachers, unqualified teachers, etc.?

The main reasons are the fault of our top educators:

♦ Teachers were never properly educated in our schools of education.

♦ Our reliable research on what an effective teacher is and does has been inadequate.

♦ The national programs and reform movements presented to them have been largely a series of fads and untested programs.

Edmund's Partial List of Teachers' Problems

Teachers have a multitude of problems that have been studied, "researched," written about, but for which they have never been given adequate guidance and help. Some of these mentioned in the literature are:

Change, change, change, seldom for the better
Inadequate training in teachers colleges
Unfair criticism from parents, students, the public, and everyone else
The expectation that they use new methods that are largely untested
Not enough time to do what is expected of them

Often subjected to misuse of school funds by politicians
Bored, rebellious, spoiled, distracted, demoralized students
Students promoted to them not up to grade
Worries about personal safety
Lack of respect, appreciation, and feeling of isolation
Lack of support from administrators, who have their own problems
Unrealistic expectations of parents
Large classes
Inadequate supplies
Decrepit buildings or overcrowded facilities
Excessive paperwork
Their responsibility for exceptional children with learning disabilities
Pressure to teach to the test
Threat of school closure or school choice if goals are not met
Varied racial mix
Students whose first language is not English
Impractical "pay for performance" policies and proposals for them
Need to hold a second job because of poor pay
Idea that they should be able to do everything and be everything
Hands-on learning, requiring extra time and effort
Student drug, alcohol, sexual activities
Have to do it but they are not part of the decision process
Expected to do character training that may really be main
       responsibility of parents
Lot of evening work grading papers and tests
Periodic "retraining" classes
Disruption of charter schools affecting their work
Requirement to meet the demands of federal programs
Supervision of extracurricular programs
Job stress that makes many consider another occupation
Expected to be psychologists
In the middle on evolution versus creation controversy

Endless Uncoordinated Studies of Teachers and Their Problems

Teachers have had most of the problems I list for years. These have often been "researched" and "researched." The uncoordinated studies continue. Some current examples are given below.

Coalition of National Business Groups

Education Week (February 7, 2001) reports that the National Alliance of Business released a report, "Investing in Teaching," and began a new campaign to improve teacher quality.

Carnegie Foundation for the Advancement of Teaching

Education Week (March 21, 2001) reports a 5-year, $3 million initiative to examine how prospective teachers learn and how their learning is evaluated.

National Research Council of the National Academy of Sciences

The October–November 2000 issue of the National Science Teachers Association publication reports on a National Research Council report, "Educating Teachers of Science, Mathematics and Technology—New Practices for the New Millennium."

Milken Family Foundation

This foundation currently has a Teacher Advancement Program, which aims to improve the quality of the nation's teachers. It pushes performance-based accountability, etc.

Teachers Commission

Education Week (January 22, 2003) reports that Louis V. Gerstner, Jr., former head of IBM, has stated that he will lead a new nonprofit group aimed at formulating and promoting the best policies for raising teacher quality.

Many others, such as Pew Charitable Trust, *Education Week's* Quality Counts 2003, Recruiting New Teachers, Inc., and the Fordham Foundation, also issue reports, surveys, polls, etc.

Congratulations to all of them for being interested, and they do some good. Most are sincere in their efforts, but the usual game of education goes on, that is:

♦ Lots of reports that are good, poor, or impractical. They are often just filed away and result in little of practical use.

♦ Often they push the personal agenda or advocacy policies of the supporter of the report. There is often a lot of Dr. Fox-type baloney in them.

♦ There is no coordination among the researchers. There are often no, or minor, or disorganized additions to a reliable body of knowledge on which educators can all rely.

Until we have a series of permanent specialized SM-14 type national research centers on teachers' problems based at our universities and schools of education, we lack reliable knowledge to guide actions needed. The help and studies of foundations and other types of organizations will still be needed to assist the SM-14 type research centers in their work.

Teachers' Ideas on Effective Ways To Teach Are Largely Ignored

I have been reading educational magazines since the 1940s, except for my 1975–1989 retirement period. I have always been impressed with the articles by teachers on creative ways they have devised for more effective teaching. But alas! These have been largely ignored by educational researchers and reform program designers. If you want to know how to effectively teach fractions to children, just research the teachers' magazines, and you will come up with dozens of ideas. Have the National Council of Teachers of Mathematics program designers used them? I don't think so! And so it goes, with thousands of other good teachers' ideas. However, after all these years change may now be coming. In April 2004, U.S. Secretary of Education Rod Paige announced a "Teacher to Teacher" initiative for sharing techniques developed by teachers. We also need a Teacher to Top Educator Initiative!

Look at What a Teacher Did

Harry Wong was a high school science teacher. He and his wife wrote and produced a book that has sold more than 1.5 million copies because it fills teachers' needs and is so well done. It is called *The First Day of School—How to Be an Effective Teacher*. This self-published book is, I believe, a great contribution to the science of effective teaching. Also available is a series of videotapes on teaching.

Teachers Need To Improve

While I have presented the problems of teachers in this chapter, teachers have plenty of faults and need to improve. That the Wongs have sold 1.5 million copies of their book indicates that many teachers are interested in improving. However, it is not very productive to point out all their faults and ask for self-improvement when they see all the constant disasters interfering with their effectiveness.

Nevertheless, we could use a permanent specialized SM-14 type national research center on teachers' self-improvement.

Questions about the Complex Life of a Teacher

Do we pay our teachers less than comparable professionals receive, yet expect them to be psychologists, diplomats in handling parents, nurses, character builders, counselors, fundraisers, policemen, learning disability experts, experienced disciplinarians AND pay for supplies schools can't afford AND still fill out a load of paperwork?!

Conclusions

◆ Yes, we have "bad" teachers and we will always have some, but far too much blame is placed on teachers for disasters caused at the levels above their control.

◆ We can spend billions of dollars recruiting and training new teachers, but our high turnover rate will continue until the disasters that drive them out of the teaching profession are corrected. Otherwise, the shortage problem will not be solved, even by higher pay.

We Have Millions of "Team Player" Teachers

When you research the literature on education and read of all the disasters teachers have been subjected to, the thought that pops into your mind is: Why have they taken so much? The answers probably are:

◆ Crisis is the way of life in the education field. Ever since they entered the profession, they have heard stories from the old timers— that's the way it is—one impractical program after another.

◆ Teachers want to be team players, but if they protest loudly, they are accused of being against change and reform. Being "only" teachers, their opinions don't count.

? ?

The Mystery

Why have the teachers unions been so quiet about all the fads, problems, and unfair burdens on our teachers coming from above? Shouldn't they be pushing for the use of the scientific method and using it in their own research?

? ?

Chapter 23

The Disaster of Inadequate Head Start and Early Childhood Education

---

Section 1
Inadequate Head Start

◆ Head Start Became a Political Football

◆ Another Example from My 1969 Baby Booklet

Section 2
The Disaster of Early Childhood
Education in General

◆ The Disaster of Our Kindergartens

◆ Past Disaster

◆ Present Activities

◆ The Very Favorable Economics of Early Childhood Education

◆ "The Urban Tail Has Wagged the Public School Dog"

◆ The Gap between the Rich and the Poor Will Always Be There

◆ Educational Toys, Tapes, and TV Programs

◆ Suggestions and Mystery

SECTION 1
INADEQUATE HEAD START

Head Start Became a Political Football

Fault—Our Top Educational Leaders and Researchers

Today, "research" indicates that Head Start is a valuable concept. Simple logic also indicates it. Everyone is concerned about our "bad schools," and one logical and important way to help end them is to have students better prepared when entering. Today, fewer challenge the concept that our government should make a big effort in this direction.

Some details of the history of the federal Head Start program:

♦ Head Start was launched in 1965 as a 6-week summer program serving 500,000 students. It grew to serving more than 700,000 children in summer and year-round programs.

♦ By 1977 only 325,000 were enrolled.

♦ By 2000 about 800,000 students were being served.

♦ According to the Thomas B. Fordham Foundation, in 2000 the program served about two-thirds of eligible 4-year-olds and one-third of eligible 3-year-olds (*Education 2001:Getting the Job Done*, 2000). This probably means that we are missing a million or so children who are eligible or really need it.

Here are just a few of the disasters that befell the Head Start program:

♦ In his 1961 book *Slums and Suburbs*, Dr. Conant made many recommendations to correct conditions in urban schools. But, since, in addition to other reasons, researchers are not required to use the scientific method, these were largely disregarded.

♦ In 1969 (the same year I published my booklet about an enriched environment for babies,) a "research" evaluation declared that the Head Start program was producing no lasting cognitive or behavioral gains for its participants. Others with a similar conclusion followed in 1976. As recently as 1995, the American Research Association published a study entitled "Going, Going, Gone: One Reason Why Head Start Efforts Fade Over Time." While much of the accuracy of this research has since been challenged, it all created the impression that there was no value to Head Start. This misled our political leaders and the public, and gave those who opposed Head Start false ammunition. Head Start became a political football.

♦ Why did these researchers waste government funds on this type of research instead of discovering the defects in the program that needed improvement?

♦ The Head Start program was initially placed in the Department of Health and Human Services. As a result, a good part of the effort went into social, psychological, nutritional, and health activities. The National Head Start Association, founded in 1973, has been fighting for more and better Head Start programs. Its web site, www.nhsa.org, reports:

> One of the biggest errors made with the program during the early years was to tout its impact with purely cognitive measures such as I.Q. scores. During most of its existence, program staffs have been guided by Head Start Bureau "experts" that warned them against an emphasis of such issues as reading and learning numbers. As a result, programs are now being criticized for not doing what they were told not to do.

♦ You will recall that in Chapter 14 on the Science Teaching Disaster I pointed out the terrible job the National Academy of Sciences and its operating unit the National Research Council did on setting the 1995 National Science Education Standards. Well, the disasters at the top never end. Here is what the National Head Start Association reports:

> Now, the National Research Council (NRC) has recommended that all early childhood teachers have a Bachelor's degree in early childhood. While each of these efforts is admirable, they ignore the greater issues of ensuring positive outcomes for children by improving interactions between teachers and children. . .

> The potential cost of requiring early childhood teachers to attain a Bachelor's degree could be staggering and continuous. Not withstanding the actual cost (probably at the expense of the teacher) of the education, it would likely increase the operating costs of early childhood programs dra-

matically, since obviously—teachers with a Bachelor's degree will be able to demand higher wages. The current average annual teacher's salary in Head Start is $19,600, while the average elementary school teacher—whose position requires a Bachelor's degree—earns more than $30,000 per year. It would be difficult for Head Start programs to retain a teacher qualified to teach in public school without offering competitive salaries and benefits.

Look at the impracticality of the National Research Council's recommendation and of others who recommend bachelor's degrees for all early childhood teachers:

♦ There is talk of a teacher shortage at present and in the future for regular school teachers. This proposal would also displace existing experienced personnel.
♦ It could double the existing cost of early childhood education. Even now we are only covering about half the children who need to be covered, so costs could as much as quadruple.
♦ It is highly unlikely that tax funds would be available, or some other area of education funding would be reduced.
♦ It would adversely affect privately operated early childhood schools.

The logical alternative in this age of specialization is to:

♦ Research and develop several basic structured model courses for pre-schooling for which people can easily be trained. We already have a great deal of experience, knowledge, and ideas.
♦ Establish various job classifications requiring 3-month, 6-month, and on up to the present 2-year associate degree in early childhood education from community colleges.
♦ Remember that more than 150 different languages are encountered in Head Start classes. These have to be provided for.
♦ Use the college graduates with bachelor's degrees mainly in supervisory and training positions where funds are in short supply.

I could go on about other disasters about our Head Start program (and kindergarten, too), but what they all add up to is:

♦ Our top educators in the very beginning did not adequately define the problem and set proper goals.
♦ There was never a permanent specialized SM-14 type national research center set up on Head Start, kindergarten, and early childhood education in general.
♦ The scientific method has not been properly applied to the problem.

Another Example from My 1969 Baby Booklet

Remember that Head Start commenced in 1964. In my 1969 booklet, I offered parents material for a child's enrichment. I present below some of the advertising copy that appeared in that booklet to give you an idea of the state of knowledge and material that was available way back then.

1969 Advertising Copy

"HOW TO RAISE A BRIGHTER CHILD" by Joan Beck

Joan Beck, author of the syndicated newspaper column "You and Your Child," has now written this fascinating book. She provides the latest theories, facts, guidelines, amazing case histories, and suggestions on how you can raise a brighter child.
Here are some of the chapters: "Your Child's First and Best Teacher...You" (17pp), "Why You Can Raise a Brighter Child" (28pp), "How the Atmosphere in Your Home Can Foster Intelligence" (13pp), "How to Raise a Brighter Baby...Birth to 18 Months" (24pp), "The Insatiable Drive to Learn...18 Months to 3 Years" (15pp), "How to Stimulate Intellectual Growth in 3-to 6 yr. Olds" (43pp), "Should You Teach Your Preschooler to Read" (40pp), "How You Can Encourage Your Child to Be Creative" (19pp), plus four others.
[Still in print, 2004]

My Suggestions

We should make a big effort to make Head Start and other pre-school programs available to all or most children in below-poverty-level families. Be practical about the cost of this, and don't insist that teachers have a bachelor's degree. Establish various classes of teachers or caretakers in affordable salary ranges.

Since I have not studied the matter fully, the best I can suggest is that, with a good summary of the scientific method now available in *The Scientific Method Today*, those interested in or operating Montessori schools should investigate the scientific method and how its stages, methods, etc. should be incorporated into their program.

The use of standardized special limited trained personnel can be successful just as it is in industry.

What America needs are some scientifically designed preschool programs for Head Start and kindergarten in which the best ideas are accumulated and tested before they are introduced nationally.

SECTION 2
THE DISASTER OF EARLY CHILDHOOD EDUCATION IN GENERAL

The whole field of early childhood education has never been properly understood, analyzed, developed, and summarized, even with the billions of dollars spent on educational research in the second half of the 1900s. I discussed Head Start first because it is the best known of our efforts to improve preschooling.

Before I proceed, let's consider very briefly how we have done with our kindergarten efforts. There is no doubt that they have improved over the years and that they have been outstanding in some schools.

The Disaster of Our Kindergartens

Again our top leaders have done a disastrous job.

In the Spring 2001 *Curriculum Update*, the Association for Supervision and Curriculum Development reports:

> Education experts have pointed out that there has never really been a consensus on just what should be taught in kindergarten, even going back to its earliest days in U.S. schools in the latter part of the 19th century. But experts do agree that with the current ferment and public interest in early childhood education, the opportunity to improve kindergarten for all children shouldn't be squandered.

The real problem we have is no permanent specialized SM-14 type national research center on kindergarten.

You Can Start Teaching the Scientific Method Early

I pointed out that the scientific method is a natural problem-solving method that humans have used unknowingly in some manner from the beginning in order to survive (Chapter 2).

In *Learning All the Time* (1989), John Holt points out:

> Children are born passionately eager to make as much sense as they can of things around them. The process by which children turn experience into knowledge is exactly the same, point for point, as the process by which those whom we call scientists make scientific knowledge. Children observe, they

wonder, they speculate, and they ask themselves questions. They think up possible answers, they make theories, they hypothesize, and then they test theories by asking questions or by further observations or experiments or reading. Then they modify the theories as needed, or reject them, and the process continues. This is what in "grown-up" life is called the—capital S, capital M—Scientific Method. It is precisely what these little guys start doing as soon as they are born. If we attempt to control, manipulate, or divert this process, we disturb it. If we continue this long enough, the process stops. The independent scientist in the child disappears.

Past Disaster

Besides Holt's comments, I previously told you about how much we knew of the ways to improve and enrich a child's early years.

From the September 2000 issue of www.electronic-school.com:

> In 1966, in a landmark report for the U.S. Department of Health, Education, and Welfare titled *Equality of Educational Opportunity*, James S. Coleman researched thousands of children and concluded, "Studies of school achievement have consistently shown that variations in family background account for far more variation in school achievement than do variations in school characteristics."

There is nothing very questionable about this 1966 study. Just a little curious observation of urban schools shows that the material coming into them is not well prepared compared to suburban schools. It is an extremely difficult burden on these schools, even if they are efficiently run, which in most cases circumstances have prevented.

Coleman's work was quotely widely, but little action resulted. Urban schools continued have the big disadvantage of less-prepared students.

So all the efforts in the past have not been sufficient to prevent the disaster in early childhood education in regard to both number of children covered and reliable programs presented.

Present Activities

At present we have a much better recognition of the need for early childhood education.

Look at All the Activity Now in Favor of Early Childhood Education

In addition to Head Start, there are a lot of other activities going on in early childhood education. There are so many that I gave up the idea of listing them here.

Utilize Older Sisters and Brothers Already in School

It seems to me I read somewhere of a plan for older children to help their preschool siblings. They could be utilized to take them teaching toys, books, and lending library materials. Perhaps they should be provided with computers if they also use them to teach siblings or neighborhood preschoolers. These could be toy type or low-cost standard computers.

The Number of Children Being Served by Early Childhood Classes

In April 2003, the U.S. Department of Education stated that 35% of public schools have classes available, but that does not mean that everyone eligible was attending.

An article in the September 25, 2002 issue of *Education Week* states:

> By contrast, fewer than half of children whose families fall below the poverty line attend preschool, not because their parents don't want them to, but because we haven't created enough Head Start programs. To serve all the eligible children, we'd need twice as many as we have. Once again, we're talking the talk when it comes to helping poor children, but not walking the walk. And, largely for that reason, the gap will not only *not* disappear, it will grow.

The Very Favorable Economics of Early Childhood Education

The National Institute for Early Education Research at Rutgers University says that society receives a $4.00 return for each dollar spent on high-quality preschool.

An article in the October 10, 2001 issue of *Education Week* about the Chicago Child-Parent Centers reports a $7.00 return for every dollar spent.

I claim that if our top leaders and researchers properly use the scientific method on the problem and establish a permanent specialized

SM-14 type national research center or a series of them, the return on dollars spent on early childhood education could be from 10- to 100-fold. No matter how great our teachers, schools, and programs are, if the raw material coming in is unprepared, there are huge problems that last for years and upset the whole system of education and many other areas of society.

"The Urban Tail Has Wagged the Public School Dog"

This statement by Professor Larry Cuban of Stanford University appeared in an article in the May 30, 2001 issue of *Education Week*. It seems correct. Our whole educational effort is being distorted and harmed by the needs of our urban and rural low-achieving schools. So my claim of a 10- to 100-fold return by innovative improvements in early childhood education could be correct. The public must be sold on the need to drastically improve what is happening. National educational reform programs are designed for all schools. When there is a large group of low-achieving schools in urban and rural areas, it is difficult to have programs that don't adversely affect suburban schools. So people in suburban areas also must demand that the problem of early childhood education be solved.

The Gap between the Rich and the Poor Will Always Be There

In this book I am strongly supporting the views of many that we must better prepare our children for school. This is sometimes referred to as closing the gap between the rich and the poor. However, this is not accurate—the gap is really that between those above the poverty level and those below.

Let's be practical about the problem:

◆ The National Center for Education Statistics reports that 76% of 4-year-olds from households with incomes of more than $50,000 per year are enrolled in preschool. In 2001, the median income of a family with two earners was $64,552. Therefore, many families with modest incomes are seeing to it that their children get preschooling.

◆ Families with modest incomes are buying good educational toys and computers, and making enriched environments available to their children. This includes reading to their children, taking them to museums, and giving them crayons and coloring books at an early age. Thus, they come to school better prepared. This trend is likely to continue and widen the gap.

◆ Many parents in higher-income families were poor in their youth. It often takes several generations for the poor to advance above the poverty level.

◆ Historically, the United States has had various waves of poor immigrants. We continue to attract poor people who speak a variety of languages. These people will, for a period of time, fill the low-paying jobs and live in poverty by our standards.

◆ **The gap will most likely always be with us and may increase.**

We must then permanently:

◆ Use the scientific method in permanent specialized SM-14 national research centers on early childhood development to originate, refine, extend and apply practical and tested programs on how to preschool, in various ways, all our children.

◆ Spend the money wisely to implement these programs, as the economies of proper use of taxpayers' money favors doing so.

◆ Prepare for the fact that new immigrants will constantly be arriving with children of all ages, speaking a variety of languages and, for the most part, living in poverty.

◆ Prepare to have tracking of some type in early grades because of the wide differences in readiness. Our better-off children will come ever better prepared in most cases (with new immigrants a special problem), but there will still be a gap. It will hurt our country if they are all lumped together, and early readers will be bored to death.

Educational Toys, Tapes, and TV Programs

Educational Toys

In reviewing the professional literature on teaching and learning to read, I am always surprised at how few mentions are made of the vast numbers of new and well-designed educational toys we have today. I remember that way back in 1920, I had only a set of wooden ABC blocks. Today if you tour a large toy store, you see an amazing array of educational items for children. Our more well-to-do are using these to help their children. Considering the many hours children spend outside of school and the need to teach them self-education, we are not utilizing these toys enough, especially for those living in poverty.

One of the activities of a permanent specialized SM-14 type national research center would be to evaluate all these and promote their use.

Teaching Toy Collection in Wealthier Areas

At garage sales in wealthier areas, a huge number of teaching toys are often sold. Many of the people who are selling them would donate them to collections for poor children.

Give or Loan Educational Toys and Tapes to Poverty Families

In looking at some of the toys available, I believe that the economics of our responsibility to prepare children for school would favor giving or loaning the more effective educational learning aids to children raised in poverty. These children are said to regress during summer vacation. A toy and tape program could prevent this.

Sesame Street and Similar Teaching TV Programs

We have accumulated a large inventory of these programs. Strategies to better utilize them should be developed.

Suggestions

End the disasters that continue in the early childhood education field.

1. Better educate the public to the social needs and economic value of early childhood education and the adverse effects on all schools of neglecting the needs of students raised in poverty.

2. Require the use of the scientific method whenever public funds are used in this field as well as others.

3. Establish a series of permanent specialized SM-14 type national research centers on early childhood education. These would
     - provide continual evaluation of existing efforts, programs, and ideas
     - provide materials on which U.S. agencies, Congress, and states could base their actions
     - provide aid and guidance to all organizations, day care centers, and public and private schools active in early childhood education on children's social skills, self-help skills, literacy, and medical needs; locating and affording high-quality

early education is of concern to all parents. Parents need more guidance too.

4. Let's have fair competition and understanding. Stop threatening low-achieving schools with vouchers and closing. Help them overcome their major problem—unprepared raw material—which causes enormous problems.

? ?

The Mystery

With all we have known for so long about the value of early childhood education, why haven't our top leaders done more intensive development, summarized more successful programs, and given early childhood education greater priority?

? ?

Head Start Should Begin in the Crib

Here is an idea I presented in my 1969 Baby Booklet. I like it so much that I can't resist including it here. All my grandchildren and great-grandchildren have been raised with these lights, and all have done well in school.

A week or so after birth, the baby lies in its crib with little to watch. So position strings of Christmas tree **randomly** blinking assorted-color lights (C-7 size) at a **safe** distance from the baby and above the baby's eye level. Use standard precautions for lights of this type. The baby is fascinated; the baby's eyes will follow the lights.

I claim that it helps to develop the baby's brain and eyes.

If your local store doesn't have standard C-7 sets of 24 colored bulbs, you can find them on the Internet by using Google Froogle.

This idea can be expanded in many ways. For example, how about someone researching a set for the ABCs and numerals for an older baby?

We Knew a Lot Way Back in 1969 about a Head Start

When Nicole Edmund, my first grandchild, was born, an article in *Life* magazine about an enriched environment for a baby attracted my attention. With the help of my son-in-law, James W. Husted, then a medical student, I researched the concept and wrote a 16-page, 8 1/2- by 11-inch booklet entitled *Smarter, Healthier, Happier Babies Through an Enriched Environment.* This was for the purpose of alerting new parents to the opportunities available to them. I sent out about 20,000 free copies and tried to support the venture with items in the booklet that we added to our product line. It was not successful businesswise, so I gave up on the project. The material in this booklet was presented in easy-to-read comic book style. In reviewing the material now, it is still largely technically correct. In reduced size, I reproduce a few of the illustrated blocks below.

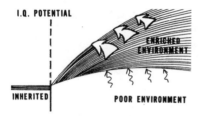

While heredity may play a part in how intelligent we will be, it is environment that determines how well we develop our innate potential.

Providing the proper environment for children of all economic backgrounds might help solve many of the major social problems facing us today.

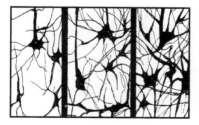

Early and repeated stimulation of the baby's senses builds a foundation for all learning. His brain will form many new pathways—adding "intelligence."

Babies are curious. Everything in your world is a novelty to Baby and worthy of his investigation. You need to encourage rather than discourage his explorations.

Remember, I wrote this booklet in 1969—36 years ago.

Chapter 24

The Disaster of Our Urban Schools

Urban or great city schools have been an enormous problem for many years. Numerous reports and articles concerning their problems have been published but have not been heeded enough, for we still have big problems today.

There are many remarks in the literature that, because of the recent flood of immigrants and other factors, the problem of urban schools has greatly increased. Offsetting this to some extent have been the recent availability of funds under the federal Title I program, the public's greater interest in education, the No Child Left Behind Act, and improvements to the federal Head Start program.

In this chapter I will show that

- urban school problems will not be adequately solved until our top leaders and educational researchers start to apply the scientific method to all the problems of urban schools
- we need expansion and improvement in preschooling
- we need a series of permanent specialized SM-14 type national research centers on urban school problems

---

Some Statistics on Great (Large) City Schools

- Why Are So Many of Our Urban Schools Still Low Achieving?
- The Unfavorable Conditions Urban Schools Face
- The Faults of Urban Schools, Students, and Communities
- More Self-Help Is Needed
- Urban Schools Especially Need Vocational and Technology Courses
- Learning Systems and Integrated Curricula
- Summary—"Children as Pawns"
- Mystery

Some Statistics on Great City Schools

The Council of Great City Schools is a coalition of 60 of the nation's largest public school systems. Its web site, www.cgcs.org, gives these characteristics of great city schools:

Total student enrollment: 7 million

African American: 38.4%; Hispanic: 31.4%; White: 23.2%
Asian/Pacific Islander: 6.4%
Alaskan/Native American: 0.7%
Eligible for free/reduced price lunch: 61.9%
English language learners: 17.9%
Students with individualized education programs: 12.9%

Number of languages spoken: 120

Number of teachers: 409,633

Early in 2003 the Council issued a report, *Beating the Odds*, claiming significant gains on statewide assessment exams. However, it also reported that urban schools are still below national averages.

Teacher Turnover in Urban Schools

Here are a few quotes on what Touchton and Acker-Hocevar (*International Journal of Education Reform*, vol. II, no. 4, Fall 2002) call a "revolving door for teachers."

John Merrow (*Education Week*, October 6, 1999):

> Many who become teachers don't stay long. An estimated 30 percent leave the field within five years; in cities, the exit rate is an astonishing 50 percent.

Dale Mezzacappa (*Philadelphia Inquirer*, March 12, 2003) in an article "Teacher Attrition Sapping Urban Schools":

> A study by Betsey Useem of the nonprofit Philadelphia Education Fund followed 60 teachers in seven high-poverty middle schools hired for the 1999–2000 school year. Forty-three percent were no longer teaching in Philadelphia after four years, while an additional 25 percent had left their original schools for another assignment in the city.

Why Are So Many Urban Schools Still Low Achieving?

After decades of time and "research" and billions of dollars spent, only a little progress has been made in solving the problem that so many of our urban schools are low achieving.

I claim that our top educational leaders have failed to properly and adequately analyze the problems of urban schools. They have failed to offer adequate guidance and initiate needed programs that really make substantial progress. This is especially true in preschooling.

In reviewing what has been done, I found many articles and books about urban school problems along with case histories of successful urban schools. However, books, articles, and the efforts of the U.S. Department of Education are not sufficient to get the methods and ideas being used by successful ones analyzed and widely distributed.

In my research, what I found missing was a complete list of all the major unfavorable conditions that urban schools face. If one exists, it has not been well publicized. Many articles and books list some of the conditions, but a complete analysis is lacking.

It is basic to solving a problem to know all the major factors that may be causing it. Therefore, I have accumulated from the literature a reasonably complete list of the major unfavorable conditions facing urban schools.

Edmund's List of 35 Unfavorable Conditions Urban Schools Face Compared to Suburban Schools

Remember that it is not that suburban schools do not have some of these conditions, but rather a matter of degree. I am also sure that suburban schools have problems that urban ones do not have. Because there are so many conditions, I explain a few very briefly and just list the others.

Some of My Conclusions before You Read the List

◆ Our lack of progress to date is because of these conditions. Until we adequately improve all of the conditions or at least the major ones, we will not solve the problem.

◆ The threat and concept that charter schools, vouchers, and school choice are the way to go is shortsighted and tragically unfair.

- ◆ The scientific method has not been adequately applied to these unfavorable factors.

- ◆ There has been no permanent specialized SM-14 type national research center on these problems to accumulate and communicate reliable knowledge about them.

The 35 Unfavorable Conditions That Urban Schools Face

As I stated, all these conditions have been mentioned in the literature, and many have been "researched" and discussed. However, they have not been adequately presented in total anywhere that I could find in a limited search. Here I attempt to do just that. Policymakers need to look at the total picture in planning urban school reform, and they should study all these conditions to get the big picture.

Children start school less prepared. While Head Start and other efforts have helped some, it is still a major problem and has been made more difficult in recent years by an influx of students whose first language is not English. I cover this problem in greater detail in Chapter 23.

Budgets are usually lower. Over the years urban school budgets have been lower than those of suburban schools. While much progress has been made in recent years, many urban school budgets are still lower.

Urban school budgets should be higher than those of suburban schools, but they are not. Urban school budgets actually should be higher than those of suburban schools. At the state level, this is probably politically difficult to achieve. While federal contributions have been a help, they are still far from adequate.

School facilities are poorer. They are older and less adequate. Repairs are often needed.

School superintendent turnover is high. Superintendents and principals are often dismissed and replaced with new "white knights," who are expected to overcome huge difficulties.

The effects of fads are greater. The effects of the fad of the whole language method of teaching reading, incorrect math programs, and other fads show up in the poor achievement of students in all grades.

Demoralizing remarks are made in the media about the low status of teachers.

Political interference, poor school board and district management, and patronage are factors.

Extended administrative hierarchy causes inefficiencies.

Curriculum is watered down out of necessity.

There are lower expectation of students.

College-oriented curricula are unsuitable.

Tests are not appropriate for poverty students.

Class management is a greater problem.

Class size is often larger.

Discipline is a bigger problem.

Principals have a more difficult job.

It is harder for teachers to diagnose students' requirements.

There are inadequate after-school care and activities available.

Poverty is greater. This has enormous ramifications and results in many of the things that follow.

There are more students whose first language is not English.

The racial mix is greater. This makes for more conflict and problems.

Students change schools frequently.

Administrative clerks are lower paid and often of lower ability.

Teenage pregnancies are more frequent.

There are more exceptional students.

The dropout rate is higher and absenteeism is much higher.

Drugs and gang violence are bigger problems.

Nutrition and health care are bigger problems.

206 END THE BIGGEST EDUCATIONAL AND INTELLECTUAL BLUNDER

Schools are located in environmentally poor areas.

There is less parental support.

Reforms and improvements divert staff from their real jobs.

There are fewer educational resources.

There is less cultural identification with teachers.

Social promotion is more frequent.

There are fewer qualified teachers. The last item on my list is one of the most important. While it is claimed that qualified teachers are of major importance, urban schools usually have lower paid and less experienced teachers, with a high turnover each year. They often have great difficulty filling vacancies and have to take whoever is available at the last minute for a variety of reasons.

On Top of These Unfavorable Factors, We Have All the Other Disasters I Have Described

I purposely made this chapter and the one about Head Start the last major ones in the disaster section. On top of all the unfavorable factors facing urban schools are all the disasters that have harmed most schools and have often increased the problems of the unfavorable factors I list.

Faults of Urban Schools, Students, and Communities

In this book, I have placed the major blame for the ills of education and our schools on our top educational leaders, even though they have had no direct control over them. In fairness and also to help see the big picture, I try to briefly cover some of what may or may not be the fault of urban schools, students, their parents, and their communities.

"Urban Schools Will Not Change"

This charge is made repeatedly. I have shown you all the fads and disasters that have been thrown at them over the years and the additional unfavorable conditions they face. To say that "will not change" is a correct charge against them I find hard to justify. Nevertheless, there is the question of whether they have made enough effort.

Parental Support Is Low

The literature describes many reasons that poverty, poorly educated parents, parents who work two jobs, etc. result in poor parental support for students and schools. But again, regardless of everything, it is a parental duty to help children and their schools.

Unqualified District Superintendents, Principals, and Teachers

It is difficult to say to what extent this is the fault of local school boards, shortages, etc. Nevertheless, improvement is needed.

Racial Gap

The March 12, 2003, edition of *Education Week* contains an article entitled "Meager Effort Said to Fuel Racial Gap." This reports on a book by noted anthropologist John U. Ogbu, in which he argues, according to *Education Week*, "that African-Americans' cultural attitudes toward education, their generally minimal involvement in schools, and black students' own lack of effort contribute to the persistent achievement gap."

An article entitled "Why the Black and White Test Gap Exists," by John McWhorter, appeared in the *American Experiment Quarterly* (Spring 2002). The abstract states:

> In *Losing the Race: Self-Sabotage in Black America*, John McWhorter writes that as the common cold is caused by the rhinovirus, so black students do poorly in school, decade after decade, because of a virus of anti-intellectualism—a byproduct of slavery and racism—that infects the black community.

I am not qualified to evaluate the extent of this problem. But to the extent that it exists, we must make efforts to end it.

Hispanic Communities in Urban Areas

These, too, have their special problems, especially one of language added to the burden of urban schools.

On March 12, 2001, President George W. Bush established the President's Advisory Commission on Educational Excellence for Hispanic Americans. The commission's objectives:

As such, the Commission shall develop a multi-year action plan aimed at closing the educational achievement gap between Hispanic students and their peers. In doing so, they will ensure that the fastest growing segment of the United States population not only graduates from high school at the same rate as their peers but that *they also go on to enroll and complete a college education*. [emphasis mine]

It is my claim that a permanent specialized SM-14 type national research center would recognize that many Hispanics as well as others are or should be headed for vocational and technology courses and not for college. The current high dropout rate of Hispanics is evidence that supports this claim.

More Self-Help Is Needed

There has been a reluctance to spend what is necessary to bring urban schools up to par. I mentioned the need to equalize urban and suburban school budgets. In fact, we should spend more on urban schools because of the many unfavorable conditions they face. To overcome the reluctance of many to spend extra funds on urban schools, more self-help would be influential.

The need for this was called to the attention of the public in May 2004 by Bill Cosby. He pointed out that many young and low-income African-Americans use poor English and have little ambition, a poor attitude toward education, parental failures, and a number of other issues. In his keynote speech at the Democratic National Convention in July 2004, Barack Obama also spoke of the need for more self-help.

There have been a number of articles about the self-help efforts already being made by minorities and urban communities. These efforts must be greatly expanded to alert the public that extra guidance and financial help is merited.

For example, the December 13, 2000 edition of *Education Week* describes the work of the National Urban League and Howard University with civic partners to improve literacy and achievement of African-American students. There is also the annual National African-American Read-In, sponsored by the Black Caucus of NCTE and by NCTE. There is an excellent article in the *New York Times Magazine* (June 20, 2004) about Geoffrey Canada's Harlem Children's Zone Project.

Urban Schools Especially Need Vocational and Technology Courses

In the United States we have had an influential group of top educational leaders who have pushed an academic curriculum for all high school students. Today we still have students reared in poverty and those whose first language is not English. Vocational and technology courses and courses to prepare children for a career right after high school are logical plans for some students. The insistence on high-stakes testing, teaching everyone algebra and other academic courses is causing dropouts and students who are not ready for the real world. Advocates of the need for all students to take college preparatory courses must analyze the reality of the situation. The educators advocating vocational, technology, etc. courses have to fight a constant battle for better understanding of the real needs of students who are not college material.

In *Beyond College for All—Career Paths for the Forgotten Half* (2001), Professor James Rosenbaum states:

> A crisis is emerging in the American labor market. Young people who do not get college degrees have been called the "forgotten half" because society offers them no way to enter adult roles (Howe 1988). They either experience enormous difficulty getting jobs or take dead-end jobs that offer low status, little training, and pay too low to support a family...Among new high school graduates, 26 percent of whites and 56 percent of blacks still had no job four months after graduating from high school.

The February 6, 2002 issue of *Education Week* reported on a meeting hosted by the Spencer Foundation, January 24–25, 2002. The report stated that Richard Rothstein, an economist who writes on education matters for the *New York Times*, offered the group this advice:

> "We cannot seriously believe that school can fully compensate for the educational disadvantages of children from lower social classes," he said.

> Yet the national debate swirling around education—for instance, the idea that college and high academic standards are for everyone—suggests that schools can do just that, he added. Unless such "out of balance" convictions are set right, he added, schools will inevitably be seen to fail.

I may be right or wrong. This important question and a recommendation for a national policy should long ago have been made by a permanent specialized SM-14 type national research center on vocational, technology, and career preparation courses.

Learning Systems and Integrated Curricula

In his excellent book *Fix Schools First* (2001), Jack E. Bowsher states that learning systems and integrated curricula are essential for all schools. There should be an integrated curriculum for the whole school district and specific course material for each grade. Here is Bowsher's definition of a learning system:

> A learning system integrates systems design principles and instructional design methods to produce a set of group learning sessions, individual learning models, interactive tutoring, and high-quality motivational course materials. All of these elements are essential to enable *all* students to become successful learners by achieving learning objectives derived from educational standards.

For a complete description, see the book. This approach may be especially needed in urban schools for these reasons:

♦ The high rate of teacher turnover and the large number of inexperienced teachers

♦ The large number of students who are constantly changing schools as parents move

♦ To simplify the heavy burden of urban school principals and superintendents

♦ What we have done in the past has not been successful

♦ Today's pressure of tests and accountability that will close non-performing schools requires extraordinary measures

I agree with Bowsher's comment about opponents:

> Unfortunately, many educators want to continue living in the world of almost no structure and few assessments. They make speeches and write articles emphasizing how each teacher must customize learning for each student based on

the individual needs of a local school and students. This theory sounds well-meaning until one realizes that this lack of structure and little management results in failure rates between 25 and 75 percent. It means that teachers and administrators within inner-city schools must continue to work in a "no-win" situation.

Summary—"Children as Pawns"

I gave you my conclusions about why so many urban schools are low achieving. And don't forget the misguidance school districts have received from our top leaders.

I admire Hacsi's book *Children As Pawns*. I think this phrase hits the nail on the head! Hacsi is a researcher at Harvard's Graduate School of Education. While he does not cover the scientific method in his book, he gives an excellent description of the disastrous history of Head Start, bilingual education, class size, and school funding.

In not using the scientific method better to solve the problems of urban, rural, and suburban schools, ignoring my efforts to correct *the* **BLUNDER**, and maintaining their organized interest, our top leaders are really using our

Children as Pawns

? ?

The Mystery

Blame, blame, blame put on our urban schools, teachers, principals, school districts, etc. Certainly they have their faults, but when you look at all the unfavorable conditions they face, their task is appalling and heart breaking. They are being given some help, but far from enough, considering the size of the task and the poor guidance they have received and are receiving from our top leaders. Why do so many people still blame, mis-analyze, and threaten them with closing, school choice, and charter schools?

? ?

Chapter 25

Other Disasters in the Educational Field

My purpose in writing this book is not to belittle people, but to initiate a major change in education—proper acceptance of the scientific method. All the disasters I describe are cause for change. You should demand change of the right type so that you don't get "more of the same" for your children, grandchildren, and society in general.

In this chapter I cover other disasters more briefly. This does not mean that they are not important, but simply that it was not practical or there was no time to go into detail.

- The Disaster of the Progressive Education Movement
- The Disaster of Piaget and the Scientific Method
- The Disaster of the Misapplication of Capitalistic Principles
- The Disaster of Ignoring Published Books on School Reform
- The Disaster of Our Local School Boards
- The Disaster of School Administrations
- The Disaster of Alternative Teacher Certification
- The Disaster of Current Educational Reform Centers and Educational Research Centers
- The Disaster of U.S. Presidents Adding to Education's Disastrous Mess
- The Disaster of Not Teaching the Scientific Method in Our Community Colleges
- The Disaster in the Transfer of Learning
- The Disaster of the Inadequate Teaching of Creativity
- The Disaster That Isn't the Disaster It Is Claimed To Be: America's Performance in the Third International Mathematics and Science Study (TIMSS)
- The Disaster of Not Teaching the Scientific Method in Our Liberal Arts Colleges
- The Disaster of the Writing of Essays
- The Disaster of Not Building Students' Intuitive Base
- The Disaster of Adult Education Not Teaching the Scientific Method
- The Disaster of Vocational and Technical Education
- The Disaster of the Report *Our Schools and Our Future* by the Koret Task Force on K-12 Education
- The Disaster of Our Principals and School Superintendents
- The Disaster of School Size
- The Disaster of the Term "Critical Thinking"
- The Undescribed Disasters

The Disaster of the Progressive Education Movement

The progressive education movement existed from about 1917 to about 1954. It was killed or fractured into miscellaneous movements by its opponents, by its deficiencies, and by events of the 1950s.

In reading about the movement's objectives other than teaching the scientific method, it is difficult to determine which were excellent, good, bad, or impractical. Even though 40 years have passed, many of the issues it raised have never been settled.

The Progressive Education Movement and the Scientific Method

In the *Handbook of Research on Science Teaching and Learning* (1994), edited by Dorothy L. Gabel, there is a discussion of the progressive era, which includes the following statement:

> There was also a strong commitment to scientific method as a means of developing general problem-solving skills that could be used in the solution of social problems.

The Progressive Movement Should Never Have Been Killed

Education must ever be progressive—keeping up with the application of constant certified practical improvements. The knowledge explosion, the tremendous changes, etc. since the 1950s are proof of this. Instead of being killed, progressive education should have had the scientific method applied to test its objectives, originate new objectives, refine others, and, after pilot programs, extend the certified ones. Its demise was caused by too many arrogant opinions by those both for and against it rather than scientific research.

The big disaster is: the movement promoted the teaching of the scientific method, and if this promotion had continued, *the* **BLUNDER** would never have occurred.

Disputes Never Settled

Because of the lack of permanent specialized SM-14 type national research centers and educational courts, important disputes about various issues are never settled. This has resulted in fads and in disastrous trial and error programs. All this extended the immense harms caused by *the* **BLUNDER**.

The Disaster of Piaget and the Scientific Method

Jean Piaget was a famous Swiss psychologist who has often been quoted by educators. There is even a Jean Piaget Society, which recently had a 25th anniversary symposium. I have read many comments on his work. In my library, I have six of his books, but in past years I was only motivated to spend about 2 hours on them, so I am definitely not very qualified to give opinions of his work.

However, because of how often Piaget has been quoted and my research into the scientific method, I believe that he contributed to **the** BLUNDER. According to an article in *Education Week* (February 4, 1998), Piaget stated:

> The principal goal of education is to create men [and women] who are capable of doing new things, not simply of repeating what other generations have done—[people] who are creative, inventive, discoverers.

> The second goal of education is to form minds which can be critical, can verify and not accept everything they are offered. The great danger today is of slogans, collective opinions, ready-made trends of thought. We have to be able to resist individually, to criticize, to distinguish between what is proven and what is not. So we need pupils who are active, who learn early to find out by themselves, partly by their own spontaneous activity and partly through materials we set up for them, who learn early to tell what is verifiable and what is simply the first idea to come to them.

To the best of my knowledge, Piaget never recommended the teaching of the scientific method, yet:

- It is the method and guide to doing new things, being creative, inventing, and discovering.

- Critical thinking is problem-solving thinking.

- Verification of information is done by applying the scientific method, with its demand for evidence, alternative ideas, and verification of hypotheses.

Thus, Piaget failed to understand and teach the main method or guide to accomplish his goals of education.

The Disaster of the Misapplication of Capitalistic Principles to Public K-12 Education

Educational ills and disasters are not by any means all the fault of our professional top educational leaders. In our top educational leadership group we have leaders and opinion makers from many domains who shape, control, and often dominate public debate about education.

Here, because of its great importance to and influence on *the* **BLUNDER**, I point out the disaster below, which may be added to by people in all domains as well as by those in business and industry.

The Misapplication of Basic Business Principles to Education

Business leaders and others look at what has gone on in education and the many poorly trained graduates who enter the workforce. They are shocked and dissatisfied, and rightly so.

Remember that before I became an educational researcher I had 40 years of business education and experience. In addition, I am a great believer in the capitalistic system. Only because I specialized for 15 years in researching the scientific method and its application to education am I able to explain more clearly the way the misapplication of capitalistic principles to public education on the national front has contributed to the ills of education.

I claim that they have been misapplied in the following important ways.

The Major Fault Is Usually at the Top

When a company or industry is in distress, the first element examined is its top management. Usually, the major fault is there. Our educational system is broken, but many of our top business leaders and others have not recognized that the main fault lies at the top.

Analyze and Define the Problem

A basic business principle is to thoroughly analyze and define a problem before attempting to solve it. However, many capitalists are accepting prevailing opinions that the trouble with schools is bad teachers, bad schools, bad unions, and bad students, and that pressure on schools and teachers is the best tool to fix the problems. They have not made any thorough analyses of the big picture of education.

Testing and Pilot Implementation of Major Programs

The idea of standards, testing, and accountability of some type is sound, but, as I point out in Chapter 14, The Disaster of Standards, Testing, and Accountability, the implementation has been a disaster.

Few big businesses will implement a major program without thorough evaluation, pilot implementation, feedback, etc.

Competition of School Choice, Charter Schools, and Vouchers

Many business leaders, organizations, and others have gone to great lengths to push the competition of school choice, etc. But, as I explain in Chapter 13, The Disaster of the Charter School, Voucher, and School Choice Movement, these actions have limited practical application. Those who are aggressively pushing them are violating basic business principles of fair competition and analysis of what is really wrong with education.

Well-Designed and Well-Tested Compensation Plans

Business leaders and others have been pushing for incentive pay for teachers. Basically, the idea may be good, but, as I explain in Chapter 22, teachers' compensation is a very complex matter. Business and industry learned long ago that incentive plans must be designed very carefully. Yet in the education field, plans are being proposed right and left. Poor incentive programs do more harm than good.

Again, basic principles are being violated.

Business Media

The basic principle of fair and accurate reporting of education is constantly violated by many of our business papers and magazines. They publicize and praise the work of business organizations and authors whose work on education is not based on real research, detailed analysis, and accurate basic business principles. Thus, they are distorting the basic principles of capitalism, free enterprise, and fair competition.

That's Enough

I could give some other examples, but that is enough. You will see that education reform is an exceedingly complex matter.

The Disaster of Ignoring Published Books on School Reform

Education has had and still has so many ills and troubles that every year many books are written and published about school reform. In August 2004, a search on "education reform" on Barnes and Noble's web site listed more than 6,000 books. I quote from many of them in this book.

Just a few others that have been published in recent years are:

Fix Schools First (2001) by Jack E. Bowsher
Why National Standards and Tests? (1998) John F. Jennings
The Academic Achievement Challenge (2000) by Jeanne S. Chall
Underground History of American Education (2000) John Gatto
Spinning Wheels (1999) by Frederick M. Hess
The Schools Our Children Deserve (1999) by Alfie Kohn
Class and Schools by Richard Rothstein (2004)
Inventing Better Schools (1997) by Phillip C. Schlechty
All Children Can Learn (2000) edited by Pankratz and Petrosko
Beyond College For All (2001) by James Rosenbaum
Ensuring Student Success (2000) by Myles I. Friedman
Charter Schools and Vouchers (2002) by Seymour Sarason
The Kind of Schools We Need (1998) by Elliot W. Eisner
One Size Fits Few (1999) by Susan Ohanian

In my library, I have an enormous number of books on school reform. In my judgment, they range from poor to good to excellent. Often the authors have done substantial research and have spent years of effort pointing out deficiencies in our educational efforts. I have read a lot of these books, and many have influenced points I discuss in this book.

I have seen no one make a detailed analysis of these books. It may be that no one can get a grant from our top educators to do it!

The disaster, then, is that people spend years of effort trying to bring the problems of our educational system to the attention of educators and the public and making recommendations for improving the system. However, they attract little attention. I estimate that the lack of utilization of these books by our leaders has cost taxpayers billions of dollars and has done great harm to educational progress. If we had a system of permanent specialized SM-14 type national research centers, one of their responsibilities would be to review these books and new ones that are published. Much of what I have said also applies to magazine articles on educational reform.

We Can't Agree on What's Wrong or Who's To Blame

We examined just some of the recent books on educational reform to determine the authors' positions in regard to two questions: What is the problem? Who is to blame? Here are the results.

What's Wrong with Our Schools?

Public education does not foster basic skills or literacy.
Schools don't teach basic information.
Traditional schooling is unproductive and unappealing.
American students lag behind their foreign counterparts.
American students are not well prepared for global competition.
There are social, institutional, and organizational obstacles to success
There is a dumbing down of the curricula.
Schools don't educate all children.
Cognitive research has not been applied to school reform.
Student achievement is too low for our technological society.
The American public school system is undemocratic.
Schools have curtailed children's ability and desire to learn.
We "stopped doing the right thing."
Education is more than what happens at school.
Our children are not prepared for the 21st century.
American schools have low academic standards.
Old programs are presented with new names.
There is an obsession with intelligence testing.

Who or What Is To Blame?

Social changes
Policies not supported
    by the public
Education professors
School administrators
Education establishment
Liberals
Conservatives
Elephantine bureaucracies
Groups defending their power
Educational foolishness
Social foolishness
Colleges
Universities
Education bureaucracy
Teachers unions
Schools
Reformers
Educational community
Traditionalists
Relativists
Advocates of testing
Parents
Teachers
Lack of academic standards
Lack of integration
Lack of discipline
Media

The Disaster of Our Local School Boards

America has a tradition of local control of schools. Good or bad, that is the existing situation. However, local control is not complete because federal financial aid and regulations, state regulations, and other factors—for example, that students need to be educated to meet the requirements of national tests, college entrance examines, etc.— enter into the decisions that school boards must make.

The Disaster of the Inadequate Problem-Solving and Decision-Making Qualifications of School Board Members

In our democracy, school board members are elected from all walks of life. They are called on for all sorts of important decisions.

Because of *the* **BLUNDER**, they were not taught the complete method of creative problem solving and associated thinking skills across the curricula and from kindergarten through university. Therefore, they often are not qualified to solve problems and make the decisions their positions require. The same situation exists for all our citizens in other public activities, such as serving on juries, etc.

The Disaster of School Board Members Not Having Reliable Knowledge on Which To Base Their Work

Since there are no permanent specialized SM-14 type national research centers, school board members have no reliable sources of information accumulated based on the scientific method.

Let me give you an example of this from the November 2001 issue of the *American School Board Journal*. The title of the section "Reviews—What school leaders are reading" is "Champions of Choice Look into Crystal Balls." This section has reviews of three current books on school choice and vouchers.

The title is exactly right—it is all looking into crystal balls to know what is best. So how are local school board members going to make long-range intelligent decisions? In January 2003, the Progressive Policy Institute issued a helpful report. This is not enough. We need a permanent specialized SM-14 type national research center on school boards that will continually provide the best and latest knowledge. We have a disastrous situation with school boards. Many political fights develop based on the lack of availability of reliable knowledge. These fights retard progress in achieving good schools.

The Disaster of School Administrations

There are so many stories of teachers' problems existing for years—really for decade after decade—with no solutions. These problems constantly interfere with teachers' ability to properly teach students.

Examples:

Supplies—Teachers have to pay out of their own pockets for some supplies that they desperately need. It has been estimated that the average teacher spends $400 of his or her personal funds on supplies each year. In some school districts, some teachers are now given a personal allotment for supplies.

Telephones—Teachers are expected to keep in touch with parents, school offices, etc. yet there are usually no telephones in classrooms, and a limited number of phones are available for teachers' use. In some classrooms, teachers can use e-mail, but not all parents have an e-mail address, and e-mail communication is often not as effective as telephone communication.

Classroom, building, and equipment repair—Teachers often have problems with leaking roofs and windows, building damage and broken equipment, and these problems are slow to be repaired. They often must also contend with old buildings and temporary classrooms.

Textbooks—Textbooks are often in short supply or out of date. Requests from teachers for new books are often held up because of disputes about which books to purchase or because the funds have not been allocated to purchase them.

Classroom discipline—Teachers often do not have the support of the school administration in dealing with behavior problems. Teachers are faulted for sending too many students to principals' offices, and they are criticized for their inability to keep their students in order.

School administrations—These in turn have had many problems to contend with. Administrators have often been unable to fire bad teachers. Their budgets have often been inadequate.

In general, the disaster is that the problems of teachers, principals, and school administrators have not received the attention from our top educators that they deserve. We have a great deal of knowledge, but it is not summarized by an authoritative body.

The Disaster of Alternative Teacher Certification

"Teacher Certification Needs Dispassionate Analysis" is the subject of a letter to the editor of *Education Week* (November 7, 2001) from Ray Bacchetti, former education program officer at the Hewlett Foundation. The disaster is that this is an urgent need. Instead, we have for years had a raging debate, with all sorts of claims and counter claims by proponents and opponents of alternative certification. This is typical of what goes on constantly in the educational field. Debate about a problem goes on for years.

Most teachers, having been required to attend schools of education and pass certification tests, are demoralized by claims that anyone with a bachelor's degree in a subject area should be allowed to teach that subject.

Many leave the teaching profession for other jobs for various reasons. So too should we have provisions for job changers to enter the teaching profession, but in a way that is fair to current teachers.

The "teaching shortage" is constantly mentioned as the reason for alternative certification. This book shows that a large part of this is due to the unfair working conditions for teaching that exist because of the blundering of our top educators. I hope that in years to come the use of the scientific method will greatly decrease these unfair conditions and help retain many of the teachers who now quit in disgust.

There may be a place for properly designed alternative certification. I was impressed with the case for its use in poor urban schools made by Martin Haberman, Distinguished Professor at the University of Wisconsin. His address "Alternative Certification: Intended and Unintended Consequences" was made to the first National Center on Alternative Certification Conference (February 2, 2004). A copy is available from the Haberman Foundation at www.altcert.org. He also pointed out the poor job our schools of education are doing. There have been many reports about the need for alternative certification for hard-to-fill vacant positions for physics teachers and other specialties.

The only way to end this disaster is to establish a permanent specialized SM-14 type national research center on certification, where dispassionate analysis can provide us with reliable knowledge on what we should do about regular and alternative certification. Again, it must be a permanent center, as the need for teachers in various specialties is constantly changing.

The Disaster of Current Educational Reform Centers and Educational Research Centers

I am making an impassioned plea in this book for permanent specialized SM-14 type national research centers in the educational field.

We already have research centers in name. Many of them, I believe, are disasters compared to what they should be. As I have made no study of them, I must qualify my claim. I believe that some of them are doing a good job, but we have no system to identify them.

Here are the strikes all or most of the centers have against them:

♦ In the present state of educational research, the quality control method of the scientific method is not standard. Thus, their research may or may not be reliable. I have noticed in their reports that many ignore the evidence that the scientific method exists.

♦ I have sent my literature to some of them, and it has also been ignored, even though they claim to be "research centers."

♦ They are funded by someone they dare not offend for fear of loss of financing.

♦ Often they are not permanent, and therefore the scope of work is limited.

♦ Since the big picture of education is not known, their work suffers.

♦ Many try to cover too wide a field.

♦ They issue costly reports, but little action ever results.

♦ Some are strictly advocacy centers rather than the "research" centers they call themselves. This tarnishes the image of other, more reliable centers.

In Chapter 58 I lay down strict standards for permanent specialized SM-14 type national research centers. In Chapter 55 I describe what scientifically based research means. Existing research centers will have to conform, I believe, to a standard such as the one described. If they do not, they will not be eligible for government contracts once the full implications of the No Child Left Behind Act requirement for "scientifically based research" are understood.

The Disaster of U.S. Presidents Adding to Education's Disastrous Mess

U.S. presidents usually add to education's disastrous mess, as well as helping education in some ways, despite good intentions.

These are the reasons:

♦ The President is usually not an educator, and education has become extremely complex in recent years.

♦ The President depends on his limited personal experiences, stories in the media, and education "expert" advisors.

♦ No one knows the big picture of education, and much of educational research is unreliable; therefore, the advice from these "experts" is not reliable.

♦ Usually, untested programs are advocated, resulting, as the title of Professor Sarason's book tells us, in *The Predictable Failure of Education Reform* (1990).

♦ Political considerations often enter the picture. These often are bad, because the big picture of education is not known. Thus, pressures of various types build up, adding to the mess.

I will not go into detail on this subject, as this book explains many of the reasons why presidents end up with poor advice on education.

The solutions are:

♦ Require the use of the scientific method (SM-14) by all educators and especially those who advise our presidents.

♦ The establishment of permanent specialized SM-14 type national research centers, including one on the Big Picture of Education, that will also guide or provide reliable knowledge about education to our presidents, Congress, and state officials.

♦ Business, industries, think tanks, and other domains that put pressure on presidents for educational reforms must also use the scientific method in formulating their advice and demands of presidents. At present these pressures result in defective programs that harm our students, teachers, schools, and society. It is time to reform the reformers.

The Disaster of Not Teaching the Scientific Method in Our Community Colleges

Anyone who is going to take a 2-year college course may be at a disadvantage in competing with those who take a 4-year course to earn a degree. This disadvantage can be offset to some extent among community college attendees if they learn and practice the scientific method for use in their careers and in real-world situations.

Employers Want Graduates with Excellent Problem-Solving Skills

Employers already sense the growing need for employees who can identify and solve problems quickly and make decisions efficiently and effectively. The U.S. Department of Education's May 1995 *Community Update* reports that

> A reflection of problems in education from the business world was offered by Alan Wurtzel, vice-chairman of Circuit City Stores. He said that when Circuit City recruits workers for its retail stores, 15 to 20 people must be interviewed for every job that is filled. These positions do not require a college education, but, according to Wurtzel, most people interviewed lack the basic abilities to read, write, interact with the public, and *think and solve problems.*

It is thus a disaster that we don't help the students in our community colleges adequately learn the scientific method.

Overview of Basic Community College Course Schedule

A review of a course schedule for any community college reveals some basic subjects like:

business	education	criminal sciences
technology	economics	medical arts, nursing
engineering	management	science and math

It is not efficient for no methods or different methods to be taught for all these subjects when they all have the scientific method in common. For example, the scientific method is the method of police work and investigation, while it is also the method of medical diagnostics throughout the health care industry. It is the method for all the courses listed above. Community colleges have a golden opportunity to end this disaster by giving their students the edge by quickly offering courses on problem solving and decision making.

The Disaster in the Transfer of Learning

High on the list of the objective of education, as I have previously explained, should be the teaching of problem solving and the associated thinking skills. Here is one of the main reasons for this—the transfer of learning. Another neglected area in education is an analysis of what knowledge will stay in students' minds.

You learned a lot of subject matter in school. You got good grades. You were expected to learn to think as you were taught subject matter—and you did to some extent. You might even have been taught critical thinking skills. Out into the cold world of reality you go—the real world, where it isn't tests but actual actions that show your real worth.

What matters?

1. How much you know, your experiences, and your personal attributes
2. How well you can look up knowledge in the library or on the Internet, etc.
3. How well you can think and in a practical manner apply what you know

Numbers 1 and 2 are important, but they are of limited value if you don't know how to apply your knowledge and abilities efficiently.

It is only through teaching the scientific method and then assigning projects or, even better, letting a student pick problems or areas for investigation that you get them engaged in thinking efficiently. Without the scientific method, they wander in all directions.

In *The Process of Education* (1960), Jerome S. Bruner states:

> The first object of any act of learning over and beyond the pleasure it may give is that it should serve us in the future. Learning should not only take us somewhere; it should allow us later to go further more easily.

"It should allow us later to go further more easily" is exactly what the scientific method does. You have a body of knowledge gained through education and experience. To transfer this to new situations, you follow the guide of the scientific method. It is a disaster to the transfer of learning that the method is not adequately taught.

The Disaster of the Inadequate Teaching of Creativity

The big picture of creativity shows that it is an extremely important factor in America's success and in the advancement of society in general. While there are claims that you are born with creativity—that it cannot be taught—our body of evidence shows that a person's creativity can be improved and that it is important not to stifle a child's creativity early in life. The No Child Left Behind Act may do this.

Even though comparisons of American students to those of other nations (which I criticized previously) show that we do not fare well, the United States is still the leading nation of the world. This is true for the following reasons.

Our Workers. It is a tribute to our workforce that, on the whole, they are industrious, willing to earn more, subjected to competition, and eager to embrace new ways and technologies. Witness our rapid advancement in the use of computers.

The United States Is a Democracy and a Capitalist Nation. The resulting freedom and prosperity we have is a major factor. It attracts immigrants who help us remain the world's leading nation.

Our Intellectual Elite, Creative People, Entrepreneurs, and Other Gifted and Talented People. These people are another major reason for our leadership. We have fostered a receptive climate for them, although it is somewhat slanted toward those with high IQs because:

- they are easier to identify
- they are more apt to be in charge of education or in positions of authority, dictating what tests cover and what is taught in our curricula

In reading school magazines, I have learned of many teachers' efforts to improve students' creativity. Gifted programs, entrepreneurship programs, and science fairs all help. Some schools even offer classes on creativity. However, on the whole, we make only a small effort.

Creative Education Foundation

This organization has been promoting the teaching of creativity and offering extensive material since the 1950s. However, our top leaders, business, industry, and foundations on the whole have not aided their efforts to any great extent, thus adding to this disaster.

The Disaster of Not Teaching the Scientific Method in Our Liberal Arts Colleges

While it is a disaster that the scientific method is not taught in all colleges and universities, I call special attention to the disaster as it affects our liberal arts colleges.

My research indicates and I believe logic supports:

♦ As is presently done, a liberal arts student needs education in the arts, humanities, sciences, and social sciences.

♦ Liberal arts students should be taught and trained to be specialists in the scientific method—the complete method of creative problem solving and decision making for all domains.

Because of *the* **BLUNDER**, liberal arts (as well as other) students are not given extensive training in the scientific method. This is logically wrong. The logical reasoning is:

♦ Knowledge without training on how to apply it is of limited value.

♦ As generalists, liberal arts students must be specialists in the method, which in all fields is used to originate, refine, extend, and apply knowledge.

♦ Education in bits and pieces of problem solving and decision making is not enough.

♦ Liberal arts students should be well trained in what historically has been determined by numerous researchers to be the method or guide found superior to all other methods or guides—the scientific method—which is also the complete method of creative problem solving and decision making for all domains.

Those in charge of liberal arts colleges and courses and the students themselves should study the situation. This entire book supports the need to learn and teach the scientific method. Those who question the value of a liberal arts education will be less able to challenge its value if the scientific method is taught extensively.

That the liberal arts colleges or courses are not stressing the above is a gigantic disaster in terms of wasted time, money, and effort that stems from *the BLUNDER.*

The Disaster That Isn't the Disaster It Is Claimed To Be: America's Performance in the Third International Mathematics and Science Study (TIMSS)

Our top educational leaders are teach-subject-matter minded, not method or creative minded. Millions of dollars a year have been spent on TIMSS (which measures achievement in science and mathematics by students in the United States and in a number of other countries). There has been a great deal of publicity about the poor performance of America's schools in comparison to those of other nations. The value of this comparison is accepted without question by many of our top leaders. The "blame" is largely placed on our "bad schools, bad teachers, and bad unions." Almost never is blame placed on our top leaders and their bad programs and bad research.

There is no real purpose or need for this comparison, which is of questionable accuracy. Our educational system has produced disaster after disaster but in the actual everyday world, our graduates still out-perform those of other nations. For example, this appeared on the front page of the *Wall Street Journal* on January 18, 2001:

> Does the rest of the world want to emulate the U.S. and its remarkable economic success, or doesn't it? The unequivocal answer from abroad: Yes.

There are many reasons for America's success. One is pointed out in the *Wilson Quarterly*, Winter 2001:

> "Managers, professionals, and technical workers, who are increasingly involved in creative activities," now make up 33 percent of the work force, almost double the proportion in 1950. There are six times as many "creative professionals": Scientists, engineers, architects, writers, designers, artists, and entertainers now number 7.6 million.

Certainly we should watch foreign nations for ideas we can adopt to improve our methods. For example, math textbooks from Singapore have become popular. Seeking foreign ideas and methods better than our own is productive, but questionable statistics that frighten us have no real value. Our objective should be to look for ideas, not doubtful statistics.

Then America could rise to much greater heights of prosperity.

The Disaster of the Writing of Essays as a Test of Students' Abilities

Centuries ago (actually, as far back as the "dark ages"), it became a custom to require students to write essays to help determine their abilities and knowledge. Time passed, and the scientific method was recognized and developed. Then came the tragedy of Conant's claim that it does not exist, so progress on its use in education slowed dramatically, and no standard formula (such as SM-14) was developed.

Thus today we still have the ancient requirement that students write essays as a major test of their abilities and knowledge.

An article in the *American School Board Journal* (March 2004) entitled "Words on Paper" asks: "Is writing at risk? Written expression is the result of ordered thought and the product of good teaching. . ." You get "ordered thought" from following the stages of the scientific method (SM-14).

Ask yourself:

Is an essay by a student about his or her trip to Uncle Sumner's farm—or even about a more serious subject—any real test? Compare it to being required to write a short report on, for instance, how he or she originated and solved a problem, or made a decision following the scientific method (SM-14) formula.

Students in elementary and high school should not be required to write just essays but also to write reports following the scientific method that will help prepare them for those they will write in the real world.

Employers want people who can write well; they especially want well-thought-out and well-written reports on decisions and problem solutions. Imagine—even in these modern times, we are still practicing an ancient custom when we place such great emphasis on essays from applicants to college!

Another inefficiency in education caused by *the* BLUNDER.

It is often stated that colleges and universities are slow to change. I believe that the idea I present here is very logical. To determine its validity and to speed its development, I suggest that a study group research the idea for its application to all schools.

The Disaster of Not Building Students' Intuitive Base

In his excellent book *The Process of Education* (1960), Harvard Professor Jerome S. Bruner states:

> ... formalism. Unfortunately, the formalism of school learning has somehow devalued intuition. It is the very strong conviction of men who have been designing curricula, in mathematics and the sciences particularly, over the last several years that much more work is needed to discover how we may develop the *intuitive gifts of our students from the earliest grades onwards.* [emphasis mine]

Unfortunately, Bruner's promotion of teaching and building an intuitive base was never followed. Our curricula have had a heavy slant toward subject matter.

At one time it was claimed that intuition was a gift that only highly creative people possessed. Today we know that such a capacity is a common ingredient in everyday thinking. It can be developed if attention is paid to understanding how it works.

The Value of Training in the Scientific Method to Your Intuitive Base

Instantaneous Decisions and Problem Solutions

In the course of a day you make hundreds of simple decisions and problem solutions, usually based on your intuition. They are called by such names as:

Intuitive decision	Quick guess
Instantaneous decision	Snap judgment
Gut feeling	Trial and error solution
Leap of understanding	Good enough
Habit decision	Emotional decision
Hunch	Off the top of your head
Arbitrary guess	Immediate apprehension
Jumping to a conclusion	Arbitrary guess
Hasty decision	Subconscious mind
Sixth sense	A visualized solution

Many of these solutions and decisions are really simple, unimportant, and in the habit-type class. Others are of varied importance that you may make instantly because of time frames, a good-enough answer will suffice, or you have confidence in your intuition.

Some may be important, so too many errors can hurt your success, relationships, or reputation. Therefore, it is important to develop your intuitive base.

Your Intuitive Base

Your intuitive base depends on a great number of factors that you retain in your working and long-term memory:

Body of subject knowledge	Patterns
Experiences	Ideas
Reading of others' experiences	Methods
Discriminating thinking	Concepts
Knowledge of basic principles	Relationships

A stress-free moment, rest, selective forgetting that may occur with sleep, or working on a different problem often help your intuition and imagination function better.

Your intuitive base may be harmed by the following:

Lack of experiences	Prejudices
Mental laziness	Biases
Superstitions	Reliance on authoritarianism
Dogmatism	Irrationality
Stubbornness	Fanaticism

Knowledge of the Scientific Method Is Essential to Your Intuition Base

If you are trained in all the stages of the scientific method and its associated thinking skills, your intuitive base is greatly improved. A simple example: When important matters arise, instead of jumping to a conclusion, your intuition will tell you that this is a complex matter. Then you know you must use the scientific method as your guide. In addition, when trained in the scientific method, you have a body of experiences from solving many problems following the complete method of creative problem solving and decision making. Thus your intuition tells you that any intuitive thought should be considered tentative and, if time permits, should be put through all the stages of the scientific method. Thus, *the* **BLUNDER** has been a disaster to building our students' intuitive base. They usually go out into the world not as well prepared as they would be if they were taught the scientific method.

The Disaster of Adult Education Not Teaching the Scientific Method

Adults take educational courses to complement what they have already learned in school, remind them of what they have forgotten, or because of technological changes. We know that, because of *the* **BLUNDER**, they were never adequately taught the scientific method. In this period of information explosion and change, change, change, they badly need to know the method of change, the complete method of creative problem solving and decision making—the scientific method.

I recommend for grades K-12 that educators study my claims before instituting changes, as they have gone ahead in the past with so many fads and false concepts and piled these into an already overburdened system. I believe they must study changes more scientifically.

In adult education I suggest going ahead immediately with teaching the scientific method. Anyone who reviews this book should realize:

♦ Adults do not have time to wait for studies. They are mentally mature and if offered the material can see for themselves the value of it. They need it in their personal lives as well as in their careers.

♦ Employers are asking for problem solvers, decision makers, and entrepreneurs. The scientific method trains people to meet these challenges.

The famous management specialist Peter Drucker states in an article in *Forbes Global* (May 15, 2000):

> Engineers tell me that they need a thorough refresher course in their specialties at least every other year and a "reimmersion"—their word—in basics at least every four years.

> So do millions of other knowledge workers. The market for continuing education is already much bigger than most people realize. A good guess is that it already accounts for 6% of GNP in the U.S. and is rapidly getting there in other developed countries. It is going to get a lot higher. . .

> Why this explosion of demand? We live in an economy where knowledge, not buildings and machinery, is the chief resource and where knowledge-workers make up the biggest part of the work force.

The Disaster of Inadequate Vocational and Technical Education

The new term for vocational education is "career technical education." Don't think of the old woodworking shop when you see vocational education discussed today. The whole field has changed dramatically. It should no longer be thought of as a second-rate high school experience, even though I call it a disaster area. Those who advocate career technical education are ignored to a great extent. The automobile industry constantly complains about the lack of mechanics. The "college for all" group is largely in power and controls the situation.

Professor James Rosenbaum spent many years studying the problem and wrote *Beyond College for All—Career Paths for the Forgotten Half* (2001). In Chapter 1 he states:

> A crisis is emerging in the American labor market. Young people who do not get college degrees have been called the "forgotten half" because society offers them no way to enter adult roles (Howe 1988). They either experience enormous difficulty getting jobs or take dead-end jobs that offer low status, little training, and pay too low to support a family (Osterman 1980; Althauser and Kalleberg 1981; NAS 1984). Among new high school graduates, 26 percent of whites and 56 percent of blacks still had no job four months after graduating from high school (NCES 1993, 82). Moreover, another study found that most graduates who got jobs (58.3 percent) were only continuing the same dead-end jobs that they already held during high school (Nolfi 1978). Obviously, high school graduation does not give these students access to better jobs. Moreover, their difficulties do not end quickly, and their early problems may hurt their career many years later (D'Amico and Maxwell 1990; Lynch 1989). Even at age thirty, a large portion of high school graduates continue to hold low-paying, high-turnover jobs (Osterman 1995).

He also points out:

95 percent of seniors plan to attend college, but only 28 percent of young adults ages 30–34 have a BA degree or higher and another 8 percent have an associate's degree.

An article in the July 8, 2003 edition of the *Christian Science Monitor* by Marjorie Coeyman states in part:

Today, concerns that technical education could be a means of sidelining some kids are very much alive. At the heart of the 2001 No Child Left Behind federal education law is the belief that all high school graduates should be ready for college, whether they choose to attend or not. But that focus on core academics means other kinds of learning will necessarily be harder to fund and tougher to squeeze into a busy school day. . . The debate over the value of vocational education in America's public schools has been raging at least since 1917, when the federal government first began funding such classes.

So there you have another gigantic educational blunder that has existed since 1917. The important matter is debated and researched, and billions of dollars are spent on it, but a clear, definitive solution is never achieved. Many of our authoritative top leaders push their views on the desirability of college for all whether it is practical or not. Thus, vocational and technical education suffers.

From Howard Gardner's work on multiple intelligences and Mel Levine's *A Mind at a Time*, research on learning styles, and our experiences with dropouts, we know that "college for all" is a false concept and not practical. All the disasters I have described in this book have contributed to the number of students who should be helped with vocational courses. In some school districts, a good job is being done, but overall we have a disaster.

The October 2004 issue of *Phi Delta Kappan* contained an article entitled "Is High School Career and Technical Education Obsolete?" It states in part:

> One way to sort out public education's core challenges is to examine what happens to today's students during and after their public school experience and what programs of study do or do not improve their situation. Let's take a hypothetical class of 24 first-graders and, using national data, see what happens to them over the next 12 to 16 years. The results are rather different from what might be assumed on the basis of our current rhetoric and policies and suggest that CTE [career and technical education] may in fact be more in line with the real issues than its critics would have us believe.

For the sake of society and the lives of many who are really not college material, we need a permanent specialized SM-14 type national research center on career and technical education to advise the public and our top educational and legislative leaders.

The Disaster of the Report *Our Schools and Our Future* by the Koret Task Force on K-12 Education

Background

In 1999, the Hoover Institute at Stanford University organized a group of 11 scholars with the purpose, among others, of presenting key facts on the current condition of American education. A recent publication is a book *Our Schools and Our Future . . . Are We Still at Risk?* (2003). It reviews the state of American education 20 years after the report *A Nation at Risk*.

Our Schools and Our Future states: "The Koret Task Force renews the call for excellence but also asks the country to bring accountability, choice and transparency into the structure and operation of its public schools." A symposium was held in Washington, D.C., on February 26, 2003 to mark the release of the book. The report has not received very much attention.

A Nation at Risk (1983)

While many have claimed that this is a great report, my opinion, which many others share, is that is a very imperfect one.

The Hoover Institute

While I have made no detailed study, my opinion is that, in its educational activities, the Hoover Institute is more an advocacy group than a think tank that uses the scientific method to reach conclusions. Thus, they cannot be relied on for guidance.

The Eleven Scholars

They are all well-known, authoritative top educators. I recognize some as individuals I would classify as belonging to what I call the Harvard/Conant group and misguided followers (or whoever they are).

The Report Raises the Question, Are We Still at Risk?

My answer is yes, the nation is very much at risk because of top educators who do not realize the need to acknowledge that the scientific method exists and
- teach it across the curriculum
- require that our top educators and educational researchers use it in achieving excellence

The Disaster of Our Principals and School Superintendents

To properly understand this disaster, you must be familiar with the many problems that our principals and school superintendents face every day. Please see the list on the next page.

This is another one of the disasters at the very top national levels, resulting in overwhelming problems for principals and school superintendents at a lower level.

Many articles claim that there is a shortage of qualified principals, but one pinpoints the shortage in urban schools, southern schools, sunbelt schools, and rural schools. It is easy to understand why there is a shortage when you consider the heavy load of problems and a job that requires a 10-plus-hour day and weekend work. In some places, the pay for a principal is not much higher than that of a teacher.

But the real disaster is the workload of principals, with so many frustrating problems. Principals need the guidance of a permanent specialized SM-14 type national research center on their problems and a number of centers on subject matter areas of the curriculum.

The training of new principals is improving, with several foundations and some universities offering special courses. The National Association of Elementary Principals and the National Association of Secondary Principals have been presenting the principals' perspective for years. These efforts will help, but, as several articles state, we need a combined national effort of professional organizations, community and business leaders, political leaders at all levels, and cooperative teachers.

Suggestions

For the efforts mentioned above to be successful, we must also have

- top leaders and educational researchers using the scientific method
- the establishment of permanent specialized SM-14 type national research centers in many areas

Years ago principals had few legal problems. In my mail recently was a newsletter titled *School Principals Legal Alert* from the Alexander Hamilton Institute, Inc. The school legal problem is so bad, this newsletter is published once a month. We need a permanent specialized SM-14 type national research center on school legal problems.

Problems of Principals and School Superintendents

I have compiled this list from a variety of articles.

Expected to be "leaders of learning" without time or proper assistance
Politics and bureaucracy
Daily emergencies
Insufficient budget
Mandate after mandate, often not funded
Insufficient time to do all the things required
Take a barrage of criticism from many sources
Medical "emergencies" and new safety concerns
Answering anonymous complaints
Building, space, and overcrowding problems
Constant discipline problems
Prisoners of paperwork
Increased responsibility for exceptional (often disabled) students
Changing expectations for the position
Extraordinary demands and threat of charter schools
Worry about violence
Stressful conditions and lack of needed resources
Limited and ineffective recruitment of teachers
Shouldering responsibility that once belonged at home
New before and after school programs, breakfast and lunch programs
Facing possible termination if their schools don't show results
Too little control over resources and staffing
Litigation and threats of legal action
Can't exercise instructional leadership alone
Insufficient professional development funds
Dealing with union grievances and disgruntled parents
Difficult to remove failing teachers
Dealing with requests for data and statistics
New pressures of NCLB act accountability
New pressure of NCLB act report cards to the public
New pressure of NCLB act tests
New pressure of NCLB act on "Effective Teachers"
Problems increase and resources diminish
No time for professional development courses
School bashing by the media and public officials
No time for home life and their own children
Supervisory load approximately three times that of a middle manager
Threats of school closing or takeover
Threats of charter schools
Breakfast and lunch programs

The Disaster of School Size

School size is another of the many educational problems that have been handled in a disastrous way.

By 1959, there was a movement toward large schools. Then, in his book *The American High School* (1959), Dr. James Conant recommended that schools should be "comprehensive" and large. Within a decade of the release of this book, says Thomas Toch in *In the Name of Excellence* (1991), "the number of public school systems shrank from over 40,000 to under 18,000."

With size came many unforeseen problems. From the Education Writers Association Backgrounder #13 report (August 1999):

> The argument against large schools started as early as 1964. But the real small schools movement began in New York City a decade later.

In its January 2002 issue, *Education Digest* mentions that, in 1996 "Susan Cotton reviewed more than 100 studies and found student attitudes, behavior, and attendance are better at smaller schools."

Also in 1996, *Educational Leadership* magazine (September issue) contained an article by Deborah W. Meier giving seven reasons for smallness.

The March 25, 2003, edition of the *Washington Post* reports that the Bill and Melinda Gates Foundation has committed more than $400 million in the past 3 years to making American high schools smaller.

There is even a movement to break big schools into several smaller ones, all located in the same building.

Look at the disaster: first, a big movement in 1959 to consolidate and build large schools that continued for years and years. Questioning the wisdom of large schools started as early as 1964 and increased in intensity in the 1990s.

Because we did not have a permanent specialized SM-14 type national research center on school size, taxpayers' dollars by the billions have been wasted by our top educational leaders. Students, parents, and teachers have been seriously harmed over the years by the disaster of not knowing what size schools should be.

The Disaster of Small Class Size

There is little doubt that smaller classes, especially in the lower grades, are more effective than larger ones. A number of studies have shown this, and simple logic makes the idea seem correct.

Thus, there are numerous articles and movements in favor of small class size. Florida voters even passed a constitutional amendment mandating small classes by a certain date.

The September 2003 issue of *Educational Leadership* contained an article entitled "Class Size Reduction—A Fresh Look at the Data." The authors report favorable results in a Wisconsin program.

The problems are: where is the money to come from? Is the public willing and able to make the sacrifices involved in financing the extra cost? Are enough teachers available? Are there enough classrooms? What other problems does such a change create?

The matter is so very complex, is this really the most practical change and the best use of taxpayers' money?

I am, of course, no expert on the subject. However, as I point out throughout this book, we do not know the big picture of education and therefore we constantly waste billions of dollars every year.

Small class size is desirable but will not make up for the other disasters currently going on that are covered in this book. We particularly need the following:

- better parental preparation of children for school, especially in poverty areas
- most children receiving pre-schooling
- improvement in pre-schooling and kindergarten teaching
- greater understanding and application of student motivation and discipline principles
- improved teacher training
- greater use of good structured programs
- better understanding and aid for children with reading difficulties

I don't like to be a parrot, and my editorial consultant thinks I mention it too much, but here again a permanent specialized SM-14 type national research center on class size is needed to really guide our local and state educators.

The Disaster of the Term "Critical Thinking"

Throughout this book I point out the very inadequate teaching of the scientific method—the complete method of creative problem solving and decision making *and* the important need for teaching the supporting thinking skills.

Most of our top educational leaders have been mainly concerned with teaching subject matter. A brief review I made of the National Educational standards set since 1994 shows that none of these puts much emphasis on teaching thinking skills. In the standards set after 1995, there are a few insignificant mentions of the scientific method.

However, for many years a number of individuals and organizations have existed that have promoted the teaching of thinking skills, problem solving, or critical thinking. They all deserve praise for their efforts.

These progressive people have been hindered in their efforts by:

◆ never having been taught the scientific method during their education over the years

◆ being taught that the scientific method does not exist, so they should not include it in their programs

◆ realizing the importance of the scientific method but knowing that if they include it they would endanger their grants or bring down on their work the disapproval of the Harvard/Conant group and misguided followers (or whoever they are)

Here are just some of the terms being applied to thinking skills:

reflective thinking	logical thinking
productive thinking	analytical thinking
effective thinking	directed thinking
decision-making thinking	real-life thinking
scientific thinking	practical thinking
problem-solving thinking	higher-order thinking

The leading term today is critical thinking.

This term began to be used more often in the early 1940s. In 1946, Professor Max Black wrote *Critical Thinking—An Introduction to*

Logic and Scientific Method. The term "critical thinking" has, in recent years, been increasingly used by those who realize the need to teach thinking skills. But, for the various reasons mentioned previously, they don't specify the need to teach them as an essential part of the scientific method.

The use of this term is a disaster for these and other reasons:

♦ There is no clear-cut definition or understanding of what critical thinking is. Many definitions are long and not practical to teach.

♦ When it is used, there is usually no reference to the scientific method or problem solving.

♦ "Critical" is often interpreted as analytical, and there is far more to a complete act of thought.

♦ Students who are often subjected to criticism are turned off by the term and don't clearly see its relationship to their future life.

A more detailed criticism of the term is found in *Critical Thinking and Education* (1981) by John McPeck. I especially like his statement:

> Purporting to teach critical thinking in the abstract, in isolation from specific fields or problem areas, is muddled nonsense; thinking of any kind is always 'thinking about X'. Critical thinking cannot be a distinct subject.

The Undescribed Disasters

Those in the art, geography, history, civics, and some other domains will be disappointed that I didn't cover the disasters in their fields. There is also a growing interest in addressing the disasters that exist in our high schools (see *Education Week*, January 26, 2005). I have covered some of these disasters, but I just could not cover everything. The lack of teaching the scientific method and the lack of its use by educators harms all areas of education.

Summary of Part 5

While we will never have perfection in public or private education, all the disasters I have described have caused unnecessary and tremendous heart-breaking situations for students, parents, teachers, and others.

I don't want to bore you by repeating and repeating, but there is no better summary for this part of the book than the summary for Chapter 6. Here it is again.

A Killed —
     The widespread teaching of the scientific method

B Killed —
     The proper use of the scientific method by top
     education leaders, educational researchers,
     and others in the education field

C Killed —
     The development of the science of education
     and establishment of permanent specialized
     SM-14 type national research centers

This all ends up with. . .

DISASTERS AT THE SCHOOLHOUSE
FROM THE GREATEST INTELLECTUAL AND EDUCATION
BLUNDER IN HISTORY

To close this part of my book, I repeat my warning:
If you don't want more of the same, read on and take action to ensure that my recommendations in Part 11 are followed.

Introduction to Part 6

Contributions to *the* BLUNDER

The **BLUNDER** has been perpetuated not so much by individuals operating on their own as by the collective effects of misguided top leaders in operating their organizations. Here I cover a few individuals but many organizations and domains. I did not do a complete analysis, so there are others that should have been included. However, I have covered enough to give you an idea of the far-reaching extent of *the* **BLUNDER**.

I have told you the story of the misunderstanding and false claims about the scientific method that misled so many intelligent people, even though they were motivated to improve science, education, and the advancement of knowledge. Many didn't even know that there was a dispute about the existence of the scientific method. I didn't realize what was happening until I was accidentally led into specialized research on the scientific method. So as I tell these stories, it is not a case of my being "holier than thou." Rather, my research woke me up. My lack of success in waking others up has made me become a crusader for the scientific method.

The little known, the famous and prestigious, regardless of status, all seem to have participated in *the* **BLUNDER**. My reasons for claiming that it has been the biggest educational and intellectual blunder in history rest on solid ground. To do my duty, I have had to name organizations, regardless of their status. To show the extent of *the* **BLUNDER,** for historical reasons, and for members of the organizations about which I have written, I often go into a lot of detail. If it bores you, do a little skip reading.

Remember that the top leaders of many organizations have changed since I last wrote to them several years ago. The organizations, etc. are not arranged in any particular order, although I start with Harvard, where, in my opinion, *the* **BLUNDER** began.

Chapter 26

Contribution of Harvard University to *the* BLUNDER

I present here my opinion of Harvard's major contribution to *the* **BLUNDER**.

- ◆ Harvard's Ties to *the* **BLUNDER** as an Institution
- ◆ The Perpetuation of *the* **BLUNDER** by Harvard Professors
- ◆ Minor Exceptions to the Lack of Teaching of the Scientific Method at Harvard
- ◆ Harvard's Refusal To Study the Scientific Method Situation
- ◆ The Harvard Business School
- ◆ My Suggestions for Study
- ◆ The Big Mystery

To be fair to Harvard, I first point out that all our colleges and universities have contributed to *the* **BLUNDER**. I found none that has a policy of actively promoting the scientific method and teaching it across the curriculum.

However, there are individual professors who believe in the scientific method and actively teach it. In addition, our scientists and engineers are trained in the method, usually by apprenticeship.

The scientific method and a short formula for it appear in a high percentage of science textbooks and in a very low percentage of textbooks in other fields. It does not appear in any national educational reform program of 1995.

Here I single out the special contributions Harvard as an institution and through its professors has made to *the* **BLUNDER**.

As an institution, Harvard has declared no policy that I know of that denies the scientific method, but it has no program that I know of that includes thorough teaching of it. Harvard has programs, such as law, business, medicine, etc. that I believe should include the direct teaching of the scientific method and a formula, but do not. What seems to be the universal acceptance by colleges and universities of no need to teach the scientific method shows the extent of the blunder.

Harvard's Ties to *the* BLUNDER as an Institution

In Chapter 3 I discuss the origination of *the* BLUNDER. Here is a brief review of Harvard's ties to it as an institution.

♦ In 1946 Harvard President James Conant delivered the Terry Lectures at Yale University. He claimed that there is only an alleged scientific method. He published several books while still president that claimed that the scientific method does not exist.

♦ According to Fletcher G. Watson (*Journal of College Science Teaching*, May 1988), the Harvard Committee on General Education was delighted to have Conant teach a general education science course after his Terry Lectures and the publication of *On Understanding Science* (1947).

♦ Harvard received a grant from the Carnegie Corporation to support Conant's teaching of a general science education course.

♦ In 1948, Harvard University Press published *Harvard Case Histories in Experimental Science*, General Editor James B. Conant. The copyright owner was the President and Fellows of Harvard College. In the Introduction, Conant stated, "There is no such thing as scientific method."

♦ In *Modern Science and Modern Man* (1952) Conant, still President of Harvard, stated that historians of science and philosophers (and thus others by inference) would be doing a public service to emphasize that there is no such thing as "*the* scientific method."

♦ In May 1995, Harvard declined my challenge to appoint a panel to study the scientific method situation.

The Perpetuation of *the* BLUNDER by Harvard Professors

Throughout history, many great thinkers have blundered. Fortunately, those mistakes usually are not perpetuated but are ignored or corrected by the peer review process of science and its method. The trouble with this blunder is that Conant was President of Harvard. I know of no Harvard professor who challenged him on his false claims, except Easley in 1958. This is easy to understand, as Conant presented the scientific method as something it was not and then belittled it. At the same time, there were no really good definitions or formulas to confront him with. In the course Conant taught (Natural Science 4) based on his Terry Lectures, Professors Watson, Kuhn, and Nash assisted him.

In 1955, B.F. Skinner, a Harvard psychologist, belittled "the method" in a President's speech at the Eastern Psychological Association meeting. Although Skinner was correct to say that young psychologists receive little training in the scientific method, his patronizing of the method echoed Conant's dismissal of it.

In 1952, in *Introduction to Concepts and Theories in Physical Science* (section 12.3, The Lack of a Single Method), Professor Gerald Holton stated "if by scientific method we mean" and went on to give some of the erroneous thoughts used by Harvard groups to support the non-existence of the scientific method.

In 1962, Thomas Kuhn's writings and his book *The Structure of Scientific Revolutions* were a major support to **the** **BLUNDER**. See Chapter 33.

In 1965, in *Substance, Structure and Style in the Teaching of Science,* Professor Paul Brandwein stated "the steps in the spurious 'scientific method'..." and in general belittled the idea of a method.

In 1994, I received no response to my Special Report—A Study of Harvard's Apparent Position on the Scientific Method from any of the more than 50 professors to whom it was sent.

Minor Exceptions to the Lack of Teaching of the Scientific Method at Harvard

Harvard Center for Risk Analysis

On December 12, 2002, the web site of this Center showed one class offering "management science (frequently referred to as operation research)." Operation research is just one of the many names for the scientific method.

Department of Economics

Harvard Professor of Economics Gregory M. Mankiw published *Principles of Economics* in 1997. On page 18 of this textbook it says "The essence of science, however, is the *scientific method*—the dispassionate development and testing of theories about how the world works." However, that is the only mention, and no formula is given.

Harvard's Refusal To Study the Scientific Method Situation

By 1958, in spite of Easley's paper, Conant's concept that the scientific method does not exist was well on the way to becoming a tradition, policy, firmly accepted concept, or a fixed belief at Harvard. The professors as a whole (with minor exceptions) acted in one of many unfortunate ways: they fell in line, repeated Conant's false concept, remained silent, mentioned it lightly, or did not include the scientific method or a formula for it in their teaching, books, research, and design of educational reform programs. This process, to the best of my knowledge, continues today, with minor exceptions.

In 1992, I sent the first editions of my booklet, *The General Pattern of the Scientific Method*, to the President of Harvard and a few of its professors in the hope of having it studied.

In 1994, Harvard was listed in my booklet, *Edmund's Idea and Research Report on the General Pattern of the Scientific Method*, as one of several I publicly challenged to appoint a panel to study the scientific method and the misunderstandings surrounding it.

After completing the Idea Booklet, I reasoned that if I could get Harvard to admit that a mistake had occurred, its prestige and press coverage would result in substantial steps to end it. So I spent months preparing a special report for Harvard on the scientific method and its current situation. In November 1994, a copy was sent to each member of the Board of Overseers and to about 50 professors. I asked that they assign someone to study the matter. Harvard refused to do so in a letter to me in May 1995. If an independent panel were to review this report, I believe that they would agree with me that it contained sufficient evidence that Harvard should have studied the situation.

Harvard's Refusal Was a Major Perpetuation of *the* BLUNDER

If Harvard had accepted my report and challenge to study the scientific method situation and had then taken steps to correct **the BLUNDER**, it would have ended it. Harvard's prestige, press coverage, and efforts would probably have been enough to get the wheels going nationally. The matter would no longer have been a "deep, dark secret." Harvard did not do so, so I had to continue my crusade unsuccessfully, finally resorting to writing this book to try to end **the BLUNDER**. I hope that more detailed evidence in this book will encourage Harvard officials and professors to now study the matter more thoroughly.

Harvard Business School

In the Preface I pointed out the importance of the direct teaching of the principles of the scientific method.

There is an interesting book, *Teaching and the Case Method* (1987), by C. Roland Christensen with Abby J. Hansen, published by Harvard Business School and describing its activities.

It brings out this point: In 1909, the first dean of Harvard Business School advised engaging MBA students in a practice-oriented, problem-solving instructional mode.

As I understand it, beginning in 1909, Harvard Business School developed a case history-problem method involving discussion-oriented teaching.

They have ignored:

◆ The small body of knowledge existing in 1909 on the scientific method and problem-solving formulas and the big advance with the publication of John Dewey's book *How We Think* in 1910

◆ The additional great advances in knowledge of the scientific method that have occurred from 1910 to the present

◆ My Special 1994 Report to Harvard

The only clue I found why this may be was in *Teaching and the Case Method* (1987), on page 3 of the Introduction:

> Lectures about judgment typically have limited impact. Reading about problems or memorizing principles does little to prepare the practitioner—architect, doctor, or manager— to apply concepts and knowledge to the complexity of real-life problems. Discussion teaching achieves these objectives better than alternative pedagogies.

I take this to mean that they do not believe in teaching the principles of problem solving and thus the principles of the scientific method.

To emphasize the need for problem-solving knowledge and principles by all business school graduates, I call your attention to the poor record of problem solving and decision making that exists in the business field. See Chapter 46.

My Suggestions for Study

For Harvard and Its Professors

This book contains a great deal more evidence than my earlier reports to some of you. I believe that Harvard and its individual professors should study the scientific method situation.

For Harvard Students

Since the idea that the scientific method does not exist seems to have become a tradition at Harvard, I suggest that you study the evidence I present in this book. Whether I am right or wrong about the details of *the* **BLUNDER** is not as important as ending it.

During the course of my research on Harvard, I read of many rebellions for various causes by Harvard students. If Harvard officials do not study the matter of the scientific method, I believe that you should take some action to encourage them to do so. Your future education is at stake, for it should include your being taught the scientific method, the greatest idea of all time.

For Harvard Graduates

Before jumping to the defense of Harvard, I hope and suggest that you will study the scientific method situation carefully. In most cases, you were misled or improperly educated in it while attending Harvard. Thus, you should study the matter before reaching a conclusion about it. The future welfare of Harvard and its students is deeply involved in a correct analysis of the scientific method situation. My claims of a blunder are based on more than 15 years of specialized research.

For All Colleges, Universities, and Their Students and Graduates

While I have singled out Harvard for special analysis, remember that *the* **BLUNDER** has affected almost all our colleges and universities. This includes my own alma mater, the University of Pennsylvania, to which I sent several letters, unsuccessfully. Thus, these suggestions apply to all.

I hope that those who rate colleges will start to examine how thoroughly they teach the scientific method formula and the supporting ingredients. Students should investigate the programs for the scientific method at schools they plan to attend.

? ?

The Big Mystery: Why No "Method" at Harvard?

This important question has puzzled me from the beginning of my research. It took me days to determine how to present to you the apparent reasons for "no method at Harvard."

In 1870, the Dean of Harvard Law School, Christopher Langdell, designed a new way of teaching law by the case history method. It became fabulously successful and was widely imitated. However, it did not include the scientific method.

In 1909, Harvard Business School was established by President Charles Eliot. It used the case history method and problem method. However, again it did not then and still does not include the teaching of the scientific method.

In 1946, Conant belittled the scientific method and then advocated the teaching of science by the historical case history method. This was done for about 3 years and was then dropped. I know of no instance in which it has been imitated successfully.

In 1985, Harvard Medical School began to use the problem method in teaching medicine, but again the scientific method is not taught.

I do not know to what extent the case history method is used in other schools at Harvard.

I think that the Big Mystery boils down to this:

We have a huge body of knowledge on the value of method and learning basic principles.

Why, when the case history-problem method with the presentation of problems is used, is a problem-solving method or guide for the stages of mental activity not employed?

? ?

Chapter 27

Contribution of the Social Sciences to *the* BLUNDER

This book is primarily about how *the* **BLUNDER** has affected one of the social sciences—education. In this chapter I cover the contribution of the whole field of the social sciences to *the* **BLUNDER.** I include the humanities in the social science classification. In subsequent chapters I will cover some of the social sciences individually.

◆ The Natural Sciences

◆ The Social Sciences

◆ Conant Asks "Are the Social Sciences Really Sciences?"

◆ Evidence That the Social Sciences Debate Rages On

◆ In Defense of the "Social Scientist"

◆ The Claims of "Social Scientists" That They Do Not Have To Follow the Natural Sciences in Research Procedures

◆ But Here Is the Great Harm That Results from All the Claims

◆ A Quote from a Recent Book on the Social Science Debate

◆ National Standards for Social Studies Teachers

◆ Summary, Suggestions, and Mystery

The Natural Sciences

Generally, these are regarded as the natural sciences.

Biological or Life	Physical
botany	physics
zoology	chemistry
human physiology	geology
bacteriology	astronomy

The Social Sciences

This would leave most other domains in the social sciences. For example, the Yahoo directory lists the following under social sciences:

anthropology	library and information science
archaeology	linguistics
criminology	demography
economics	environmental studies
education	peace and conflict studies
migration	political science
futures studies	popular culture
gender studies	psychology
ethnic studies	recreation and leisure studies
geography	social work
gerontology	sociology
history	urban studies

There may be others that should be added or there are subdivisions of one of those listed above. Indeed, I notice that philosophy is not listed for some reason.

Conant Asks "Are the Social Sciences Really Sciences?"

Before proceeding, I would like to call your attention to the importance of this matter, as it covers many domains. In his book *On Understanding Science* (1947), Dr. Conant stated:

> Are the social sciences (psychology, anthropology, sociology, political economy, economics, and history) really sciences? If not, can they become so?

> The answers to these and many related questions are *of supreme importance* to the future of the free people. Our educational procedures on the one hand and our collective actions in regard to a variety of social, economic, and political problems on the other, are *all tangled up with this current debate about the social sciences* [emphasis mine].

There is no doubt that the question of whether the social sciences are really sciences or can become sciences is "of supreme importance."

In this book I show that

◆ the social sciences can become sciences

◆ at the present time they *really are not*

"All Tangled up with This Current Debate about the Social Sciences" (Conant)

Although more than 54 years have passed since Conant raised the question of whether the social sciences are really sciences, the debate still rages on. My research indicates that it cannot be settled until *the* **BLUNDER** about the scientific method is corrected.

Our social sciences and improvements to society's social welfare suffer as a result of the debate continuing without a solution to the problem, which is of "supreme importance" (Conant).

Evidence That the Social Sciences Debate Rages On

Numerous books and articles report on the debate. An example is:

In the *Chronicle of Higher Education* (August 11, 2000), in an article entitled "Toward Sociology as a Science, Maybe," Professor Theodore D. Kemper states:

> An indicator of the underdevelopment of sociology as a science is its lack of focus on specific problems. . .
>
> Another reason sociology lags as a science is that sociologists have a distressingly low regard for cumulative knowledge. Rather, they prize originality to a fault. All too often, the fulcrum of research is that no one has previously focused on a particular problem, or done so in a particular way. That obsession with novelty is especially prevalent in dissertations.

I have given an example of these points in the chapters on education. The many disasters explained there result because problems are never solved, and fads—both new and recycled—are thrown at schools without proper research and testing. Originality is needed, but evaluation, challenge, and testing must follow. *We must do a far better job of accumulating reliable knowledge.*

The Terms "Scientific Study" and "Research"

The situation in the social sciences that prevails is that there is not enough understanding that research means the use of the scientific method.

Long ago, in *Foundations for American Education* (1947), Professor Harold Rugg clarifies these terms with this statement:

> We pause a moment to connect two frequently used terms—namely, "scientific study" and "research." In most instances, in this book, I have chosen to use the terms "scientific study," or *"the scientific method of inquiry and work,"* instead of the term "research." The two, however, mean the same thing. Both mean careful inquiry or investigation with the aid of the best-known technical instruments and methods [emphasis mine].

Research that does not follow the scientific method has the possibility and probability of being unreliable!

In Defense of the "Social Scientist"

Proponents of the scientific method were denounced. Conant, the greatest authoritative figure in the 1950s, claimed that the scientific method does not exist. Popper and other philosophers claimed that there is no scientific method. These factors, along with the work of Kuhn, created a very confusing situation for social scientists. It was made substantially worse because the Harvard/Conant group and misguided followers (or whoever they are) were in control of funding, awards, jobs, memberships, etc.

Thus, while many authors continued to write about and teach the scientific method, the opposing forces prevailed. *The* **BLUNDER** has been a very major factor in the failure of the social sciences to be "sciences." The profession as a whole, or its leaders, seems to have been misled. Let us examine the claims of social scientists that resulted from those events.

The Claims of "Social Scientists" That They Do Not Have To Follow the Natural Sciences in Research Procedures

These claims fall into three main categories.

The Scientific Method Does Not Exist, So They Do Not Have To Use It

Throughout this book, I have shown that the claim of non-existence is false. The social scientists are merely echoing the claims of the Harvard/Conant group and misguided followers (or whoever they are).

They make the usual false claims about the scientific method (see Chapter 7).

Since none of these claims is correct, there is no reason that the scientific method, as defined by the SM-14 formula or description, should not be used in the social sciences, including education. Some social scientists even claim that, instead of the scientific method, they operate under Kuhn's paradigms.

Claims That the Social Sciences "Are Different" and Therefore They Do Not Have To or Cannot Follow the Natural Sciences

These claims include:

◆ Human behavior and social sciences are too complex.
◆ You cannot predict about humans.
◆ You cannot verify theories in the social sciences.
◆ You cannot falsify theories in the social sciences.

In *The Scientific Approach—Basic Principles of the Scientific Method* (1967), Professor Carlo Lastrucci discusses and refutes the above claims. I also refute the claims in this book.

Claim That Is Not Possible To Arrive at Truth in the Social Sciences

Following is a falsification of the claim of some social scientists that they should not have to use the scientific method because you cannot arrive at the truth in the social sciences as you can in the natural sciences. They do not say what "truth" means.

Big Point—Which Immediately Falsifies This Claim:

Even the scientific community does not claim that you can arrive at the truth. Any person who claims that you can attain the truth following the scientific method misunderstands this great method. The misunderstandings about obtaining "the truth" are responsible in part for the continuing debate about evolution and creationism.

A correct view of a conclusion is: "On the evidence available today the balance of probability favors the view. . ."

Thus, claims of not using the scientific method in the social sciences because you cannot arrive at the truth are false for the reasons given above. Truth is a very elusive thing.

But Here Is the Great Harm That Results from All the Claims

They exempt themselves from also having to use all the important stages of the scientific method described in *The Scientific Method Today*. This results in many social scientists doing inadequate searching, exploring, and gathering the evidence. Often they ignore contrary evidence or logical alternative solutions. Scientific research requires following all the stages of SM-14 and using the supporting ingredients of the method.

Reliability Not Improved Much—Even If "Peer Reviewed"

They submit a conclusion to "professional" journals in the social sciences whose editors and reviewers are not real practitioners of the scientific method. Then what is finally filtered through them cannot be accepted as reliable knowledge, even if it is published in a peer-reviewed professional journal!

So the "truth," as near as it can be determined, is much less than if the scientific method system were followed.

Thus, it is a lot of baloney that social scientists should not have to follow the scientific method or guide! These claims are based on a misrepresentation of what the scientific method or guide really is!

Long ago it was recognized and discussed that at times, as a result of using the scientific method, because of uncertainties and inability to test or experiment, the conclusion should be multiple hypotheses.

Historically, T.C. Chamberlin, a geologist, is famous for his paper "The Method of Multiple Working Hypotheses," first published in the *Journal of Geology* (1897; vol. v, pp. 837–848). A copy of this paper is included in *Physical Science: Men and Concepts* (1962), where I first read it.

Social scientists should keep this in mind when they claim that they cannot use the scientific method. There are many more stages to it than the conclusion. That is one of the reasons that it is the greatest quality control method ever recognized and developed.

All Else Being Equal

There are plenty of social "scientists" who sincerely try to and do arrive at reliable conclusions. However, until the "profession" as a whole really embraces and teaches its members and its students the scientific method and holds them accountable to the requirements I outline in Chapter 55, they cannot really be social "scientists" or professionally credible. *The* BLUNDER must be ended to enable them to use the greatest quality control method ever recognized and developed—the scientific method.

A Quote from a Recent Book on the Social Science Debate

The Uncertain Sciences (1998) by Bruce Mazlish, Professor of History at the Massachusetts Institute of Technology, is the best book I have found on the question of whether the social sciences are or can become sciences. I like this statement of Mazlish's:

> What is true for the natural sciences is true for the human sciences. They are bound by the same allegiance to scientific method that we are treating as the essence of science—the combination of sustained observation, accumulation of data, experimentation, testing of results, establishing of theories, logical inferences, use of mathematics if suitable, return to data gathering, weighing and interpretation of materials and findings, and so on—although the forms and details of that method must be adapted to the phenomena under consideration.

National Standards for Social Studies Teachers

As I report in Chapter 14, the idea of standards may be good. However, the way they have been executed or imposed by our top educational leaders has been a grand disaster.

I briefly reviewed the 1997 National Standards for Social Studies Teachers by the National Council for the Social Studies. The task force that worked hard for 3 years to prepare the standards consisted of seven professors, one state official, and one teacher. I found no mention of the scientific method and one minor mention of problem solving, critical thinking, and decision making.

How are social scientists of the future and the public to learn the scientific method's application to the social "sciences" when it is not included in the standards? This disaster is not the basic fault of those who prepared the standards. The fault is that of our top educational leaders, who started and have perpetuated *the* BLUNDER.

Summary

The BLUNDER Continues into the 21st Century

When I began to research the scientific method in 1989, I knew little about it. However, I sensed that it was something special that needed promotion and explanation. My main concerns grew to be to explain it and to see that it was accepted as existing and taught.

I have not been successful.

It all amounts to misunderstandings, confusion, and inefficiency of a blundering degree that extends to the social sciences and continues into the 21st century. Until the Harvard/Conant group and misguided followers (or whoever they are) acknowledge *the* BLUNDER, stop failing to fund research on the scientific method and stop other efforts to prevent its use in the social sciences, there will be little improvement in the social sciences.

Suggestions

If social scientists really want their domains to be a "science," they must study this book and the scientific method thoroughly. This problem should be reviewed in all the social science journals. Study groups should be appointed. Codes of professional ethics should be established by the various professional organizations that call for the use of the scientific method.

? ?

The Mysteries
How can a matter of "supreme importance" (Conant) be blundered about for more than 54 years?

Why aren't the recent books by Professor Fuller and Professor Mazlish and my actual presentation of the method in *The Scientific Method Today* and its predecessors stimulating debate and action?

? ?

Chapter 28

Contribution of the National Academies: National Academy of Sciences, National Academy of Engineering, Institute of Medicine, and Their Operating Unit, National Research Council, to *the* BLUNDER

The big picture I am going to paint of the participation of the top leaders of the National Academy of Sciences in *the* **BLUNDER** is not pleasant. However, as a specialized researcher of the scientific method, I must follow the instructions of Einstein, which appear on his statue at the National Academy of Sciences headquarters: *The right to search for truth implies also a duty; one must not conceal any part of what one has recognized to be true.*

- Some History of National Academy of Sciences
- The Internal Politics of the National Academy of Sciences
- History of the National Academy of Sciences' Position on the Scientific Method
- Publicly Stated Policy of the Leaders of the National Academy of Sciences Is That the Scientific Method Does Not Exist!
- The Educational Activities of the National Academy of Sciences
- The 1995 National Science Education Standards
- My (Failed) Efforts To Prevent the Blunder of Presenting "Science As Inquiry" with No Method of Inquiry
- Other Educational Activities of the National Academy of Sciences
- The Terrible Spreading of the Blundering
- Ethics Involved
- Suggestions and Mysteries

Some History of the National Academy of Sciences

The Royal Society of London

The Royal Society of London is the most famous national scientific society. It was founded in 1661 by Sir Francis Bacon (1561–1626) and his associates. In *How We Think* (1910), Dewey states:

> These characteristics are displayed in the attacks made upon the early work of the Royal Society, which was founded in

the seventeenth century. The birth of this celebrated society is a landmark in the history of the scientific method.

Many nations today have national academies of science under various names.

The U.S. National Academy of Sciences

From its literature:

> To help science better serve American society, Abraham Lincoln and Congress created the National Academy of Sciences (NAS). Since then, the NAS and its sister organizations—the National Academy of Engineering and the Institute of Medicine—have served as advisers to the nation, helping to guide public policies related to developments in science, technology, and health care.

Note that education is not mentioned.

The members of the National Academy of Sciences select new members and today number something less than 2000 of our most prestigious scientists. Although it is chartered by Congress, the National Academy of Sciences is an independent organization and is not part of the federal government.

However, its charter provides that "the Academy shall, whenever called upon by any department of the Government, investigate, examine, and experiment, and report upon any subject of science or art."

The National Academy of Sciences prepares numerous technical reports for government agencies using the unpaid services of its members and paid consultants. It is paid for these services.

I am not qualified to judge these technical reports. The National Academy of Sciences is generally considered to be a prestigious organization and makes this claim in its literature.

Recently the National Academy of Sciences has been greatly expanding its educational activities.

♦ The top leaders of the National Academy of Sciences have not kept its members informed about their position on the scientific method and my reports, letters, and challenge to them about the scientific method. Therefore, I believe that the members do not know what has occurred.

♦ Neither have the top leaders of the National Academy of Sciences informed Congress and the public about their policy and the reasons for the policy. They have not provided Congress with an accurate definition of science.

In its literature, the National Academy of Sciences refers to itself as a prestigious organization, which, according to the dictionary, is one held in a high level of honor or esteem.

I will show here that in this matter of great public concern, the top leaders are acting in a very unprestigious and unscientific way.

The following is from *Kindly Inquisitors* (1993) by Jonathan Rauch:

> First, the skeptical rule. If people follow it, then no idea, however wise and insightful its proponent, can ever have any claim to be exempt from criticism by anyone, no matter how stupid and grubby-minded the critic. The skeptical rule is,
>
> > *No one gets the final say:* you may claim that a statement is established as knowledge only if it can be debunked, in principle, and only insofar as it withstands attempts to debunk it.

So no matter how stupid and grubby-minded I may be, the evidence I submitted that the scientific method does exist to the National Academy of Sciences on numerous occasions should have been studied. The National Academy of Sciences is not the king of science.

The Internal Politics of the National Academy of Sciences

Normally, the internal politics of the National Academy of Sciences would be of no concern to me, but, because of its refusal to study my reports, I must consider them. The Harvard/Conant group and misguided followers (or whoever they are) are, I suspect, "in control" of the National Academy of Sciences, the American Association for the Advancement of Science, the National Science Foundation, the U.S. Department of Education (at least until Secretary Paige took over), and many other organizations. (Remember that members of these organizations have not been informed of the hidden agenda of their top leaders.) They have used this "control" to further their agenda of perpetuating their claims that the scientific method does not exist. I have no valid evidence for these statements other than:

- Because of this "control," none of these organizations has included the scientific method in national educational reform programs that started in approximately 1957 and continue today, with one or two very minor exceptions. *This is very significant evidence.*

- They have not informed their members, etc. of my reports.

- It is also a continuation of a policy of "science as inquiry" of the National Science Foundation. In *NSTA Reports* (May 1991), Robert E. Yager states:

  > This is extremely alarming in view of the supposedly great attention to science-as-inquiry during the past 30 years in the NSF-supported projects.

- In 1995 the National Academy of Engineers elected a rebel candidate as President. After he took office, disputes arose, and he was "bought out." *Science* magazine (March 1, 1996) quotes one of his supporters as saying: "Liebowitz 'has been prevented from executing his responsibilities by a small group of good old boys.'" Who was right in this dispute I do not know. But the comment adds to my theory of an old boys network perpetuating *the* BLUNDER.

- These organizations have ignored or taken no action on all my special reports, letters, and booklets explaining the misunderstandings and errors. In recent years, they have even ignored my claim that the biggest intellectual and educational blunder in history has occurred about the scientific method.

It is because of their ignoring my efforts to get them to study the matter that I have been obliged to spend years writing this book.

History of the National Academy of Sciences' Position on the Scientific Method

I do not know the National Academy of Sciences' position before 1946. However, since the 1950s, its effective policy or position (based on its activities) seems to have been that the scientific method does not exist. I found no indication that the National Research Council or the National Academy of Sciences—in any of the education reform programs they have assisted with or participated in—included the scientific method.

Because of Conant's tremendous reputation, power, and activities, and the activities of the Harvard/Conant group and misguided followers (or whoever they are), it appears that almost everyone and most organizations in national circles accepted his concept without the usual critical and skeptical analysis that occurs when a new theory is presented to challenge an existing one. In this case, the prevailing theory had been that the scientific method does exist.

Why did the National Academy of Sciences probably join others in not challenging Conant? These events, abstracted from *James B. Conant* (1993) by James Hirshberg, reveal the probable reasons.

In 1947, Conant declined the presidency of the Academy, and A.N. Richards was selected. It is natural that he would then be reluctant to challenge Conant's position on the scientific method.

In 1950, Conant was nominated for the presidency of the National Academy of Sciences and accepted, but unprecedented opposition developed, and he withdrew in favor of Detley W. Bronk. Again, it would have been difficult for Bronk or the Academy to have challenged Conant's concept. These events and the universal acceptance of Conant's concept in national circles eventually resulted in the politicizing and institutionalizing of the concept that the scientific method does not exist in the activities of the National Academy of Sciences.

It is so hard for me to understand the policy of the leaders of the National Academy of Sciences that I have watched for clues other than those mentioned above. Years ago the Carnegie Corporation funded the National Research Council building, according to William Gilman in *Science U.S.A.* (1965). The Carnegie Corporation originally funded Conant's course at Harvard on Understanding Science. Whether the National Academy of Sciences feels any obligation to the Carnegie Corporation I do not know.

The Publicly Stated Policy of the Leaders of the National Academy of Sciences Is That the Scientific Method Does Not Exist!

Most organizations perpetuating and echoing Conant's false claim that the scientific method does not exist have been careful not to state so in their literature and debate the issue of the existence of the scientific method. This is why I often refer to it as a "deep, dark secret." In this case, the National Academy of Sciences did take a position in a booklet but later altered this—after my reports were issued.

In 1989, under the leadership of then President Frank Press, the National Academy of Sciences published *On Being a Scientist* (1989) for students beginning to do scientific research. In a page 2 heading, it asks "Is There a Scientific Method?" It then goes on to deny that there is one and to claim that scientists use "a body of methods." In the second edition (1995), the only mention of the scientific method is made indirectly on page 3:

> Throughout the history of science, philosophers and scientists have sought to describe a single systematic procedure that can be used to generate scientific knowledge, but they have never been completely successful. The practice of science is too multifaceted and its practitioners are too diverse to be captured in a single overarching description. Researchers collect and analyze data, develop hypotheses, replicate and extend earlier work, communicate their results with others, review and critique the results of their peers, train and supervise associates and students, and otherwise engage in the life of the scientific community.

This statement is of course "true" in some part, but it is basically incorrect. Just look at *The Scientific Method Today*, which I abstracted and compiled from books by scientists, philosophers, and others. Also remember that the U.S. Supreme Court stated in the 1993 Daubert decision that there is "the scientific method."

In Chapter 53 on the legal status of the scientific method, I report on how the joint *amicus* brief of American Association for the Advancement of Science and the National Academy of Sciences to the U.S. Supreme Court in the 1993 Daubert case claimed with quotations from Feynman and Ziman that the scientific method exists.

The National Academy of Sciences publication *Responsible Science: Ensuring the Integrity of the Research Process* (1992) acknowledges the existence of the scientific method (pages 36, 38, and 39). In addition, the "research process" (note the singular "process") is just another name for the scientific method.

It should be embarrassing to the Academy that groups within the organization admit the existence of the scientific method.

However, despite the information above, the main educational activities of the National Academy of Sciences disregard these admissions that the scientific method exists, even though one of the admissions was presented to the Supreme Court and was probably instrumental in some of the Court's findings.

How does the National Academy of Sciences explain this?

In all my efforts, I am continually amazed at the determination of the Harvard/Conant group and misguided followers (or whoever they are) to prevent the teaching of the scientific method.

The Educational Activities of the National Academy of Sciences

For many years the Academy had a minor science teaching program jointly with the Smithsonian Institution. However, the Academy became involved in the national science education standards movement. The Academy's major blundering here that has caused me to devote so many pages to the Academy.

The 1995 National Science Education Standards Blundering at its Worst by the National Academy of Sciences and the National Research Council

The National Academy of Sciences and the National Research Council received contracts and government and foundation funds to guide the preparation of the National Science Education Standards.

The standards were published in book form in 1996. The book is available from the National Academies Press. The standards can also be found at www.eric.ed.gov.

I am not qualified to comment on the subject matter teaching involved in the standards, but I am qualified to comment on science as inquiry.

The *National Science Education Standards* (National Academy Press, 1996) present science as inquiry, but include no method of inquiry or formula for the scientific method. Presenting "science as inquiry" is a continuation of an erroneous movement that has been going on for quite a while. It rejects "scientific method" with this statement on page 121 of the final standards:

There is a logic behind the abilities outlined in the inquiry standard, but a step-by-step sequence or scientific method is not implied.

Based on more than 15 years of specialized research on the method of science and what science is—its method—the scientific method, in the interest of public debate, I make these claims about the standards:

I am normally a calm individual, but I now state that presenting science as inquiry without presenting the method of inquiry, the scientific method, is

an intellectual blunder
an educational blunder
a legal blunder
a science of science blunder
a Harvard-based blunder
a blunder that should never have occurred
a blunder based on arrogance
a science teaching blunder
a blunder caused by poor leadership
a blunder that wastes billions of dollars each year
a blunder that perpetuates Conant's blunder
a blunder by the National Academy of Sciences
a blunder that Edmund alerted them to beforehand

Teaching Science As Inquiry without Also Presenting the Method of Inquiry—the Scientific Method

This is non-logical for the following reasons:

♦ It is being done to perpetuate the claim of the Harvard/Conant group and misguided followers (or whoever they are) that the scientific method does not exist.

♦ Our body of knowledge as expressed in the literature shows inquiry to be a prominent feature of science, but that science is fundamentally and basically its method—the scientific method.

♦ **To teach just inquiry leads to wandering aimlessly. In actual practice, inquiry leads to process, and the process is the scientific method.**

♦ The claim that "inquiry" is some big overriding theory of science is a "red herring." The overriding theory of science is the method of inquiry—the unity of science, the scientific method.

Were Professional Politics Involved?

Why was responsibility for the National Science Education Standards assigned to the National Academy of Sciences?

In 1991 the National Academy of Sciences received its first grant to support start-up activities on the National Science Education Standards. Why was it awarded to the National Academy of Sciences rather than the National Science Teachers Association?

Was it to be sure that *the* **BLUNDER** was perpetuated and scientific method was not taught? Was it to help the finances of the National Academy of Sciences?

In an article in the *Chronicle of Higher Education* (April 7, 1993) about her tenure (1991–1993) as Assistant Secretary for the Office of Educational Research and Improvement (OERI) in the U.S. Department of Education, Diane Ravitch says:

> The politics of educational research is strange: every program has its own constituency, which battles for its own small slice of the pie. . .In support of goals that pledge improved student achievement from kindergarten through high school, we used our few discretionary dollars to award grants to independent organizations (such as the National Academy of Sciences and the National Geographic Society) to bring together teachers and scholars to develop voluntary national standards in the sciences, the arts, history, civics, geography, English, and foreign languages. We modeled our support on the successful collaborative work of the National Council of Teachers of Mathematics, which published mathematics standards for elementary and secondary schools in 1989.

The National Academy of Sciences is mainly concerned with and qualified in regard to science, engineering, and medicine, not teaching or education.

I think that the award of the contract by OERI to the National Academy of Sciences was a mistake. From the news reports at the time, I got the impression that NSTA protests were quickly squelched, and there were tongue-in-cheek announcements by the National Academy of Sciences that the NSTA had "unanimously" voted to ask the National Research Council to take the job. It would be interesting to hear these "unanimous" people testify under oath.

Another indication of the high-handedness of the leaders of the National Academy of Sciences is this from *Education Week* (December 7, 1994):

> The long-awaited release of the science standards provoked an unexpected controversy.
>
> The executive director of the National Science Teachers Association charged that the document failed to acknowledge the organization's pioneer standards-setting efforts. Bill G. Aldridge said the new standards dishonestly singled out a reform effort of the American Association for the Advancement of Science while ignoring the N.S.T.A.'s Scope, Sequence, and Coordination of Secondary School Science project.

All this is just another indication of the overall mess, politics, and waste of billions and billions of dollars on how to teach science. It continues even in 2004. It reinforces my contention that a permanent specialized SM-14 type national research center on teaching science is needed.

Comments on Statements in *National Science Education Standards* (1996, Published by National Academy Press)

"Now All Must Act Together in the National Interest"

> Individuals from all of these groups were involved in the development of the *National Science Education Standards*, and now all must act together in the national interest. Achieving scientific literacy will take time because the *Standards* call for dramatic changes throughout school systems.

Those responsible for the standards, after blundering badly, say that "all must act together." The injustices to our science teachers continue. I think that it is a terrible thing to present such an erroneous program and then ask for national support for it.

Here Is One for Ripley's Believe It or Not

I (and my editorial assistant, Karen Simon) examined the *1995 National Science Education Standards* (National Academy Press, 1996) looking for a clear, teachable definition of science. Neither of us could find one! Another part of the blunder of the standards.

My (Failed) Efforts To Prevent the Blunder of Presenting "Science as Inquiry" with No Method of Inquiry

Here I show in a somewhat self-righteous tone what I did to try and prevent the blunder that the Standards stress inquiry instead of the scientific method.

I feel that all the efforts I put forth with reports and letters should have succeeded. However, they did not, so I must have goofed in not doing more. For reasons of money, age, health, bashfulness, etc., I did not run advertisements, employ an attorney, go to meetings, make personal visits to people, make telephone calls, make speeches, etc.

This is abstracted from page vi of my *Special March 1995 Report to the National Academy of Sciences on the Scientific Method*:

A REVIEW OF MY EFFORTS TO GET THE ACADEMY TO SELF-CORRECT

October 5, 1992: I sent Dr. Press (President of NAS) a letter with <u>five sets</u> of my first edition booklets—one for him and four for his staff. All five sets were returned. When I inquired as to whether this was censorship or an error, I was assured it was an error. I was asked to return the booklets. It seemed peculiar that Dr. Press did not retain at least one set for his files.

September 15, 1992: I sent Dr. Florio at the National Research Council a set of my booklets, since he was working on science standards.

December 9, 1992: I sent E.K. Stage a set of my booklets, since she also was working on science standards.

November–December 1992: I sent a set of booklets to all members of the Education Writers Association and the Science Writers Association, including all who had a National Research Council or National Academy of Sciences address.

May 17, 1993: I sent a set of my first edition booklets to Dr. Alberts (their new president) at his California address and a duplicate set to his Washington, D.C., National Academy of Sciences office.

July 14, 1994: I sent Dr. Alberts (with a copy to Dr. Merrill) a set of my 2nd edition booklets. I called his attention to my challenge to the National Academy of Sciences to appoint a panel to properly define the scientific method and requested an answer.

August 22, 1994: I sent Dr. Alberts (with a copy to Dr. Merrill) a letter and enclosed one I had received from the U.S. Department of Education, which stated that "You must seek acceptance for your ideas within the scientific community and by working with organizations like the National Research Council."

As of January 30, 1995, I had received no answers to my three letters to Dr. Alberts. In *Her Study Shattered the Myth that Fraud in Science is a Rarity* (New York Times, November 21, 1993), Dr. Sazey calls this type of thing "structured silence." I realize that I have been constructively criticizing the National Academy of Sciences. It may be an extra-sensitive matter, since Dr. Alberts inherited this problem from his predecessors and received his Ph.D. from Harvard. However, a serious problem exists, and it must be faced!

To be fair, I report that I received a reply to a letter I sent in 1999 about an oversight committee. I failed to follow up on the information.

Distribution of My Special March 1995 Report to the National Academy of Sciences

This was sent to the officers and council of the National Academy of Sciences and included a copy of my booklet *Edmund's Idea and Research Report on the General Pattern of the Scientific Method (SM-14)* (2nd edition, 1994). I received no answer or acknowledgment. *All of the preceding were sent from 1992 to January 1995, before the National Science Education Standards were finalized.*

My 1994 Challenge to the Proposed National Science Education Standards

In the second (1994) edition of *Edmund's Idea and Research Report on the General Pattern of the Scientific Method (SM-14)* I abstracted from the February 1993 *National Science Education Standards: An Enhanced Sampler* their charts of formulas for the nature of science.

Perhaps I should have kept quiet. In the 1994 draft of the standards, these had all been dropped, and science as inquiry—with no method—was stressed. Who was responsible for dropping them? I don't know.

My Follow-Up Reports after March 1995

I sent a *Special June 1997 Report to the Council of the National Academy of Sciences on the Scientific Method*. Again it was ignored, and I received no acknowledgment or comment about it. In addition, there has been no change in the policy of the leaders of the National Academy of Sciences about the scientific method.

This report included some of my strongly worded Reports and Briefs that should have provoked some action. For example:

Report #5: Research Report on "The Scientific Method"
Report #6: Research Report: False Claims about "The Scientific Method"
Report #7: Research Report: Have Unlawful Activities Occurred in Connection with False Claims about "The Scientific Method"?
Report #8: Research Report: What Is "Science"?

New short essays included were:

HELP STOP THE BIGGEST INTELLECTUAL BLUNDER IN HISTORY
Junk Science at National Science Foundation, U.S. Department of Education, American Association for Advancement of Science & National Academy of Sciences
AAAS's $300,000 Whitewash of Project 2061
Injustices to Our Teachers of Science
Why Psychologist and Psychology Organizations Should Accept the Challenge To Study "The Scientific Method"
Why We Must Teach Complete Creative Problem Solving

Other Educational Activities of the National Academy of Sciences

Here are some comments on some of the National Academy of Sciences' other educational reports.

Improving Student Learning (issued April 1999): In April 1999 I was working on my blunder book when I received the National Academy of Sciences report called *Improving Student Learning*. This so disturbed me because of erroneous statements and positions that I stopped everything to write

Special Report #19, *Shame on the National Academy of Sciences*

This report was sent registered mail to the officials and council members. I found that compiling a list of members was very time consuming, so I did not send them copies. Again I received no response.

National Research Council Report *Scientific Inquiry in Education*

This was issued in November 2001 and contains nothing about the scientific method or a method for inquiry. It has 24 pages of citations of books and other documents. I recognize only a few as proponents of the scientific method. That they ignore the thousands of books acknowledging the scientific method is another example of unscientific research, ignoring contrary evidence, and what they call "the culture of science." Therefore, I claim that the report is not reliable and further perpetuates **the BLUNDER.**

National Research Council Report *Scientific Research in Education*

The National Academy of Sciences had contract ED-00-00-0038 with the U.S. Department of Education National Educational Research Policy and Priorities Board. Here is my critical and constructive review of the publication, *Scientific Research in Education* (2002), that resulted from the contract.

It contains a misrepresentation inferring that there is no scientific method and false claims of its nature.

Nowhere does this report say that the scientific method is involved in research. Therefore, as a critical reviewer of this report, I claim:

◆ None of the material in it can be accepted as reliable based on its discussion of research with no correct description of the scientific method (on which research is based). Since the "facts" are wrong at the beginning, what follows is not reliable.

◆ In Chapter 41, I show how they are pushing science as a "culture" instead of a method. There is no doubt that there is a "culture" to science. However, you must be able to identify the culture easily. When you try, you find that you are describing the scientific method and its supporting ingredients.

The Terrible Spreading of the Blundering

On February 6, 2002, the U.S. Department of Education held a seminar to discuss the meaning of scientifically based research. They were terribly misled. Attending this meeting were two representatives from the National Research Council. They distributed a few copies of the report *Scientific Research in Education* and offered more copies later. They discussed this report. There was nothing about the scientific method. It is only fair to point out that none of the other speakers mentioned the scientific method either, according to a transcript available on the Internet at www.ed.gov/ nclb/methods/whatworks/research/index.html.

In 2003 the Academy Recommends a Network of State-Based Centers

From *Science* magazine (April 11, 2003):

> The National Academy of Sciences (NAS) wants the nation to invest $500 million in research on how to improve student learning. In a report issued last week, an academy panel proposes a novel, state-based structure to funnel new research findings into the classroom—and to make them readily available to educators all over the country. If adopted, the initiative would also give a major shot in the arm to educational research, which has traditionally been a scientific stepchild.

They envision a network of a half dozen or more centers financed by public and foundation sources. My opinion is that this idea is *again* very impractical and again illustrates that NAS is not qualified to engage in national educational activities.

Ethics Involved

Of all professions and occupations, I sincerely believe that scientists have the best record and are doing the most to improve and teach the ethics of conducting research. But this does not extend to many top leaders of their professional organizations' educational activities. I do not enjoy the difficult roles that I am now having to play to correct misunderstandings about the heart and soul of science and the basic way we originate, refine, extend, and apply knowledge—the scientific method. **While correction may hurt now, in the long run science and society will benefit tremendously.**

It Is the Top Leaders—Not the Members

The top leaders of the National Academy of Sciences have not kept its members informed about their policy. Therefore, I believe that the members do not know what has occurred.

Suggestions to the National Academy of Sciences Members

This book gives the National Academy of Sciences a black eye because of its top leaders' educational activities. If you rise to their defense without a serious study of the situation concerning the scientific method, the reputation of your organization will only be hurt further. I urge you to appoint a study group to devote full time to the task. My library is available.

Suggestions to Congress

If the National Academy of Sciences reacts promptly to the challenge of this book and studies the scientific method and does an unbiased job, then there is no need for action on your part. You might even finance their report, since it is the duty of the National Academy of Sciences to advise you on science. If the National Academy of Sciences does not react to the challenge and study the matter promptly, then I recommend that you ask them for a correct definition of science and scientifically based research.

? ?

The Big Mysteries

Why have letters and reports sent to the Academy been ignored?

Why did the Academy tell the U.S. Supreme Court that there is a scientific method but deny it in setting the 1995 science standards?

Why do the top leaders ignore the fact that the Academy's publication *Responsible Science: Ensuring the Integrity of the Research Process* acknowledges the scientific method?

Why hasn't the Academy informed its members about my reports and challenge, especially "Shame on the National Academy of Sciences"?

? ?

Chapter 29

Contribution of the American Association for the Advancement of Science to *the* BLUNDER

"Give 'em hell Harry" Truman told AAAS in 1948 that "science means a method of thought." Here "Give 'em heck" Edmund tells them that the method of thought is the scientific method.

- ◆ Information about AAAS

- ◆ Who Is the Boss of *the* BLUNDER?

- ◆ Internal Politics of AAAS

- ◆ The Operating Policy of the Top Leaders of AAAS Regarding the Scientific Method

- ◆ AAAS Educational Activities and the Teaching of Science

- ◆ Science Textbook Surveys

- ◆ No Code of Ethics Enforced in Educational Research

- ◆ My Attempts To Get AAAS To Study the Scientific Method Situation

- ◆ The Effects of the Blunder on the Regular Activities of AAAS

- ◆ Suggestions and Mystery

Information about AAAS

The following information about the American Association for the Advancement of Science is abstracted from an article about its 150th anniversary (*Science*, December 18, 1998).

The American Association for the Advancement of Science (AAAS) is America's largest federation of scientific and engineering societies and has become the preeminent professional society worldwide. It began in 1848 in Philadelphia, Pennsylvania. It was the first permanent U.S. organization to promote the development of science and engineering at the national level and to represent the interests of all of its various disciplines. AAAS now has more than 145,000 members. (The AAAS website indicates that AAAS affiliates include 272 societies and academies of science, serving more than 10 million members. Its magazine, *Science*, established in 1880, has a circulation of more than 150,000.)

The 4-page article also recites some of the great historical accomplishments and current important activities of the Association. It made me proud to be a member (for a total of about 35 years) of such a great organization, even if I am disappointed with its educational activities. If you read the Association's magazine *Science*, you will be impressed by their many activities on behalf of science and society.

The article ends with a quotation from Harry Truman's 1948 speech at the Association's 100th anniversary meeting:

> "Now and in the years ahead, we need more than anything else the honest and uncompromising common-sense of science. *Science means a method of thought.* That method is characterized by open-mindedness, honesty, perseverance, and above all, by an unflinching passion for knowledge and truth. When more of the peoples of the world have learned the *ways of thought* of the scientist, we shall have better reason to expect lasting peace and a full life for all." [emphasis mine]

It is interesting to note that President "give 'em hell Harry" Truman knew that science means "a method of thought." It is just *what* "stupid and grubby-minded" old Edmund is trying to get across to our top educational leaders and the Harvard/Conant group and misguided followers (or whoever they are).

Remember that page 3 of my booklet *The Scientific Method Today* says "Each stage 1-11 represents a different type of mental activity." These stages represent a "method of thought" and Dewey's "complete act of thought." It is strange that, with America's great intellectual community, the stages of mental activity involved in the scientific method were not better identified and put into a standard formula long ago.

If "give 'em hell Harry" were still alive, I would enlist him in my crusade with top leaders to "give 'em hell" that we are not teaching in our national educational reform programs that science is a method of thought, and the method is the scientific method.

The Buck Stops Here

It is a funny coincidence, but "give 'em hell Harry" had a sign on his desk saying, "The buck stops here."

This is also my big theme in this book—the blame for the mess that education is in belongs to a great extent to our *top* educational leaders. It's time for them to reassess their position.

Who Is the "Boss" of *the* BLUNDER?

In 1992, the National Science Foundation advised me to present my ideas to the principal professional societies. I had already done this.

In 1993, the U.S. Department of Education advised me to present my ideas to the National Academy of Sciences and the American Association for the Advancement of Science. I had already done this.

Is *the* **BLUNDER** being perpetuated mainly by the big professional societies, or are the government agencies just trying to protect their backsides? Or is there a "boss"?

Internal Politics of AAAS

There are indications, as I mentioned in Chapter 28 about the National Academy of Sciences, that the American Association for the Advancement of Science is under the "control" of the Harvard/Conant group and misguided followers (or whoever they are). By itself, the "control" of organizations by old boys networks, cliques, etc. is common. I like to try to be practical. I realize that if you eliminate an old boys network, you usually get a new old boys network. These types of cliques are usually limited to favoring friends and institutions with jobs, grants, promotions, etc. They are not usually involved in big, historic, expensive blunders.

One comment that I found about the inner workings of AAAS appeared in *Science: U.S.A.* (1965) by William Gilman:

> It has its tight inner government . . . But, though accused of being run by a clique and its secretariat, AAAS is more outgoing than that.

My complaint—to review it again—is that in a matter of "supreme importance" a group is injecting a false concept about the scientific method, the greatest idea of all time, into all our national educational reform efforts.

Again, I find it hard to understand why the top leaders of AAAS are taking the position they are other than the influence of the Harvard/Conant group and misguided followers (or whoever they are).

Conant Was President of AAAS in 1947

This means that he was President-elect in 1946, which is the year in which he first made erroneous false claims about the scientific method. Many of the people at AAAS I mention here, such as Dr. Nicholson and Dr. Rutherford, are Harvard graduates. The Carnegie Corporation, an old supporter of Conant, has supported many Association projects over the years.

The Intensity of Top Leaders' Injection Worries Me

The determination of those in control to keep injecting the false concept that the scientific method does not exist worries me.

Not the Members

Again I want to stress, as in the case of the National Academy of Sciences, that the members have never been informed about what is going on. If they had reviewed the reports I sent to the Association in *Science*, the members would have been informed of the situation. It would probably have caused some debate.

The Operating Policy of the Top Leaders of AAAS Regarding the Scientific Method

As mentioned in Chapter 28 on the National Academy of Sciences, organizations perpetuating *the* BLUNDER tend to keep it a deep, dark secret. The operating policy of the top leaders of AAAS that the scientific method does not exist can be seen in several ways.

An Editorial by Richard S. Nicholson "On Being a Scientist" (*Science*, October 20, 1989)

In Chapter 28 about the National Academy of Sciences I explained how its 1989 publication *On Being a Scientist* denied the existence of the scientific method.

As stated in the editorial by AAAS's then Executive Officer mentioned above, the publication was prepared

> under the leadership of Academy President Frank Press [now at Carnegie Institute] and written by a very distinguished panel headed by Francisco Ayala [who became president of AAAS in 1994].

While the editorial itself does not mention the scientific method, *On Being a Scientist* is praised and endorsed as good reading and pushed to be used by professors for graduate students and postdoctoral candidates. Thus, the leaders of AAAS are endorsing and perpetuating the idea that there is no scientific method.

Teaching Activities

AAAS has never included the scientific method in any of its science teaching programs, including Project 2061.

Science Magazine Articles

AAAS has done a terrific job for the advancement of science by making all issues of *Science* and the old *Scientific Monthly* available on the Internet to its members. I did a search for "scientific method" in the titles of articles, and found approximately 16 articles published before 1946. Some were very interesting and showed a good understanding of the scientific method. There was an especially good one in 1895. After 1946, only 14 articles with "scientific method" in the title were published, yet it is "the greatest idea of all time."

An article in *Science* (May 12, 1944, page 385) indirectly quotes Dr. Cattell as saying "that all men should have a good workable knowledge of scientific method." This is of special interest, as Dr. Cattell was "the dominant figure in AAAS" for more than 50 years, from about 1894 until his death in 1944.

However, since I renewed my membership in about 1989 and started skip-reading the magazine again, I cannot recall any article of great importance about the scientific method. Worst of all, there have been no articles calling the attention of the members to my special reports.

In my opinion, there is little doubt that the Harvard/Conant group and misguided followers (or whoever they are) have "control" of the

American Association for the Advancement of Science and are injecting their agenda on the scientific method into its activities.

AAAS Educational Activities and the Teaching of Science

Remember that one *extends* scientific (and all other types of) knowl-
edge through the scientific method. President Truman's Scientific
Research Board, created in 1947, requested the assistance of the
American Association for the Advancement of Science. Thus, the
Association became more active in science education.

I did not research exactly what occurred in AAAS teaching activities
from 1847 to 1967. I will begin in 1967.

Science—As a Process Approach (SAPA)—1967

This AAAS science teaching program describes science as what it is—
a process. The process is, of course, the scientific method.
Unfortunately, the designers did not understand that the process is
the scientific method. Thus, while the program is good in some
respects, it really was not what was needed. By 1970, it was being used
in about 9% of the school districts surveyed (according to DeBoer).
Eventually, like most fadish educational reform programs, it faded
away. Along came a bigger and more fadish program—Project 2061.

Before discussing Project 2061, I want to state that there should never
have been a Project 2061 because of the injustice to science teachers
caused by all the ill-planned, erroneous science teaching programs
forced on them over the years. In the beginning—or at least at some
later time—there should have been established a permanent specialized SM-14 type national research center on science teaching.

Project 2061

Project 2061 has been AAAS's big science education reform effort in
recent years.

Science magazine (October 27, 1995) describes the project as follows:

A Decade of Science Education Reform

In 1981, AAAS put science literacy at the top of its priority
list and began exploring possibilities for a large-scale project
that would bring deep and lasting reform to science educa-

tion. Next month is the 10th anniversary of the launch of that initiative: Project 2061.

Project 2061's work has provided the foundation for curriculum reform in many states and school districts and has influenced the development of national science education standards and other reform efforts. The project conducts numerous workshops around the country and continues to develop new reform tools for educators and curriculum developers.

The director of Project 2061 was Dr. F. James Rutherford (also Chief Education Officer of the American Association for the Advancement of Science) until his retirement in 1998. He was a professor at the Harvard Graduate School of Education (1964–1971) and director of the National Science Foundation educational programs (1977–1980). These organizations have been perpetuators of Conant's concept that the scientific method does not exist. His successors since 1998 have continued not to include the scientific method in any of their literature to improve science teaching.

Two Blunders in Project 2061

Blunder #1—The Program Does Not Include the Scientific Method. This erroneous statement appears on page 9 of its *Benchmarks for Science Literacy* (1993):

> Scientific inquiry is more complex than popular conceptions would have it. It is, for instance, a more subtle and demanding process than the naive idea of "making a great many careful observations and then organizing them." It is far more flexible than the rigid sequence of steps commonly depicted in textbooks as "the scientific method."

It is wrong in its description of the scientific method. It is wrong in claiming that inquiry is a superior idea. I have explained the scientific method throughout this book. What makes this project's denial of the scientific method a gigantic blunder is that Project 2061 was one of the things instrumental in the non-inclusion of the scientific method in the 1995 National Science Education Standards.

Blunder #2—Incorrect Description of Science Literacy. Its description of science literacy does not include knowledge of the scientific method. Blunder #1 leads to blunder #2.

Summary

- Project 2061 should never have been started. Overall, in my opinion Project 2061 is too complex. The "less is more" theory it praises is just another fad. We should have had a permanent specialized SM-14 type national research center on science teaching that designed one or several science teaching programs, rather than the odd assortment on which taxpayers' and foundations' dollars have been spent.
- Project 2061, with its major blunders, is not up to the quality standards of a major scientific organization like AAAS or to the standards of the scientific method.

Science Textbook Surveys

My Survey of Science Textbooks

In Edmund's Idea and Research Report of 1994 (which is still available) I made the following statement in the discussion on science textbooks:

> We should all salute the textbook authors and publishers who have included a formula for "The Scientific Method." During the decades that the controversies have existed, these have been the principal source for any knowledge which students have obtained. Formulas that appear in the various textbooks vary a great deal. To illustrate this, but not to criticize, some formulas are shown below, exactly as they appear in current textbooks.

In my report, I show six formulas from elementary, secondary, and college texts. I included a chart for a total of 15 books giving the year of publication of each book, the name of the publisher, and the number of pages (1 to 33) devoted to the scientific method. Remember that *no* federal science education reform program, since they began in 1957, has included the scientific method and a formula for it. This occurs despite the federal government spending billions of dollars a year on the improvement of science teaching. Yet the improvement of including the scientific method did not occur.

No Code of Ethics Enforced in Educational Research

In this book I point out that educational researchers have been allowed into the world where ethics are not enforced—or at least not as strictly as they are in the natural sciences.

This seems to apply even to the scientists at AAAS when they deal with education.

In my reports of 1995 to the organizations I challenged, I devoted 8 pages to the problem of ethics. I did not receive any response or publicity. This is hard to understand. Today a great deal of attention is being paid to the improvement and refinement of ethics in many domains.

I am not going to review what is covered in the 1995 reports because it would require too much space, but I am going to raise a question about Project 2061.

Lapse of Ethics?

Science magazine has done an excellent job of keeping its readers up to date on scientific frauds and ethics debates. However, in its January 31, 1997 issue, the AAAS News and Notes page mentions a favorable report on Project 2061. It cites an SRI International report *without stating that the American Association for the Advancement of Science paid for the report.*

My Attempts To Get AAAS To Study the Scientific Method Situation

My letters and reports to them were too numerous to list. I will simply highlight what was of greatest importance.

1992—I sent copies of my first two booklets to various officers, etc., at the Association. I also sent a page of special suggestions to Dr. Rutherford, Director of Project 2061.

1994—I sent copies of the 1994 edition of my booklet that challenged the Association to appoint a panel to properly define the scientific method.

1995—I prepared "A Special March 1995 Report to the American Association for the Advancement of Science on the 'the Scientific Method.'" This was about 40 pages long. It was sent to the officers, Board of Directors, and Council Members of the Association. Frankly, it was a crusader's report rather than an "if you please" one. I pointed out that "There is an emergency that calls for crass action." I was referring to the preparation of the 1995 National Science Education Standards that were soon to be finalized.

1995—As a member in October 1995 I followed procedures and submitted a resolution to the Association for consideration at its meeting on February 11, 1996, requesting study of the scientific method situation.

1996—In April I sent copies of my Reports #5, #6, and #7. I called special attention to my inclusion of Dr. Easley's paper falsifying Dr. Conant's claims of the non-existence of the scientific method. Dr. Easley was a respected member of the scientific community and was honored as a fellow of AAAS.

1997—In January I sent Report #8, "Help Stop the Biggest Intellectual Blunder in History," "Junk Science at National Science Foundation, U.S. Department of Education, American Association for Advancement of Science & National Academy of Sciences," and "AAAS's $300,000 Whitewash of Project 2061."

1997—In June I sent a copy of my Report #10, "U.S. Supreme Court Requires Use of the Scientific Method."

After 1997, there were a few letters of minor importance.

The net result of all my letters and reports was no action to study the scientific method situation. There was no change to Project 2061. In fact, the top leaders of the Association helped to ensure that the 1995 National Science Education Standards did not include the scientific method.

In fairness to AAAS, I state that my reports were not those of a Ph.D. or a Presidential Commission. However, regardless of who I am, the question is not, "*Who* is right?" but, "*What* is right?" In 1993 they published a review of my booklet *The General Pattern of the Scientific Method* in *Science Books and Films*, a publication that had a very small circulation of about 2,000. I did write to thank them for this tiny bit of publicity. However, this publication was not very influential and was subsequently discontinued. I would have liked to have been mentioned in *Science* magazine, which is sent to members of the Association.

The Effects of *the* BLUNDER on the Regular Activities of AAAS

I will not go into these in detail, but the Association should consider them. A few areas are listed here.

Guidance to Scientists

Since scientists are largely trained by the apprentice method [according to James Feibleman in *Scientific Method* (1972)], it would remove a burden from senior and junior scientists if those new to the profession already had a good background in the scientific method. In addition, the Association is encouraging scientists to go out into classrooms and speak to students. There is no better subject for these speakers than the method of science—the scientific method.

The Association's "Court-Appointed Scientific Experts"

Through the National Conference of Lawyers and Scientists, the Association has made an effort to keep junk science out of the courtroom and to help courts in handling science problems. A standardized formula for the scientific method and recognition of what it really is would greatly help these efforts.

AAAS' Guidance to Other Nations

The May 31, 2002, issue of *Science* states:

> As a first step, the Board has rephrased the historic AAAS mission, which now reads, "To Advance Science and Innovation Throughout the World for the Benefit of All People."

I point out that *To Advance Science and Innovation* requires use of the scientific method.

"A Landmark AAAS/UNESCO Forum Explores Science Education." This was a headline in *Science* (June 25, 2004). The forum, held in Paris and organized by AAAS, calls on "political leaders world-wide to make systematic improvements necessary to properly educate children in science and technology." There was no mention of teaching the scientific method.

Suggestions to Members of AAAS

Normally, members of scientific organizations should support their elected leaders—if they are carrying out their duties properly. I do not say that the Association's leaders are not doing a great job in most of their activities. However, as I have shown here, they are doing a very bad job in educational activities. This is based on my research of the public issue of the existence of the scientific method, the need to teach it in our public schools, and the need for educational researchers to conduct scientifically based research under the ESEA. To prevent this situation from hurting the American Association for the Advancement of Science, I hope you will ask for a full-time study group to investigate and report on the claims I have made.

Suggestions to the Public

The American Association for the Advancement of Science is the largest of our private professional scientific organizations. Over the years, our scientists have made tremendous contributions to our progress and welfare and deserve your support and that of Congress in their activities. As a member of AAAS for a total of 35 years, I have always admired its contribution to science and to the United States. But I must now speak out. *The* **BLUNDER** I claim exists permeates our whole society. The American Association for the Advancement of Science is, I believe, another victim of the agenda of the Harvard/Conant group and misguided followers (or whoever they are). However, taxpayers' funds are, in my opinion, being extensively wasted by their educational activities. The activities need to be studied and the results reported to the public. This is especially important because they have been influential in the setting of the erroneous 1995 National Science Education Standards, which are still being pushed in 2004. These represent a huge perpetuation of *the* **BLUNDER**.

? ?

The Big Mystery

My 1995 report to the top leaders of the American Association for the Advancement of Science was really frank, loaded with evidence supporting the scientific method, and contained warnings about the harms and possible consequences of what they were doing. Yet it was ignored, and no action was taken.

What is the mysterious factor of such importance that this and my other reports, including a copy of Dr. Easley's article, were ignored and not revealed to the members?

? ?

Chapter 30

Contribution of the U.S. Department of Education to *the* BLUNDER

Section 1
Contribution of the U.S. Department of Education to *the* BLUNDER
before January 2001

- The Internal Politics of the U.S. Department of Education Regarding the Scientific Method
- The Operating Policy of the Top Leaders and the Bureaucracy of the U.S. Department of Education Regarding the Scientific Method
- My Unsuccessful Attempts To Get the Department to Study the Scientific Method Situation
- The National Commission of Mathematics and Science Teaching for the 21st Century (Glenn Commission)
- The Second Term of President George W. Bush
- The Basic Fault Is the System

Section 2
Contribution of the U.S. Department of Education to *the* BLUNDER
after January 2001, When George W. Bush Became President

In this chapter I report on both historical and current activities. In the case of the U.S. Department of Education, we have had major changes since January 2001.

- President George W. Bush took office with a librarian wife and his ideas on education reform.

- Congress has passed legislation requiring "scientifically based research" in education programs and has revamped the Office of Educational Research and Improvement into the Institute of Educational Sciences.

SECTION 1
BEFORE JANUARY 2001

Before 1980 we had a Commissioner of Education in the Department of Health, Education and Welfare who was in charge of national educational efforts. The U.S. Department of Education was established on May 4, 1980, by Congress in the Department of Education Organization

Act. The department has 4,710 employees and an annual budget of approximately $54 billion.

The Internal Politics of the U.S. Department of Education Regarding the Scientific Method

It is difficult to show how the Harvard/Conant group and misguided followers (or whoever they are) "control" the U.S. Department of Education's policy on the scientific method. In his autobiography, Conant tells of the difficulty of improving Harvard's School of Education and his desire to find a new dean for it from the social sciences. He chose Francis Keppel. Years later, Keppel served as the U.S. Commissioner of Education (1962–1965). In 1967 a friend told Conant that Keppel had social scientists in dominant positions. In Chapter 27 I explain how social scientists have not followed or promoted the use of the scientific method to any great extent.

Of the past six Secretaries of Education, only one was a Harvard graduate or professor. Harvard graduates serve in many other positions.

I can show very well, however, that the operating policy of the U.S. Department of Education since its inception in 1981 has not included promoting the teaching of the scientific method.

The Operating Policy of Top Leaders and the Bureaucracy of the U.S. Department of Education Regarding the Scientific Method

The secretaries of the department come and go with the wishes of the current President and Congress. The department's bureaucracy, however, is more stable and has probably contributed to *the* BLUNDER.

The U.S. Department of Education Has Sponsored No Research Studies on the Scientific Method

In response to my inquiry I received a letter dated January 15, 1993, saying that, to the knowledge of the writer, the department had never supported research studies on "the scientific method per se." In my research, I never found a record of any such studies.

U.S. Department of Education's Stated Opinion of the Scientific Method

I do not recall seeing any published opinion of the scientific method by the U.S. Department of Education. However, on July 30, 1993, I

CONTRIBUTION OF U.S. DEPARTMENT OF EDUCATION to *the* BLUNDER 293

received a letter from the Learning and Instruction Division. One of my letters to Secretary Riley had been referred to this division. The letter from the Learning and Instruction Division contained many misunderstandings of the scientific method and ended with the usual brush-off. I wrote again to Secretary Riley about this letter, and this time my letter was sent to the Mathematics and Science Education Division. The response contained the comment that the Office of Educational Research and Improvement had received four letters from me in the past year. The letter recommended that I contact national professional associations and state education agencies.

Educational Standards of 1995

The department made no attempt to have the standards include the scientific method.

Eisenhower Mathematics and Science Education Program

This was established by Congress and administered by the Department of Education. It had a large budget for a number of years. It never included anything about the scientific method. It certainly should have, since science is its method.

U.S. Department of Education's Office of Educational Research and Improvement

This office is headed by the Assistant Secretary for Educational Research. OERI was established in 1980 as part of the original Department of Education.

The following was taken from the website www.ed.gov/offices/OERI in 2001:

> The Assistant Secretary for Educational Research and Improvement serves as the principal advisor to the Secretary on educational research, statistics, and practice, as well as on the dissemination of information to improve the quality of education.

Even though the head of OERI is the advisor to the Secretary, apparently none of them has ever called *the* BLUNDER to the attention of the various Secretaries, despite my letters and reports forwarded to OERI. They have also ignored all the material about the scientific method I mention in this book, such as Easley's falsification of

Conant's 1947 claims that the scientific method does not exist and the numerous books from which I quote. As our top educational research facility, they should have been familiar with all this material and evidence.

So what did OERI do from 1980 to 2001?
◆ It failed to research the scientific method or have others do so.
◆ It did not use the scientific method in its own activities.
◆ It perpetuated *the* **BLUNDER**.
◆ From 1992 on, it brushed off and ignored my attempts to get it to study the matter.

It Is Not All Bad at OERI

There is no question that OERI has done a lot of good. We must remember "that OERI has been too easily controlled by the political whims of whatever administration is in power" (*Education Week*, July 13, 1994). Actually, the entire U.S. Department of Education has a difficult time functioning anywhere near efficiently because of political interference. An interesting book about this is *Conflict of Interest— The Politics of American Education* (1988) by Joel Spring.

In 1994 Congress reauthorized and revamped the OERI, but this did not overcome the institutionalizing and politicizing that had befallen the scientific method.

The Regional Laboratories and Research Centers of the U.S. Department of Education

To the best of my knowledge, none of these organizations has ever researched or approved the teaching of the scientific method.

Goals 2000 of 1994

This was another major program that did not include the scientific method, even though the scientific method is a subject that should be taught across the curriculum. Whether a Republican or Democrat was President, the scientific method was neglected.

National Educational Research Policy and Priorities Board

The following was taken from the website www.ed.gov/offices/OERI/NERPPB in 2001:

> The National Educational Research Policy and Priorities Board works in cooperation with the Assistant Secretary and OERI to determine research priorities and evaluation standards. In addition, the Board works to determine priorities that ultimately guide the work of OERI and provide guidance to Congress in its oversight of OERI. Public members of the board are appointed by the Secretary and represent educational researchers, school-based professional educators, and parents.

This board was established by Congress in 1994. It held its first meeting in March 1995. I goofed in finding out it existed and never sent it any reports or letters. Apparently OERI did not share those I sent.

This board did done nothing to correct *the* **BLUNDER**. It met four times a year. Apparently a lot of its actual work was done by OERI staff. In June 1999 the board issued a 37-page report with many interesting features. I suspect that it, like most other panel reports, will probably be filed away, with only minor use made of it.

My Unsuccessful Attempts to Get the U.S. Department of Education to Study the Scientific Method Situation

I give only the highlights here. My attempts were quite numerous.

When you are just an individual attempting to correct what you perceive to be wrong in a large organization, you can expect this: you write to a person, the letter is answered by a secretary, who says that your letter has been referred to another person or department. Then you get a thank you and a brush-off type of letter from the person to whom your letter was referred.

1992—I sent a letter and my booklets to Secretary Alexander, who sent my letter to OERI. I received a brush-off type letter.

I sent a letter to Assistant Secretary of Education Diane Ravitch, who sent it to Programs for Improvement of Practice. I received a brush-off type letter.

1993—I wrote to the new Secretary of Education, Richard Riley. I received another brush-off letter.

I sent a letter and booklets to President-elect Clinton. They were sent to OERI. I received the usual brush off.

I wrote to Michael Cohen, consultant to Goals 2000, by certified mail. I received no reply.

I sent Secretary Riley a copy of my Rainbow Report, which went to all the members of Congress. It was referred to the Learning and Instruction Division of OERI.

1994—I sent the same challenge to the U.S. Department of Education that I sent to NAS, AAAS, etc.

1995—I sent the same report to the organizations I had publicly challenged. This went to 44 people at various offices in the U.S. Department of Education, the National Education Goals Panel, and chairpersons of various education-related panels of Congress. I goofed, as previously mentioned, in not sending it to the National Educational Research Policy and Priorities Board.

1996—I sent copies of Reports #5, #6, and #7. I included a copy of Dr. Easley's 1958 essay in which he falsified Conant's claims about the scientific method. This mailing went to the same list as the 1995 report.

1998—I sent a few more letters.

2000—I tried unsuccessfully to get the addresses of the members of the Glenn Commission from the Department. They wanted any materials for the Commission sent to the Department.

The National Commission on Mathematics and Science Teaching for the 21st Century (Glenn Commission)

The following description of the commission is from the Department of Education's *Community Update* (September 1999):

U.S. Secretary of Education Richard W. Riley recently announced the appointment of 25 members to the new National Commission on Mathematics and Science Teaching for the 21st Century, to be chaired by former U.S. Senator and astronaut John Glenn. As part of the U.S. Department of Education's mathematics initiative, *America Counts*, the commission will consider ways to improve the recruitment, preparation, retention, and professional growth of K-12 teachers who provide math and science instruction.

It Never Should Have Been Appointed

In Chapter 20 I discuss the waste of money, time, and effort in temporary big-name panels versus permanent specialized SM-14 type national research centers. The 25 members of the commission are all great people from all parts of the country. They are very busy individuals, and I won't say a word against them. They are very distinguished, well known, intelligent people. However, they are also people who, because of *the* **BLUNDER**, were never adequately educated about the scientific method.

Comments on the Unreliability of the Content of the Report

Blunder #1—The report does not include a recommendation to get back to teaching the scientific method. It mentions "skills of scientific approach." Of course, the scientific approach is just another name for the scientific method! However, this is not recognized or acknowledged.

Blunder #2—Page 5 of the report states:

> . . . the Commission has concluded that the most powerful instrument for change, and therefore the place to begin, lies at the very core of education—*with teaching itself.*

The blunder is that the "place to begin" is at the top leadership of education. We must end the "control" of the Harvard/Conant group and misguided followers (or whoever they are) that is preventing the Commission members and almost everyone else from realizing the need to teach the scientific method.

These Two Points Are Enough

I could go on, but these two blunders are enough to show that the report is not reliable, even though it is beautifully written, professionally presented, and budgeted at $800,000.

Summary of Section 1

I believe that the preceding is sufficient to show that the Harvard/Conant group and misguided followers (or whoever they are) have been able to keep their agenda of preventing the teaching of the scientific method going, even in the U.S. Department of Education, despite the fact that the department has a "research" division and had a Policy and Priorities Board.

SECTION 2
CONTRIBUTION OF THE U.S. DEPARTMENT OF EDUCATION TO *THE* BLUNDER AFTER JANUARY 2001, WHEN GEORGE W. BUSH BECAME PRESIDENT

In approximately 1999 I made the decision to stop my program of writing letters, briefs, reports, and special reports to organizations to try to correct *the* BLUNDER. I was accomplishing nothing of any significance. I decided instead to write a book on *the* BLUNDER for the general public. The objective was to bring the misunderstandings to the attention of the public in the hope that this would cause change to occur. I held to this course, with a few minor exceptions.

When President Bush appointed Rod Paige Secretary of Education, I was delighted, as he clearly was not a Harvard man and had worked in many levels of education. Early in his term (in 2001) there were remarks in the media that, being an outsider, he would not survive and would probably resign when confronted by the bureaucracy of the Department of Education. He proved to be strong enough to survive.

I was faced with the decision of whether to flood him with reports on the scientific method, putting him in the position of having to ignore my reports or sticking his neck out to correct *the* BLUNDER, along with handling all his other problems. One of these is his responsibility to carry out the President's policies. I decided to continue to write my book, since *the* BLUNDER is so widespread.

Comments on the 2003 Changes in the U.S. Department of Education

While I have been working on this book, there has been a major change in the U.S. Department of Education that involves the end of the Office of Educational Research and Improvement. The new Institute of Educational Sciences seems to be an improvement. However, it will be a poor substitute for a series of permanent specialized SM-14 type national research centers scattered around the country in our colleges and universities. There is also the worry of political appointments and influence affecting its work.

You cannot achieve in Washington the many requirements I have specified for a large number of specialized individual research centers with their continuity of personnel, accumulation of books and files, etc. The continuation of temporary grants with the usual reports does not result in the systematic accumulation of reliable knowledge and its proper use. There are far too many areas that require continuous study rather than jumping from one project to another.

I have noticed more 5-year grants awarded by the Department of Education. While this provides more continuity of research, it is still not as efficient as the permanent specialized SM-14 type national research centers I recommend in Chapter 58.

The Bush administration's emphasis on the Reading First Act seems to be a step in the right direction. While the establishment of the National Center for Reading First Technical Assistance sounds good, we still need a permanent specialized SM-14 type national research center on reading.

NSTA Reports (February/March 2003) tells us that the "Bush Administration Plans New Math/Science Initiative." We continue to blunder on the teaching of math and science because of the lack of individual permanent specialized SM-14 type research centers on math and science.

In Chapter 55 I comment on the No Child Left Behind Act administered by the U.S. Department of Education.

It's a huge task to research and analyze all the developments going on, but on the whole I conclude that the U.S. Department of Education continued to perpetuate *the* **BLUNDER** while Rod Paige was Secretary of Education.

The Second Term of President George W. Bush

During his second campaign, President Bush praised his sponsorship of the No Child Left Behind Act, even though it has provoked a great deal of negative commentary in the press.

Margaret Spellings is now the Secretary of Education. News reports indicate that she was the principal architect of Bush's first-term educational program, including the No Child Left Behind Act. Although some say that she lacks the educational background for the position, most comments have been favorable. Her job is to carry out the education policies of the Bush administration.

In the chapters on educational disasters, I show that they have largely continued during Bush's presidency. Who do I blame? Do I blame the President and his Secretaries of Education? The scientific method must not become a political football. Its use should be a goal of both political parties. I did not blame President Clinton for the ills of education during his administration, and I do not blame President Bush and his Secretaries of Education for the current situation.

The Basic Fault Is the System

Presidents and political parties adopt educational goals and programs based on prevailing "knowledge" and advice from top educational leaders and advocates. Because of *the* **BLUNDER**, the prevailing educational "knowledge" is not reliable, nor is the advice of so-called top educational "experts," leaders, and the advocates of many causes.

It is my basic contention, shown throughout this book, that until Recommendations 1 and 2 (Chapters 57 and 58) are followed, there will be no real and continuing progress in improving education at the national level.

???

The Mystery

Why has our top government agency on education, which has spent so many billions of dollars, ignored the scientific method all these years?

???

Chapter 31

Contribution of the National Science Teachers Association to *the* BLUNDER

◆ Information about NSTA

◆ The Internal Politics of NSTA

◆ The Operating Policy of NSTA as It Concerns the Scientific Method

◆ My Unsuccessful Attempts To Get NSTA To Study the Scientific Method Situation

◆ Suggestions and Mysteries

You may say, "Hold on, Edmund. In Chapter 11 you claim a great injustice has been done to our teachers of science, and now you are criticizing "their" association!" You will have to read my story to understand what is going on.

As part of their agenda, the Harvard/Conant group and misguided followers (or whoever they are) had to "control" NSTA. Otherwise, the scientific method would be widely taught, since, as Conant said in 1948, ". . . the scientific method has been put forward . . . as one of the primary aims of modern education."

Information about NSTA

The following information is from the website www.NSTA.org.

Founded in 1944, NSTA has a current membership of more than 55,000, including grade school science teachers, professors of science, science supervisors, administrators, scientists, business and industry representatives, and others involved in and committed to science education. It has a full-time staff of more than 100.

NSTA has seven affiliated organizations of professors and others above the level of grade school science teachers.

302 END THE BIGGEST EDUCATIONAL AND INTELLECTUAL BLUNDER

In addition, NSTA has 59 state chapters and 28 associated groups.

NSTA has a wide range of activities to promote excellence and innovation in science teaching. These are described on the website. Other than in regard to the scientific method, it has made a great contribution to the teaching of science.

NSTA has not been a major originator of *the* **BLUNDER**. In the hierarchy, it ranks below NAS, AAAS, NSF, and the U.S. Department of Education. However, because it provides leadership and advice to science teachers, it has been an important perpetrator of *the* **BLUNDER**.

The Internal Politics of NSTA

In many organizations, the paid executive director dominates, rules, guides, and advises the operation of the organization to some or a great extent. Therefore, this is a key position in NSTA and one the Harvard/Conant group and misguided followers (or whoever they are) I believe "controlled."

The president of NSTA serves a 1-year, unpaid term and is usually not a big factor in its operations. The president's term is short, and he or she keeps working at his or her usual job. The actual operation of the organization is left in the hands of the salaried full-time executive director.

Because of the name of the association, I and others have viewed it as an organization of grade school science teachers. However, it also includes college professors of science, consultants, and state officials. It is logical that they exert considerable influence. On nominating committees and executive committees, K-12 teachers seem to be in the minority, although they make up the majority of members. It is very strange! An estimated 55% of NSTA members teach the scientific method a little. Yet NSTA leaders ignore the method.

Executive Director Bill G. Aldridge

Aldridge became executive director in 1981 and retired in 1996. He built a small organization into the major one it is today, with a staff of more than 100. He received NASA's Distinguished Public Service Medal for his accomplishments. I believe that he is a Harvard graduate, and I suppose that he was trained in the theory that the scientific method does not exist.

Executive Director Gerald Wheeler

When Aldridge retired in 1996, Gerald Wheeler was selected to replace him. Wheeler had been working at AAAS, so I believe that he was considered "safe" as being opposed to the scientific method.

A Little Story. I was not able to get any publicity about my research in the local newspaper (*Sun-Sentinel*). Then, in 1998 my secretary-assistant met a reporter for their weekly entertainment give-away newspaper. She interviewed me and did a nice reporting job. To present a rounded view, she called NSTA Executive Director Wheeler. She reports:

> Wheeler says he's not surprised by the time and energy Edmund's devoted to his undertaking.
>
> "There are a number of people," he says, "who have a particular passion for the way they feel things ought to be in the world, and they write letters. I don't want to put him on the level of kooks. Edmund's not that far out. But he does have this thing where he's saying the world is wrong and I am right and I'm gonna keep mailing things until I get their attention.
>
> "He's not a kook, and he's not crazy. But he does have a passion for this thing."

From this you have confirmation that I am not a "kook." This tickled my sense of humor. (I was, though, afraid to ask my wife what she thought about my being a "kook"!)

Wheeler thinks that the Harvard/Conant group and misguided followers (or whoever they are) are "the world." It is correct that they have built quite a "world of their own making" in the national education community and even in the international education community. One tells the other that the scientific method does not exist, and it goes around and around. This is perpetuated by their control of grants, honors, professional journals, jobs, etc. However, it is all built on a foundation of ignoring contrary evidence and keeping the matter a deep, dark secret. It cannot withstand the studies I am requesting. Therefore, they have refused to do them. In this book I have shown that an honest search of the literature shows that the realistic world acknowledges the existence of the scientific method as do millions of people.

I readily admit that we do have a huge group that has been misled, causing the scientific method to be inadequately taught.

The preceding quote also confirms that Wheeler received my mailings. However, despite my efforts, I did not get a panel appointed at NSTA to study the matter, so it's another reason I've had to write this book. Since so many science teachers use textbooks that contain information about the scientific method, I am surprised they do not challenge NSTA's policy.

Operating Policy of NSTA as It Concerns the Scientific Method

Although NSTA publications occasionally have an article written by a teacher about the scientific method, the association has, to my knowledge, never promoted teaching it. Beginning in 1989, Aldridge designed a new program for teaching science called Scope, Sequence, and Coordination (SS&C). It was supported for many years by the U.S. Department of Education and NSF. It contained nothing about the scientific method by name, but it did include a section on the processes of science, with features from the scientific method. This program, while quite different, competed with AAAS's Benchmarks—Project 2061, launched in 1985. There were professional jealousies involved, according to one report in *Education Week* (December 7, 1994, page 9). NSF funding for SS&C was cut off in 1996.

Since 1996, under the leadership of Wheeler, NSTA has continued to support the policy of the Harvard/Conant group and misguided followers (or whoever they are) of ignoring the scientific method. Examples follow.

Year 2000 NSTA Position Statement: The Nature of Science

The NSTA bimonthly newspaper, *NSTA Reports*, presented a prospective position statement for review by its membership. It states in part:

> 2. Although no single universal step-by-step scientific method captures the complexity of doing science, a number of shared values and perspectives characterize a scientific approach to understanding nature. Among these are a demand for naturalistic explanations supported by empirical evidence that are, at least in principle, testable against the natural world. Other shared elements include observations, rational argument, inference, skepticism, peer review and replicability of work.

Here is another denial of the scientific method, despite my reports, letters, booklets, and our vast body of knowledge about it. This is a disgrace to science teaching and yet another result of *the* **BLUNDER** and the "control" of the Harvard/Conant group and misguided followers (or whoever they are).

Stage 10 of SM-14 calls for an open mind. Indications are that they not only do not approve of the scientific method, they also do not keep an open mind about it.

On June 13, 2000, I sent a registered letter to NSTA protesting the position statement, with additional literature explaining the scientific method. I requested an answer but never received one.

1995 Science Education Standards

NSTA participated in the setting of the science education standards. After the standards were approved for implementation, NSTA urged its members to participate in implementing them. NSTA never made any attempt to have the scientific method included in the standards. My reports and letters to the officers and the board were kept a deep, dark secret from the members.

My Unsuccessful Attempts To Get NSTA To Study the Scientific Method Situation

1992—I sent the first edition of my booklet.

1994—I sent the same challenge I sent to other organizations.

1995—I sent my March 1995 Special Report to those I challenged to study the scientific method. This went to the board of directors, the executive secretary, the president, and division and district directors.

1996—I sent the same follow-up letter with additional reports that I sent to the others I had challenged.

1997 and on—I sent additional letters of minor importance.

I was very disappointed that officials of an association that has had so many injustices done to its members (one erroneous program after another) made no effort to even study *the* **BLUNDER** so plainly described to them.

Suggestions to the Members of NSTA

◆ Quickly establish an investigative study group to review the serious claims I have made. The group should be small and devote full time to the task.

◆ Your association should recommend the establishment of

> a permanent specialized SM-14 type national research center for teaching science and technology (with satellite centers for particular subjects at various universities)

◆ Individual teachers can proceed now on a small scale to teach the SM-14 formula. Because the SAT, ACT, and other tests have nothing about the scientific method, you cannot devote much time to it yet. However, when you come to the part with the erroneous material in the 1995 standards foisted on you to teach science as inquiry, let your students know that inquiry leads to process. The process leads to the scientific method. The best example of this is SM-14, explained in *The Scientific Method Today*.

I hope that a foundation or company will finance sending you a free copy of *The Scientific Method Today*. Before long someone will turn it into a good manual for teaching the scientific method. You can also find it on the Internet at www.scientificmethod.com.

Suggestion to Industry and Foundations

By all means continue your help to the teaching of science, but aid in the establishment of a permanent specialized SM-14 type national research center for science teaching so that you are reliably guided on how to spend your funds more efficiently.

? ?

The Mysteries

Why didn't the top leaders of NSTA, who received copies of my strong report of March 1995, take any action? Why did the Executive Committee that reviewed my material fail to take any action? Why didn't the full board review it? Why didn't they report on it to their members? Who or what influenced their lack of action?

? ?

Chapter 32

Contribution of the National Science Foundation to *the* BLUNDER

◆ Information about NSF

◆ Internal Politics of NSF

◆ The Operating Policy of the Top Leaders of NSF Regarding the Scientific Method

◆ NSF Educational Activities and Teaching of Science

◆ Natural Scientists Are Held to a Strict Code of Ethics, But No Adequate Code of Ethics Is Enforced in Educational Research at NSF

◆ NSF-Paid Appraisals of NSF Programs

◆ My Unsuccessful Attempts To Get NSF To Study the Scientific Method Situation

◆ One of the Troubles with NSF

◆ NSF Launches Five New Centers in a $100 Million Project

◆ Suggestions and Mysteries

Information about the National Science Foundation

The National Science Foundation has done an outstanding job of aiding the development of science in the United States in many ways. The following information about the National Science Foundation (NSF) is abstracted from its website (www.nsf.gov).

> By the National Science Foundation Act of 1950 the Congress established the National Science Foundation to promote the progress of science; to advance the national health, prosperity, and welfare; to secure the national defense; and for other purposes. The President approved the act on May 10, 1950.

> The National Science Foundation (NSF) is an independent agency of the U.S. Government. . .
>
> The Foundation consists of the National Science Board of 24 part-time members and a Director (who also serves as ex officio National Science Board member), each appointed by the President with the advice and consent of the U.S. Senate. Other senior officials include a Deputy Director who is appointed by the President with the advice and consent of the U.S. Senate, and eight Assistant Directors.

Eventually NSF's activities were specifically described to include promoting education in the sciences. Internally, its Directorate for Education and Human Resources is in charge of this. Vannevar Bush, James Conant, and others fought hard for a number of years to get the foundation authorized by Congress. Its budgets in the first years were very meager. Following the Sputnik mission in 1956, its budget was greatly increased.

In its regular activities, NSF has made a great contribution in the areas for which it was founded. However, in education, it is a different story. According to *Science* magazine (November 16, 2001) its 2002 educational budget was $875,000,000. Since 1952, NSF has spent almost $6 billion on education and human resources.

I spent so much time preparing the chapters on NAS and AAAS that I must make this and future ones shorter. Since the basic blunders are the same, I need not go into such great detail again.

Internal Politics of NSF

The factors that have prevented the teaching of the scientific method given in Chapter 29, Contribution of the American Association for the Advancement of Science to *the* BLUNDER, also apply to NSF.

Conant's Influence Shows Up at NSF Too

Conant was the first director of the National Science Board. After serving as director for one year, he served two more years as a board member. It is my opinion that his false claims about the scientific method have become institutionalized and politicized into NSF through the efforts of the Harvard/Conant group and misguided followers (or whoever they are).

The Operating Policy of the Top Leaders of NSF Regarding the Scientific Method

In my research, I found no direct statements by NSF that the scientific method does not exist. However, it is very obvious that this is the policy. In all the years since its inception, I found no evidence that it has supported specific research on the scientific method or promoted the use of the scientific method, despite the fact that the scientific method is mentioned in a least a few pages in most science textbooks. This strange situation alone is proof that NSF is following the Harvard/Conant concept that the scientific method does not exist.

In Its Own Teaching Activities

NSF's own Statewide Systemic Initiatives Program in classrooms does not include the scientific method.

My Claim Is Further Supported

In a letter to me dated May 25, 1995, returning (refusing to accept) my March 1995 report, Luther S. Williams, then Assistant Director of NSF, stated:

> I assert that NSF's position is that trained scientists do their professional work by a variety of methods which share a number of features in common.

Summary

Here again there is little doubt that the Harvard/Conant group and misguided followers (or whoever they are) are in "control." NSF's policy and treatment of the scientific method match those of NAS, AAAS, and many other national organizations.

In addition, my special reports and letters produced no study of the scientific method situation.

NSF Educational Activities and Teaching of Science

The first national science teaching programs in the 1956 era supported by NSF were the Physical Science Study Committee and the Harvard Physics Project. These set the tone for those that followed. It was an era in which Conant's books with false claims about the scientific method were published and circulated. Conant had been

Director of the National Science Board, so you can be sure that early NSF programs did not include the scientific method, nor have any other major NSF projects or grant since then—a terrible record!

The Ring around the Rosie

Both NSF and the U.S. Department of Education advised me to pursue my ideas with the professional societies if I want change about the scientific method. However, NSF and the U.S. Department of Education are the ones who control grants needed by the professional organizations to help cover their overhead and educational activities. Thus, they, too, keep pushing the same false theme as NSF and the U.S. Department of Education. It becomes institutionalized and politicized in all of them. It is like the old song—ring around the rosie—but what an expensive and tragic one for society.

Tremendous Number of Teaching Programs

Over the years, NSF has aided so many programs, projects, grants, etc., regarding science education that I will not attempt to cover them. There is no doubt that overall NSF has aided science teaching, but has been unsuccessful on a cost/benefit basis. The lack of inclusion of the scientific method has meant a huge waste of billions of dollars and misdirection of programs. Report after report, article after article report on the U.S. lag in the teaching of math and science and the lack of science literacy among students and the public. My claim is that this can be traced to *the* **BLUNDER**. Remember that *the* **BLUNDER** continues in 2005.

NSF's Statewide Systemic Initiative Program (SSI)

Remember that NAS, AAAS, and the National Science Teachers Association had programs to reform science teaching. In 1991 NSF launched its own direct Statewide Systemic Initiatives (SSI). The details of this program are too complex to review here. It is another expensive program that should never have been started. You can be sure it did not include the scientific method and a formula for it. Thus, it is another blunder.

NSF's Long, Long Push for Teaching Science as Inquiry

In this book and in my reports and briefs, I constantly complain about teaching science as inquiry without also teaching the method of inquiry—the scientific method. In Chapter 31 I quote Professor Yager, past president of NSTA, who in 1991 complained of NSF-supported projects giving great attention to science as inquiry for 30 years. His comment and all my reports and efforts did not change anything among the Harvard/Conant group and misguided followers (or who-ever they are). The 1995 National Science Education Standards were approved with science as inquiry with no method of inquiry—the scientific method—thus perpetuating *the* **BLUNDER**. The NSF provided part of the funding for the Standards.

Inquiry as part of science goes way back in history. The theme was popularized in the 1950s to 1960s by Professor Schwab. In *A History of Ideas in Science Education* (1991), George DeBoer states:

> One forum that allowed Schwab (1962) to present his ideas concerning the teaching of science as "enquiry" was the Inglis Lecture at Harvard University in 1961.

I am sure that Schwab was welcome at Harvard, as he was opposed to teaching the scientific method. So you can see that the theme of science as inquiry goes back many years. In his essay protesting the non-teaching of the scientific method, Professor Easley compares the views of Dewey, Conant, and Schwab on the scientific method.

Dr. Vannevar Bush's Statement about the Scientific Method

The National Science Foundation credits Bush with its establishment by Congress. I found nothing in his books about where he stood on the scientific method. Finally, I ran across a statement he made in an address at the George Westinghouse Educational Foundation Forum in Pittsburgh, Pennsylvania, May 16–18, 1946, published in *Science* (May 31, 1946) and reported by Good and Scates in *Methods of Research* (1954). Bush said, *"I am decidedly not one of those who speak* of the scientific method as a firm and clearly defined concept" (emphasis mine). He seems to be echoing Nobel Laureate Percy Bridgman of Harvard, who stated: *"I am not one of those who hold* that there is a scientific method as such" (emphasis mine).

Natural Scientists Are Held to a Strict Code of Ethics, But No Adequate Code of Ethics Is Enforced in Educational Research at NSF

In this book, I have mentioned several times that government enforcement of prudent judgment and a code of ethics on government contracts seems to be lacking in the educational field. Steve Fuller claims that the educational field gave up the scientific method in favor of following paradigms as a result of Kuhn's works (Chapter 33).

It is neither good science nor prudent judgment to ignore contrary evidence in **completing** government contracts, as is constantly done in the educational field.

Is This the Answer?

This quotation from *Restructuring Science Education* (1990) by Richard A. Duschl may give one reason why this is allowed to happen:

> The NSF sought from the beginning to guarantee that the principal drive, design, and growth of the precollege programs would come from outside the Foundation. By design, NSF's involvement in science projects was administrative only. Once a project was approved by a peer review panel, implementation of the program or grant project was the responsibility of the university, college, or institution that received the award. The assumption was that the individuals awarded the grants for basic research were experts in their respective fields and should not be held to strict guidelines for the direction of the goals of the research or be governed by strict timeframes for completion of the research.
>
> The NSF applied the same administrative policy to its education grants as a way to avoid "the curriculum control" argument brewing in Congress. The policy was essentially to allow institutions or individuals awarded grants to make all decisions related to grant-supported activities.

This seems to indicate that NSF is pushing responsibility onto the educational grant recipient for the quality of work performed, which does not sound practical or legal. I don't really know what the answer is. It needs to be clarified.

NSF's Own Program Record Is Bad on the Scientific Method

As time passed, NSF instituted its own educational programs in some cooperating schools. The designers of these programs did not, in my opinion, use good judgment concerning the scientific method. After all, it is in about 65% of science textbooks and is covered extensively in the general literature.

Congress' New Requirement

Time has passed, and now Congress is requiring "scientifically based research" in the ESEA. If Duschl's 1990 description is correct, NSF had better realize that the days of the Harvard/Conant group and misguided followers (or whoever they are) are waning and issue some new guidelines to educational grant holders. This is of special importance now that the U.S. Supreme Court has acknowledged the existence of the scientific method.

NSF-Paid Appraisals of NSF Programs

In Chapter 29, I complain about AAAS's lapse of ethics on a report of Project 2061. NSF has also paid for outside reviews of its programs.

While these NSF-financed reports may not always be 100% favorable, they are too subject to bias toward NSF, which is paying for them, to be worthwhile. None has reported on the exclusion of the scientific method from their programs.

An article entitled "That Glowing Report on Company X Isn't What You Might Think" appeared in the *Wall Street Journal* on June 24, 2002. The article uses the phrase "praise for pay." I do not claim that NSF, AAAS, and others are doing this in the educational field, but I do say that the system of hiring people to appraise your own work is flawed and a waste of taxpayers' money.

My Unsuccessful Attempts To Get NSF To Study the Scientific Method Situation

I give only the highlights here.

1992—I sent a copy of my first two booklets to Dr. Walter Massey, Director, and four extra for his staff and members of the board.

1994—I sent a letter and a copy of the 1994 edition of Edmund's Idea and Research Report challenging NSF to appoint a panel to properly define the scientific method to Dr. Neal F. Lane, Director.

1995—I sent the same Special March 1995 Report that I sent to NAS, AAAS, and others I had challenged in my 1994 Idea and Research Report. This was sent to the officers and also to members of the National Science Board.

1996—In April I sent copies of Reports #5, #6, and #7. I included a copy of Dr. Easley's 1958 essay in which he falsified Conant's claims about the scientific method.

1997—In January I sent Report #8, which was also sent to NAS, AAAS, and other organizations.

After 1997, a few more letters were sent. Despite all my letters and reports, NSF took no action to study the scientific method situation. **The BLUNDER** at NSF continued. Because of NSF's high budget for science education, it radiated out all over the education field.

One of the Troubles with NSF

Vannevar Bush, who is usually given most of the credit for founding NSF, wrote a report for President Franklin Roosevelt, *Science, The Endless Frontier* (1945), and a book, *The Endless Horizons* (1946). I quote from this book on page 33 of *The Scientific Method Today* regarding how science has done so much for human welfare.

I think that NSF carries the "endless frontier" over into education and jumps from one experimental program to another and another. Education is not an "endless frontier" to anywhere near the degree of the natural sciences.

It is not easy for a government agency to operate efficiently. NSF got off to a bad start in its educational activities when it was under the influence of Conant. I believe that it is still under the influence of the Harvard/Conant group and misguided followers (or whoever they are).

"NSF Hands $216 Million to Enhance Math, Science"

Here we go again with more junk science. The October 8, 2003 edition of *Education Week* reports, under the above heading:

> The National Science Foundation announced last week that it would be giving $216.3 million in grants to improve student achievement in mathematics and science.

> This is the second round of grants the independent federal agency has awarded under its Math and Science Partnerships program, which pairs experts from colleges and universities with state departments of education and individual school districts.

NSF generates one new educational program after another, year after year. I am an advocate of a big permanent specialized SM-14 type national research center on science education with satellite centers. However, the centers must be SM-14 type—not like those described. These will not be required to follow the scientific method under present NSF policy. Thus, what we can expect is a lot of junk science (no scientific method included) along with some good work!

Suggestions

Suggestions to the Officers and the National Science Board

This book shows with a great deal of evidence that *the* **BLUNDER** has caused educational research, including math and science, to become a grand mess. Regardless of your personal beliefs, political pressures, and obligations to others, the good of science, the United States, and the rest of the world requires that *the* **BLUNDER** be studied. This should be done promptly.

Remember that I have spent 15 years accumulating a specialized library on the scientific method. It now contains some excellent books and files that would facilitate your study.

Whether it is under your care or some other arrangement, we need

a permanent specialized SM-14 type national research center for science and technology teaching

a permanent specialized SM-14 type national research center for math teaching

Suggestions to Congress

You made a great step forward when you required "scientifically based research" in the ESEA. The same provision should be added for appropriations for NSF educational activities. In addition, you should define this term to mean following the scientific method (SM-14 type). We also need a system of

permanent specialized SM-14 type national research centers

In the next congressional agency review of NSF, you should pay special attention to whether the scientific method is in its science and math education activities.

Suggestions to the Public

NSF has performed an essential job in promoting scientific research in the natural sciences. Because of its efforts, our scientists, engineers, and others have tremendously improved your welfare. They deserve your continued support and that of Congress.

The record of NSF, along with the records of almost all the other organizations involved in educational activities, is bad. I am not qualified to say what part NSF should play in a revision of our educational activities. The immediate need is to demand that NSF study the scientific method situation.

? ?

The Mysteries

Why does NSF have a closed mind about the scientific method? I have shown a strong conviction that the scientific method exists, but this is backed up by more than 15 years of specialized research and *communicated* evidence to back up my views.

◆ Why has NSF never explained its reasons for not including the scientific method?

◆ Why will they spend $100 million on their own Statewide Systemic Initiative science teaching program, but not even a few thousand dollars to check the detailed evidence I submitted?

◆ Why has NSF spent almost $6 billion from 1952 to 2002 without any specific program about the scientific method?

◆ Has the grant-making power of NSF been used to perpetuate ***the*** **BLUNDER**?

◆ Is NSF afraid of some faction in Congress?

What are the answers?

? ?

Chapter 33

Contribution of the Philosophy Domain to
the BLUNDER

◆ The Philosophy Societies

◆ My Research Releases Philosophers from the Obligation under Which Conant Placed Them

◆ A Review of the Aims and Goals of Philosophy of Science

◆ Sir Karl Popper

◆ Paul Feyerabend

◆ Thomas Kuhn

◆ The Inability Thus Far of Philosophy To Become a Science

◆ Suggestions and Mystery

The Philosophy Societies

I made no effort to research these. There seem to be many small specialized societies. I do not know what part they played in *the* BLUNDER, except that they seem to have participated in it.

The Philosophy of Science Association publishes a quarterly journal. After reading a few issues, my impression was that they are under the "control" or influence of those perpetuating *the* BLUNDER. However, in this chapter I go into a little detail about three famous philosophers of science who contributed to *the* BLUNDER.

My Research Releases Philosophers from the Obligation under Which Conant Placed Them

Remember that I reported in Chapter 3 that in *Modern Science and Modern Man* (1952), Conant publicly stated:

> It would be my thesis that those historians of science, and I might add philosophers as well, who emphasize that there is

no such thing as "the scientific method" are doing a public service.

Admittedly, Conant was a great and extremely influential scientist and educator. Few have dared to directly challenge his claims, even though they were erroneous and thus false claims. I have read of no one who has publicly released the philosophers and historians of science (and all other domains by inference) from doing "the public service" of emphasizing that there is no such thing as "the scientific method." While it may be a little unusual, I think the matter is so important that I hereby state that my research releases them from the obligation under which Conant placed them. The research concerning the scientific method in this book is of sufficient reliability that philosophers (and anyone else) are no longer under the obligation to follow Conant's "thesis." His "thesis" has been falsified by my research and by Easley's research in 1958.

A Review of the Aims and Goals of Philosophy of Science

In the Introduction to *Philosophy of Science Today* (1967), edited by Sidney Morgenbesser, with contributions from many famous philosophers, such as Max Black, Paul Feyerabend, and Ernest Nagel, Morgenbesser states:

> Thus, five major goals of the philosophy of science are: to clarify the nature and aims of science; to specify the structure of particular scientific theories; to criticize and to comment critically on scientific claims in the light of epistemological and ontological theses; to assess claims about the possible reach of science; and to buttress or test various epistemological theses on the basis of scientific results. These objectives have been shared by the great philosophers of the past.

The aims and goals of philosophy of science as they affected *the* **BLUNDER** and education have been influenced by three prominent philosophers of science whose work I now discuss.

Sir Karl Popper (1902–1994)

Because his views about science are so frequently mentioned in the literature, I explain here in some detail how Popper contributed to *the* **BLUNDER** in a number of ways. These quotes give you an idea of his prominence in the second half of the 20th century.

In *Nature of Science* (1983), Dr. Henry Ellington says:

> The influence of Popper on the work of scientists had been
> profound, and it has been publicly acknowledged by many
> well-known figures, including Nobel Prize winners such as
> Sir Peter Medawar, Jacques Monod, and Sir John Eccles.
> Indeed, Eccles' advice to his colleagues is "to read and med-
> itate upon Popper's writings on the philosophy of science
> and adopt them as the basis of operation of one's scientific
> life." More and more scientists are now accepting this
> advice.

However, Popper's concepts were also very controversial. For example, Imre Lakatos (1922–1974) said in a lecture delivered in 1973 and
published in *For and Against Method* (1999), edited by Mateo
Motterlini:

> I think that the fact Popper's philosophy survived for so long
> is a sociological mystery.

A summary of Popper's views about science is given by Thomas
Nickles in *Scientific Discovery: Logic and Rationality* (1980):

> Popper, in his life-long attack on inductivism, has of course,
> tried to eliminate all inductive elements even in the theory
> of confirmation or, rather, "corroboration" (as he terms it).
> Despite their difference over scientific justification, how-
> ever, Popper and the positivists (for the most part: see
> Section II) agreed that what made theories scientific was
> their relation to test results, not how they were generated.
> Since (1) the method of discovery was strictly irrelevant,
> since (2) there was no reliable logic of discovery anyway, and
> since (3) the business of philosophy was to articulate the
> *logic* of scientific inquiry, Popper and the positivists agreed
> that discovery fell outside the proper domain of philosophy
> of science. Philosophy of science was essentially a logic of
> confirmation-corroboration.

In accordance with these claims, Popper claimed that science started
with problems and the hypothesis. Instead of advocating or admitting
the existence of the scientific method, he advocated following his
hypothetical-deductive scheme. He called it "scheme"; others
referred to it at times as method or process. His scheme is not practical to teach to students instead of the scientific method.

Thus, by denying the existence of the scientific method, Popper reinforced the claims of Conant and his followers.

Because Kuhn and Popper had a well-publicized debate about each other's positions and books, Kuhn's and Popper's views received more publicity than they otherwise would have. Thus, we have two nonbelievers in the scientific method adding to its woes. Looking back, it is amazing how much attention was paid to these men.

Summary of the Logic of Discovery Controversy

From previous explanations and quotations, you know that Popper and most other philosophers of science have claimed that, since there is no logic to discovery, this area does not belong to philosophy. In SM-14, the first six stages that are in Part 1 represent the context of discovery. In the context of confirmation, you begin with the hypothesis, with which philosophers like Popper claim science starts.

While Hanson is mentioned frequently in the literature for challenging Popper's position, I found Nobel Laureate Herbert Simon's explanation easier to understand. Recently, an even better article by Martin Gardner has appeared.

Evidence That It Was All One Additional Big Intellectual Blunder

Here is a more up-to-date review of Popper's work. The well-known Martin Gardner, writing in *Skeptical Inquirer* magazine (July, August 2001) in an article entitled "A Skeptical Look at Karl Popper," says:

> Sir Karl Popper, who died in 1994, was widely regarded as England's greatest philosopher of science since Bertrand Russell, indeed a philosopher of worldwide eminence. Today his followers among philosophers of science are a diminishing minority, convinced that Popper's vast reputation is enormously inflated.

> I agree. I believe that Popper's reputation was based mainly on his persistent but misguided efforts to restate commonsense views in a novel language that is rapidly becoming out of fashion.

In summary, if you hear of or read any claims that the scientific method does not exist based on Popper's statements, do not believe them.

Paul Feyerabend (1924–1994)

Since Feyerabend's works have been widely quoted and have contributed to *the* **BLUNDER**, I explain here what I found from reviewing only three of his many books, which is not a good sampling; I cover his best-known work, *Against Method* (1975).

Feyerabend was a student of Karl Popper who, in his book, disclaimed Popper's basic theory. Feyerabend was very familiar with Popper's misleading claims of "no scientific method," etc. and quoted him on these without clarifying how they related to *the* scientific method.

While the title *Against Method* indicates that Feyerabend is against *the* scientific method, this is probably not so. He did not have a clear idea of what the method really is.

Feyerabend is against rules, rigid methods, fixed thoughts, Popperism, Kuhnism, logical positivism, and other isms, fixed step-by-step methods, rational standards, etc. Thus he is not against method or guides, but rather he is against rigidity and more for "anything goes."

Feyerabend misunderstood the scientific method. Here are some quotes pertaining to his views of it in *Against Method*:

> Occasionally, the laws of scientific method, or what are thought to be the laws of scientific method by a particular writer, are even integrated into anarchism itself.

> The idea of a method that contains firm, unchanging, and absolutely binding principles for conducting the business of science meets considerable difficulty when confronted with the results of historical research. We find, then, that there is not a single rule, however plausible, and however firmly grounded in epistemology, that is not violated at some time or other.

His claims of "laws of scientific method" and "idea of a method that contains firm, unchanging, and absolute binding principles for conducting the business of science" are false representations of the scientific method.

Thus, Feyerabend cannot be claimed to be against *the* scientific method unless we can accept as accurate his mis-definitions of what it consists of. They are wrong.

The effect on education of Feyerabend's works has been:

He helped those perpetuating the false claim that the scientific method does not exist.

He influenced educational researchers and educational leaders against the scientific method.

Thomas Kuhn (1922–1996)

Even though Thomas Kuhn is known more as a philosopher and historian of science than as an educator, I devote a number of pages to him because he was also a major contributor to the spread of *the* **BLUNDER** to the education system and other domains.

In my research I found Kuhn to be one of the most quoted authors in the natural sciences and social sciences.

While I have shown that it was mainly Conant's influence, starting in 1947, that caused educators and others in the social sciences not to use or have to use the scientific method in their work, Kuhn, a protege of Conant, contributed to this with his book *The Structure of Scientific Revolutions* (1962) and his other works and activities.

Thus, Kuhn's book gave further justification to those in education, the humanities, and other social sciences to follow Conant's claim that the scientific method does not exist. He provided them with the excuse that they were following paradigms.

To give you an idea of Kuhn's influence and the respect he gained with many people, I present this quotation.

The following information about Kuhn comes from www. emory.edu:

> Of the five books and countless articles he published, Kuhn's most renowned work is *The Structure of Scientific Revolutions*, which he wrote while a graduate student in theoretical physics at Harvard. Initially published as a monograph in the International Encyclopedia of Unified Science, it was published in book form by the University of Chicago Press in 1962. It has sold some one million copies in 16 languages and is required reading in courses dealing with education, history, psychology, research, and, of course, history and philosophy of science. *Structure* has also generated

a good deal of controversy, and many of Kuhn's ideas have been powerfully challenged.

As mentioned above, his ideas have been "powerfully challenged." Almost all of the challenges to Kuhn have failed to point out the major reason for the success of his book: his close association with James B. Conant and Harvard University.

An exception is philosopher and professor Steve Fuller, who states in *Thomas Kuhn: A Philosophical History for Our Times* (2000):

> This enabled *Structure* to be accorded a charitable reading in diverse quarters once it appeared.

> In Kuhn's case, the power of his diffuse network of acquaintances came from a common culture that centered on the vision and actions of Harvard president James Bryant Conant. In Granovetter's terms, then, Kuhn had a singularly strong tie to Conant, who in turn had many weak ties to opinion leaders in American society. Indeed, Kuhn's dependence on the Conant network did not elude the Harvard General Education committee that denied him tenure.

Note from this statement in *James B. Conant* (1993), by James Hershberg, Kuhn's close relationship to Conant:

> For the next three years, Conant annually taught Nat Sci 4, reprising his old table-top demonstration lecture techniques, collaborating with up-and-coming scientists and historians of science (including I.B. Cohen, Thomas S. Kuhn, Gerald Holton, and Leonard K. Nash) who helped to design and teach the course.

Kuhn's Distorted View of the Structure of Science

I have shown that Conant influenced Kuhn to believe that the scientific method does not exist. Since most philosophers who challenged Kuhn have also supported the nonexistence of the scientific method or have said that it begins with the hypothesis, there have been few calling attention to the fact that Kuhn's views are incorrect because of the basic defect of his belief that the scientific method does not exist.

One author (Bruce Mazlish in *The Uncertain Sciences*, 1998) who realized this states:

By focusing on the changing results, the paradigms, *they are ignoring the constant feature: the scientific method*, which, though it changes and adapts itself in its particulars to the phenomena with which it must deal, *remains a consistent method in its essentials.*

Evidence of Kuhn's Lack of Knowledge of the Scientific Method

In his book *The Structure of Scientific Revolutions*, which also involves the whole structure of science, Kuhn ignores the scientific method, as it was reported to be in the literature by others than Conant and his misguided followers. He did make one reference to it in *The Essential Tension* (1977):

> Traditional discussions of scientific method have sought a set of rules that would permit any *individual* who followed them to produce sound knowledge. I have tried to insist, instead, that, though science is practiced by individuals, scientific knowledge is intrinsically a *group* product and that neither its peculiar efficacy nor the manner in which it develops will be understood without reference to the special nature of the groups that produce it. In this sense my work has been deeply sociological, but not in a way that permits that subject to be separated from epistemology. . .

This "traditional discussion" was very early in the history of the scientific method. Much more was known in 1977. In the 20th century very few claim that the scientific method consists of a "set of rules." This comment, and because Kuhn mentions nothing else about the scientific method in his books, is clear evidence that he is following Conant's false claims that it does not exist. All other conclusions about paradigms, movements, etc. have to be seriously questioned if Kuhn's basic foundational views of science crumble.

Kuhn's "Normal Science"

Kuhn attempted to differentiate between "normal science" and men whose research is based *on a shared paradigm*. His definition of normal science seems to be talking about scientific knowledge, whereas science is basically its method.

Now look at the tragic results of this false shared paradigm concept:

In his book *Thomas Kuhn: A Philosophical History for Our Times* (2000), Steve Fuller states:

All of these revelations induced a collective sigh of relief from practitioners of the humanities and the social sciences, who had a hard enough time making sense of each other, let alone agreeing on a common method. They quickly latched on to Kuhn's ideas and declared that they too were respectable knowledge producers laboring under paradigms.

Conclusion on Kuhn—A Tragedy of Errors

Even before reading Fuller's book in 2000, I was convinced that *The Structure of Scientific Revolutions* was a disaster to the proper understanding of the scientific method, and a book about the structure of science ignoring the scientific method should never have been written. Fuller does not write much about the scientific method, but his book is remarkable in the frank investigation and appraisal it presents of Kuhn and Conant that most other authors have failed to make.

Here is what Fuller says:

> I believe that a similar comedy of errors has marked the history of the reception of *The Structure of Scientific Revolutions* and its author, Thomas Kuhn. . . . A fundamental premise of my book, then, is that the impact of *The Structure of Scientific Revolutions* has been largely, though not entirely, for the *worse*.

I wholeheartedly agree that Kuhn's book and, more importantly, **the BLUNDER**, has been a comedy of errors or actually, because of its harm to education and other fields:

A Tragedy of Errors!

The few benefits from Kuhn's works have been dwarfed by their contribution to the perpetuation and spreading of **the BLUNDER**.

The Inability Thus Far of Philosophy To Become a Science

What we have now is constant disagreements among philosophers that continue year after year. We have no movement among them that clarifies issues and says "this is philosophy you can trust."

About the issue of whether philosophy should attempt to be a "science," Jean Piaget has this to say in *Insights and Illusions of Philosophy* (1965):

> From these premises Jaspers draws the following conclusions, which are precisely ours: "In philosophy there is no consensus of opinion, establishing a definitive knowledge... Contrary to science, philosophy under all its forms ought to dispense with a consensus of opinion, this ought to be implicit in its very nature."

There was even debate about philosophy becoming a science in Dewey's time. Alan W. Richardson wrote an article entitled "Engineering Philosophy of Science: American Pragmatism and Logical Empiricism in the 1930s," which appeared in the journal *Philosophy of Science* (September 2002).

Suggestion to Philosophers of Science

There is a great deal of irony in an amateur philosopher like me giving professional philosophers advice, but I did some study to arrive at my conclusions. The rule is "not who but what."

The fight for funding for research becomes more competitive all the time. Unless you work on something of real value to society rather than too much rehash of old controversial items, philosophy will suffer as a profession. It is this amateur's opinion that philosophy needs a modernization movement.

The theory that philosophers should not be concerned with the logic of discovery should be thrown out the window completely. Follow Professor Thomas Nickles and others in exploring discovery. Recognize, learn, and follow the scientific method (SM-14 type) to determine the best future for philosophy.

Thanks again to the many philosophers, dead and alive, for the help your works provided to me in the writing of *The Scientific Method Today*.

? ?

The Mystery

How could so many philosophers, who are historically supposed to tell scientists how science should be done, have been so wrong about the scientific method during the second half of the 20th century?

? ?

Chapter 34

Contribution of the Psychology Domain to *the* BLUNDER

Psychology is one of the social sciences, and I devoted many pages to the social sciences in general in Chapter 27. However, because of the importance of psychology to society, I cover it here separately.

- ◆ Unreliable Research in the Field of Psychology

- ◆ The Operating Policies of the Psychology Organizations

- ◆ My Unsuccessful Attempts to Get the Psychology Organizations to Study the Scientific Method Situation

- ◆ The Study of the Scientific Method Probably Belongs to Psychology

- ◆ Suggestions and Mystery

The psychology domain has not been as responsible for the origination and perpetuation of *the* BLUNDER as some others. However, because thinking and behavior are so involved, psychologists should never have allowed *the* BLUNDER to continue so unchallenged.

Many introductory college psychology textbooks briefly mention the scientific method. Others ignore it. Some authors of books on psychology cover it in greater detail. Examples are *Scientific Method in Psychology* (1955) by Clarence Brown and *Psychology's Scientific Endeavor* (1989) by Christopher Monte.

However, on the whole, the field has not adequately studied, used, and taught the scientific method. This is another reason a science of psychology has not developed.

Unreliable Research in the Field of Psychology

Examples of Psychologists' Misunderstanding of Research

I explain in Chapter 5 that to research is to use the scientific method (SM-14 type). As a result of *the* BLUNDER, the profession has not really adopted the scientific method. Again, because of *the* **BLUNDER**, there has not been adequate information available to psychologists. In addition, there is the probability of funding being cut off if they actively promote the scientific method. Here is an example of the misunderstanding and confusion.

The Task Force on Statistical Inference Initial Report (Draft) to the Board of Scientific Affairs of the American Psychological Association (www.apa.org/science/tfsi.html) as of August 23, 1999, states:

> (2) The need for theory-generating studies
>
> In its recent history, psychology has been dominated by the hypothetico-deductive approach. It is the view of the task force that researchers have too often been forced into the premature formulation of theoretical models in order to have their work funded or published.

The hypothetico-deductive approach or method is most often associated with a method that starts with the hypothesis. The Task Force realizes that this guidance is wrong, but fails to suggest the use of the scientific method. When a profession does not follow the scientific method (SM-14 type), there exists the usual situation of the unreliability of its research.

In a *Science News* (June 7, 1997) article entitled "Null Science," Bruce Bower reports:

> Geoffrey R. Loftus, a psychologist at the University of Washington in Seattle, experiences "a certain angst" about his discipline these days. Over the past 30 years, he has built a successful scientific career and now edits the journal Memory and Cognition. From this lofty vantage point, Loftus sees with dismay a research landscape dotted with dense stands of conflicting data that strangle theoretical advances at their roots.

Harm to the Field of Testing

Psychologists are often involved in preparing tests. To the extent that they do not follow the scientific method (SM-14 type), the reliability of these tests is questionable. The field of education, in particular, has been plagued with over-rated tests and important decisions made based on bad or partially incorrect tests.

Harm to the Nation's Thinking Overall

In 1910, John Dewey wrote a great book *How We Think*, pushing the scientific method. But, after Conant's false claims in 1946 that the scientific method does not exist, books on thinking were largely diverted away from basing programs on it. Thus, a "critical thinking movement" started rather than the development of a greater scientific method movement.

A Famous Psychologist Contributes to *the* BLUNDER

In 1955, B.F. Skinner, a famous Harvard psychologist, delivered an address of the President at the Eastern Psychological Association meeting. The address was entitled "A Case History in Scientific Method." Dr. Skinner said:

> But it is a mistake to identify scientific practice with the formalized constructions of statistics and scientific method. These disciplines have their place, but it does not coincide with the place of scientific research. They offer *a* method of science but not, as is so often implied, *the* method. As formal disciplines they arose very late in the history of science, and most of the facts of science have been discovered without their aid.

These comments, I believe, were in support of Conant's 1946 statements, which were intended to divert us from the scientific method in an attempt to promote case history studies. Thus, Skinner contributed to psychology's lack of use of the scientific method.

The Operating Policies of the Psychology Organizations

I did not conduct a thorough examination of the activities of these organizations. However, they seem to be going along with the existing situation, in which professional organizations are not recognizing the existence of the scientific method to any extent and are not promoting its teaching. In the case of the American Psychological Association, I found some references to it, but of a minor nature.

American Psychological Association

From the website apa.org:
> Based in Washington, DC, the American Psychological Association (APA) is a scientific and professional organization

that represents psychology in the United States. With more than 155,000 members, APA is the largest association of psychologists worldwide.

> The object of the American Psychological Association shall be to advance psychology as a science and profession and as a means of promoting health and human welfare. . .

Its position on the scientific method is shown by its National Standards for High School Psychology and Code of Ethics.

National Standards for Teaching of High School Psychology

The American Psychological Association estimates that 800,000 students take psychology courses every year. The APA's national standards, published in 1999, state: "Central to the objectives of a well-designed psychology course is an emphasis on scientific method." But that is the end of it. The standards discuss methods and research methods, scientific reasoning, etc. There is no clear presentation of the scientific method. It is to their credit that they did not deny its existence. In *The Scientific Method Today*, I quote Charles R. Foster (*Psychology for Life Today*, 1966). He points out that the word thinking is usually applied to mental processes that we identify as problem solving. The scientific method is the best problem-solving method known. The standards should cover it thoroughly.

Code of Ethics of the American Psychological Association—Great and Also Incomplete

To the great credit of the association, it has an extensive ethics code. The code, adopted June 1, 2003 (a revision of the original 1992 code), available on its web site (www.apa.org), contains nothing requiring the use of the scientific method. Instead, in Section 2.04, it says:

> Psychologists' work is based upon established scientific and professional knowledge of the discipline.

From my research of the scientific method, I make this observation:

This is not a clear enough definition. It must include a requirement that the research must be based on following the scientific method (SM-14 type).

My Unsuccessful Attempts to Get the Psychological Societies to Study the Scientific Method Situation

American Psychological Association

1997—I issued Challenge #16 to APA to study the scientific method situation. A report was sent to the officers, Board of Directors, and the six Members at Large.

No reply or action resulted.

Cognitive Science Society

From the website cognitivesciencesociety.org:

> The Cognitive Science Society, Inc. brings together researchers from many fields who hold a common goal: understanding the nature of the human mind.

The society has more than 1,000 members.

In *Thought and Knowledge* (1989), Diane Halpen states:

> Although psychology has been concerned with the way people think for much of its 100+ years of existence as an academic discipline, cognitive psychology, the branch of psychology that is concerned with thought and knowledge, has virtually dominated the field of psychology over the last 15 years. Psychologists have been concerned with learning about the skills and strategies used in problem solving, reasoning, and decision making and the way these abilities relate to intelligence. All of this interest in human thinking processes has given birth to a new area of psychology that has come to be known as cognitive process instruction. Its goal is to utilize the knowledge we have accumulated about human thinking processes and mechanisms in ways that can help people improve how they think.

Since the scientific method is essentially a problem-solving and decision-making method, you would think that cognitive psychologists would be especially interested in it. From what I have read, there appears to be a shocking lack of interest, which is contributing to the perpetuation of *the* **BLUNDER**. It is important that cognitive psychologists promptly recognize the scientific method.

I tried unsuccessfully to get the Cognitive Science Society to study the scientific method situation.

1997—I sent the society's Chair and Secretary/Treasurer a Special 1997 Report on the Scientific Method and Challenge #17 to study the scientific method situation.

American Psychological Society

This organization split off from APA in 1988. Its 12,000 members are more interested in psychological science.

I tried unsuccessfully to get the American Psychological Society to study the scientific method situation.

1997—I sent Challenge #15 to study the scientific method matter and a special report to two of the officers.

I received no answer. If they are especially interested in the science of psychology, then it is essential for them to study and promote the scientific method. To neglect to do so perpetuates *the* BLUNDER.

The record is bad! Not one of these organizations is promoting the scientific method, nor did any take action after receiving my reports. In spite of this, look at what I award them!

The Study of the Scientific Method Probably Belongs to Psychology

In Chapter 38 I reviewed and commented on which should be the home domain of the scientific method. Since no one aggressively and loudly claims it, I boldly took the initiative and awarded it to psychology. I explain why in Chapter 38.

However, the psychology field must show a much greater interest in the subject. In *Complex Problem Solving* (1991), Sternberg and Frensch state:

> Although complex problem solving has emerged as a field of psychology in its own right, it is a field that usually occupies a single chapter in textbooks on thinking, a part of a chapter in textbooks on cognitive psychology, and a part of a part of a chapter in textbooks on introductory psychology. The literature on complex problem solving is far-flung, and is

sometimes so technical that it is difficult for nonexperts to plow through.

Best Book on the Scientific Method by a Psychologist

In my 15-plus years of researching the scientific method, I hunted for books on the subject. The best book I ever found was by a social psychologist—*The Scientific Approach* (1967) by Carlo L. Lastrucci, a professor at the (then) San Francisco State College. This is to the credit of the profession, even though the book was not reviewed, accepted, and used to any extent in the field of psychology or by any domain.

The Next Great Advance in Psychology

More than 30 years ago I read a forecast by a psychologist that the next great advance in psychology would probably come from an outsider. I remember it because of my great interest in personal attributes.

I would now like to step up and say as an outsider that the next great advance in psychology is *a step back* to the 1920s, 1930s, and 1940s, when the profession was working toward the use of the scientific method until it was stopped by the Harvard/Conant group and misguided followers. So much has been learned since then about the scientific method system that it will be a great re-advance when psychology is redirected to the right path.

Suggestions to Psychologists

It is easy for me to suggest that people who are under what I believe is the domination of those perpetuating *the* **BLUNDER** should stick their necks out. Nevertheless, it is necessary for all domains to study the scientific method situation.

Therefore, I suggest that the psychology organizations, either individually or jointly, appoint a study panel to investigate the scientific method situation. This should also be done in self-interest. Psychologists thoroughly trained in the science of problem solving and decision making will be in great demand.

I remind all psychologists that

♦ Psychology will not really be a science until it meets the requirements I outline in Chapter 55.

- As an individual, you will not really be a scientist until you use the scientific method (SM-14 type).

- Review the article in the *New York Times* (March 9, 2004) "Defying Psychiatric Wisdom, These Skeptics Say 'Prove It.'" Public disputes like this between the members of the American Psychological Association and the American Psychological Society would not occur if all members of both organizations followed the scientific method.

Suggestion to the Public

Think about this quote I found in *Toward a Psychology of the Scientist* (1981) by Sonja C. Grover. The quote is from *The Subjective Side of Science* (1974) by I. Mitroff:

> We can no longer afford to ignore psychology in any future accounts of science. . .[and] that one of the greatest purposes of [science] is as much—perhaps more so—to learn about ourselves as it is to learn about nature.

If you do not undertake a study of the scientific method situation, there will be no complete end to the biggest intellectual and educational blunder in history. It is preventing us from obtaining more reliable knowledge about ourselves.

? ?

The Mystery

In editing this chapter it occurred to me that I should be claiming that *the* BLUNDER is also one of the biggest behavioral blunders in history. The fact that for a half century so many in the world did not really challenge *the* BLUNDER to any extent should be studied. So the mystery is:

Why, on a matter of such "supreme importance," (Conant) have so many people followed poor leaders?

And a question: How fast will those whose profession concerns mental processes start to help correct *the* BLUNDER?

? ?

Chapter 35

Contribution of the Carnegie Corporation to *the* BLUNDER

During Dr. Conant's time, famous foundations such as the Carnegie Corporation, the Ford Foundation, and the Rockefeller Foundation were frequent supporters of his educational activities. This is understandable, as he was a famous and influential man in his day. The Carnegie Corporation was more directly connected to Conant and his claims that the scientific method does not exist. Therefore, here I review their contribution to *the* BLUNDER. Please understand that they have done a tremendous amount of good in their many years of activity, but not for the scientific method.

- ◆ The Carnegie Corporation Was Involved in the Start of *the* BLUNDER

- ◆ The Harms of the Influence of the Carnegie Corporation

- ◆ My Efforts To Get the Carnegie Corporation To Study the Scientific Method Matter

- ◆ Suggestions and Mystery

The Carnegie Corporation Was Involved in the Start of *the* BLUNDER

In his biography *James B. Conant* (1993), James Hershberg states:

> Conant now [1946] proposed creating a commission to study how to teach the "tactics and strategy of science" within the larger context of "General Education in a Free Society." The goal, he explained, would be to inculcate among lay students not the content or principles of science "but rather an appreciation of how scientific research is really done . . . the difference between controlled and uncontrolled observation and experiment; the difference between basic research and applied research; and the relation of both to development and production." To raise funds for this project, he approached the Carnegie Corporation in New York, which soon signed on to

the venture, now scaled down to a plan to instigate the teaching of college-level courses and the development of suitable research materials.

At Harvard, Conant volunteered to take on this assignment himself, and inaugurated a new undergraduate course, Natural Sciences 4: "On Understanding Science. . ."

This course was based in part on Conant's book *On Understanding Science* (1947). You will recall that this is the first book in which Conant claimed that the scientific method was only an "alleged method" and that he wanted to teach "the tactics and strategy of science" via the historical case history method, which never proved to be practical.

Because of Conant's great reputation, it is easy to understand how the Carnegie Corporation agreed to support him. Nevertheless, great harm has resulted. I believe this created the atmosphere at Carnegie that the scientific method does not exist that influenced all its subsequent activities, even down to 2005.

Another event that may have influenced the Carnegie Corporation was Professor Peter Caw's book, *The Philosophy of Science* (1966). The Carnegie Corporation granted him leave from his regular duties near the completion of the book. This book belittles and misrepresents what the scientific method really is. Whatever his employment with the Corporation was, he may have added to the erroneous opinions held by the officers and trustees about the scientific method. The book could also have sent another signal to researchers and educators of the Carnegie Corporation's position on the scientific method.

Chapter 48 gives you an idea of what was known about the scientific method in the 1800s and early 1900s. A great deal more was known by 1946. The irony of the situation is that the major method of understanding, advancing, and applying knowledge, and understanding the reliability of knowledge, is the scientific method. Yet the Carnegie Corporation supported Conant in his denial of its existence.

It is my opinion in this public matter of great importance to society that, by supporting Conant in the 1940s and ignoring my letters and reports to them about *the* BLUNDER in 1996, they have done the opposite of their mission statement, which Carnegie set in 1911:

the advancement and diffusion of knowledge and understanding

Normally, whether or not the organization is accomplishing its mission statement would be no concern of mine. However, because of its preeminent status in the philanthropic and education fields and the influence it wields by its grant making, it may be influencing other people or organizations that do not want to offend the Carnegie Corporation as far as the scientific method is concerned. Grant seekers have such a hard time obtaining funds that they must be sensitive to the beliefs of grant makers.

The Harms of the Influence of the Carnegie Corporation

I started to list how the influence of the Carnegie Corporation may have perpetuated *the* **BLUNDER**. However, the foundation has done so much and helped so many, that I cannot see what I would accomplish. It is sufficient to say that the Corporation has made numerous grants to Harvard, the American Association for the Advancement of Science, the National Academy of Sciences, *Education Week*, and many others who have helped perpetuate *the* **BLUNDER**. I have no way of knowing how great the Corporation's influence has been on these organizations.

I mention in Chapter 53, Legal Considerations of the Scientific Method, the Carnegie Corporation's help to projects in the legal field that have not responded to my efforts to get the scientific method recognized.

My Efforts to Get the Carnegie Corporation to Study the Scientific Method Matter

In 1992 I sent the Carnegie Corporation a letter and a copy of my first booklet. I never received a reply.

A Special 1996 Report to the Carnegie Corporation was sent to then president David A. Hamburg and to the trustees. I challenged them to appoint a committee, panel, etc. to study the matter of the scientific method. To make it easy to read for busy people, it was only five pages long and included a copy of the 1994 edition of my small booklet *The General Pattern of the Scientific Method*. I offered to provide more of my reports and challenges to various organizations.

The only thing I ever received in return was a letter stating that my request for a grant could not be considered as part of the Carnegie Corporation's program. I had not asked for a grant, so I do not know if this was simply inefficiency or a brush off.

I am shocked that I received no reply from the trustees of the Carnegie Corporation. In my crusade, I have found that directors, trustees, and officials seem to take their organizational responsibilities very lightly, despite my warning to them about doing so.

Suggestions to the Carnegie Corporation

Since I sent you my special 1996 report, your new President, Vaartan Gregorian, stated in his pamphlet *Some Preliminary Thoughts* (1997):

> Some of the questions I have posed to my colleagues and the trustees are: What are we doing? Why are we doing it? How well are we doing it, especially in relation to the work of other foundations? How does it serve Carnegie Corporation's overall mission to advance and diffuse knowledge and understanding?

It is my contention that you cannot adequately "advance and diffuse knowledge and understanding" without the use and promotion of the method of knowledge—the scientific method.

To avoid the waste of your corporate grants, my recommendation to you is that you should study this book and the evidence in it concerning the misunderstandings and blunders about the scientific method and take action to spread a correct understanding of the scientific method.

? ?

The Mystery

Among the trustees of the Carnegie Corporation are attorneys, college officials, professors, foundation officials, publication officials, etc. Yet I received no replies to my report.

Why not?

? ?

Chapter 36

Contribution of Historians of Science and the History of Science Society to *the* BLUNDER

◆ The History of Science Society

◆ My Unsuccessful Attempts to Get the History of Science Society to Study the Scientific Method Situation

◆ History of the Scientific Method

◆ Suggestion and Mystery

As I conducted my research, I was shocked to find that the historians of science seem to devote all their efforts and writings to the product of science and very little to the way scientific knowledge is produced. The scientific method is largely ignored. In my early 1992 efforts, the History of Science Society was the only complete association membership to whom I sent a mailing. I limited the mailing to about 1,993, those with addresses in the United States. I probably wanted to be sure that they paid attention to the efforts I was making to correct the mistake most top leaders in national education reform were making so that history could be reported accurately.

The History of Science Society

From one of the society's brochures:

> The History of Science Society is the world's largest society dedicated to understanding science, technology, medicine, and their interactions with society in their historical context. Founded in 1924, the Society now serves more than 4,000 individual members and institutions as both a learned society and a professional association. Its primary role, to advance research and teaching in the history of science, is achieved through its publications, its national meetings, and sponsorship of awards and lecture programs. As a professional association, HSS provides its members with information about research trends, grants, fellowships, and jobs. HSS also works to inform government agencies, Congressional

committees, and private foundations about the uses and needs of the field.

Internal Politics—Largely Influenced by George Sarton

The society was formed in 1924 by a historian of science, George Sarton (1884–1956), who was a professor of the History of Science at Harvard University from 1920 to 1951. He was also the founder of the society's magazine, *Isis*, which became its official journal. According to Richard Duschl in *Restructuring Science Education* (1990), Sarton established a style of doing history of science.

In writing history, it is far easier for historians just to recite what happened and give the results than to show how the results were achieved through the scientific method. However, history is far more useful if it shows science in action and if the discovery process and method used are included. Sarton readily admitted that he was not very familiar with methods, for in *The Study of the History of Mathematics (1936)* he states:

> There are a great many books dealing with the methods of science, and I could not tell which are best, as I have read only a few.

He then lists about 10 books such as Pearson, Poincare, Westaway, Ritchie, Whitehead, Campbell, etc. concerning scientific method. Yet in just a few places in his books he seems to sense the importance of the experimental method, which is the earlier name for the scientific method. The following are abstracted from Sarton's *History of Science and the New Humanism* (1937):

> The central method of science is the experimental method, but it has taken thousands of years to discover it.

> The experimental method is in appearance the most revolutionary of all methods. Does it not lead to astounding discoveries and inventions? Does it not change the face of the world so deeply and so often that superficial people think of it as the very spirit of change?

> New inspirations may still, and do still, come from the East, and we shall be wiser if we realize it. In spite of its prodigious triumphs, the scientific method is not all-sufficient.

Thus Sarton and other historians of science who followed his example made major contributions to **the BLUNDER***.*

Sarton taught Conant and had a close relationship with him during Conant's graduate school days and when Conant became President of Harvard.

If Sarton and other historians of science, in their writings and teaching, had properly stressed the method of science—the experimental method—the scientific method—along with the accomplishments of science, then Conant would not likely have been able to say that the method does not exist.

On its website, the American Historical Association claims that "history helps us understand change and how the society we live in came to be." It is my claim that historians of science have blundered badly in not properly reporting science—"and how the society we live in came to be"—by the scientific method.

Operating Policies of the History of Science Society

In reading some of the issues of the society's newsletter and the journal *Isis*, I found no discussion about the scientific method. I believe that this results from Sarton's style and then Conant's statement (Chapter 3) that the historians of science who emphasize that there is no such thing as the scientific method are doing a public service. Thus, the society appears to have paid little or no attention to the scientific method.

My Unsuccessful Attempts to Get the History of Science Society to Study the Scientific Method Situation

1992—I sent the first edition of my booklet to 1,993 members.

1995—I sent a few letters.

1996—I sent Challenge #11 to appoint a panel or committee to study the misunderstandings and disputes about the scientific method and issue a scholarly report. I included my Reports #5, 6, and 7 and the 1994 editions of my two booklets.

Even a wide distribution (1,993) to all U.S. members in 1992 and a variety of reports elicited no reaction to my research and then my challenge.

History of the Scientific Method

I found no book on the 20th century history of the scientific method. I find this rather amazing, but again it is a result of *the* **BLUNDER**.

As far as the 19th century goes, there is an excellent article by Laurens Laudan, with a lengthy bibliography, in *History of Science*, volume 7 (1968), edited by Crombie and Hoskins.

At the end of the article, Laudan points out that the article terminates at 1900 and there is a need for someone to supplement it from 1900 to 1935. I would add 1935 to 2000 and on. The obvious reason that this very important work has not been done is that there are no grants available and the fear of the Harvard/Conant group and misguided followers (or whoever they are).

Suggestion

To end their contribution to *the* **BLUNDER**, the historians of science should realize their responsibility to science and history and really fully study my claims and the scientific method. They should then fully report on the method when writing history, to the extent that it can be done.

? ?

The Mystery

Why, after sending a report to 1,993 members of the History of Science Society, did I get no response or action?

? ?

Chapter 37

Contribution of Teachers Unions to *the* BLUNDER

Here I, as a proponent of the scientific method, must try to be unbiased despite the opinions I had about unions before I started to research the scientific method in 1989.

The teachers union situation is complex. I have not had time to study it in great detail, but I present some thoughts about it.

Effect of *the* BLUNDER on Unions

The BLUNDER has caused so many educational fads, ignoring of teachers' needs, and poor and unreliable educational research that it has enabled the teachers unions to grow faster and larger than might otherwise have been the case. Evidence of this is their size today. Unions are not noted for educational research, but they have done some to support their claims. In recent years they have started to do more, claiming that the educators' current research is unsatisfactory or incomplete. How good their new research is remains to be seen.

There is criticism that the research done by unions is biased. When all students and adults have been properly educated in the scientific method, I hope we can also expect better research from the union researchers. In addition, the public and educators will be much better judges of the research offered after *the* BLUNDER is corrected.

Contribution of the Teachers Unions to *the* BLUNDER

From my research it is hard to specify any great contribution of the teachers unions to *the* BLUNDER about the scientific method, other than the fact that they have participated in it, and often restrictive union contract provisions harm education.

I did send just a few letters about the scientific method to the teachers unions and received no replies.

Blaming Teachers Unions for the Ills of Education

Many authors, business people, educational leaders, members of the public, etc. in books, editorials, magazines, speeches, and newspapers, place major *blame on the teachers unions for failing schools, bad teachers, and opposition to reform efforts.* This is not where I found the major blame to be in my research. In this book I show that

343

- Our top educational leaders are the ones most responsible for the ills of education that are preventable or correctable.

- Union policies preventing removal of "bad teachers" have been heavily criticized. While they seem wrong, we really don't have a fair system of identifying "bad teachers."

- Unions often seem to stand in the way of reform, but the claim that unions are opposed to reform efforts is only partially correct. My complaint is the opposite, that teachers unions allowed so many fads and disastrous reforms to be instituted.

Incentive Compensation Plans for Teachers

Many business leaders and others have been pushing for incentive compensation plans for teachers based on the theory that they work in business and should be used in schools. However, incentive plans that are not carefully designed are failures. The unions have, to a great extent, opposed them, with some minor exceptions.

We have many incentive, bonus, etc. plans now being implemented. There are already complaints about them based on experience. Basically, what is happening is that we are again dashing ahead with a "reform" without adequate research, testing, and follow-up. There is a need for a permanent specialized SM-14 type national research center on teacher compensation. This center should examine and closely follow all existing plans. It should design a few incentive plans for careful pilot testing. Instead, we are dashing ahead haphazardly with a wide variety. The center should examine the whole field of teacher compensation.

Conflicting Missions

The book *Conflicting Missions* (2001), edited by Tom Loveless, former public school teacher and professor at Harvard University, now director of the Brown Center on Education Policy at the Brookings Institution, states:

> . . . a serious gap exists between what we think we know about teachers unions and what we really know.

The problem is that his book, like other books on education reform, will not be read by enough people. Some or many of its conclusions will not be studied further and applied if found reliable.

The American Federation of Teachers' advertisement about "Redesigning Schools to Raise Achievement" in the January 21, 2004 issue of *Education Week* sounds impressive. It merits study and expansion if it is as good as it is described.

Do We Have a "Good Old Boys Union"?

There is so much bashing of teachers unions that my mind keeps jumping from thoughts about my opponents to the existence of the scientific method. There seems to me to be a "union" of old boys or someone who is "blackballing" my attempts to correct *the* **BLUNDER**. This is evidenced by the lack of acceptance of my many challenges to study the scientific method situation and no publicity about my campaign and reports in the educational and professional journals. So those concerned about education and who bash unions in their desire to improve education I invite to aid me in my fight against the "good old boys union" perpetuating *the* **BLUNDER**.

Suggestions

◆ Teachers unions should study the scientific method situation. It holds the promise of ending some of the numerous injustices done to teachers over the years. It has the potential to improve the working conditions of teachers more than almost anything else. If they use the scientific method in their own educational research and reform recommendations, they could become a major party to efficient educational reform.

◆ Teachers unions are here to stay. Considering again that education is a half-trillion dollar to a trillion-dollar-a-year industry, it is unfortunate, as shown by the book *Conflicting Missions*, how little reliable information is known and has been accumulated about teachers unions.

Therefore, I suggest the establishment of a

permanent specialized SM-14 type national research center
on teachers unions

If we want concessions and changes from teachers unions, we should furnish reliable knowledge from the application of the scientific method to the ills of education.

Chapter 38

Contribution of No Home Domain for the Scientific Method to *the* BLUNDER

♦ Reminder of the Importance of Scientific Method

♦ The Reason No One Is Really Claiming the Scientific Method

♦ An Analysis of Most Appropriate Home Domains

♦ I Boldly Award It to Psychology

Reminder of the Importance of the Scientific Method

Science is its method. On page 33 of *The Scientific Method Today* and at the beginning of this book I quote Dr. Vannevar Bush on the value of science. Throughout this book I stress its value. It has been a massive gold mine for society—the golden method of knowledge. (Each of us has our own gold mine in his or her "mind.") But the scientific method got lost in our educational field and other fields as a result of *the* BLUNDER.

It Is a Universal Method—It Belongs to All Domains

While scientists have been the leaders in using, recognizing, and developing the scientific method, other domains have helped. It is the complete method of creative problem solving and decision making for all domains.

The supporting ingredients used at the various stages of the method, which include creative, non-logical, logical, and technical methods, can be used in all domains or altered to a specific domain's requirements. Each domain will also have specialized methods, techniques, procedures, and skills specific to its requirements. Thus, all must aid in the use, development, and teaching of the scientific method. As the scientific method is a universal method, it needs a home domain. Completely divided responsibility often results in confusion. The misunderstandings we have had for more than 40 years probably would not have occurred if one domain were officially responsible.

The Reason No One Is Really Claiming the Scientific Method

At present the Harvard/Conant group and misguided followers (or whoever they are) are in control of a lot of government spending, and, claiming that the scientific method does not exist, are providing no funds for its study. So no one really cares in which home domain it is, or they are reluctant to speak out. Before long this will change, and then perhaps it will be fought over. However, the fighting could take decades or more. In recent years knowledge has increased much faster. We know a lot about the scientific method today. There is no reason we should not settle the issue quickly.

I present here some thoughts and quotations concerning the domain-in which the main responsibility for analysis, summarization and teaching of the scientific method belongs. I consider the following:

natural sciences	sociology
technology	psychology
philosophy	history of science
education	liberal arts

Before considering them individually, the words of John Ziman, a physicist, are of interest. The following appears in *Public Knowledge—The Social Dimension of Science* (1968):

> By assigning the intellectual aspects of Science to the professional philosophers we make of it an arid exercise in logic; by allowing the psychologists to take possession of the personal dimension we overemphasize the mysteries of 'creativity' at the expense of rationality and the critical power of well-ordered argument; if the social aspects are handed over to the sociologists, we get a description of research as an N-person game, with prestige points for stakes and priority claims as trumps. The problem has been to discover a unifying principle for Science in all its aspects.

This illustrates that it is not easy to find an ideal home domain for the scientific method—the intellectual aspects of seeking knowledge.

An Analysis of Most Appropriate Home Domains

The Natural Sciences

In *Scientific Method: Function in Research and Education* (1932), Truman L. Kelley states:

We must grant to scientists the right to say what the scientific method is, just as we must grant to philosophers the right to say what philosophy is, provided in each instance performance is in line with the claim.

Just as you often hear that philosophers tell scientists "what they ought to do," you also hear that "science is what scientists actually do." The recognition and development of the scientific method have mainly been done by natural scientists, with help from other domains. The stages of the scientific method are natural ones and are not likely to change to any extent. It is a different story for the supporting ingredients. There are, in addition to the old basic ones, new techniques, new procedural principles, new thinking skills, new ethics, new understanding of how the brain works, and personal attributes being called for all the time.

In *Out of My Later Years* (1956), Albert Einstein makes this comment, an indication of the universal nature of the scientific method:

> The whole of science is nothing more than a refinement of everyday thinking. It is for this reason that the critical thinking of the physicist cannot possibly be restricted to the examination of the concepts of his own specific field. He cannot proceed without considering critically a much more difficult problem, the problem of analyzing the nature of everyday thinking.

Scientists have not been interested in studying and analyzing the scientific method. This comment has been made by many authors. They say that they are too busy doing science. In *Scientific Method* (1972), Feibleman states:

> At the present time science is taught largely on the apprentice method, and the scientist is not particularly aware that he is following any established procedure; rather is he always occupied with some specific problem involved in that procedure, guided chiefly by past experience, by accepted tradition, training, memory, and imitation.

While natural scientists' past achievements, experience in, and development of the method should be carefully utilized, it appears that the natural sciences is not the best home domain for the scientific method—the complete method of creative problem solving and decision making.

Technology

Most of the reasons that apply to the natural sciences domain also apply to the technology domain. Technologists have been great appliers of theories, etc. using the scientific method and furthering our knowledge in the process. Technology has done an excellent job on standardization. To be taught universally, the scientific method needs some standardization, but, of course, none that restricts its flexibility. In addition, new and better ways to teach it are needed. Our technologists' input on this is important. But, once again, it does not appear that technology should be the main home domain for the scientific method.

Education

While a very important feature of the scientific method system is the need to be taught, the domain of education does not seem to be the one for the further development of the method. However, the input of educators will surely be needed in helping to develop the way it should be taught.

History of Science

Historians of science are too concerned with the past. The scientific method is more devoted to the future. Therefore it appears that this domain is not qualified.

Sociology

While the science-technology-society movement and thinking about the social nature of science have been growing rapidly, it still does not appear that this is the home domain for the scientific method.

Philosophy and Philosophy of Science

There is frequent mention in the literature that it is the duty of philosophers to tell scientists how science ought to be done.

For a more detailed outline of philosophy of science, see Chapter 33. Based on the points covered in that chapter, I do not think that philosophers of science are the ones to be mainly responsible for the scientific method for these reasons:

◆ We have only a relatively small number of philosophers.

◆ Since Conant's statements and Popper's claims, they have largely abandoned any interest in a full formula for the scientific method.

◆ Philosophy is not taught to any extent below the college level.

◆ A great amount of the deep thinking about the scientific method has already been done. It is now a job of abstracting, clarifying, refining, and extending knowledge and learning how the brain works. Philosophers may not be qualified or want to do this.

Therefore, I believe that philosophers have disqualified themselves, even though they have been famous throughout history for thinking and their intellectual pursuits.

Psychology

In *Scientific Method* (1968), M. Weatherall, former professor at the University of London, states:

> Scientists today pursue knowledge with such specialization that a physicist, a medical scientist, and a psychologist are likely to find each other's work incomprehensible. But all science has a common foundation which may be understood by any of them and which is not difficult for a non-scientist to grasp. That foundation is not any particular body of factual knowledge but a way of thinking and acting which together form scientific method. Science, in fact, is what scientists do. Study of scientific method is the study of how they do it, and is properly a branch of psychology, particularly important to all practising scientists and to anyone who is interested in scientists and science.

The key words above are "thinking" and "acting." Thus, it appears to me that the home domain for the scientific method should be psychology. Another reason is that we have far more psychologists than philosophers. Many people will be needed to teach it.

I Boldly Award It to Psychology

Since no domain is loudly and aggressively claiming the scientific method, and since no one else is talking about where it belongs, I hereby boldly take the initiative and award it to psychology.

Chapter 39

The Contribution of Business and Industry
to *the* BLUNDER

It is important for business and industry to help in the education of our students. Many companies and their officers and personnel are making important contributions in money and time to education. Their scholarship efforts and help to local schools have been especially effective. In my criticism of some of their other national efforts, I do not want to discourage their work, but hope my comments will lead to their help in ending *the* **BLUNDER** and more effective use of their money and time.

HARMS TO BUSINESS AND INDUSTRY CAUSED BY *THE* BLUNDER

- Business and Industry Are Not as Efficient as They Should Be

- Business and Industry Action on the Need for Thinking

- *The* **BLUNDER**'s Effects on Education Are Discouraging Some Business and Industry Leaders from Helping Education

CONTRIBUTION OF BUSINESS AND INDUSTRY TO *THE* BLUNDER

- Many Business Leaders and Business Organizations Are Active in Education

- The Misapplication of Basic Business Principles to Education

- Hooray for Business!

- My Attempts to Inform Business and Industry Organizations about *the* **BLUNDER**

- Summary, Suggestions, and Mysteries

HARMS TO BUSINESS AND INDUSTRY CAUSED BY *THE* BLUNDER

Because the scientific method has not been taught to any extent in our schools, it has also affected the education of our business and industry leaders. This has resulted in great harm in these domains. I cover this in more detail in Chapter 46, Harms to Business and Industry.

Business and Industry Are Not as Efficient as They Should Be

A direct result of not being adequately taught the scientific method and its associated thinking skills is that business and industry are not as efficient as they otherwise might be. The book *The Professional Decision Maker* (1983) by Ben Heirs has a page on

America's Future—A Declaration on Behalf of our Brain

A few points Heirs emphasizes are:

—To face our day-to-day responsibilities, how should we best manage our brain?

—In practical terms, what does it mean to "think"?

These are questions to which all of our managers should know the answer, but few do.

As a consequence, this failure is causing many of our most important managers and leaders in the United States to make a fundamental mistake. They are not taking practical *thinking* anywhere near as seriously as they should—that is, the kind of thinking we have to use to operate and guide into the future our government organizations, business corporations, educational systems and private lives.

Remember, the scientific method encompasses all the mental activity stages of a complete act of thought. It is the greatest quality control method ever recognized and developed.

Business and Industry Action on the Need for Thinking

While our managers and leaders are still not familiar with the need for the scientific method, they are well aware of employees' lack of proper education and thinking abilities, as shown by this quote from the *Wall Street Journal* (March 1, 1990):

'C' Stands for Company, Turned Into Classroom

Companies learn they have a lot to teach.

Within the next three years, 93% of the largest U.S. companies will be teaching employees the three R's and other basic work skills, according to a survey by the American Society for Training and Development.

Corporate Curriculum

Percentage of companies planning to teach these skills in the next three years

Teamwork	39%
Problem solving	38
Oral communication	34
Creative thinking	31
Writing	28
Reading	23

Note that 38 percent and 31 percent plan to teach problem solving and creative thinking. For this to be done effectively, the scientific method should be taught. However, it is not. At least I know of no corporation that includes it in its training program. This is understandable, as so many leaders have been taught that it does not exist.

The BLUNDER'S Effects on Education Are Discouraging Some Business and Industry Leaders from Helping Education

USA Today published an article by Del Jones on September 18, 2002, that stated:

> Many businesses and corporate foundations say they have grown so frustrated with the pace of public education reform that they are ready to cut back on contributions to public schools.

> These businesses saw themselves as the cavalry in the 1990s, riding to the rescue and injecting public schools with business practices of standards and accountability. Now those companies, after giving billions of dollars to public schools over the last decade, are falling back on perhaps the first rule of business: Don't throw good money after bad.

Correcting *the* **BLUNDER** should stop this slow-up in their helping education.

THE CONTRIBUTION OF BUSINESS AND INDUSTRY TO *THE* BLUNDER

Many Business Leaders and Business Organizations Are Active in Education

Louis V. Gerstner, President of IBM, wrote a book *Reinventing Education* (1994) and sponsored the Educational Summit of 1996. An earlier president of IBM, John F. Akers, headed a 1991 task force of America's largest corporations at the request of President George Bush. The National Alliance of Business sponsored the Business Coalition for Education Reform Educational Initiative. The list of those active in education goes on and on.

In general, business leaders were campaigning for a variety of objectives, with the main emphasis on:

> standards   school choice
> testing   accountability

They made no mention of improving the quality of the work of our top educational leaders.

The No Child Left Behind Act of 2001. Business leaders were influential in the passage of this act, and most have supported its implementation.

Subject Matter versus Creativity. In the past, our curriculum has been heavily weighted toward teaching subject matter rather than creativity, problem solving, decision making, and entrepreneurship. Despite this, some teachers and organizations have made efforts to promote creative activities in their classes.

I and others warn our business leaders that there are indications that the No Child Left Behind Act causes so much time to be devoted to "teaching to the test" that creative teaching activities are suffering in our suburban schools, where they have largely occurred in the past. Despite repeated claims by many business leaders of the soundness of the basic principle that students should be problem solvers and decision makers, I will show in this chapter how my efforts to get the scientific method accepted by them have been a failure.

The Misapplication of Capitalistic Principles to Education

In Chapter 25 I covered "The Disaster of the Misapplication of Capitalistic Principles to Public K-12 Education." I hope that our business and industry leaders will study this situation carefully. We want our teachers to teach the value of the capitalist system.

Hooray for Business!

In this chapter, I have been highly critical of the practicability of many of the efforts of business to help education.

However, here I congratulate them—even if the action is years late, at least it is now on the right path. The *Wall Street Journal* (May 7, 2003) reports:

> The Business Roundtable is calling on state and federal governments to rethink the way they provide and fund early-childhood education, saying early intervention is the only way to narrow the gap in achievement between students from lower- and higher-income families.
>
> The group of chief executives called on states to "take the lead in developing and funding a coherent early childhood education system" from today's patchwork approach. The federal government, it said, "should make high-quality early childhood education a national priority...focusing on the children most in need."
>
> The group, which joined with Corporate Voices for Working Families, a nonprofit advocacy group for working families based in Bethesda, Md., plans to formally announce its position today. It said that universal education programs for three- and four-year-olds will help lower long-term education costs by reducing the number of children who need special education services while improving high school performance and graduation rates. Without government commitment to preschool education, it said, schools won't produce an adequate work force.
>
> "These are guys who care about the bottom line, and this is a smart, bottom-line investment," said Amy Wilkins, president of the Trust for Early Education, a nonprofit education advocacy group in Washington.

"Rethink" the way states and the federal government provide and fund early childhood education is the important point. The key, as the report points out, is that only 47 percent of low socioeconomic status kindergartners are likely to have attended a center-based program (including Head Start) before entering kindergarten. Until close to 100 percent of urban 3- and 4-year-olds are in good programs involving parent and community participation, the problem will not be substantially improved. How much effort will business put into accomplishing this? It will take a lot of money.

I may have to take back my "Hooray for Business," because, since this announcement, I haven't seen business organizations following through to any extent.

My Attempts to Inform Business and Industry Organizations about *the* BLUNDER

I could not cover all business and industry groups, but I do report on a few that I tried to influence to study the scientific method situation.

Business Roundtable

In a *Wall Street Journal* (March 20, 1991) article "Let's Get to Work on Education," John Akers, Chairman of IBM Corporation and the Business Roundtable Education Task Force, stated:

> The nation's 200 leading corporations, members of the Business Roundtable, are pledging their resources for 10 years to work with Secretary of Education Lamar Alexander and the 50 governors and their legislatures and schools to help America reach the national education goals of President Bush.

I had high hopes in 1992 when I wrote to the Business Roundtable about my efforts to get the scientific method situation studied. Business is often praised or said to be efficient.

However, all that resulted was that the executive director (an educator) advised me to contact the National Research Council, which I had already done.

My observation is that Harvard, which does not teach the scientific method, indirectly exerts a strong influence on the activities of business and industry.

In *The New York Times* (June 18, 2000) David Leonhardt reported:

> If there is an intellectual center of big business, it is the immaculately maintained faux-Georgian campus of Harvard Business School, for nearly a century the training ground for the people who run and advise the world's largest companies. From turning out future chief executives of I.B.M., Merck and Procter & Gamble to being the home of strategy gurus like Michael E. Porter, Harvard has practically stamped its crest on the large industrial companies that defined the 20th-century economy.

Other Groups Contacted in 1992

The first editions of my booklets were also sent to:

American Management Association
American Productivity and Quality Center
Chamber of Commerce of the United States
Committee for Economic Development
National Alliance of Business
Triangle Coalition for Service and Technical Education

1996 National Education Summit

This appeared to me to be a very important meeting, so I went to a lot of trouble to try to reach the people involved. Each governor was to bring a corporate guest to the summit. This is what was on the agenda, according to the Summit's literature:

> Thank you for your interest in the 1996 National Education Summit. Hosted by Louis V. Gerstner, Jr., Chairman and CEO of IBM Corporation, Wisconsin Governor Tommy G. Thompson, Chairman of both the National Governors' Association and the Education Commission of the States, and Governor Bob Miller, Vice-Chairman of the National Governors' Association, the Summit will provide an opportunity for Governors and business leaders to recommit their energy, time, and resources to improving student achievement through significantly higher academic standards and accountability and through the effective use of information technologies. The goal of the Summit is to build commitment among participants for prompt actions that will help states and communities build consensus and develop and

implement high academic standards, assessments, and accountability. The Summit will also serve as a catalyst for other discussions and activities on these important issues.

A Record of What I Did

1996—To each of the 50 governors I sent two copies of a 20-page report, A Special Report to Those Attending the Education Summit in March 1996, one copy for the governor and one for the corporate guest. I have no way of knowing whether the extra copy was passed on to the corporate guest.

Again, no action resulted from my calling their attention to "The Biggest and Most Expensive Blunder That Has Ever Occurred in the History of Science and Education."

I received a number of letters acknowledging receipt of the report. However, the Summit ignored the report in the actions taken at its meeting.

I also wrote to

American Enterprise Institute (1995)
National Association of Manufacturers (1998)
American Society of Training Directors (2000)

Council on Competitiveness

If anything is of major importance to America's competitiveness, it is the education in and use of the complete method of creative problem solving and decision making. Consider the situation today. The complete method of creative problem solving and decision making is known. However, it is taught in bits and pieces and not as an entity. This interferes with getting the most out of our human resources. This situation influenced my decision to send a large mailing to the Council on Competitiveness in 1997.

Who They Are

The Council on Competitiveness is a private, nonprofit advocacy organization comprised of 150 CEOs from industry, academia, and labor that is dedicated to improving the competitiveness of U.S. companies and workers in world markets.

Record of My Attempts

1992—I sent a set of the first edition of my booklets.

1997—I sent to 202 members and officers a copy of my small booklet, *The General Pattern of the Scientific Method*, and a six-page Special Public Service Research Report to Business and Industry on Complete Problem Solving and Decision Making.

The 202 people who were sent the report were very busy presidents, CEOs, chairmen, etc. I received a few acknowledgments of receipt of the report. However, nothing resulted. It was just another of my failed efforts.

The 1999 National Education Summit

Because of the lack of response in 1996, I made no attempt to influence this sparsely attended summit. *NSTA Reports* (April 2001) says the following:

> A coalition of leading business organizations, including The Business Roundtable, the National Alliance of Business (NAB), the National Association of Manufacturers, and the U.S. Chamber of Commerce, has issued a new report and long-term agenda that would virtually reconfigure the teaching profession and require substantially new investments in teaching.

> The report, titled *Investing in Teaching*, resulted from the 1999 National Education Summit, at which businesses, governors, and educators pledged to improve the quality of teaching with "significantly increased investments in teachers and accountability for results." The business groups behind this report vow that the effort to improve teaching will be similar to the campaign businesses undertook to raise academic standards in the states.

Note that there is

◆ no recognition that *the* **BLUNDER** exists

◆ no reform plan for top educators

But there is praise for the campaign to raise standards in the states.

That program may be needed, but its implementation and analyses have been varied.

Achieve, Inc.

This organization's literature states:

> Achieve is an independent, bipartisan, nonprofit organization created by governors and corporate leaders to help states and the private sector raise standards and performance in America's schools. Founded at the 1996 National Education Summit, Achieve has sponsored two additional Summits in 1999 and 2001.

Its first president was a Harvard professor. While I have not written to Achieve, Inc., I sent its first and current presidents my literature in their past activities.

Summary

In general, business and industry have not properly analyzed the problems of education. Their influential efforts on the national level have contributed to the perpetuation of *the* **BLUNDER**.

Education Week (September 18, 2002) published an article by A. Hernandez and M. Mahoney entitled "Is the Private Sector Qualified to Reform Schools?" One of the points raised is:

> A generic management approach to service in schools can do more harm than good. Education policies that fail to consider the needs and concerns of teachers have little hope of adoption. Teachers are inundated with such mandates year after year, a situation that breeds frustration among professionals and ultimately undermines service to students.

I believe that business and industry can make a major contribution to improving education if they follow the suggestions below.

Suggestions

First an Appeal to Leaders of Business and Industry

In an article in *Forbes Global* (March 5, 2000), Peter Drucker stated that he believes the United States now spends about $1 trillion per year on education and training. In this book, I have impartially pointed out that billion-dollar decisions are constantly being made based on authoritative opinions, resulting in little progress in education. I have shown that the blame for poor progress has been put on those at the bottom, with almost none on those at the top, where a great deal of the blame belongs.

In more than 100 places, the No Child Left Behind Act requires scientifically based research. I have shown that this means following the scientific method. I again appeal to you to study my suggestions promptly and take appropriate action.

Suggestion #1

I ask you to immediately follow my suggestion of alerting all those in your organizations to the fact that they too should use the scientific method (SM-14 type) in their research, planning, goals, etc., and not depend so much on authoritative opinions. It is long past the time for the greatest quality control method ever recognized and developed to be widely applied to the operation of businesses.

Suggestion #2

Business and industry are advocating many things about education. Some of them sound good in theory. But the contribution of businesses to education in many areas on the national scene has been based too much on authoritative opinions. Many business-oriented organizations are pushing theories, policies, and laws detrimental to education.

My suggestion is that businesses should set up a permanent specialized SM-14 type national research center on education to determine what policies and actions should be recommended by business and industry.

Suggestion #3

A press release on "Early Childhood Education: A Call to Action from the Business Community" (Business Roundtable, May 2003) states:

> The BRT also strongly supported the passage of the No Child Left Behind Act of 2001, which creates a national imperative to raise student achievement and close the achievement gap,

and the Roundtable's Task Force on Education and Work-force is actively involved in the law's implementation.

I have pointed out that this act is based largely on authoritative opinions and no pilot test program. It is basic business procedure, upon the introduction of a large-scale, complex program, to arrange for careful feedback and adjustment for unanticipated defects.

I suggest that the Business Roundtable and other business leaders endorse my suggestion in Chapter 14, The Disaster of Standards, Testing, and Accountability, that an impartial, nonpolitical study group (not a big name panel) be established to monitor and report to the public and political leaders on the successes and failures of the No Child Left Behind Act.

Suggestion #4

Because students know that employers do not usually request a transcript of their grades, many don't make much effort to achieve—only enough to graduate. Business and industry groups should urge their members, when hiring, to request grade transcripts and SAT and ACT scores and widely advise students of the importance of good grades in securing a job.

? ?

The Mysteries

Our top business leaders are highly intelligent and talented people. Normally, they don't have the time to research educational issues. They have the funds to hire the best advisors, but often hire the same old educators, who are responsible for the present disasters. In my opinion, their efforts at the national level to improve education have been largely based on authoritative opinions, simple solutions, and theories that sound good. But when these are reduced to practice, they don't solve education's problems. There is insufficient analysis and defining of the basic problems.

Is the reason for this mysterious situation that they and their advisors have never been adequately educated in the scientific method? Why, as I show in Chapter 25, are capitalistic principles so often misapplied to efforts to mold educational reform?

? ?

Chapter 40

Contribution of Foundations to *the* BLUNDER

◆ Importance of Foundations to Education

◆ Harm to Foundations from *the* BLUNDER

◆ Contribution of Foundations to the Perpetuation of *the* BLUNDER

◆ My Efforts Regarding Some Foundations

◆ Suggestions and Mystery

Importance of Foundations to Education

America is fortunate in having numerous foundations that are contributing large amounts of money to education. It is important that they continue to do so. For example, according to the Foundation Center, foundation grants to K-12 education increased to $1.4 billion in 2001.

Giving away money effectively is not an easy task. Because giving is so complex, foundations have a Council on Foundations and are even more progressive, with an affinity group called the Grantmakers Evaluation Network. However, when I look at the organization's website, I see a report *Creating a Culture of Inquiry*. As I have shown elsewhere, inquiry leads to process, and the time-tested process is the scientific method.

Here I will point out the harm *the* BLUNDER has done to foundations and how some foundations have contributed to the perpetuation of *the* BLUNDER.

Harm to Foundations from *the* BLUNDER

Foundations Have Been Hurt by Not Being Better Problem Solvers and Decision Makers

While it is wonderful to give, it is really hard to give efficiently and effectively. Most of those charged with the duty of operating foundations have never been adequately taught the scientific method. They are like almost everyone else: they are victims of **the BLUNDER.** Because it is a deep, dark secret, they probably do not know it is occurring. Thus, they are not doing as good a job as they otherwise could and are wasting millions of dollars. To operate effectively, they must solve their complex problems using the scientific method. Foundations and individuals who have been financially successful could make a great contribution to urban schools in poverty areas by building a new school. Many of the present buildings are in very poor condition, and cities are without the funds to correct the situation.

Self-Regulation

Foundations exist largely as a result of tax encouragements in our income and estate tax laws. They also receive yearly tax exemptions of a great deal of their income. In recent years, their activities have been increasingly regulated by the government. By using the scientific method in their own self-regulation activities, they will prevent the harm of even more government regulation.

For example, one bad situation that exists is what I call "wolf in sheep's clothing foundations." In my research I have seen what appear to me to be foundations claiming that they are helping education and, in the name of philanthropy, push a view, project, etc. that current evidence shows to be wrong. If they have any personal financial reasons to do so, they should reveal their real motivation. If they are doing it from arrogance or lack of research to justify their views, then to me this too is unethical. Foundations have a duty to taxpayers to operate efficiently and for the benefit of the country.

All foundations should be using the scientific method, which entails following a code of ethics. This includes honesty and not trying to make efforts or grant projects look better than they really are. If foundations effectively use the scientific method, they are less apt to have to polish up their results.

Contribution of Foundations to the Perpetuation of *the* BLUNDER

They Try to Help the Teaching of Science, But Fail

For example, I explain the disaster of the teaching of science (Chapter 11). Many foundations have made misguided efforts to improve science teaching, none of which included teaching the scientific method. They support organizations that claim that the scientific method does not exist. Thus, they contribute to *the* BLUNDER.

Many Foundations Are Harvard Oriented

Normally, there would be nothing wrong with this, but it makes it more difficult to end *the* **BLUNDER**. The April 18, 1997 edition of the *Chronicle of Higher Education* reports that:

> Several newcomers have cracked the current edition's list of colleges. But the Harvards, Princetons, and Cornells have long-standing ties to foundations and their board members, and traditions of calling on them for support, that make them perennial favorites.

In *Education Week* (June 23, 1999) there is a note that a Harvard professor heads one of the foundations to which I wrote. This foundation underwrites the monthly research section of *Education Week*. This paper has not published one word about news of my crusade, adding to keeping it and the scientific method dispute a deep, dark secret.

My Efforts Regarding Some Foundations

In 1995 I wrote to the 10 highest foundation contributors to education, asking specifically *not for a grant* but stressing the national need to establish a foundation for promoting problem solving and quoting Nobel Laureate Herb Simon "that there appears to be at present no foundation for which decision making and problem solving are a major focus of interest."

I received either no reply or a brushoff as if I were requesting a grant.

Our Lack of a Big Picture of Education

Support for my claim that no one seems to see the big picture of education is this news note from *Education Week* (November 15, 2000):

> Ellen Condliffe Lagemann, an education historian and the president of the Chicago-based Spencer Foundation, opened the conference on a sobering note, telling the 200-plus attendees that philanthropists have poured untold millions into education for decades.
>
> But Ms. Lagemann contends that those demonstration projects, new curriculum materials, and commissions established to study the problems have produced little of lasting effect. "When one looks at the history of philanthropy in

education, one is hard pressed to come up with projects that have had enduring success," she said.

There have been and still are many foundation direct grants, etc., that have helped various schools and groups. However, Ms. Lagemann is looking at the overall picture and is, I believe, correct. The only way to end the bad situation is to require the use of the scientific method and to support a series of permanent specialized SM-14 type national research centers.

Summary of Foundations' Contribution to *the* BLUNDER

It is my claim that they are causing harm by wasting billions of dollars and often perpetuating *the* BLUNDER by

♦ not making enough effort to see the big picture of education

♦ not applying the scientific method to their own activities

♦ not requiring the organizations' researchers or program designers, etc., whom they support, to teach and use the scientific method

Suggestion

Therefore, I recommend that this book be read and studied thoroughly. All foundations should use the scientific method in their work and should promote its use everywhere they expend funds.

? ?

The Mystery

Why, as Noble Laureate Simon asks, has there been no foundation "for which decision making and problem solving are a major focus of interest"?

? ?

Chapter 41

Other Contributions to *the* BLUNDER

Since *the* BLUNDER has been so universal, there are innumerable contributions to it. Rather than go into too much detail, I have limited those that follow to a few pages. There are many others, but I present only these.

Contribution of the Educational Testing Service

By not including questions about the scientific method in tests, our testing companies have contributed to *the* BLUNDER.

Two Major College Entrance Tests

SAT—designed by the Educational Testing Service (ETS, founded in 1947), taken by about 1.3 million students each year. I challenged it with a special report in 1995.

ACT—designed by ACT, Inc. (a nonprofit corporation started in 1959). This test is taken by about 1 million students each year. I sent ACT, Inc. copies of my first booklets in 1992, but never challenged it.

ETS was founded in 1947, at the urging of Conant, by the American Council on Education, the Carnegie Foundation for the Advancement of Teaching, and the College Entrance Examination Board. It is an independent nonprofit corporation. *The Future of Education* (1994), edited by Nina Cobb, states:

> The College Board is a national nonprofit association that champions educational excellence for all students through the ongoing collaboration of more than 2,900 member schools, colleges, universities, education systems, and associations. The Board promotes—by means of responsive forums, research, programs, and policy development—universal access to high standards of learning, equity of opportunity, and sufficient financial support so that every student is prepared for success in college and work.

I sent the College Board copies of my first booklet in 1992, but I have not challenged it directly. I suppose that I should have done so, or at least sent copies of my report to ETS.

Why I Included ETS in My Challenges

I had read of Conant's connection in 1947 with the founding of ETS. The content of tests so often influences the content of instruction that they serve as "gatekeepers of knowledge." ETS, along with most other test preparers, has not included any questions in its tests about the scientific method, even though it is of great importance in originating, refining, extending, and applying knowledge in all fields. Thus, I believe that ETS set the precedent for other tests and has helped substantially in perpetuating a false concept about the scientific method. I reproduce here just one page from my Special 1995 Report to ETS:

THE EDUCATIONAL TESTING SERVICE'S APPARENT POSITION ON THE EXISTENCE OF "THE SCIENTIFIC METHOD"

In my research, I found no indication that the Educational Testing Service included any questions in their tests concerning "The Scientific Method." My letter to them, asking for confirmation of this, was not answered . . . so I must assume that this lack of being included in their test is correct. This situation seems unusual as "The Scientific Method" is included in most science textbooks to some extent. . .

Educational Testing Service—Influenced by Conant?

In 1947 there was a merger of three separate testing enterprises, resulting in the establishment of the *Educational Testing Service*. Conant was head of a committee that brought this about. Later, in 1957, he became a trustee. Also in 1957, he utilized the help of Henry Chauncey, President of ETS, in his "comprehensive high school" project.

This, combined with ETS's close association over the years with national government, educational, and scientific organizations which have accepted Conant's erroneous concept, has resulted in there being nothing about "The Scientific Method" in the ETS testing. Since so many teachers, curricula designers, and principals must test their students, there has been no incentive for them to teach "The Scientific Method," even though it is mentioned in varying degrees in most science textbooks.

The Educational Testing Service, under Grant No. NIE-G-83-0011 from O.E.R.I., produced the report *Science Learning Matters* (1988). This report does not mention or include anything about "The Scientific Method."

ETS's Reply to My Report

It took me a while to get a mailing list from ETS, so it was not until January 1996 that I sent a copy of my 1995 report to its trustees. In February 1996 Nancy S. Cole wrote to me (unlike most others I challenged), saying that "any test maker, not just ETS, works to avoid promoting any one group's educational goals." She explained their procedures for test preparation, the basis of which is what students are actually taught. My contention and answer is that the scientific method is in a few pages of most science textbooks and of such great importance that it should be included in the SAT.

ETS's Early History Set the Pace

My opinion is that, because of Conant's influence in helping to found ETS, and because its first president, Chauncey, was a Harvard man, the scientific method never had a chance of being included in the SAT. This situation just continued in the years that followed. Other test preparers were also probably influenced not to include it in their tests. Thus, the "gatekeepers of knowledge" shut the gate on the scientific method.

Curriculum designers and teachers often are under pressure today to teach to the No Child Left Behind requirements. This too works against the scientific method.

? ?

The Mysteries

Because of Conant's association with ETS, it is easy to guess why the scientific method was not included in the SAT from the beginning.

After so many years have passed, and ETS has stressed the need for students to be taught critical thinking skills, and since the scientific method is included in a few pages in most science textbooks, why is the scientific method still not included in the SAT and ACT?

? ?

Contribution of Bloom's Taxonomy

Benjamin Bloom was at one time president of the American Educational Research Association. He obtained a Ph.D. and conducted his research at the University of Chicago. In 1956 he published the *Taxonomy of Educational Objectives*. This book was eventually translated into more than 50 languages and used in the preparation of many tests. Bloom lists 34 participants who contributed to the development of the taxonomy at conferences from 1949 to 1953. Three were from the Educational Testing Service, which has never promoted the scientific method.

The taxonomy has received a great deal of publicity and is extensively quoted. On the whole, it did contribute to improving education. Yet it contributed to *the* **BLUNDER**, for there is only one mention in Book #1 of the scientific method:

1.25 - Knowledge of Methodology

47. Of the following, which represents the most important differences between the scientific method as used in the social sciences and as used in the natural sciences?

This seems to indicate that Bloom knew about the scientific method, but elsewhere he ignores it, although methodology is mentioned. In rereading the *Taxonomy*, I found place after place where logical thinking and knowledge of the scientific method calls for specifying the use of the scientific method, but it does not. For example (from the 1984 edition of *Taxonomy of Educational Objectives*):

The importance of the intellectual abilities and skills is further illustrated by our recognition of the individual's ability to independently attack his problems as a desirable sign of maturity. Individuals are expected, as they mature, to solve problems on their own and to make decisions wisely on the basis of their own thinking.

Bloom was probably influenced not to discuss the scientific method by the publicity about Conant's claims that it does not exist. These claims were prominent when Bloom wrote his book.

Because of the great recognition Bloom's book has received and the lack of direct challenges to the taxonomy, it has contributed greatly to *the* **BLUNDER** in the United States and around the world.

Contribution of America's Intellectual Community

In the *Encarta World English Dictionary* the second definition of an intellectual is

> 2. intelligent and knowledgeable: having a highly developed ability to think, reason, and understand, especially in combination with wide knowledge

There are many reports that America loves to "bash" its intellectuals. Much of this is probably from envy and some for the fun of kidding. But seriously, most people know that we owe a great deal of our progress, prosperity, and world leadership to them.

In *Betrayers of the Truth* (1982) Broad and Wade point out that

> . . . members of the elite are sheltered from the scrutiny that is supposedly applied without fear or favor to all scientists.

This, I believe, is even more prevalent in the educational field. In my crusade I have had to disregard my own family's dislike of my criticism of top leaders. The real problem is that those who depend on grants do not dare to criticize for fear of losing their livelihood. But intellectuals not under this obligation must investigate and speak out if this blunder is to be corrected.

My book provides the evidence and the grounds for my claims of intellectual blunder. While I claim that it is the greatest in history, I would not try to defend the "biggest," as this would involve opinions and it is of little difference whether it is big or biggest. Its importance is what matters.

By not actively challenging the Harvard/Conant group and misguided followers (or whoever they are), our intellectual community has contributed to *the* **BLUNDER**. Thus, it has affected most of our professional publications and organizations. No college or university makes a big effort to teach the scientific method across the curriculum. Where have our big thinkers been? It is correct that thousands of books and articles continue to mention or describe the method, but there is no big fight to debate and correct the blunder that is going on. In the last 50 years, hundreds of thousands of books have been published in which some of the contents are wrong but they will continue to be read in the future. The harm to our intellectual community caused by its being led down the wrong path has been tremendous.

My suggestions to our intellectual community are:

1. As Dr. Conant stated (see Chapter 4), the question of the existence of the scientific method is a matter of "supreme importance." I suggest that you give this matter close attention.

2. For the sake of intellectualism and society, please study my claims carefully. Even though I have done more than 15 years of specialized research on the matter, my claims need study.

3. I recently read a book review of *The Moral Obligation to be Intelligent* (2000) edited by Lionel Trilling and Leon Wieselter. The title impressed me. In my opinion, intellectuals have a moral obligation to stand up for and fight for the method of knowledge, the method of intelligence, and the method of applying knowledge— the scientific method. A great many of you have paid little attention to the scientific method or have not been familiar with what has occurred. Others have erred or blundered. I suggest that you stand up and fight for the scientific method.

4. The matter can best be corrected if everyone admits that an error or blunder has occurred and admits that we all have goofed (including me) and then takes steps to correct it.

5. Denials not supported by study and evidence will only add to **the BLUNDER** and possible loss of reputations both personally and as a community. Therefore, be careful to study the matter thoroughly.

6. There is a great need for a standardized version for teaching purposes of what the scientific method consists. I suggest that you help accomplish this.

??

The Mystery

Considering the centuries of literature, debate, research on intelligence, logic, thinking skills, method, etc., how could America's intellectual community have been so easily misled by the Harvard/Conant group and misguided followers (or whoever they are) into going along with their false concepts about the scientific method based on such flimsy and erroneous reasoning?

??

Contribution of America's Think Tanks

In its Directory of Think Tanks, the Institute for Research Advancement lists about 80 in the United States.

The *American Heritage Dictionary* defines a think tank as:

> A group or an institution organized for intensive research and solving of problems, especially in the areas of technology, social or political strategy, or armament.

Over the years, in conducting my research on the scientific method and education, I have read various reports by so-called think tanks. I was appalled at the quality of work about education of some. Have you ever seen one of their reports placing a lot of the troubles of education on top leaders and explaining clearly why? Their existence often depends on contracts, often from government agencies. Their reports, therefore, are not always unbiased.

Like all other organizations, think tanks have been harmed by *the* **BLUNDER**. The lack of teaching the scientific method and the lack of intensive development of research and problem solving have adversely affected their personnel.

Nevertheless, a think tank is supposed to be able to think and not be a "tinkering tank"! Why has not one of them recognized the blunder about the scientific method and fought for its teaching and use? This adds to my claim that the scientific method situation is the biggest intellectual and educational blunder in history.

Because think tanks have not addressed the scientific method situation, they have contributed to *the* **BLUNDER** and to the flow of unreliable and questionable reports to the public and others.

Conservative versus Liberal Think Tanks

As many issues involve the future or the unknown, there may be a reason for the conservative or liberal view. However, my observation is that, in a great many cases, *there is a great deal of ignoring contrary evidence, even in think tanks,* so much that some do not deserve to be called think tanks. If these conservative and liberal think tanks certify their reports as being based on the scientific method (SM-14 type), it will substantially narrow their differences. We need fewer advocacy think tanks with predetermined outcomes and more real research.

Any think tank that receives a government contract should be required to certify that its work was done following the scientific method (SM-14). This requirement would stop the waste of millions and maybe billions of dollars every year.

WE NEED PERMANENT SPECIALIZED SM-14 TYPE NATIONAL RESEARCH CENTERS.

At present, many issues continue to flourish, inaccurate reports are presented, and incorrect public policy is set because we do not accumulate knowledge more systematically. Special reports put out by temporary educational researchers at think tanks cannot equal the work of permanent SM-14 type research centers. Education is an example of an area in which the big picture is not known. Thus,we constantly have erroneous reports about various problems and issues from so-called think tanks and "public intellectuals."

My Reports Sent

I have sent my booklets and reports to a few think tanks, but I have received no response.

Suggestions for Think Tanks and Those Who Aspire to This Title

In this book, I quote the views on research, thinking, and the scientific method of many people. There is enough evidence that you should study the scientific method (SM-14 type) to be sure that your own research is of scientific grade. The "intensive research" in the dictionary definition of a think tank means research done following the scientific method. For greater public acceptance, you should then certify your reports as following the scientific method (SM-14 type).

Suggestions for the Public

If a group holds itself out to be a think tank, then you have the right to expect reliable information, not biased or selective research. Just as we have educational standards, we need think tank standards.

The scientific method (SM-14 type) is the best quality control method ever recognized. If think tanks do not use it and certify that they did, then they should not earn your confidence in their work or enjoy the title think tank. FAIR and the Institute for Public Accuracy publish a Think Tank Monitor. Their work or something similar should be done with a certification that the scientific method was followed.

Contribution of the National Association of Scholars

In 1994 my attention was attracted by a few advertisements "Science Is Under Attack" run by the National Association of Scholars. These pointed out that "formerly the attacks came from outside the academic and scientific disciplines. Increasingly, now they come from within."

Well, there I was, fighting the biggest intellectual blunder in history, that the method of science—the scientific method—did not exist. Some of my opponents were educator-scientists who were denying science its method. Thus, the ads appealed to me. Finally, in early 1997, I decided to try to get the help of the National Association of Scholars by challenging it.

Who They Are

From the website www.nas.org:

> The National Association of Scholars (NAS) is an organization of professors, graduate students, college administrators and trustees, and independent scholars committed to rational discourse as the foundation of academic life in a free and democratic society. The NAS works to enrich the substance and strengthen the integrity of scholarship and teaching, persuaded that only through an informed understanding of the Western intellectual heritage and the realities of the contemporary world, can citizen and scholar be equipped to sustain our civilization's achievements.

It has a membership of more than 4,000. As the name indicates, its membership includes some of our most prestigious intellectuals.

Internal Politics

I am not familiar with this, although I notice a number of Harvard graduates in the association's literature and believe that the association may be Harvard oriented.

Operating Policy

I did not research this very much. I did purchase a copy of the association's 1996 publication, *The Dissolution of General Education 1914–1993.*

My Unsuccessful Attempts to Get the National Association of Scholars to Study the Scientific Method Situation

1997—I sent the association's president, chairman, research director, and executive director Challenge #14. This included a copy of Professor Easley's essay, my reports #5, 6, 7, and 8, and copies of my 1994 booklet on the General Pattern of the Scientific Method. I also sent the 28-page supplement to Edmund's Idea and Research Report. In my letter, I made this request:

> I ask that if you are unwilling or unable to accept this challenge yourself, on behalf of NAS that you discuss the matter with your board of directors and other officers.

> If you will furnish me with their names and addresses, I will be glad to send them copies of this letter and the reports I have submitted.

I did not receive any reply. This was another of the many disappointments I have had in my crusade.

On the page of reasons why the National Association of Scholars should accept my challenge to study the scientific method, I stated:

> The Evaporation of Content
> Page 19 of your report "The Dissolution of General Education 1914–1993" seems to recognize the existence of "The Scientific Method" in the statement: "This requires, among other things, a comprehension of science as method and process, and not merely as a body of knowledge or as an oracular source of theoretical authority." Page 16, however, mentions "scientific inquiry," which is the theme the National Academy of Sciences is using in the National Science Education Standards instead of "The Scientific Method." As there seems to be no direct reference to "The Scientific Method" in your literature on the whole, I get the impression you are one of the many organizations denying its existence by not properly utilizing it for teaching purposes in your efforts to improve education and scholarly work.

Suggestions to Members of the National Association of Scholars

In my letters of January 1997 to your officers, I stated some things that I believe you should consider:

This is an unusual opportunity for the National Association of Scholars to help science and university and grade school education and to clarify the method by which we originate, refine, extend, and apply knowledge. It is also an opportunity for you to avoid being classified as one who helped perpetuate the blunder even after it was called to your attention.

My research shows that it is only through correct teaching of "The Scientific Method" and the complete system of science that the public will be better able to identify junk science, unfair attacks on science, and science literacy.

An organization such as yours cannot expect intellectual honesty from others and refuse to study this matter. I am not asking for agreement with my claims, only that they be studied. I have been forced to start describing the situation as "THE BIGGEST INTELLECTUAL BLUNDER IN HISTORY" and must continue to do so until the matter is corrected. Because the National Academy of Sciences would not study the matter, we now have millions of dollars of taxpayer money being wasted on presenting "science as inquiry" instead of science as its method—the scholarly method.

I suggest that a study group of your association review this matter.

? ?

The Mysteries

The scientific method is
the method of scholars
the method of scholarly investigation

Why then
- did its officers, to whom I sent my reports, not accept my challenge to study the scientific method situation?
- the "structured silence" of not reporting my challenge to its members?

The widespread knowledge of the scientific method is the best way to stop anti-science threats. So why isn't the association ending the claims that the scientific method does not exist?

? ?

Contribution of Sigma Xi Scientific Honor Society

In 1996, I indulged in some self-pity and pondered the fate of poor little me crusading unsuccessfully for the scientific method—the greatest idea of all time. Then I got the idea of challenging the honor society for scientists and engineers, Sigma Xi, The Scientific Research Society.

The Special March 1995 Report I had sent to the original seven organizations I had publicly challenged had a 10-page chapter on Ethics and Analogies. How all those who received this report ignored the points in this chapter mystified me beyond belief. I still cannot understand why I received no acceptances.

In that chapter I quoted from an excellent booklet published by Sigma Xi called *Honor in Science* (1984). This led me eventually to the idea of challenging the organization. This is a really good little booklet and can still be purchased from the society by calling 800-243-6534 or from the website www.sigmaxi.org. Now that Congress, in the ESEA, is requiring "scientifically based research," it is especially useful.

In 1993, in its magazine *American Scientist*, Sigma Xi published a study on scientific misconduct by Dr. Swazey et al., condemning a pattern of denial the authors call "structured silence." This is a term I like to apply to the Harvard/Conant group and misguided followers (or whoever they are) because of their failure to publicize my reports and crusade and to accept my challenges.

Who They Are

From the society's literature:
> Sigma Xi, The Scientific Research Society, was founded in 1886 as an honor society for scientists and engineers. Today more than 100,000 scientists and engineers are active members of Sigma Xi. There are over 500 chapters and clubs at universities, government laboratories, and industry research centers.
>
> Membership in Sigma Xi is by invitation. The most promising young scientists and students with demonstrated research potential are invited to join as Associate Members. Full membership is conferred upon individuals who have demonstrated noteworthy achievements in research. Each year the Society initiates more than 5,000 new members.

The Internal Politics of Sigma Xi

I did not research this. I did notice at the time of my challenge that the society's president was a Harvard graduate and among the advisors listed for *American Scientist* I recognized a Harvard man. Since Harvard has a reputation for attracting our best and brightest, I image that many of Sigma Xi's staff and members are Harvard graduates.

I noticed that in 1996 the National Academy of Sciences had renewed its contract with Sigma Xi's Grants-in-Aid of Research Program for another 5 years. In addition, two of Sigma Xi's booklets, *Partners in K-12 Science Education Reform* and *Systemic Reform in K-12 Science Education*, were made possible by a grant from the Carnegie Corporation (see Chapter 35 on its contribution to *the* **BLUNDER**).

The Operating Policy of Sigma Xi Regarding the Scientific Method

I did not research this either. I did read some of the society's literature and a few copies of its interesting magazine, *American Scientist*. Years ago, when I was operating Edmund Scientific Co., I advertised my products in this journal. I believe that Sigma Xi is following others at the top level in not promoting the scientific method and a formula for it. Its booklet *Partners in K-12 Science Education Reform* refers readers to educational programs of AAAS, NRC, and NSTA, none of which include the scientific method now nor have they since their inception.

Sigma Xi's Educational Activities

The society is engaged in a wide range of educational activities, with many local chapters participating. This is great, but it would be even greater if it were promoting the scientific method and a formula for it.

Here is what I told Sigma Xi in my 1996 Report:

> Your educational activities will be improved if they include teaching "The Scientific Method." You should remember the quote by C.P. Snow in your pamphlet *Honor in Science*, "The only ethical principle which has made science possible is that the truth shall be told all the time." I have found that practically no one has researched diligently for the truth about the existence of "The Scientific Method," therefore, a study committee is needed for you to arrive at the "truth" in this situation. Opinions are not good enough.

My Unsuccessful Attempts to Get Sigma Xi to Study the Scientific Method Situation

1992—I sent copies of my first booklets to *American Scientist*.

1996—I sent "History in the Making—A Special March 1996 Report to the Officers and Executive Board" (a total of 28).

The executive director answered but declined for the reason that there were so many issues currently affecting the research community that Sigma Xi had to devote its limited resources to those members and chapters identified as critically important.

My request for a list of Sigma Xi chapters and contacts was refused because of the reason I requested the list. I intended to go directly to some chapters. I did not know at the time, but there was a regularly published directory of chapter and club presidents and secretaries.

Suggestions to Sigma Xi Members

Since you are a scientific honor society, you should be actively seeking an answer to settling the issue of whether the scientific method exists. I feel that your officers should have brought this matter to your attention rather than make the decision to do nothing and keep such an important matter a deep, dark secret. Since this matter has a big effect on the accuracy of your educational activities and general policies, I believe that you should promptly form a full-time study group to review what should be done about teaching the scientific method. If I am right—and I have done more than 15 years of specialized research on the scientific method—then your officials' actions will be a black mark on your fine record that should be erased promptly. It is not safe for your reputation to rely on authoritative opinions rather than convene an independent study group.

? ?

The Mystery

I was disappointed once again that a challenge was not accepted—especially since a scientific and engineering honor society was involved. What is there about this mystery that even an honor society's top leaders will not participate in investigating the scientific method?

? ?

Contribution of Professional Journals

In this book, I have explained *the* **BLUNDER**. The professional journals have helped perpetuate it by not challenging the false claims of the Harvard/Conant group and misguided followers (or whoever they are) that the scientific method does not exist. They had the opportunity to publicize Professor Easley's essay challenging the false claims in 1958 and again in 1969. None of the small number of the journals to which I sent my literature called attention to my claims. They have, on the whole, made a major contribution to keeping the dispute about the scientific method a deep, dark secret.

The BLUNDER Has Harmed Professional Journals' Ethical Status

Recommendation Twelve of *Responsible Science*, prepared by the National Academy of Sciences (1992), states:

> Scientific societies and scientific journals should continue to provide and expand resources and forums to foster responsible research practices and to address misconduct in science and questionable research practices.

Science magazine (February 21, 2003) contained "Statement on Scientific Publications and Security." It states:

> **FIRST**: The scientific information published in peer-reviewed research journals carries special status, and confers unique responsibilities on editors and authors. We must protect the integrity of the scientific process by publishing manuscripts of high quality, in sufficient detail to permit reproducibility.

My observation is—and history shows—that professional journals have made a major contribution to the progress of professions and the "sciences" they represent. However, I believe that *the* **BLUNDER** will be a major "black eye" on their record.

My Message to Professional Journal Editors and Staffs

This book shows that there is much evidence that not teaching and acknowledging the scientific method system is extremely questionable. Claims of the non-existence of the scientific method are not reproducible. You should stop keeping this matter a deep, dark secret and encourage open discussion of it in your journals.

Contribution of Other Professional Societies

In this book I review the work of a number of specific professions and professional organizations. In fairness, I must say that my choice was haphazard, based on what I found in my research. There are others I should probably have reported on.

The *American Heritage Dictionary* defines the noun "professional" as

> 1. A person following a profession, especially a learned profession. 2. One who earns a living in a given or implied occupation: *hired a professional to decorate the house.* 3. A skilled practitioner; an expert.

While I have in mind our "learned professions," what I say here also applies to all professions or even crafts that want to qualify as scientific, or even as a profession.

In Chapter 55 I explain that any profession that wants to be considered a science must follow the scientific method.

Consider further:

◆ Knowledge origination, refinement, extension, and application make specialized professions possible. Professionalism could be greatly improved if there were greater use and understanding of the scientific method (SM-14).

◆ Professionalism exists because there is a method of arriving at "the truth" rather than continual argument about what is correct.

Considering other professional societies and organizations, I make the statement that almost all of them have participated in *the* **BLUNDER**! By this I mean that not one has challenged the Harvard/Conant group and misguided followers (or whoever they are), explained that the scientific method does exist, presented a formula for it, and specifically urged the teaching of the scientific method. This certainly contributes to the magnitude of the blunder (the biggest).

Suggestions to All Professional Organizations

Any organization that claims to be a "professional" one should study this book carefully and appoint a study group on the scientific method situation.

Contribution of Historians in General

The Method of History is the Application of the Scientific Method

In his book *In the American Province* (1985), David Hollinger states:

> What matters most about the discipline of history is its abil-
> ity to distinguish good history from bad history, accuracy
> from confusion, truth from fraud. However diverse and
> complicated the aims of doing history, we are at least
> dependent upon this activity for knowledge about certain
> things. While we care about the ways in which history is rel-
> ative, we care even more about the ways in which it is true.

This shows clearly that a historian must follow the best guide to
investigation that our intellectual elite has recognized—the best quality control method to ensure accuracy (for we know that the "truth"
is often unattainable)—that is, the scientific method, following a
complete formula such as SM-14. Claims that the method cannot be
used in historical research are based on misunderstandings of what
the scientific method really is. The many misunderstandings about
the scientific method have seriously harmed K-12 education, but, as
seen here, the ill effects have filtered down into other domains.

While history is a meaningful record of peoples' past achievements, its
importance is far greater to us. It enables us to understand the present,
what other people have done to solve problems, and to learn from
experience. Their successes and failures are a guide to our future
efforts. Thus it is important that all those engaging in historical
research be thoroughly familiar with the scientific method as well as
the specific techniques or methods peculiar to professional historians.

Our historians seem to have contributed to *the* **BLUNDER**. While I
made no detailed search, indications are that they have, on the whole,
followed other domains and do not teach the scientific method or
acknowledge its usefulness to historians. There are exceptions to this
claim, and I quote a few of these historians in this book.

I examined the *National Standards for United States History* (1994)
for grade schools. While it includes "Standards in Historical
Thinking," there is no reference to the scientific method. This overall
situation is surprising, as we have intellectual historians who should
be using the method of intelligence—the scientific method. We have
a history of ideas, even a *Journal of the History of Ideas*, yet the greatest idea of all time and all ages is neglected.

The BLUNDER Includes Books That Should Have Been Written But Were Not

As I do my research and writing on the scientific method, I refer to and read many books that are really good in many respects, but the authors have misunderstood or are not familiar with the scientific method as a result of *the* **BLUNDER**. Therefore, many of their conclusions are erroneous or the information given is not complete. This includes the very important subject areas of thinking, problem solving, and decision making themselves and as they relate to many other areas of life. Of course, this is part of the disaster.

But just as bad or even worse are the books that should have been written but were not because of *the* BLUNDER.

Here is an example. In *Edmund's Idea and Research Report on the General Pattern of the Scientific Method* (1994), I included two pages of a plan for teaching SM-14. The following was part of it:

Section D: Specific Subject Areas from The Arts to Zoology
Each domain, in addition to aiding in teaching general thinking skills and methods, would teach special skills, techniques, and methods peculiar or especially important to their field.

The Arts	English	Science	Other Domains

So, because of *the* **BLUNDER**, rather than these and an orderly progression of books on the subject of the scientific method and its associated thinking skills and other supporting ingredients, we got only a few. So hundreds and thousands of books that would have advanced and communicated our knowledge still remain to be written. We have been operating all these years without the full benefit of this knowledge that is so important to society.

Contribution of the World Future Society

The Who and What from Its Website

The World Future Society is an association of people interested in how social and technological developments are
shaping the future. The Society was founded in 1966 and is
chartered as a nonprofit educational and scientific organization in Washington, D.C., U.S.A.

What Does the Society Do?
The Society strives to serve as a neutral clearinghouse for
ideas about the future. Ideas about the future include forecasts, recommendations, and alternative scenarios. These
ideas help people to anticipate what may happen in the next
5, 10, or more years ahead. When people can visualize a better future, then they can begin to create it.

Distribution of My Booklets at Its Annual Meeting in 1994

I love the idea of this society and believe it serves a vital need. Its
founder is a Harvard man. While I was in Cambridge, MA, in July 1994
to distribute my booklets at the Sixth International Conference on
Thinking, I did the same a few days later at the annual meeting of the
World Future Society. I accomplished nothing. The society has made
only a very small contribution to *the* **BLUNDER**, but, because of the
effort I made and to show how little understanding there is of the
method of prediction—the scientific method—I have included it.

To make my point about the need for the scientific method in prediction across in a small space, I offer this short quotation from *The
Nature of Scientific Thought* (1963) by Marshal Walker:

Every time the word *science* or *scientific* appears, the idea of
prediction is explicitly or implicitly involved. . . Men have
always valued the ability to predict future events, for those
who can predict events can guard against them.

**Today's current events illustrate vividly the need for our top leaders
to be better predictors of the results of their actions.**

By not endorsing and promoting the use of the scientific method, the
World Future Society is contributing to *the* **BLUNDER** and the inac-
curacies of predictions.

Contribution of Other Federal Agencies

Early in my research, I saw a pie chart of how federal education dollars were spent by government agencies. The National Science Foundation and the U.S. Department of Education were the largest, so I focused my attention and efforts on them.

However, as other agencies are also concerned with education, I did try a little to educate them, again unsuccessfully. It is my impression that the Harvard/Conant group and misguided followers (or whoever they are) have been successful in spreading their theories into all government agencies.

Here are the efforts I made:

1992—I sent the first editions of my booklet to the National Institutes of Health.

1995—I sent just one copy of my Special March 1995 Report to the U.S. Department of Labor.

1996—I also sent my 1996 follow-up reports to the U.S. Department of Labor.

1997—I sent a set of my literature to the National Assessment Governing Board.

1998—I sent a set of my booklets to NASA.

I sent a set of my literature to the National Human Genome Research Institute of the National Institutes of Health for its work on curriculum for high school biology.

Considering its importance and size, I should have sent the National Institutes of Health more of my literature and even a special report. The scientific method is of great importance to our health and lives.

2002—I sent 10 copies of each of my booklets to the U.S. Department of the Army, the U.S. Department of the Navy, the U.S. Department of the Air Force, the U.S. Marine Corps Headquarters, the FBI, and the CIA. They were not addressed to any individual. This was not a smart thing to do, and I consider it to be one of my goofs.

Contribution of What Seems to Be But Isn't

The BLUNDER has caused a tremendous amount of misunderstanding about the problems of education. To give an example, I present these two quotations. I will not identify the source, for you cannot blame the organization—it is one that normally presents a far more unbiased picture of education than others. It is merely reporting on what is accepted as general knowledge at the end of the year 2001.

> But education experts are virtually unanimous in saying that the quality of teachers is the single most important factor in raising student achievement. [December 14, 2001]

> School reform advocates hope that making student achievement data available to the public will encourage parents and citizens to demand more of their schools. [December 21, 2001]

Education "Experts" Are the "Single Most Important Factor"

In this book I point out and provide evidence that the single most important factor in raising student achievement is raising the quality and achievements of the top education "experts." We will never achieve adequate teacher quality until this is done. Our top education experts have done a terrible job of

- providing correct leadership on programs, student motivation, standards, tests, etc. used in our schools by our teachers

- providing correct training of our teachers

Reformers Hope That "Parents and Citizens Will Demand More from Their Schools"

There exist tremendous arrogance, lack of self-insight, and denial on the part of many educational reformers. Our top educators continually fail to acknowledge the tremendous goofs they have committed in the past. This misleads the public into blaming schools and teachers.

Parents and citizens must demand more of our top educators. They must demand that all educators study the matter and start using the best quality control method ever recognized and developed—the scientific method. Parents must also contribute more. But again they need more practical advice from our top leaders.

Contribution of "No Revolution"

A long-ago claim in 1903: A revolution must be effected to teach scientific method.

In *The Teaching of Scientific Method and Other Papers on Education* (1903), Henry Armstrong, talking about British schools, said:

> But a revolution must be effected in our schools if scientific method is to be taught in them. I have no hesitation in saying that at the present day the so-called science taught in most schools, especially that which is demanded by examiners, is not only worthless but positively detrimental. All who are acquainted with the facts know this to be the case; and if we ask ourselves the simple question—whether what is done tends to develop the wits, to develop the power of self-help, we must all admit the very opposite to be the case. Schools, in fact, are engaged in fashioning our youth to require leaning-posts, not in training them to act on their own account; examinations have made self-help impossible. No employer, go where you will, is satisfied with the product the schools turn out.

We did have the beginning of a revolution in the United States: the progressive education movement began in the first half of the 20th century and started to change things so much that in 1948, in *Education in a Divided World*, Conant complained:

> Indeed, in the last twenty-five years, indoctrination in the scientific method has been put forward with more and more insistence as one of the primary aims of modern education.

But the revolution was squelched by the Harvard/Conant group and misguided followers (or whoever they are) to such an extent that even in 2004 only a tiny bit of the scientific method is being taught, usually just a few pages in most of our science textbooks. They are even trying to stop this by insisting that textbooks conform to the 1995 National Science Education Standards. These claim that the scientific method does not exist!

It should be noted that, just as in 1903, you can still say:

"No employer, go where you will, is satisfied with the product the schools turn out." (That's 100 years later.)

All the States Have Contributed

Early in my research I found that the origination of *the* **BLUNDER** and the perpetuation of it was at the national level. Therefore, I directed my efforts and attention there.

The **BLUNDER** has just filtered down into our states and local schools.

I did not find any state that had a policy of promoting the teaching of the scientific method. This, of course, contributes to *the* **BLUNDER**.

This is not surprising for several reasons:

♦ Many state officials and their advisors are members of the Harvard/Conant group and misguided followers (or whoever they are). So many people at all levels have been miseducated about the scientific method and misguided that they are everywhere.

♦ State people and organizations are at times reluctant to challenge federal officials and indeed are often forced to follow federal requirements to receive needed federal financial help.

♦ I believe that most state people and organizations are influenced by a desire to a great extent to coordinate state activities with federal activities to accomplish our country's educational goals. This is good only if the federal activities are reliably correct.

♦ It should also be remembered that, in 1965, Dr. Conant was one of the founders of the Educational Commission of the States, an organization described on the next page.

♦ *The* **BLUNDER** has been kept such a deep, dark secret that most state and local educators probably do not even know it is a problem that needs investigation and study.

The efforts I made at the state level to correct *the* **BLUNDER** are described below.

State Governors

As described in Chapter 39, an Educational Summit was held in 1996. It was attended by 43 governors. Before the summit, I sent all 50 governors a copy of a special report.

Educational Commission of the States

Its literature states:

> ECS is a national, nonprofit organization that helps gover-
> nors, legislators, state education officials and others identify,
> develop and implement public policies to improve student
> learning at all levels. A nonpartisan organization, ECS was
> formed in 1965 and is located in Denver, Colorado.

The co-founder of the Education Commission of the States was Dr.
Conant. Every year this organization presents the James Bryant
Conant Award to an individual who has made a notable contribution
to the nation's education system. Bill Clinton received this award
when he was governor of Arkansas.

This organization ignored my reports on the situation in the educational field in 1993 and 1997. I agree that this organization should
respect its co-founder, as he was, in his day, a great man with many
achievements to his credit. While he blundered on the scientific
method, it has been his followers who have done the greatest damage
in perpetuating his false claims. This organization must realize that
its first duty is to

society, state residents, and citizens of the United States

Minor Letters

I sent special letters to a few people at the state level at various times,
but nothing of any great importance.

Suggestions for Study

All state officials should study the scientific method situation.
However, until federal programs, SAT and ACT, the 1995 Education
Standards, etc. are corrected to include it, you are limited to what you
can do in your grade schools. Nevertheless, I suggest that you study
the situation with a view to starting to teach the scientific method to
a far greater extent than is presently done. State-supported colleges are
in a much freer position to start teaching the scientific method than
are grade schools.

I predict that the states that teach it best will be those whose student
graduates will be in the greatest demand.

Contribution of Great Britain

In the early days of my research, I gained a lot of respect for the British for their pioneering work on the recognition and development of the scientific method and parts of it. Important work was done by Bacon, George, Westaway, Strong (including lectures of McDougall and Gotch), Wolfe, Locke, Pearson, and Armstrong.

It is not that France, Italy, and other countries did not contribute to the advancement of knowledge about the scientific method, but Great Britain seems to have made the greatest contribution. However, I must point out that I only read and write English and did very little research on the contribution of other countries to the method.

After my Special March 1995 Reports to U.S. organizations which I had publicly challenged in the 1994 edition of *Edmund's Idea and Research Report on the General Pattern of the Scientific Method*, I decided I should send a report to Great Britain. It was headed

A SPECIAL MAY 1995 REPORT TO GREAT BRITAIN
The Royal Society
The Royal Society of Chemistry
Association for Science Education
Association of British Science Writers
Association of Commonwealth Universities
Association of Learned & Professional Society Publishers
London Association of Science Teachers
National Association of Teachers of Further & Higher Education
Society for Protection of Science & Learning
Society of Schoolmasters
Society-Research into Higher Education
on
"THE SCIENTIFIC METHOD"

In the introduction to this report, I mentioned the challenges in my 1994 Idea and Research Report to U.S. organizations. I said that I believed that Great Britain had lost its leadership in researching and recommending the teaching of the scientific method. I also mentioned the positions of Conant, Popper, and Medawar. The report included my two 1994 booklets on the scientific method, supplement to Edmund's Idea and Research Report, and a few other pages.

Also in 1992 I had sent copies of the first edition of my booklets to the Royal Society, the Royal Society of Chemistry, and the Association of

Learned and Professional Society Publishers. I sent a few copies of the 1995 report to others in Great Britain at a later date. To make a long story short, I got no action from Great Britain.

Popper and the British Philosophers of Science Were Probably the Biggest Influence

In Chapter 33 I describe Sir Karl Popper, the famous philosopher. He became very influential, so much so that he was probably the most influential person responsible for Great Britain's contributing to *the* **BLUNDER**.

British Historians of Science

As in the United States, these historians of science have failed to prevent *the* **BLUNDER** by properly reporting science. They are more active and even influential in what is in the science curriculum in Great Britain. They often quote Conant's belief in the value of historical case histories.

Conant Was Very Influential in Great Britain

From the outbreak of World War II in 1939, Conant was outspoken in favor of Great Britain and the need to prepare for war and aid Great Britain. This was not a popular position at the time, but, as history proved, it was foresighted.

On February 15, 1941, Conant went on a dangerous journey to England to coordinate our joint scientific activities. As mentioned in Chapter 3, he returned to the United States. We then helped the British to further develop radar for their benefit and ours.

In this book I am highly critical of Conant's actions concerning the scientific method. But I remind my readers that he made a tremendous contribution to our country during World War II and the Cold War. He recruited scientists to help in the war effort, the development of radar, the atomic bomb, etc.

There was also a lot of discussion in Great Britain of the views of Conant's protege, Thomas Kuhn.

Joint blunder? If Great Britain had not blundered, America's blunder could not have continued, and vice versa.

The Royal Society of London

Here is a famous old society that has done so much for science and the scientific method. I am in the same position as I am with the U.S. National Academy of Sciences. I must point out that the Royal Society has blundered badly! I will not make a big point of its ignoring my special 1995 report, as I only sent two copies. However, this should have been enough!

New British Book Illustrates the Extent of *the* BLUNDER

Professor Gower of Durham University wrote *Scientific Method—An Historical and Philosophical Introduction* in 1997. In the Preface he states:

> Those of my friends and colleagues who knew that I was writing a book about scientific method often expressed their surprise. Why, they said, should anyone wish to revive such a long-expired steed?

Suggestions to the British

In Chapter 33 I point out that Popper's theories on the scientific method have now been challenged more than ever. It is time for you to study my book and the literature and end your part of *the* **BLUNDER**.

I point out that, with your national curricula, you could quickly start teaching the scientific method in all your schools and a study of the scientific method by your adult population and beat the United States to this stage by years. Think, too, how this would improve your world competitiveness!

? ?

The Mysteries

Are the British reasons for no action the same as or similar to those of the United States? How and why, concerning the scientific method, did the Royal Society fall for the reasoning of Popper and the other philosophers of science, Medawar, and the Americans in the Harvard/Conant group and misguided followers (or whoever they are)?

? ?

Contribution of the Association for Supervision and Curriculum Development

The content of our curriculum is of great importance to the success of education. Therefore, ASCD deserves special attention. This is a description of the organization from one of its brochures:

> ASCD, the largest professional leadership organization in education, has more than 120,000 members worldwide. Thirty-seven percent are principals, and the other two-thirds are district superintendents, supervisors, teachers, professors, and school board members.

> Founded in 1943, ASCD is an international education association, apolitical in nature, committed to quality in education for all students.

> ASCD initiates leadership in all areas of supervision and instruction, integrating specific values within the culture and curriculum of the learning environment.

> ASCD supports a balanced curriculum, cultural pluralism, equitable educational opportunities for all groups, self-direction for individuals, professional collaboration, democratic education, social responsibility, global education, and thoughtful learning.

> Fifty-nine affiliate units of ASCD are located in every state, Europe, Canada, and the Caribbean, offering educators regional collaboration on current education issues.

This is the reason I gave ASCD for challenging it in my March 1995 Special Report to the association:

> There are many other educational organizations in the same position as the ASCD who are following the prevailing erroneous concept that "The Scientific Method" does not exist. I included the ASCD in the first group to be challenged because of their preeminent position, their progressiveness in curricula development, and because they are concerned with the whole curriculum. THE GENERAL PATTERN OF THE SCIENTIFIC METHOD (SM-14) is something that should be taught across the curriculum, in all grades . . . not just in science classes.

The Part ASCD Plays in *the* BLUNDER

In ASCD's literature, I did not find any denial of the scientific method, or any acknowledgment of it and the need to teach it. I get the impression that the ASCD has just gone with the tide of the Harvard/Conant group and misguided followers (or whoever they are) and has not attempted to challenge them. It appears to me that ASCD is afraid or reluctant to do so.

My Unsuccessful Attempts to Get ASCD to Study the Scientific Method Situation

1992—I sent copies of the first edition of my booklet.

1994—I notified ASCD of my challenge.

1995—I sent 20 copies of my Special 1995 Report to headquarters rather than to individuals (at the request of ASCD) for distribution to officers and members of the board of directors.

1996—I sent a follow-up letter and Reports 5, 6, and 7. I included a copy of Dr. Easley's article.

I never received any answer to my letters and reports except for ASCD's refusal to furnish names and addresses for my 1995 report and a subsequent notification that the reports had been forwarded.

Suggestions

ASCD should appoint a study group to examine my claims on the scientific method and what part it should play in teaching the scientific method across the curriculum.

? ?

The Mystery

The ASCD is another important organization that has been unwilling to study the scientific method situation.

Why?

? ?

Contribution of the National Association for Research in Science Teaching

From the association's literature:

> The National Association for Research in Science Teaching (NARST) is the division affiliate of NSTA that focuses on research concerning the teaching and learning of science. Its members represent universities and colleges, school districts, and classroom teachers, as well as state and national agencies.

Its mission is to improve science teaching and learning through research. In 2000 it had about 1700 members.

Internal Politics

I do not know and did not take the time to research the internal politics of NARST. I have been a member since about 1991.

It has been sad to read the *NARST News* and its *Journal of Research in Science Teaching*. There is almost no recognition of the scientific method. This is an organization that should be in the forefront of promoting the scientific method and all the details about it. NARST is a small, poorly financed association, with a volunteer executive secretary. It is trying hard, but it is hampered by *the* BLUNDER. Who is to blame internally for its position I do not know. It may be that it is just following the position of NSTA and others that the scientific method does not exist.

Some of the NARST articles I have read are excellent. Others, because they ignore the scientific method, are unreliable.

Not Very Influential

It has been my observation that not much attention is paid to NARST's research. This is also mentioned in the association's own literature at times. When viewed as part of the big picture of education:

- A lot of NARST's efforts are futile because of *the* BLUNDER, as part of their research is unreliable.
- Even what is good is also largely futile, as it is not listened to very often by our top leaders. The continuation of this situation is a waste of money and NARST's earnest efforts.

◆ NARST's efforts should be funneled into a permanent specialized SM-14 type national research center for science teaching.

The blame for this whole situation I again place on the Harvard/Conant group and misguided followers (or whoever they are).

My Unsuccessful Attempts to Get NARST to Study the Scientific Method Situation

1992—My first mailing of booklets went to 22 members of NARST.

1993—On a membership input form I suggested that NARST have the nerve to challenge Conant's followers.

1996—I issued a challenge to NARST to study the scientific method. Reports went to the officers and executive board.

1998—I wrote to William C. Kyle, Jr., editor of the *Journal of Research in Science Teaching*, suggesting that he call his readers' attention to my research.

Again my efforts were unsuccessful. No action was taken, and I received no publicity.

Suggestions for Study

NARST members should study this book, especially Chapter 55 on scientifically based research. They must become well versed in the scientific method. There should be a complete overhaul in the choice of articles accepted for the journal. It seems to me that, once this is accomplished, NARST needs better financing and a plan for better utilization of its research by the science teaching community. Continual improvement in science teaching is important to America's progress.

? ?

The Mystery

Why did *the* **BLUNDER** extend so deeply and completely into the science teaching research community?

? ?

Contribution of the Legal Profession

If you go to a lawyer to have legal papers prepared, or if you are involved in court proceedings, do you want an attorney educated in the basics of problem solving and decision making as well as law to represent you? Sorry, but lawyers and judges, like almost everyone else except scientists, have not been adequately trained in the scientific method.

The lack of training and lack of recognition of the need for training have resulted in the legal profession making a major contribution to *the* **BLUNDER**. For example, if long ago the legal community had required those fulfilling government contracts on educational research to do *real research* (see Chapter 55), *the* **BLUNDER** would never have occurred or continued. For a review of the education of our lawyers, see Chapter 53 on the legal status of the scientific method.

I believe that the evidence indicates that the teaching of the scientific method (SM-14) should be a substantial part of a legal education. There have been a few individuals who realized that lawyers should be using the scientific method.

In *Law and the Modern Mind* (1970), Jerome Frank states:

> While lawyers would do well, to be sure, to learn scientific logic from the expositors of scientific method, it is far more important that they catch *the spirit of the creative scientist*, which yearns not for safety but risk, not for certainty but adventure, which thrives on experimentation, invention and novelty and not on nostalgia for the absolute, which devotes itself to new ways of manipulating protean particulars and not to the quest of undeviating universals.
>
> The experimental approach would be peculiarly serviceable in law. For the practice of law is a series of experiments, of adventures in the adjusting of human relations and the compromising of human conflicts.

That the scientific method has not been taught in law schools has caused and is causing great harm to the proper performance of lawyers and great harm to our welfare. As lawyers are often involved in investigations, Chapter 42 on public safety and the method of investigation will be of interest to those concerned with proper justice for all.

Contribution of the American Educational Research Association

What It Is (From the Organization's Web Site):

AERA is the most prominent international professional organization with the primary goal of advancing educational research and its practical application. Its 20,000 members are educators; administrators; directors of research, testing or evaluation in federal, state and local agencies; counselors; evaluators; graduate students; and behavioral scientists.

The broad range of disciplines represented by the membership includes education, psychology, statistics, sociology, history, economics, philosophy, anthropology, and political science.

Controlled or Influenced By Those Opposed to the Scientific Method

Although I made no detailed study, in reading AERA's literature I found no approval or recommendation of the scientific method. I did find comments against it, such as the following from an article in the *Educational Researcher* (vol. 31, no. 8, November 2002) entitled "Scientific Culture and Education Research":

In approaching the highly contested terrain of method in educational research, the NRC report makes two major points for our purposes. First, it dispels the myth that science is synonymous with a particular method. Although method is key to science, method does not uniquely define science and choices of method are often highly nuanced.

AERA's Contribution to *the* BLUNDER

Because I discuss educational research throughout this book and I cover the nonacceptance of the scientific method by the social sciences in Chapter 27, I will not go into detail here. It is sufficient to say that, as a professional organization, AERA has not really developed educational research into a real profession and one that has earned the respect and confidence of the public, government officials, and even of many of its members.

This book, with its insights into how educational research means research done following the scientific method (SM-14), should provoke this organization into an internal review of its policy and efforts.

Contribution of the Biological Science Curriculum Study

From the BSCS newsletter:

> BSCS seeks to improve students' understanding of science by developing exemplary curriculum materials, by supporting their widespread and effective use and by promoting professional development. BSCS materials preserve the integrity of scientific content, promote understanding of the nature and methods of science and involve students in their own learning by using inquiry as the organizing instructional approach.

This organization was formed in 1958. In the beginning and over the years, the National Science Foundation (NSF) has been its principal funder. In view of the great advances in biology and biosciences, it has been excellent that NSF has provided this support. However, the problem is that BSCS has always presented "science as inquiry" and not as its method. BSCS's 1960 list of themes includes "science as inquiry." Professor Joseph Schwab, who followed Conant's lead, was an active member in the early 1960s. He was noted for advocating science as inquiry and not scientific method.

Three BSCS textbooks in my library do not include the scientific method, and I believe that this is typical of all those this organization published. Personnel from BSCS were active in setting the 1995 National Science Education Standards, which did not include the scientific method, and promoting them. The organization claims to have had a widespread influence on the teaching of biology and science. One of its mottos is "Setting the standards in science education since 1958." I sent BSCS my booklets in 1992 and again in 1999.

Thus, through its activities, BSCS has made a substantial contribution to the perpetuation of *the* **BLUNDER**.

It has been my claim that, despite the billions of federal dollars spent on how to teach science, little has been accomplished in relation to the amount spent. BSCS's monthly magazine had this note (Fall 2002):

> About 70 percent of American adults do not understand the scientific process and many believe in "pseudoscience" like psychic powers, according to the National Science Foundation's (NSF's) biennial report on the state of science understanding.

Contribution of Our Colleges and Universities in General

In this book, I have concentrated mainly on showing the harm to K-12 education caused by *the* BLUNDER. In establishing the authenticity of my claims about *the* BLUNDER, I have covered the contribution of Harvard University, several domains, and others above the K-12 level to *the* BLUNDER. I also covered individually the disaster of not teaching the scientific method in our community colleges and liberal arts colleges. Of course, it has been a disaster that it has not been adequately taught in all colleges and universities.

The scientific method has been taught to our scientists, engineers, doctors, and others by the apprentice method. It has been taught by some individual professors. It has been taught under such other names as problem solving, decision making, creative problem solving, guided design, operation research, and others. But still it has all been to a very inadequate extent, considering its importance. In my opinion, this situation has resulted from the influence of the Harvard/Conant group and misguided followers (or whoever they are).

Nevertheless, our colleges and universities should have challenged their ideas and influence. That they did not means that they have made a major contribution to *the* BLUNDER.

It is not within the scope of this book to explore this situation in detail. However, I briefly point out some of the harms caused by it above and beyond the non-teaching of the scientific method.

No Permanent Specialized SM-14 Type National Research Center on the Big Picture of Our Colleges and Universities Exists

It appears to me that no existing organization presents the big picture. Basically, this would be an advisory or research summarization organization and would not interfere with the autonomy or academic freedom of colleges and universities. Because it does not exist, many issues remain unsettled for years, even decades.

Academic Freedom

This is an essential part of our college and university system. But academic freedom is constantly harmed by wild-eyed claims not based on accurate problem definition, analysis, research, and open-mindedness. Widespread use and knowledge of the scientific method would contribute to academic freedom.

College Curriculum—What Should It Be?

This issue never gets the intensive research that a permanent specialized SM-14 type national research center on curriculum would give it. Thus, there is a big dispute about what a student should learn.

The Thinking Ability of College Graduates

In an October 14, 2003 article in the *Christian Science Monitor,* "Rethinking Thinking," Mark Clayton wrote:

> College classes that make one think—it's a basic concept assumed as a given. But many grads walk away with a diploma yet still lack critical-thinking skills. That's why some educators are asking students to close their textbooks and do a little more reflecting.

There are plenty of other articles indicating that our college graduates are not adequately taught thinking and problem solving. This condition results from *the* BLUNDER. Another result of *the* BLUNDER is from an article by Stephen Bird (*Chronicle of Higher Education,* July 11, 2003):

Bush's Next Target?

> The president would also reprimand colleges for allowing too many students—especially low-income and minority students—to drop out and remain without the skills and knowledge they need. In addition, he would question the quality of education that most students receive.

College Dropout Problem

First, if the scientific method is widely taught in higher education and also taught in K-12, we should have fewer dropouts. Second, if it is widely taught in the first year of college, the college dropout rate should decrease greatly. In addition, those who do drop out will already have had some education about the scientific method.

Better Education for All Students

All students would get a better quality education if they and their professors were taught the scientific method, as everyone has been harmed by *the* BLUNDER.

Summary of Part 6

Contributions to *the* BLUNDER

In my research, I selected and reported on the major organizations and many of the minor ones I believed contributed to *the* BLUNDER. However, in fairness to all, I would like to remind my readers that there are probably many others that I did not cover.

I hope members of various organizations will encourage their leaders to examine and study their positions on scientific method and help in correcting *the* BLUNDER.

I also remind my readers that I, too, have contributed to *the* BLUNDER. For example:

♦ In 1963, when I read Dr. Crooks' article on the scientific method, I did not carry through on my idea of writing a booklet based on the article.

♦ In 1975, when I retired and had the time to write a booklet, I put it off until 1989.

♦ In 1992, when I published my first booklets and made a substantial effort to get the misunderstandings corrected, I was not successful.

♦ While my first formula for SM-14 was not bad, it was not until January 1997 that I really got it correct.

♦ My many efforts from 1992 to 1999 to get *the* BLUNDER corrected were not successful. So I goofed in not coming up with the right methods or ideas about how to accomplish its acceptance.

♦ It has taken me from 1999 to 2004 to write this book.

? ?

The Mystery

Will this book end the biggest educational and intellectual blunder in history as I predict it will?

? ?

Introduction to Part 7

Harms in Domains Other Than Education

This book is primarily about the harm of *the* **BLUNDER** to the domain of education. However, it has affected every domain, some to such an extent that, if I had time, I could write many more books.

To give you a small picture, I have written several chapters about certain domains and an assortment of short reports about others. The size of these reports does not necessarily correspond to their importance. I have not covered all domains that were harmed.

The main reason for my calling these to your attention is to impress upon you the big overall need to teach the scientific method across the curriculum so that we end *the* **BLUNDER**. Read on to see the harm that has been done to your welfare in all these areas. Remember this saying: "Defective problem solving is the cause of all disorders in the world."

The story told in this book is almost unbelievable. It is not a pleasant duty to have to call it to the attention of our leaders and the public. This book and my booklets and reports support my statements. Remember, I make no claim

> that even with the universal teaching of the scientific method we will have a perfect society. While the scientific method is basically an efficient method, it is used by humans and therefore results will vary, with perfection not obtained.

Protect your family's welfare (and our country's) by doing your part to correct the matter. Study *the* **BLUNDER**'s effect on your domain and others and take action based on your evaluation.

Chapter 42

Harms to Public Safety

In presenting the harms to domains other than education, I begin with public safety because of its great importance to our lives. The public's health, lives, prevention of problems and crime, justice, etc., all involve using the method of investigation, which is the scientific method.

Since September 11, 2001, America has a new war. The terrorist threat demands that all our citizens and residents, especially our public safety officials, know the method of prevention, the method of inquiry, the method of investigation—all of which are the scientific method.

Much of the information I present here applies to all the domains mentioned in this book, for the method of investigation should be used in every domain.

◆ The Method of Investigation—the Scientific Method—Is Needed in America's War on Terrorism

◆ A Standard Method of Investigation Formula Is Needed in the Public Safety Field

◆ National Research Council Report on *Fairness and Effectiveness in Policing: The Evidence*

◆ Mystery

The Method of Investigation—The Scientific Method—Is Needed in America's New War on Terrorism

Attention All Law Enforcement Agencies and Officers, All National Defense and Intelligence Agency Personnel, and the Public

The **BLUNDER** has prevented our security officers from being properly educated in the complete method of creative problem solving and decision making—the scientific method. This has caused harm to our nation's public safety, including law enforcement, crime prevention, and national security.

Scientists and others over the centuries recognized and developed the scientific method in their investigations of the natural world. The creative, non-logical, logical, and technical methods used at the various stages of the scientific method vary in different types of investigations. The stages, while used flexibly, do not. You cannot efficiently investigate by proceeding by chance, just "doing your thing," or using miscellaneous formulas. The scientific method should be your guide.

These are the reasons the scientific method should be used:

◆ Investigation is basically a problem-solving and decision-making activity, which can be broken down into stages.

◆ The scientific method (SM-14) is the complete method of creative problem solving and decision making for all fields. Thus, it is also the method of investigation.

◆ The scientific method provides the 11 stages of mental activity, usually aided by physical activities, that are essential in any investigation of a complex problem.

◆ The scientific method has been used and tested over the centuries against all other methods and found superior to all other methods.

◆ There is a large body of reliable knowledge concerning the scientific method available to those who want to seek it out. *The Scientific Method Today* is the best summary currently available.

◆ When properly used, the scientific method provides the most constructive, penetrating, and reliable results in the most efficient manner and time.

Be Careful

Keep in mind:

◆ *The stages of the scientific method* represent a guide to the type of mental activity involved.

◆ *The techniques actually used to solve the problem* are the creative, non-logical, logical, and technical methods. These are used at the various stages as required. Examples of some of the technical methods in the field of investigation are criminalistics, forensic medicine, fingerprinting, DNA profiling, psychological profiling, etc.

◆ There are wheels within wheels. Whenever you apply one of the more complex techniques, you must again follow the stages of the scientific method. Another example of wheels within wheels is breaking down complex problems into sub-problems and sub-sub-problems. The scientific method must be followed for all.

To those in the law and defense fields, Robert J. Marzano's presentation of types will be interesting. The following is from *A Different Kind of Classroom, Teaching with Dimensions of Learning* (1992):

> There are three basic types of investigation. *Definitional investigation* involves answering such questions as "What are the defining characteristics of. . .?" or "What are the important features of. . .?" *Historical investigation* involves answering such questions as "How did this happen?" and "Why did this happen?" And *projective investigation* involves answering such questions as "What would happen if. . .?" and "What would have happened if. . .?"

You Can't Beat Science and Its Method

Dr. Vannevar Bush, a well-known scientist who aided in the World War II effort and the establishment of the National Science Foundation, aptly described the value of the scientific endeavor. I quoted him at the beginning of this book, but I repeat it here because it is a wonderful description:

> Advances in science when put to practical use mean more jobs, higher wages, shorter hours, more abundant crops, more leisure for recreation, for study, for learning how to live without the deadening drudgery which has been the burden of the common man for ages past. Advances in science will also bring higher standards of living, will lead to the prevention or cure of diseases, will promote conservation of our limited national resources, and *will assure means of defense against aggression*. But to achieve these objectives—to secure a high level of employment, *to maintain a position of world leadership*—the flow of new scientific knowledge must be both continuous and substantial. [*Emphasis mine.*]

So we must put the method of science to use in training for defense against aggression and terrorism if we are to maintain our world leadership and our safety.

Who Has Not Heard of Sherlock Holmes?

In *Introduction to Logic* (1982), under the heading "Scientists in Action: The Pattern of Scientific Investigation," Dr. I.M. Copi states:

> As the term "scientific" is generally used today, it refers to any reasoning which attempts to proceed from observable facts of experience to reasonable (that is, relevant and testable) explanations for those facts. The scientific method is not confined to professional scientists: anyone can be said to be proceeding scientifically who follows the general pattern of reasoning from evidence to conclusions that can be tested by experience. The skilled detective is a scientist in this sense, as are most of us—in our more rational moments, at least. The pervasive pattern of all scientific inquiry is expressible in terms of the steps illustrated in the preceding section.

In his preceding section, Dr. Copi describes how Sherlock Holmes used the general pattern of scientific research in solving cases.

Here are two interesting comments from science books on detective work.

Way Back in 1903—Similarity Recognized

The similarity of the scientific method and the method of investigation has long been recognized.

In *The Teaching of the Scientific Method and Other Papers on Education* (1903), British author Henry Armstrong states:

> In pointing out how to practise in peace times, he [Baden Powell, founder of the Boy Scout movement] strongly recommends would-be scouts to read *The Memoirs of Sherlock Holmes*, by Conan Doyle, and see how, by noticing a number of small signs, he "puts this and that together" and gathers important information. This, again, is precisely our method—the scientific method: in fact, I have for years past urged upon my students that the method adopted by the detective is that of the scientific worker and the only possible one to adopt in studying science as a mental and moral discipline. If heads of schools will but regard science from such a point of view, they will have little difficulty in understanding its importance and value as an essential factor in

education; they will then also understand the spirit in which it must be taught to be of use in schools.

Important Evidence from Ritchie Calder

Ritchie Calder was a chairman of the British Association of Science Writers. In *Science in Our Lives* (1954), he states:

> There is a very good reason why scientists are addicted to detective fiction: a well-written "whodunit" is a leisure-hour scientific thesis. For crime-detection depends essentially on the scientific method—observation, hypothesis, experiment, theory and proof. *Observation* is the collection of the available facts; *hypothesis* is the tentative assumption made from these facts; *experiment* is the testing of the facts in the light of the assumption; *theory* is the hypothesis when it has become respectable enough to justify holding the suspect; and the *proof* is what the prosecutor needs to support the theory before a jury.

If not for **the BLUNDER**, the scientific method would have been extensively taught in schools training our police officers, defense personnel, and other investigators. However, it has not been adequately taught, so there are frequent cases of

lives lost
the innocent convicted unfairly
the guilty escaping punishment
and other tragedies

For more information on the scientific method, read my pamphlet *The Scientific Method Today*, in the appendix.

A Standard Method of Investigation Formula Is Needed in the Public Safety Field

I have provided evidence of the importance of the scientific method to investigators for both problem solving and decision making. Due to the misunderstandings about the scientific method for the past 50 years, those in the criminal and defense fields have not been properly educated in the method. Professors, trainers, authors, and others have offered either no formula or a variety of inadequate formulas for the stages of the scientific method. Therefore, we have had a force of investigators not as well trained as they could easily have been.

There is a need for a standard formula for the stages of the scientific method, such as SM-14, for these reasons:

♦ There are many advantages to standardizing on the usual mental activity stages of the scientific method. Thus wandering, chance, and other disadvantages of not using a method or guide can be avoided. Instead of introducing rigidity, the opposite—intelligent flexibility—is provided. The stages are used in a flexible manner; one may skip, backtrack, loop, stop, etc. in following the guide or method.

♦ The evaluation of testimony of expert or ordinary witnesses should be based on the scientific method. In *Daubert v. Merrell Dow Pharmaceuticals, Inc.*, 509 U.S. 579 (1993), the U.S. Supreme Court ruled:

> But, in order to qualify as "scientific knowledge" an inference or assertion must be derived by the scientific method.

This ruling alone requires a standard method. It will be more accurately implemented by adopting a standard formula, such as SM-14.

♦ Investigators must work together all over the country. Therefore, they should be working with an understanding of the same basic formula. It facilitates progress and teamwork.

♦ The thinking skills involved in problem solving and investigation all relate to use at the various stages of the scientific method. Thus, they are more clearly and easily taught when a standard formula is used. So-called "critical thinking" is actually problem-solving thinking.

♦ The miscellaneous formulas frequently used are usually incomplete. SM-14 represents more than 15 years of research for a correct formula, and it may be used freely.

National Research Council Report on *Fairness and Effectiveness in Policing: The Evidence* (2004)

In this book I have had to criticize the work of the top leaders of the National Academy of Sciences in the social science field because of their lack of understanding of the scientific method—an amazing and blundering situation! A few months ago I got a guilty conscience about it and decided to tone down my comments. After reviewing them, I decided that they were warranted and made no changes. Here I go again, for the matter of public safety is all important!

This NRC report was produced by the Committee to Review Research on Police Policy and Practices 2000–2003 and the Committee on Law and Justice. It is evident that those who worked on the report were inadequately educated in the scientific method—a result of *the* **BLUNDER** and its harm. There are only two incidental mentions of the scientific method. The report covers problem-oriented policing and states that there is a growing body of research evidence that it is an effective approach. On problem solving the report states:

> The desirability of a problem-solving approach to policing has taken hold in many police agencies in the United States (Scott, 2000). A conference devoted to problem solving, sponsored annually by the Police Executive Research Forum, is attended by members of hundreds of departments from around the nation. Surveys of police agencies suggest that the popularity of this approach is widespread (Maguire and Mastrofski, 2000), yet it too suffers from the same measurement difficulties as does community liaison and mobilization.

? ?

The Mystery

When will our top leaders understand that the war on terrorism and crime and that justice for all require good old Sherlock Holmes-type work and the complete method of creative problem solving and decision making?

Problems, problems, decisions, decisions—that's what we have—but almost no scientific method in the field of public safety!

? ?

Chapter 43

Harms to the Field of Economics Caused by *the* BLUNDER

Economists like to be considered separately from business, industry, and the social sciences in general. For this reason and because of its great importance, I cover economics separately. Its practitioners advise our presidents, Congress, and business and industry, so there is little doubt of its importance and the need for this domain to provide reliable knowledge.

It is the responsibility of each domain to operate efficiently. From the standpoint that the domain of economics has not adequately embraced the teaching and use of the scientific method, it has contributed to *the* BLUNDER.

I report here mainly on the harms to economists and our economic welfare caused by *the* BLUNDER.

Is Economics Really a Science?

In the literature, I found these descriptions or names for economics:

The Dismal Science
The most "exact" of the social sciences
The science of the production of wealth
Economic thinking is scientific thinking
Economics is a soft science—not as successful as physical sciences
Economics is the queen of the social sciences
Economics is the most human of of social sciences
Economics is a science of choices
Economics is the maximizing science
Economics is the most quantitative of the social sciences

The Domain of Economics Is Not a Science Today, Although It Should Be

While economics may be classified as a science in the literature, it is my claim that it is not qualified to be a science at the present time.

In Chapter 55 I explain what a "science" consists of. While economics meets most of the requirements, its group of practitioners is not adequately educating its members in and using the scientific method thoroughly enough to deserve to be classified as a "science"—just like most or all of the "social sciences." However, they often do a good job of using some of the techniques essential to their work.

I am not qualified to judge the reliability of the principles of economics or its techniques—the creative, non-logical, logical, and technical methods specific to the domain. However, I claim to see the big picture of the scientific method, so I will review here the status of the scientific method in the field of economics.

In *The American Economy* (1972), Sampson et al. point out that economics is probably the most exact of the social sciences. They state:

> For this reason, people have a right to expect a higher degree of reliability from economics than from most of the other social sciences.

Since they do not adequately teach and use the scientific method in the economics field, it is questionable to what extent they reach a higher degree of reliability. This inadequate teaching and use of the scientific method I claim is the biggest blunder in the history of economics.

The field of economics may be the most quantitative of the social sciences, but it needs lots of qualitative logical reasoning. In complex problem solving and forecasting, it is necessary to

- use the method that has been found after centuries of study to produce the most reliable knowledge—the scientific method—which is also the best quality control method ever recognized and developed

- follow the established scientific method because it is far more reliable than "doing your thing"

Figures can deceive, so quantitative methods and techniques are most reliable when they are applied following the scientific method (SM-14 type or comparable).

Economics Textbooks

A key to the extent of knowledge and the use by economists of the scientific method is gained by examining the textbooks used in economists' education and those for students who study but do not specialize in economics.

John Maynard Keynes (1883–1946)

From the website cepa.newschool.edu/het/profiles/keynes.htm:

> John Maynard Keynes is doubtlessly one of the most important figures in the entire history of economics. He revolutionized economics with his classic book, *The General Theory of Employment, Interest and Money* (1936). This is generally regarded as probably the most influential social science treatise of the 20th Century, in that it quickly and permanently changed the way the world looked at the economy and the role of government in society. No other single book, before or since, has had quite such an impact.

I did not review his works, but a number of authors quote him as saying economics was "a method rather than a doctrine, a technique of thinking, which helps its possessor to draw correct conclusions."

However, I believe that he never went on and specifically recommended the scientific method. During his lifetime (1883–1946), there was only a small body of knowledge on it compared to what we have learned since his lifetime.

Here I present the number of pages devoted to the scientific method in the more recent past and present bestselling college textbooks on economics.

Book title	Author	Range of copyright dates	No. of pages that specifically mention the scientific method
Economics	Samuelson, Nordhaus	1948–1985	2
Economics	McConnell, Brue	1963–1993	0
Economics, Principles and Policy	Baunol, Binder	1979–1984	0
Principles of Economics	Mankiw	1998	2

While there are reported to be more than 40 economics textbooks actively marketed today, I only reviewed a few older ones in my library. These too were the same, with at most a few pages devoted to the scientific method.

My Attempt to Influence Economics Textbook Publishers

In 1997 Professor Gregory Mankiw of Harvard University received a $1.4 million advance for his textbook on economics. This book contained only a few pages on the scientific method. In November 1997 I wrote to six of the major textbook publishers, giving 10 reasons why textbooks on economics should cover the scientific method more thoroughly. I received no answers to my letters.

The Harm Extends to High School National Content Standards in Economics K-12

These standards were produced by the National Council on Economics Education. An examination of the standards (2nd printing, 1998, original copyright 1997) showed no mention of the scientific method or a formula for problem solving or decision making. This probably reflects the college education in economics received by those who prepared the standards and a general lack of teaching of the scientific method. This is another harm of *the* BLUNDER in K-12.

A Simple Rule of Economics Applied by Edmund to Education

If you correct or prevent errors at the top of a system, the cost is substantially lower than if you allow the error to permeate the system and then try to correct it in numerous ways in many places at the bottom of the system. It is the continual violation of this rule in the educational field that is responsible for the waste of billions of taxpayers' dollars. **Why haven't economists spotted this and advised substantial changes at the top level of education?**

Economists Are Becoming More Active in Education

The October 25, 2000, edition of *Education Week* contained an article by Bess Keller entitled "More Practitioners of the 'Dismal Science' Casting an Eye Toward Education." The impression I got from reading the article is that economists do not understand the point I make above. Some seem to realize that the voucher movement is harmful to education in general, as I mention in Chapter 13, The Disaster of the

Charter School, Voucher, and School Choice Movement. Other prominent economists have promoted the voucher system. Until economists begin to adequately use the scientific method, their opinions and "research" on education cannot be considered reliable.

Suggestions for Study

Today everything is more complex. No longer can economics professors expect students to depend on authoritative statements of economic principles and methods that appear in textbooks.

A permanent specialized SM-14 type national research center on economics is needed for both college and high school teaching of economics. Those majoring in economics must be taught very thoroughly the scientific method.

Edmund Should Be Awarded a Nobel Prize

The very serious and critical nature of this book has prevented me from injecting much humor into it. However, before I leave economics, I have a few words to say, some true and some humorous, that bring out other points about economics.

I write this on February 27, 2001, my 85th birthday, prompted by a front-page article in today's *Wall Street Journal* by two economists who advise President George W. Bush about the national budget. I dislike arrogance—it has been responsible for many educational ills—but nevertheless, since it is my birthday, as a little present to myself, I nominate myself for a Nobel Prize. There is none for education, so that's out. There is one for physics and one for chemistry. It is "true" that if students are taught the scientific method and go on to become scientists that knowing the scientific method early rather than learning it by the apprentice method should substantially increase their productivity. But I'm not interested in the physics or chemistry prize. You know from reading this that I would never qualify for the prize in literature, and certainly not for the peace prize—this book may provoke a "war." My first career was as a businessman, so I'm after the Nobel Prize in Economic Sciences. Now you know why I said all those critical things about economists. They don't qualify, but I do!

I'm a little worried, as a recent recipient, when asked if surprised, said no, since there were only 1,000 or so economists (I guess he meant good ones). Maybe they can be convinced to give the prize to an ordinary person.

Here are the grounds for my Nobel Prize in Economic Sciences:

♦ When finally the scientific method is adequately taught to all students and when our adult population learns to use it a great deal more, economists will have to factor this into their models and forecasts. It is not a perfect method because it is used by humans, but it is still "the greatest idea of all time." For example, just as computers have increased our national productivity, the scientific method, when more widely used, will increase productivity and prevent disasters and to some extent major wrong decisions in all fields. In addition, it will promote greater creativity and entrepreneurship. It will be a while before this SM-14 productivity factor has to be considered, but the time is coming.

♦ The better use of the scientific method by economists will help prevent the wide variances in their present forecasts. The future is hard to predict, but experienced students of the scientific method can better apply their knowledge. It may even turn a "dismal science" into a happy one. I bet economists would even be happy to see me get the Nobel Prize for helping them so much!

♦ The recent literature that talks about a firm's intellectual capital or human capital being the knowledge of its personnel is incorrect. The proper formula is its personnel's knowledge of subject matter plus its ability, experience, and know-how in applying its knowledge following the scientific method. Economists should understand this. (I'm getting closer to the prize.)

♦ The current interest of economists in education and social problems will result in many unreliable results unless they follow the scientific method and realize that social scientists as a group have not been acknowledging the existence of the scientific method.

♦ The knowledge explosion is creating increased complexity of life and economics. We should start to build a complexity index.

♦ A practical forecast scale should be adopted along the lines of the one in my booklet *The Scientific Method Today*.

The administration of the Nobel Prize is in the hands of the Royal Swedish Academy of Science and its committees. There is an old saying that flattery gets you everywhere. So I tried to think of something nice to say here about the Royal Swedish Academy to help me get a Nobel Prize. But, darn it, I'm actually disgusted with them.

In the Spring-Summer 1998 issue of *Science Link* I read that the Royal Swedish Academy and the NSRC, a venture of the Smithsonian Institution and the National Academy of Sciences, had agreed to translate and adapt the Science and Technology for Children (STC) for use in Sweden's elementary schools. Since top leaders of our National Academy of Sciences are among the big perpetuators of the false claims that the scientific method doesn't exist, I knew that the program did not include teaching it. In addition, NAS ignored all my efforts, challenges, and special reports to them.

I knew that our intellectuals were greatly interested in the Nobel Prizes, so I reasoned that if I could get the Royal Swedish Academy interested in preventing Swedish students from being taught science incorrectly, I might make some progress in America.

I spent several weeks preparing a special report for the Royal Swedish Academy and sent copies in September 1998 to the Secretary General, the President, and the coordinator of the education project with a request that they and their council review it and a member be assigned to make a detailed study of the material I sent. *I didn't even get an answer!* This made me very unhappy, so even if they offer me the prize, I'll decline. I'm bashful and not very good at speeches, so it is just as well I don't accept.

However, the really bad thing is that America is exporting its false concept about "the greatest idea of all time" to other countries, and these countries are swallowing it hook, line, and sinker because of our reputation.

February 27, 2003—An Update on My Nobel Prize Claim

Gosh, two more birthdays have rolled by, and I'm still writing this book. It makes me think again that I deserve the Nobel Prize. After all, writing critical things about everyone is hard work—even dangerous. Who knows what will happen to me when this book is published! But my chance for a Nobel Prize is improving. In October 2002, the Swedish Academy awarded the Nobel Prize in Economics to a psychologist rather than an economist. Good for them! Maybe I'm eligible after all! I take back those disparaging remarks about the Royal Swedish Academy of Science. I bet the Swedish mail clerk at the Academy never gave them my reports!

I just read a very interesting article in *Education Next* (Fall 2002) by Eric Hanushek. It is called "The Seeds of Growth." Hanushek says that if gross domestic product per capita were to grow at 1 percent each year, it would increase from \$34,950 in 2000 to \$57,480 in the year 2050. However, if it were to grow 2 percent per year, it would reach \$94,000 in 2050! This increases my hopes for a Nobel Prize!

Remember that when SM-14 starts to be taught across the curriculum and to present workers, I'm turning all educational researchers, top leaders, economists, lawyers, and business people into full-fledged "scientists." All the information and "knowledge" on the internet will be much more reliable when it is certified as done following the scientific method.

Even allowing for human nature and that some might not develop into good "scientists," this change alone ought to increase gross domestic product by 2 percent in 10 to 50 years. All the top influential misguided leaders I have been talking about will be so grateful that I told them about their blunder that they will write to the Royal Swedish Academy and nominate me for the Nobel Prize. Now I know I'll get a Nobel Prize! Oops—I just remembered that they don't award the prize posthumously, and I'll be dead before my theory is proven. Oh, well! I guess I'll go back to being disgusted with the Royal Swedish Academy for not taking action on the report I sent them.

Well, if I can't get the Nobel Prize, I bet I could qualify for one of the booby prizes I read about. After all, I accidentally discovered and then started publicizing the misunderstandings back in 1992. All my efforts to correct them have been flops! Yet I claim to be more creative than most people! Well, if you know of any booby prizes, please submit my name as a big goofer.

Back to Reality—Summary

Throughout this book, I have explained the need for method and the use of the scientific method and its associated thinking skills.

Many economists have become experts in many of the creative, logical, and technical methods used at the stages of the scientific method. Thus, they have been successful many times. But economists' work involves much decision making, predicting, and problem solving. All these activities are greatly improved by applying the scientific method—the greatest quality control method ever recognized and developed. It is important to our society that they use it more adequately.

Chapter 44

Harms to Capitalism

The scientific method and capitalism have this in common: The scientific method is an imperfect system but phenomenally successful compared to other knowledge systems. A capitalistic system is a very, very imperfect system but still phenomenally successful compared to other economic systems.

+ The Scientific Method Can Aid the Big Advantages Capitalism Has Over Socialism and Communism

+ The Scientific Method Is the Method of Creating Wealth

+ The Scientific Method Aids Free Markets, Limited Government, and Individual Liberties

+ Competition Is the Lifeblood of Capitalism and Is Aided by the Use of the Scientific Method

+ Summary and Mysteries

The Scientific Method Can Aid the Big Advantages Capitalism Has over Socialism and Communism

Motivated to Make More Effort to Be Productive

At the beginning of this book I quoted Dr. Vannevar Bush on the value of science. To achieve the value, you need the capitalist system to bring them to people.

Under a capitalistic system, people are motivated to work harder and produce more for the the reward of their personal efforts. The scientific method is the method of working efficiently and more productively. Therefore, it contributes to making capitalism work better and produce more jobs and greater wealth.

Risk Taking

Under capitalism, people are more willing to take risks if they benefit personally. The scientific method, being the method of investigation, the problem solving method, etc., guides them to be more accurate and successful in risk taking. Thus, more jobs are produced.

Creativity

Under capitalism, creativity flourishes. The scientific method is the complete method of creative problem solving and decision making. Creativity leads to greater job availability and the creation of greater wealth.

Entrepreneurship

Entrepreneurship is able to flourish under capitalism and is one of the great reasons for its success. As explained previously, the scientific method is also the method of entrepreneurship. Entrepreneurs are big job producers and wealth creators.

The Scientific Method Is the Method of Creating Wealth

Numerous studies and experiences have shown that sharing and redistributing wealth is not a practical solution to poverty or society's problems. The real way to wealth is through the production of more wealth. As I show in the sections on

Scientists, Engineers, and Technologists
Business and Industry
Economics
Agriculture

the real way to producing more wealth is the more efficient use of the scientific method in these and all other domains. Through the use of the scientific method, reliable knowledge can be created. Then the scientific method can be used to efficiently apply knowledge for productive purposes.

The past popularity of socialism and communism with some people can be traced to lack of knowledge of how the application of the scientific method—when you reward people for using it—can do wonders for everyone and performs better than any other system ever tested in competition with it.

The Scientific Method Aids Free Markets, Limited Government, and Individual Liberties

Capitalism flourishes best with the above. But what happens? People use bad judgment, make bad decisions, and do not act ethically. Thus, there is clamor for the government to make laws and regulations.

Teaching it and the practical use of the scientific method tend to limit these bad activities, leading to fewer restrictions.

In 2002, we saw the bankruptcy of Enron and WorldCom because of poor ethics, poor management, poor problem solving, and poor decision making. The result has been more government laws and restrictions and the loss of the public's confidence in business.

Competition Is the Lifeblood of Capitalism and Is Aided by the Use of the Scientific Method

To compete means to do a better job than others. The way to do this is through better problem solving and decision making than others.

As the result of conspiracies, arrogance, protecting turf, secrecy about the scientific method, and lack of knowledge about methods of knowledge, there has been the biggest intellectual and educational blunder in history. The competition among our intellectuals and educators has been stifled, thereby hurting capitalism.

Those who are preventing the education of our students in the scientific method must stop for the good of capitalism and society.

Employers' Needs and Job Seekers Are Aided by the Scientific Method

One of the notebooks I keep contains articles stressing the need for problem solvers. In an editorial in *Science* (October 16, 1996), Anne Petersen made this statement:

> We also know that the 21st-century U.S. work force will require skills such as solving complex problems, dealing with uncertainty, and probing the unknown that are best acquired through discovery-based learning experiences.

All of these are best provided by an education in the scientific method. It provides employers with the workforce they need and job seekers with many of the essential skills they need. All of this helps the capitalist system to function better. When it functions better, there are more jobs and more wealth.

In 1938 Robert A. Millikan gave a speech worth reading on the contribution of the scientific method to capitalism and social justice. The speech, "Science and Social Justice, 'A Stupendous Amount of Woefully Crooked Thinking,' " was given before the New York Herald Tribune Forum, October 25–28, 1938, and published in *Vital Speeches of the Day* (December 1, 1938). In Chapter 48 I quote from this speech.

Over the centuries, all methods of originating, refining, and extending knowledge have competed. As Professor Morris Cohen states (see Chapter 53), after other methods, it is only the scientific method that is most reliable. Dr. Millikan stresses the following about the scientific method:

- It established its effectiveness 300 years ago
- It is a general method for discovering truth
- It is applicable to social sciences, although techniques are different
- In it lie all our hopes for the future of human betterment

This is straight thinking rather than the crooked, twisting, emotional thinking that falsely claims that the scientific method does not exist.

Capitalism is based not on competition but on fair competition. We have had the unfair competition of an "authoritative" group in charge of educational reform at the national level using their power to prevent the teaching of the scientific method. Thus they have hurt the growth of our economy, capitalism, and society.

? ?

The Mysteries

We have a great many organizations claiming to promote the capitalistic system, conservatism, competition, economics, and limited government interference. Yet many are participating in *the* **BLUNDER.** Are they not, instead of helping capitalism, hurting it?

Will they, as Dr. Millikan states, be a "real progressive" and use their influence to "study the problem intensively to see what kind of action does actually lead toward the economic and social well-being of the community as a whole"?

? ?

Chapter 45

Harms to and Caused by Conservatives and Liberals Battling over Education

---

- ◆ When Conservatives and Liberals Tackle a Problem, They Are Not Properly Trained in the Scientific Method
- ◆ Harm the Conservatives and Liberals Are Causing to Education

---

When Conservatives and Liberals Tackle a Problem, They Are Not Properly Trained in the Scientific Method

We have the widely used terms liberal and conservative. Normally, debates and opposite positions serve the purpose of helping to solve problems or at least hopefully presenting the issues clearly and accurately. However, almost no one has had an adequate education in the scientific method. Therefore, these debates and fights often suffer. Thus, they and the public are misled many times.

In this book, I point out that our professional educators are not solving many of the ills of education and are even creating new problems. They debate these problems in publications, usually not providing reliable information or research. Soon the news spreads. Then those outside the professional education field take a position.

It is now a double or triple whammy to society, for our conservatives and liberals take positions that are not based on reliable knowledge or the scientific method.

Since they have not been educated in the scientific method, they do not recognize that they are fighting over a disaster that should not be.

Thus, the problem is often not solved or made worse.

As is often the case, no one wins, but the public and our students suffer because of their actions.

Harm the Conservatives and Liberals Are Causing to Education

The following is from an article that appeared in *Education Week* (October 4, 2000), "Leaders Pledge to Stay the Course":

Declaring themselves the voice of mainstream America, the leaders of a growing alternative group for education leaders used their fifth annual conference here last month to stake claims in education's most challenging terrain.

On topics ranging from standardized testing and merit pay for teachers to school choice and the federal role in K-12 education, members of the conservative-leaning Education Leaders Council often derided the views of their opponents, whom they referred to as "the loosey-goosey left" and the "guardians of mediocrity."

At the opening session, this statement was made: "We have a basic philosophical battle here we need to win."

My observation is that all the major conservative and liberal groups are, as stated above, waging more a wrong philosophical battle than one based on the scientific method.

All the topics mentioned in the above quotation represent disasters I have pointed out. Thus, by not seeing or seeking out the big picture of education and investigating and using the scientific method, the conservatives and liberals are doing great harm to education.

In his book *On the Death of Childhood and the Destruction of Public Schools* (2003), Professor Gerald W. Bracey has some interesting comments on "The Rights Data Proof Idealogues" and the harm they have done to education.

When the day comes that all groups properly use the scientific method, there will be fewer differences in all their activities, and the remaining ones will be better understood and debated.

? ?

The Mystery

Will conservatives, modernists, and liberals learn to use the scientific method, or are they just interested in pushing biased views?

? ?

Chapter 46

Harms to Business and Industry
(Including Various Associated Professions)

In Chapter 39 I covered the "Contribution of Business and Industry to *the* **BLUNDER**." Here I show the harms caused to business and industry by *the* **BLUNDER**. However, in the fields of business and industry are many of our top intellectuals, who should have kept these harms from occurring.

Before my present career of 15 years as an educational researcher, I spent 35 years as a businessman. After more than 15 years of research of the scientific method, I have been able to see many of the harms to business and industry caused by *the* **BLUNDER**. These I *did not* see during my business career, although I had planned on promoting creativity and education in personal attributes after my retirement.

As this is a book primarily about the educational harm of *the* **BLUNDER**, I have tried to limit my essays on the harms in other domains. However, they are so great that books can and will be written about them by others. I give only a few short descriptions of the other great harms in the business field, each of which is of great importance.

Authors of Books on Management, etc.

There has been a flood of books for business and industry on how to improve operations, but 90 percent or more have no mention or incorporation in their advice about using the scientific method. These books may contain great ideas, but they lack the "greatest idea of all time," the scientific method.

How Leaders Make Decisions and Solve Problems

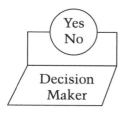

Remember the little gadget for the desks of decision makers? Just spin the coin for the correct answer!

Surprise—it works just as well as managers do!

This squib from the *Wall Street Journal* of July 25, 1996 states:

> DECISIONS GO SOUR about half of the time for managers, says Paul Nutt, a professor at Ohio State University's Max M. Fisher College of Business in Columbus. His research finds that managers fail about 50% of the time on decisions ranging from what products to sell to renovating office space.

Frankly, I find it hard to believe that decision making is poor. But here is more evidence that it is not what it should be.

In *Complex Problem Solving* (1991) Wagner states:

> Mintzberg's influential studies of what managers actually do, as opposed to what they are supposed to do, or what they say they do, provided unwelcome news to proponents of rational approaches to managerial problem solving. Mintzberg found that even successful managers rarely, if ever, employed rational approaches. Rather than following a step-by-step sequence from problem definition to problem solution, managers typically groped along with only vague impressions about the nature of the problems they were dealing with, and with little idea of what the ultimate solution would be until they found it. Isenberg reached a similar conclusion in his analysis of how senior managers solve problems. The senior managers he studied did not follow the rational model of first defining problems, next assessing possible causes, and only then taking action to solve the problem. Instead they worked from general overriding concerns, and they worked simultaneously at a number of problems.

Why Do We Have Such Poor Decision Makers?

The Harvard/Conant group and misguided followers (or whoever they are) have discouraged and prevented the teaching of the scientific method—the complete method of creative problem solving and decision making—for more than 50 years. Today team work lacks the unity of method.

Opportunity

Those who quickly learn the scientific method, use it, and teach it will be the winners of tomorrow.

Management and Planning

How to manage and how to plan are basically problems. The better your managers are trained in the use of the scientific method (SM-14), the better job they will do. Because managers are not properly trained in the scientific method, more management and planning are based on:

hunch	seat of pants
haphazard guess	uneducated guess
common sense	rule of thumb
superficial analysis	trail and error
management by exception	chaos
walk-around management	fad of the day
doing your "own thing"	outdated intuition
applying existing knowledge	pig in a poke
"we always do it that way"	quick fix

While the application of SM-14 is far superior to the above, there are times when some of these serve a useful purpose (trial and error is always a basic way to progress). Proper use of SM-14, however, should prevent so many failures and end many of the harms due to poor hunches and guesses, quick fixes, and applying the fad of the day.

Scientific Management

The BLUNDER has caused a huge misunderstanding about scientific management. It is not Taylorism. Time and motion study is just one of the technical methods or techniques used at the various stages of the scientific method.

Scientific management is the application of the scientific method to management. There cannot be management science if its practitioners are not using the scientific method.

The Harm of Unsuccessful Mergers

America needs big multinational corporations to compete in the international market place. Large size is often an advantage—but smaller, more nimble companies also have an advantage. It has been my observation that the lack of use by business and industry of the scientific method results in many unsuccessful mergers.

The July 2000 edition of the newsletter *Innovative Times*, published by Thomas E. Ollerman, Ph.D., contains an article by Scott Romeo.

He gives the following quotes:

> "Only fifteen percent of mergers and acquisitions in the US achieve their financial objectives, as measured by share value, return on investment, and post combination profitability."
>
> The American Management Association

> "Deals valued at $500 million or more showed that one-half destroyed shareholder value, thirty percent had minimal impact, and just seventeen percent created shareholder returns."
>
> P.L. Zewig—*Business Week*

> "Partners rate one half of international alliances as outright failures, and two thirds of cross-border alliances run into serious trouble within the first two years."
>
> *Harvard Business Review*

Summary

I believe that these statistics and my other comments support my claim that the lack of use of the scientific method by our financial, business, and industry top leaders and those in associated professions is very harmful to our nation.

? ?

The Mystery

Mergers affecting millions of employees and customers so often go wrong. Popular bestselling management books don't include the scientific method. Businesses have a poor record on decision making and problem solving. Poor ethics result in corporate false profit reporting.

All these things could have been largely prevented or improved had the scientific method been established long ago as the quality control method for business and industry. Why then have our business schools and intellectual leaders of business, industry, and associated professions participated in *the* BLUNDER to such a great extent?

? ?

Chapter 47

Others Harmed by *the* BLUNDER

Great Harms to Our Scientists

Natural Scientists

Because they are taught the scientific method, usually by the apprentice method, *the* **BLUNDER** has hurt them the least. They have, as you have seen, produced tremendous improvements in our health, welfare, and enjoyment of life in past centuries, and even more tremendous ones in recent years.

The harm, then, has been that they were not taught the scientific method during their education in lower levels. If those who entered these professions were adequately taught the scientific method and associated thinking skills from the beginning of Head Start or kindergarten and across the curriculum in all grades, they would be far better prepared for their college, university, fellowship, and future work.

It is my opinion that *the* **BLUNDER** has also retarded or hurt the following activities:

- the full development of the creativity of our scientists, engineers, and technologists
- appropriation of more money to science as the public does not fully understand what the scientific method and scientists, including engineers and technologists, have accomplished
- the development of a science of science and a Court of Science

"The United States Is Losing Its Dominance in the Sciences"

An article with this title appeared in the *New York Times* (May 3, 2004). As other nations realize the value of science, we are going to have more and more competition. We must be sure to spend enough money on science. Competition requires improving the efficiency of our scientists. Earlier and greater teaching of the scientific method will greatly aid the productivity of our scientists, including engineers and technologists.

Engineering and Technology

Our natural scientists have done a wonderful job of making new discoveries. Usually, it is our engineers, inventors, and technologists who take these and extend and reduce them to practice. They even make great discoveries themselves. Engineering has creative, origination, and problem-solving components just as science does. Our engineers are often included in the classification of "scientist." In their education, they get a heavy dose of math, physics, chemistry, etc.

Like the scientific method, there are many formulas put forth for the engineering method. I have been impressed by the program and problem solving material of Dr. Donald R. Woods of the Department of Chemical Engineering at McMasters University in Canada. However, as I have stated many times in this book, we have only one good basic problem origination, solving, and challenge of solution method, which is the scientific method (SM-14 type). So the mental activity stages of the engineering method are the same as the scientific method. What is specialized to engineering and design are some of the various creative, non-logical, logical, and technical methods used at the various stages of the scientific method. These techniques should be applied following the scientific method.

The **BLUNDER** has caused all the confusion about the engineering method. After all, how can an engineering professor teach the scientific method when the Harvard/Conant group and misguided followers (or whoever they are) are falsely claiming that it does not exist? This has done great harm to the engineering and technology fields, as the engineering profession has more members than any other profession except teaching.

In an article in the *Chronicle of Higher Education* (May 24, 1996) entitled "Rebuilding Engineering Education," Norman R. Augustine, president of Lockheed Martin and Chairman of the National Academy of Engineering, stated:

> First, the subject matter of engineering has changed. The company that I serve employs more software engineers than any other type, yet that discipline did not even exist when I graduated from college. Studies indicate that the half-life of material covered in many engineering courses is five to ten years. Few engineers now end their careers in the type of engineering for which they originally prepared.

This fast pace of change makes it necessary that engineers be thoroughly educated in the basic, well-defined method of engineering— the scientific method—and, as at present, the specialized engineering techniques or methods used at its various stages.

Harms to the General Media

Professional publications are covered elsewhere. Here I consider the general media, such as newspapers, magazines, television, and so on.

Media Owners, Publishers, Editors, Journalists, etc. Have Not Been Adequately Taught the Scientific Method

We all know of the importance of a free press and quality reporting and interpreting of the news.

Yet, because of *the* **BLUNDER**, our media personnel have never been adequately taught the method of knowledge, the method of investigation, the greatest quality control method ever devised—the scientific method. Like others, they have been taught parts of it, and some have been taught miscellaneous formulas for it to a small degree. But they have been taught the scientific method to a far from adequate extent, considering their need for it.

A Few of the Harms That Resulted

♦ The general reporting and interpreting of news is less accurate than it otherwise would be. You cannot take the time to apply and go through the scientific method on every problem or story. But a good education in the scientific method makes you a better solver in your everyday problem and decision activities and extremely better on complex ones.

♦ Investigative reporting has suffered. The scientific method is the method of investigation (see Chapter 42, Harms to Public Safety).

The Media Have Been Constantly Misled by "Authoritative Experts" about the Scientific Method

♦ The Harvard/Conant group and misguided followers have been careful not to reveal, inform, or encourage debate about their claims that the scientific method does not exist and should not be taught, even though Conant stated "The answers to these and many related questions are of supreme importance to the future of the free people" (*On Understanding Science*, 1947). Therefore, the media are not familiar with what has occurred.

♦ Reporters must often depend on "authoritative experts" for information. This information may not be accurate.

♦ This, along with the erroneous information given them in philosophy, psychology, science, journalism, and other college courses by authoritative people, means that they usually have been misled as to the real nature of the scientific method.

How the Media Have Contributed to *the* BLUNDER

♦ When Easley's essay was published in 1958 and republished in 1969, alert education or science reporters should have recognized its significance and reported on it. This could have stopped *the* BLUNDER long ago. Apparently, this did not happen.

♦ My special letters to some editors and publications have not produced any publicity about the scientific method situation.

♦ My news releases and special letters should have produced some publicity. This could perhaps have started a correction of *the* BLUNDER years ago.

♦ In general, those publications reaching our intellectuals have missed the boat in not recognizing that a great blunder about the scientific method was occurring.

♦ I do not know if the reason nothing has been published is a reluctance or fear to report negatively on Harvard or top educators.

My Message to the Media

The public today is really interested in education and bewildered about what is wrong. Because they have not been properly informed about the reasons for and the extent of *the* BLUNDER, *this book is news!*

Story after story has appeared placing the blame for the ills of education on bad schools and our teachers. While an ill-defined educational establishment has often been blamed, little blame has been placed on our top leaders, which is where a lot of it belongs, as I show in this book. The public needs to read news stories about my research into the problems of education.

The "power of the press" is strong. You can do a great deal to bring *the* BLUNDER to the attention of the public. Without this publicity, it may continue for a longer time, wasting more billions of dollars. Don't harm your reputation by ignoring the news stories it offers.

The Harm of Not Understanding Intellectual Capital, Knowledge Capital, and Human Capital

In recent years the terms human capital, knowledge capital, and intellectual capital have come into use. Here I discuss mainly intellectual capital, but the major point I emphasize is the same for all.

I am going to show that our top business and economic leaders and others do not always have a clear picture of what they are talking about when they discuss and define *intellectual capital.*

How Do People Define "Intellectual Capital"?

A big discussion on intellectual capital started in about 1991. Here is a quote from the Editor's Desk column of the June 3, 1991, issue of *Fortune* magazine discussing its cover story by Thomas Stewart:

> Intellectual capital. Simply put, it's the collective brainpower of everyone you work with. The knowledge that sets you and your organization apart from competitors as surely as a finger print distinguishes one person from the next.

Tom Stewart opened his book *Intellectual Capital* (1997) with

> Information and knowledge are the thermonuclear competitive weapons of our time. Knowledge is more valuable and more powerful than natural resources, big factories, or fat bankrolls. In industry after industry, success comes to the companies that have the best information or wield it most effectively—not necessarily the companies with the most muscle.

My big point in this discussion is: Intellectual capital is really

Knowledge of subject matter and memories of experiences plus:

Knowledge of the complete method of creative problem solving and decision making—the scientific method

One can have a great deal of subject matter knowledge and years of experience, but without a clear picture and knowledge of the complete method of problem solving and decision making—the scientific method—one's knowledge base is deficient in the area of intellectual capital. **You must know how to "wield it most effectively."**

Harms to People's Personal Lives

Except for us workaholics, people normally spend 8 hours daily at their occupation. Then there remain some 16 hours of their personal lives. I have covered harms to a few specific occupations and fields.

In their personal lives, people are faced with a vast array of problems to solve and decisions to make. Often these are complex.

If the scientific method were just for scientists, there would not be an enormous problem, but it is for everyone! I think it is safe to say that most people are not really good problem solvers, or at least have plenty of room for improvement.

Planning Our Lives

Another name for the scientific method is the method of planning. In *Brain Power: Learn to Improve Your Thinking Skills* (1980), Karl Albrecht describes the situation for most of us:

> The typical human life seems to be quite unplanned, undirected, unlived, and unsavored. Only those who consciously think about the adventure of living as a matter of making choices among options, which they have found for themselves, ever establish real self-control and live their lives fully.

An adequate education in the scientific method would help to improve this situation greatly.

Decisions about Where To Live Are Driving People into Bankruptcy

In the book *The Two-Income Trap: Why Middle Class Mothers and Fathers Are Going Broke* (2003), Warren and Tyagi claim, according to *Business Week* (December 8, 2003), "the culprit is the decline of public education, which has raised the price of housing in good school districts, prompting parents to overstretch on mortgages."

The Harms Are Too Numerous To Enumerate

I could go on and on about all the harms to our personal lives resulting from the lack of adequate teaching of problem solving and decision making. The cost is so great in so many ways that a dollar price cannot be put on it.

Harm to Religious Leaders

Since our religious leaders have not been adequately taught the scientific method, *the* **BLUNDER** has harmed their work.

Remember that while science is its method—applied to the natural world—the method is a general one. It is the best method ever recognized for originating, refining, extending, and applying knowledge in all fields, including our personal lives. In the past, some people claimed that it is the method for arriving at the truth. This is not correct. Rather, it is "on the evidence available today, the balance of probability favors the view. . ." Therefore, no domain should, for its own welfare and for the benefit of humanity, neglect to use it. Here are just two examples of its value to our religious leaders.

Counseling People with Problems

While many things in religion require the use of faith, there are many day-to-day matters requiring practical problem solving and decision making. Often one of the duties of religious leaders at all levels is counseling their followers, either as a group or individuals with problems, and taking positions on local, national, and world problems. To do this, you must have the good judgment that comes from a knowledge of how to make decisions and solve problems. This can best be developed from a knowledge of and practice in the use of the scientific method. Throughout the Old Testament, the New Testament, the Koran, and other religious books, many of the discussions, stories, parables, etc. concern problem solving and decision making about our personal lives.

Top Religious Leaders Must Be Good Leaders

To lead you must be an expert in your field on planning, setting goals, adjusting to changes, management, decision making, and creatively solving the vast number of problems you face every day. Some of these will be very complex. They require the scientific method.

The Complete Method of Creative Problem Solving and Decision Making

The above is just another of the many names for the scientific method. God gave us our minds to use and develop. To the extent that we use them haphazardly, creating more problems and unhappiness, we are wasting a precious gift of God.

Harms to Agriculture

Those of us who reside in American cities and suburbs often forget the debt we owe to our agricultural industry. Although we have higher labor costs than most other nations, we outproduce the world in agriculture.

The Farmer Is Essentially a Problem Solver

Farming is far from simply planting and picking. Old Mother Nature does nothing but throw one problem after another at our farmers. These, plus the whims of the public and foreign competition, make farmers' problems even worse. Farmers must make one important decision after another.

In their schooling, farmers are taught plenty of subject matter about agriculture and even some economics. However, because of **the BLUNDER**, they are not taught the fine points of problem solving and decision making. Yet these skills can often make the difference between success and failure.

Agricultural Researchers and Engineers

Our natural scientists, inventors, and engineers have been great contributors to agricultural success. They are usually people who are trained in the scientific method. But, as I have pointed out, it is not from the start of their schooling. It is by apprenticeship while they are in college and university that they are taught the method.

Rural Schools

While the problems of our urban schools get a lot of talk and attention, the severe problems of our rural schools are often overlooked. The fact that we do not have a permanent specialized SM-14 type national research center on their problems is another result of **the BLUNDER**, and this harms agriculture.

Harms to the Agricultural Industry and Society

It is difficult for me to pinpoint more exact harms than those I have mentioned without doing more research. But the items I have mentioned have caused billions of dollars of waste, heartbreaking failures, and unnecessary harm to society. Our schools of agriculture should start teaching the scientific method across the curriculum.

Harm to the Internet

The Internet has proven to be a tremendous innovation. Want to buy something? I used to have to go to a lot of trouble to find an out-of-print book I needed. Not today with the Internet. Many people have found it a great convenience for purchasing all sorts of things. Want to find information about an organization? The Internet will usually produce the information. You can go on and on about its great features.

Want "knowledge"? The Internet has it. Want reliable knowledge? That is another matter. The search engines try to bring you the "best," but it is often beyond their ability to bring you the most reliable knowledge. Many are trying in various ways to do a better rating job, but it is difficult. The reason is quite simple. While we have had a knowledge explosion, we have not had an explosion of easily identifiable reliable knowledge.

The harm is that the scientific method has not been adequately taught and thus has not been used to improve the reliability of knowledge found on the Internet. It is not a perfect method, so even the knowledge offered by humans claiming to use the scientific method comes in all degrees of reliability. However, the chance of its being more reliable than knowledge offered by those not using the method is great.

In an article written in May 2001 (formerly available at www.cisp.org) entitled "Reliance and Reliability: The Problem of Information on the Internet," Robert Wachbroit says:

> The consequences of misinformation on the Internet can be significant. The Internet is much like a broadcast medium, spreading messages rapidly, widely, and effortlessly. But unlike most broadcast media, messages can be posted anonymously or with a pseudonym so that checking the source is difficult.

Self-Certification and Certification Agencies

These could have a major impact on the usefulness of the Internet.

Please see my website, www.scientificmethod.com, for how I certify the knowledge on it. I hope that more authors will do this. Eventually, we will have certification organizations. Considering the millions of people using the Internet today, this harm represents a substantial amount of money and harm to progress.

The Harm of Two Cultures

In 1959, C.P. Snow gave a lecture (which was later published) entitled "The Two Cultures." In a second edition in 1963, he wrote *The Two Cultures and a Second Look*. His books received a lot of comments from those in intellectual fields and continue to do so.

The two cultures he claimed were

the literary intellectuals and the natural scientists

Some authors refer to the two cultures as the arts and humanities (as one) and the natural sciences.

In February 2003, it finally hit me that I am, in this book, making the big point of two cultures:

The social scientists are not using the scientific method. Therefore they are not really scientists.

and

Our community of natural scientists is using the scientific method system and process in their own fields of research (but often not when they venture into education).

In his work, Snow made no mention of the scientific method as the dividing line. **However, my claim is that today this is the dividing line.** The social scientists listened to Conant and then to Kuhn and started to claim that they were operating under paradigms. This has resulted in what I claim to be part of the biggest educational and intellectual blunder in history!

Snow made this comment:

This leads me to the major theme of what I set out to say. Let me try again to make myself clear. It is dangerous to have two cultures which can't or don't communicate.

This leads to another point I bring out in this book. While scientists are using the method, the Harvard/Conant group and misguided followers (or whoever they are) have prevented the adequate understanding and teaching of the scientific method. This must end. It is time for one culture in the sciences. Only then can we have real communication, standards, and an ethical code among all sciences.

America and Great Britain Mislead the World

One reasonable question to my claim that we in the United States have blundered badly about the scientific method is, what about other nations? Why should everyone blunder? Maybe Edmund is wrong. In my program of attempting self-falsification I had to explore this. Here are my conclusions.

Great Britain

For many years the English were the leaders in the recognition and development of the scientific method, even creating the name scientist. But in the 1940s and thereafter, changes occurred. I cover these in Chapter 3.

Other Nations

I made no special search of what has happened in other nations, but from my extensive reading, I am under the impression that other nations have followed the lead of the United States and Great Britain. They have not adequately taught the scientific method, even though France, Germany, Italy, and others made major contributions to its development.

Just a Very Few of the Ways the United States Has Misled the World

◆ Foreign students taught here return to their countries miseducated in the scientific method, and the concept spreads to their countries.

◆ In Chapter 43 I explained what has happened in Sweden, which. uses the Smithsonian/National Academy of Sciences program, which does not include the scientific method.

◆ The National Academy of Sciences received a $1.5 million grant in 2000 to aid European nations and continue support in Latin American for programs of symposia, laboratory courses, etc. NAS also has a project in China. Since the NAS is a leader in perpetuating the inadequate teaching of the scientific method, these and other of their international activities result in our misleading the world.

◆ Our Internet education programs and Internet universities, which are used worldwide, follow our curriculum and, I believe, include very little on the scientific method.

- Annual meetings of the World Forum on Education have no goals or sessions about the scientific method.

- Kuhn's *Structure of Scientific Revolutions* (1970) was translated into many languages. It belittles the scientific method.

- Bloom's *Taxonomy* was translated into 50 languages. It should have included the scientific method but did not. This is just one of perhaps hundreds or thousands of American books translated into other languages that have incorrect or inadequate information on the scientific method.

Importance to Other Countries

The *Wall Street Journal* (February 27, 2003) had an article about the opportunity that foreign nations have to leverage the age gap. They currently have a higher percentage of young people than the West. If these young people are not properly educated in the scientific method and the associated thinking skills, this opportunity to close the wealth gap with the richer countries may be lost or decreased. In an article "Barren Land" (*Education Next*, Fall 2002), William Easterly says:

> Despite pouring massive resources into expanding their education systems, poor countries have seen a steady decline in their median economic growth rates over the last four decades.

My claim is that one of the reasons for this is that teaching only subject matter is not enough to create wealth. You must teach the scientific method to show how to apply knowledge, increase creativity and the entrepreneurial spirit, and produce leaders with reliable ideas.

My Message to Other Countries

I believe that the United States and Great Britain have on the whole done a great job in helping other nations. Every country is responsible for its own educational activities. However, in efforts to help other countries, we have blundered badly in misleading you on the existence and the value of the scientific method. I advise other countries to review my claims and what your nation is doing with a view to your adequately teaching and using the scientific method.

Because of their current special needs, I review the Arab countries.

Great Opportunity for the Arab Countries—Learn to Use the Scientific Method (SM-14)

Going Back into History

At one time the Islamic countries were the foremost economic powers in the world. Their achievements in the arts and sciences of civilization were better than those of anyone else. In *What Went Wrong* (2002), Bernard Lewis gives a good description of their achievements:

> Nor was the role of the medieval Islamic scientist purely one of collection and preservation. In the medieval Middle East, scientists developed an approach rarely used by the ancients—experiment. Through this and other means they brought major advances in virtually all the sciences.

> Much of this was transmitted to the medieval West, whence eager students went to study in what were then Muslim centers of learning in Spain and Sicily, while others translated scientific texts from Arabic into Latin, some original, some adapted from ancient Greek works. Modern science owes an immense debt to these transmitters.

> And then, approximately from the end of the Middle Ages, there was a dramatic change. In Europe, the scientific movement advanced enormously in the era of the Renaissance, the Discoveries, the technological revolution, and the vast changes, both intellectual and material, that preceded, accompanied, and followed them. In the Muslim world, independent inquiry virtually came to an end, and science was for the most part reduced to the veneration of a corpus of approved knowledge.

Their use of experiment as mentioned above is often pointed to as a sign that they were originators of the experimental method—the scientific method. However, western culture usually credits Galileo with being the father of the scientific method.

Regardless of who deserves the credit, there exists a great opportunity for the Arabs to renew their interest in the scientific method as we know it today. It has the potential to decrease or end terrorism and bring prosperity to the Arab countries. However, I believe that they have been misled by *the* **BLUNDER** as to what knowledge capital, human capital, and intellectual capital are and the existence of the scientific method.

"A Blunt New Report by Arab Intellectuals"

This is the title of an article by Barbara Crossette that appeared in the *New York Times* (July 2, 2002). From the article:

> A blunt new report [*Arab Human Development Report*] by Arab intellectuals commissioned by the United Nations warns that Arab societies are being crippled by a lack of political freedom, the repression of women and an isolation from the world of ideas that stifles creativity.

The world of ideas and creativity needs the scientific method. Where it is taught and practiced, there is usually political freedom, and women's productivity is utilized. Countries that crave increased prosperity for their people must imitate the West's use of the scientific method to advance science, human welfare, and reliable knowledge.

The Scientific Method Is the Method of Self-Help

The Arab nations currently cannot compete with Western nations. While we must try to help them, it is their basic responsibility to help themselves. The scientific method is, if analyzed closely, a method of self-help. We should help them understand. But it is up to them to use it. The choice is theirs!

The *Arab Human Development Report* mentioned above is a great step in the right direction. The United Nations reports that more than a million copies have been downloaded from the Internet and that *Time* magazine cited it as the most important publication of 2002.

Arab Human Development Report 2003

This report, issued in October 2003, was sponsored by the United Nations Development Programme. I quote from the report:

> A knowledge-based society is one where knowledge diffusion, production and application become the organising principle in all aspects of human activity: culture, society, the economy, politics, and private life.

This is a great statement except that it doesn't go on and acknowledge that the scientific method is required for reliable knowledge production and application. I hope that their next report will include the scientific method. Otherwise its objectives will never be achieved.

Harm to Higher Education

In this book, I have concentrated mainly on showing the harm to K-12 education caused by *the* **BLUNDER**. In establishing the authenticity of my claims about *the* **BLUNDER**, I have covered some harms to higher education in a number of chapters. I will not repeat them here.

The harm to higher education in general is that our professors in the social sciences have not been adequately taught the scientific method in their schooling. This causes a perpetuation of *the* **BLUNDER**. The harm of this radiates into most of the curricula. To support my claim of harm to higher education, I present a few quotations.

"Why Foundations Have Cut Back in Higher Education"

This article by Mary B. Marcy (*Chronicle of Higher Education*, July 25, 2003) states:

> Little systemic innovation. I recently asked an officer from a foundation that is withdrawing support from higher education if a key reason was that relatively few colleges wholeheartedly embrace innovation in activities like assessment. She not only confirmed the point, but added that too few people on each campus are engaged in innovation, as well.

It is my contention that the lack of the scientific method—the method of innovation, the method of change—has harmed innovation in higher education. To obtain improvement, you must teach and apply the scientific method extensively and intensively.

"Bush's Next Target"

From an article by Stephen Bird (*Chronicle of Higher Education*, July 11, 2003):

> The president would also reprimand colleges for allowing too many students—especially low-income and minority students—to drop out and remain without the skills and knowledge they need. In addition, he would question the quality of education that most students receive.

First, if the scientific method is widely taught in higher education and also taught in K-12, we should have fewer dropouts. It is especially important to teach it in the first two years of college to aid those who do not continue on. The quality of education most students receive will greatly improve when *the* **BLUNDER** is corrected.

"Critics Urge Overhaul of Ph.D. Training, but Disagree Sharply on How to Do So"

From an article by Denise K. Magner (*Chronicle of Higher Education*, April 28, 2000):

> Most Ph.D.'s never land jobs at research universities, yet their training is geared precisely toward such positions. That contradiction is inspiring a growing chorus of critics to argue that American doctoral education is in need of an overhaul.

One of the big overhauls needed is to directly teach the scientific method and practice of its application intensively to all candidates for Ph.D.s. *The* **BLUNDER** has greatly harmed their careers and society. This would make them much more employable in academia, business, and industry. It would also increase the overall acknowledged value of a Ph.D.

Need for Permanent Specialized SM-14 Type National Research Centers in Higher Education

I have made suggestions about these centers in many areas of K-12 education and in some subject domains. Higher education would benefit from some of these suggestions in solving particular problems that are important.

America's Best Colleges and Universities Rankings

Those who rank our schools will eventually have to pay close attention to how well schools teach and provide practice in the scientific method. This book repeatedly points out that with the knowledge explosion, method is of greater and greater importance.

Leveling of Top-Rated Colleges and Universities

Survey after survey shows that employers are interested in problem solvers and decision makers, with the associated skills. The widespread, intensive teaching of the scientific method may prove to be a leveling factor in college rankings. Instead of a small number of top schools, we may have a much greater number of them.

The Harm of No Court of Science and No Court of Education outside the Legal System

In the literature there have been a number of suggestions for these courts or similar organizations. For example, Professor Thomas Gold, in an article entitled "New Ideas in Science," which appeared in the *Journal of Scientific Exploration* (vol. 1, no. 2, 1989), mentions science courts. I have occasionally mentioned the need for them in this book. They would have to be patterned in a different way from our present courts, where the defendants present only the evidence they want and ignore evidence unfavorable to their case.

It would probably be better not to call these "courts" in order to keep them separate from the courts that already exist. The idea and design of these would require a lot of study. Here I am more concerned with the need for them in the educational field. If we establish a series of permanent specialized SM-14 type national research centers, there would be less need for "courts" of education, since these organizations could be appealed to for help or analysis.

In the educational field, there have been many movements, issues, ideas, etc. that have gone unsettled for years and years. A typical example is phonics versus look-say or whole language. It took more than 50 years to settle this dispute and cost the country billions of dollars in wasted effort. Neither side had a "court" of education to appeal to.

In my case, I made extensive efforts in 1992 to get the misunderstandings about the scientific method corrected. I was unsuccessful. Even my subsequent efforts from 1992 to 1999, as reported in this book, were unsuccessful. Then I made the decision to write this book to present my case to the public. Since I had no "court" of education or other organization to appeal to, I have had to spend several million dollars in cash and labor plus years of frustrated efforts. In addition, billions of dollars of taxpayers' money have been wasted since 1992 because *the* **BLUNDER** continued. Even worse has been the personal harm to students and parents.

I am not alone in seeing the reforms needed in education. Our present system of everyone crusading for their ideas in the press and the haphazard, unsystematic way in which ideas succeed is wasteful and inefficient. It is not democratic either, because the powerful, authoritative, or politically connected are often the ones who succeed, whether they are right or wrong.

Harms to Parents

At the top of the list of those harmed by *the* **BLUNDER** is society as a whole. Then come our students, whose education is so distorted. Whether it is teachers or parents who are next I don't know. But, since there are many more parents than teachers, I will say parents.

All the educational disasters I have described have caused a huge number of inconveniences, emotional upsets, unnecessary waste of their time, and heartbreaks for parents. This book is written primarily to awaken them to what is basically wrong with education in the hope that they will take action to be sure that they and others don't get "more of the same." I would be a hypocrite if I placed all the blame on others and none on parents, whose help I'm depending on. I have read articles and books that place the blame for educational ills on parents. I quote from a few of them here.

Parents' Contribution to the Ills of Education

It is well known that many parents are biased and protective toward their children, and that their children are not taught that struggle is the essence of life, causing schools and teachers to have motivation and other problems. Some parents pay so little or inadequate attention to their children's schooling that again schools and teachers have problems. In addition, some parents think that, because they went to school, they are experts on education. Public Agenda's report *Where We Are Now* (2003) reports that 83 percent of teachers believe that "parents who fail to set limits and create structure at home for their kids are a serious problem."

Aids to Parents

I did not make any detailed study, but I was impressed with the catalog of The Parent Institute, P.O. Box 7474, Fairfax Station, VA 22039-7474. This organization has a series of pamphlets on how parents can help their children.

Value of Parents' Help

The Parent Institute made this statement on an envelope: "At schools with high levels of outreach—such as sending parents materials to help their child at home—reading scores grew at a rate 50% higher and math scores 40% higher, than in schools with low levels of outreach."

Beyond the Classroom—Why School Reform Has Failed and What Parents Need To Do (1996)

Beyond the Classroom by psychologist Laurence Steinberg of Temple University, with Professor Bradford Brown of the University of Wisconsin and Professor Sanford M. Dornbusch of Stanford University, represents the work of an extensive program of research conducted over 10 years.

This study

> points to a number of pervasive problems outside of school that must be addressed if any efforts at school reform are to succeed.

> The first, and most significant, problem, is the high prevalence of disengaged parents in contemporary America. . .

> The second contributor to the problem is a contemporary American peer culture that demeans academic success and scorns students who try to do well in school. . .

> These problems—parental disengagement and a peer culture that is scornful of academic excellence—are compounded by a third: an activity schedule that demands little academic energy from students when they are not actually in the classroom and permits students to devote excessive amounts of time to socializing, part-time employment, and a variety of leisure activities.

I believe that this study makes a major contribution to the big picture of education. These problems are all of major importance. There is little doubt that parents and students must do a much better job. But they will need practical help from our top educational leaders.

The authors make 10 simple, specific recommendations. The No Child Left Behind Act of 2001 probably fulfills some of them. However, I doubt that they will be enough to correct the problems described. As the authors state, it is going to require a national effort to solve America's achievement problem.

Public Agenda Report *Playing Their Part* (1999)

One of the key findings of this report was:

<u>The Well-Behaved Child Who Wants to Learn</u>
Both parents and teachers say that raising a well-behaved and motivated child is the most important aspect of parental involvement. In fact, parents say schools should be able to succeed with a child who has been taught strong values at home even if the parents haven't had much education and can't help with school work.

While we presently have some programs aimed at parents, the problem is immense. It is of such importance that our top educators must devote more time and effort to solving it.

In other chapters of this book I have covered how parents have been harmed by

◆ being forced to choose a location in which to live by school quality
◆ homework assignments that are sometimes too heavy or none at all
◆ teaching fads
◆ poor teacher preparation
◆ children not properly prepared for college entrance
◆ dropout problems

So It's Been a Disaster for Parents, Too

All the disasters I described and the contributions to *the* **BLUNDER** I told you about have added up to the foregoing and many other troubles for parents. I say again to them that unless you want "more of the same" that you have gotten in the past, you must take action on the recommendations I make in Chapters 57 and 58.

Parents' expectations of proper top leadership and reasonable efficiency in our educational system have not been met. It often appears on the surface that the fault lies with the local schools and teachers, but this book shows where it really belongs—at the top.

Suggestion

Actually, the problems described deserve permanent specialized SM-14 type national research centers.

Specifically, our top leaders should long ago have provided our teachers and schools with reliably tested programs of how to cultivate parental participation in schools, guidance of their children, and how to minimize peer pressure.

Summary of Part 7

Whether *the* **BLUNDER** will be interpreted to be the biggest in the individual domains I have discussed I leave to others to decide. But it sure was a BIG one. If you don't help to end *the* **BLUNDER**, you will suffer more of the same old confusion and harm to your life!

My forecast:

Coming: Millions of References to *The* BLUNDER

♦ Because of the magnitude of *the* **BLUNDER**, in the years ahead it will be mentioned millions of times. Whether it will be referred to as the scientific method blunder or some other name, I don't know. As I mentioned previously, for ease of reference, I started using *the* **BLUNDER**. I put "the" in italic type to reflect Conant's use of italic type in *Science and Common Sense* (1961), in which he claimed

There is no such thing as *the* scientific method.

I used bold type and capital letters for "blunder" to indicate that it is a giant one, even if it is not the biggest.

♦ Teachers and professors will have to say to students: "Remember in reading many books from 1946 to the early 2000s, *the* **BLUNDER** affected the author's reasoning and the conclusions may or may not be correct."

♦ Research papers will have to refer to it constantly.

♦ Thousands of books will explore and report on how and why it occurred and the harms done.

♦ In case history studies, it will be explored in depth.

♦ As enough time passes, people will be amazed that *the* **BLUNDER** could ever have occurred and survived for so long.

Be Careful Personally

Since this book exposes *the* **BLUNDER**, be careful not to continue to maintain that the scientific method does not exist. Don't go down in history as continuing *the* **BLUNDER**.

This Book Affects Many Current Events

The **BLUNDER** reaches into almost every aspect of current events in our personal lives and occupations. I have described many of these aspects throughout the book. Here I emphasize the effect of *the* **BLUNDER** on current events.

The No Child Left Behind Act and Disputes About It

The act is in the news a great deal today. An accurate assessment of its good and bad points cannot be made without an understanding of the big blunder that has occurred concerning how we research and plan educational reforms.

The War in Iraq Is a Major Current Event Today

Our top leaders have not been adequately educated in the scientific method. Would the war have been started if they had been? Would some aspects of it have been different?

Investigations Are Always in the News

Investigations go on every day. The scientific method is the method of investigation. Since it has not been adequately taught, what effect does it have on investigations?

Congress Changes Class Action Rules

In February 2005 the U.S. Congress passed the Class Action Fairness Act of 2005. This act will be in the news for years. Congress should have considered and covered the requirement of the U.S. Supreme Court (in the 1993 decision in Daubert v Merrell Dow Pharmaceuticals, Inc.) that expert witnesses must use the scientific method in their testimony.

Business Scandals

There are no references in these cases to the lack of use of the scientific method and its procedural requirements of a code of ethics for professionals. Because of *the* **BLUNDER**, students have not been properly taught in our business schools.

Many Other Areas

Many other current events are covered. Medical reports, psychologists' opinions, sports scandals, new scientific developments, and the constant question "what is the 'truth' and what is not the 'truth'?" The proper use of the scientific method affects them all.

Introduction to Part 8

Prevention of *the* BLUNDER

The scientific method is not only the method of originating knowledge, but also the method of prevention—the method of prevention of:

♦ unfavorable events by anticipation, falsifying, predicting, or forecasting

♦ unreliable knowledge or false claims becoming public knowledge

---

Here I devote a chapter to singling out individuals whose speeches and writings prior to Conant's 1947 book *On Understanding Science* should have been considered in evaluating Conant's erroneous and thus false claims. The people I call to your attention are:

Henry E. Armstrong	Karl Pearson
Conway McMillan	Morris R. Cohen
Ernest Nagel	Abraham Wolf
Walter Lippmann	Robert Millikan
Simon Newcomb	John Dewey

Special recognition is given to John Dewey with a separate chapter on his efforts to promote the recognition of the value of the scientific method.

There was one organization that had the potential to prevent *the* BLUNDER. I describe this organization.

After *the* BLUNDER Started in 1946

Many people continued to believe in the scientific method, regardless of the claims of the Harvard/Conant group and misguided followers (or whoever they are). In Chapter 50, I call attention to a number of these people and to the textbooks that even today include the scientific method.

Some of the Best Formulas for the Scientific Method Historically

These are shown to help illustrate that *the* BLUNDER should never have occurred.

Chapter 48

Some Early Advocates of the Scientific Method

The most famous of the early advocates of the method of science is Sir Francis Bacon (1561–1626). I will not attempt to cover the period prior to 1900 to any extent. Those interested will find a good 63-page summary in *History of Science*, volume 7 (1968), titled "A Bibliographical Review," by Larry Laudan.

Professor Henry E. Armstrong (1848–1937)

A paper Professor Armstrong presented at a meeting of the British College of Preceptors in April 1891 was published in *Science* (May 22, 1891). In 1903 his book *The Teaching of Scientific Method and Other Papers on Education* was published.

Karl Pearson (1857–1936)

The first edition of Pearson's famous book *The Grammar of Science* was published in 1892 and reprinted many times. See Chapter 52 for his formula for the scientific method.

Conway MacMillan (1867–1929)

MacMillan's paper "The Scientific Method and Modern Intellectual Life" was published in *Science* (May 17, 1895). See Chapter 52 for the formula he presented.

Morris R. Cohen (1880–1947)

Morris R. Cohen received a Ph.D. in philosophy from Harvard University in 1906 and later taught at City College of New York. In 1931 he wrote *Reason and Nature—An Essay on the Meaning of the Scientific Method*. A second edition was published in 1953 and reprinted in 1959. It contains some excellent material on the scientific method.

Ernest Nagel (1901–1985)

Nagel was a logician and a philosopher of science. He studied under Morris Cohen and John Dewey. He received a Ph.D. in 1931 from Columbia University. With Cohen, he wrote an *Introduction to Logic and Scientific Method* (1934). It contained some excellent material on the scientific method.

Abraham Wolf (1876–1948)

Wolf was Professor of Logic and Scientific Method at University College London and co-editor of the 14th edition (1929) of the *Encyclopaedia Britannica*. For years the *Britannica* contained Wolf's excellent article on the scientific method. Unfortunately, it was eventually dropped, probably as a consequence of *the* BLUNDER.

Walter Lippmann (1889–1974)

Lippmann was noted for his liberal views. He was a co-founder of the Harvard Socialist Club, but in 1914 he rejected his earlier socialism. For 30 years he wrote the nationally syndicated column "Today and Tomorrow."

Robert A. Millikan (1863–1953)

A foremost scientist in his day, Millikan was famous for his oil drop experiment. He was awarded the Nobel Prize in Physics in 1923 and was a founder of the National Research Council. Millikan served as vice president of the American Association for the Advancement of Science and chairman of the Executive Council of the California Institute of Technology; he held numerous other offices. My attention was attracted to his contribution of promoting the scientific method in his speech before the *New York Herald Tribune* Forum in October 1938, published in *Vital Speeches of the Day* (volume 4, December 1, 1938). The speech was titled "Science and Social Justice—'A Stupendous Amount of Crooked Thinking.'" Here is an excerpt that I quoted in Chapter 44, Harms to Capitalism, but it is so good that I repeat it here:

> In this progress made by science lies all our hope for the future in the field of human betterment (justice); for the rational, objective, experimental, scientific method which first began to establish its effectiveness in a large way in astronomy and physics about three hundred years ago and then was applied with amazing results in rapid succession in engineering, in chemistry, in geology, in biology, in medicine, is a general method for discovering truth, the only one that has thus far been found, and it is just as applicable to the social as to the natural sciences, though the technique is different. In the social sciences it is historical and statistical; in the natural sciences direct laboratory experimenting predominates. Until the method has been used in the social sci-

ences the word justice has no meaning save for the dema-
gogue who uses it to stir irrational emotions and thus win
unintelligent votes.

In *The American Ideology of National Science 1919–1930* (1971),
Ronald Tobey states:

> Scientific training taught emotional and individual disci-
> pline. "From my point of view," Millikan told an audience of
> teachers, "there is no training in objective, analytical think-
> ing, nor in honesty and soundness of judgment, which is
> comparable to the training furnished by the physical sci-
> ences." Millikan could sound like the pragmatists: "Life
> presents to each of us one continuous succession of prob-
> lems to be solved." And science was the best training in
> problem-solving.

Millikan's views were ignored by Conant and his followers.

Simon Newcomb (1835–1909)

Albert E. Moyer, in his book *A Scientist's Voice in American
Culture—Simon Newcomb and the Rhetoric of Scientific Method*
(1992), describes in great detail Newcomb's extensive efforts to promote scientific method in the second half of the 19th century and into
the early 20th century. Newcomb was, in his day, America's most celebrated scientist and a graduate of Harvard University. He served two
terms as President of the American Association for the Advancement
of Science. He recommended scientific method in numerous speeches
and articles. In an article entitled "What Is a Liberal Education?"
(*Science*, April 11, 1884), Newcomb stated, in reference to the small
minority who received a higher education in those days:

> Our duty to that generation is to so use and train this select
> body as to be of most benefit to the men of the future. What
> is the training required? I reply by saying that I know noth-
> ing better for this end than a wide and liberal training in the
> scientific spirit and the scientific method.

Moyer reports that, in one of Newcomb's last efforts in 1905, in an
address to the section on Social and Economic Science at the national meeting of the American Association for the Advancement of
Science:

"One of the first things to strike us in the effort to apply scientific methods to economics," he began, "is the absence of
nomenclature." As in earlier years, he went on to point out
specific instances of "defective definition." He then moved
to his more general concern, the "method of inquiry" best
suited to economics. Drawing analogies to physics and
recalling past applications of mathematical techniques to
economics, he maintained that economics could be made an
exact science even though its practitioners had to contend
with the "vagaries of human nature."

These statements impressed me, as I have pointed out the need to
teach the scientific method and that the ambiguity in our society
regarding the word "method" has contributed greatly to *the*
BLUNDER. Also note that I have drawn attention in Chapter 43 to the
fact that economists have not, as a profession, adopted the scientific
method in an effort to improve their profession. Newcomb's views did
not prevent Conant, years later, from influencing so many against
teaching the scientific method.

There Is a Solid Complete Basis for a Science of Science and a Science of the Scientific Method in the Literature

Another big advantage of the widespread use of the scientific method
in all domains is that there is a solid basis for it in the literature.
Remember that science is its method, and both science and the scientific method have centuries of analysis behind them. I believe that it
is correct to state that there has not been a good and easy-to-use summary of these subjects. The establishment of a permanent specialized
SM-14 type national research center on the science of science could
make such a summary available. It is my opinion that this summary
should be based on an 8-1/2-by-11-inch series of pages. There may be
many volumes in this project, but it is something that is needed by all
domains.

> The effects of the correction of *the* **BLUNDER** will,
> over time, be so widespread that this book covers
> only some of them.

Chapter 49

John Dewey's Efforts to Help Prevent *the* BLUNDER and His Recognition of the Value of the Scientific Method

In *How We Think* (1910 and 1933), Dewey told us to use the scientific method and associated reflective thinking skills. If our top educators had only listened and evaluated, refined, extended, and applied his claims, the greatest educational and intellectual blunder in history would never have occurred. Dewey's writing covered politics, arts, social sciences, and a variety of subjects. I have been concerned only with his views on the scientific method.

In this chapter:

◆ John Dewey (1859–1952)

◆ The Dewey Wars as They Concern the Scientific Method

◆ Dewey's Book *Experience and Education* (1938)

◆ Other Writings by Dewey about the Scientific Method

◆ Dewey's Failure

◆ The Tragedy of Dewey and the Victims—Students, Teachers, Parents, and Society

◆ Suggestions for Study and Warning

◆ Mystery

John Dewey (1859–1952)

John Dewey has been called America's most influential philosopher and educator. In my education research, I found Dewey to be the most frequently quoted individual. We even have a John Dewey Society to "keep alive John Dewey's commitment to the use of critical and reflective intelligence in the search for solutions to crucial problems in education and culture." There is a Center for Dewey Studies at Southern Illinois University.

Dewey was a prolific writer who published hundreds of books and articles. In 1894 he founded his famous Laboratory School at the University of Chicago. He left there in 1904 to become Professor of Philosophy and Education at Columbia University, where he remained until 1951.

Dewey was active in the progressive education movement but became dissatisfied with extremist zeal for corrupting progressive principles. In 1938 he wrote *Experience and Education* to publicize his criticism of the direction of progressive education. He became a very controversial figure and to such an extent that we have had the Dewey wars!

The Dewey Wars as They Concern the Scientific Method

Because of his many different progressive views of education, Dewey became a controversial figure and remains so today. Essentially, there are those who claim to be on the "educational right," or traditionalists, who believe in a traditional type of subject matter curriculum, as opposed to the modernists, liberals, progressives, child-centered advocates, etc., who advocate changes for this modern age.

It is well known in educational research circles that there are "Dewey lovers" and "Dewey haters." I am a Dewey lover because of his pioneering work in advocating the teaching and use of the scientific method.

An article appeared in the December 8, 1999, issue of *Education Week* entitled "Sorry, John. I'm Not Who You Thought I Was," by Professor Emeritus of Education William A. Proefriedt. He states:

> Of course, there are legitimate criticisms to be made of various emphases in Dewey's philosophy of education, but the fulminations of the educational right for most of this century have grotesquely distorted Dewey's positions. There is only one antidote: Read the man. Read *The School and Society* (1899); read *The Child and the Curriculum* (1902); read, if you have a summer free, *Democracy and Education* (1916); and read especially his *Experience and Education* (1938). This last is a short (91 pages) formulation of Dewey's educational thinking, abstract in the best sense of the word and readable. No one free of ideological blindness and in possession of basic reading skills would recognize the Dewey of the critics in the pages of these books. Attention must finally be paid to such a thinker.

It is from *Experience and Education* that I now present Dewey's views on the scientific method. One of the reasons he wrote it was that his theories on progressive education were being misinterpreted and misapplied.

Dewey's Book *Experience and Education* (1938)

In 1998, Kappa Delta Pi, international honor society in education, issued a 60th anniversary edition of *Experience and Education*. Here I quote Dewey from pages 107 and 108, but interrupt at points to give my comments.

> It is argued that science and its method must be subordinated; that we must return to the logic of ultimate first principles expressed in the logic of Aristotle and St. Thomas, in order that the young may have sure anchorage in their intellectual and moral life, and not be at the mercy of every passing breeze that blows.

The progressive education movement at that time was advocating the use and teaching of the scientific method. An opposition group (the education right or traditionalists) were for adhering to teaching only subject matter and traditional subjects.

I reported on Conant's 1947 complaint that for the last 25 years indoctrination in the scientific method was one of the primary aims of modern education (Chapter 3).

Dewey again:

> If the method of science had ever been consistently and continuously applied throughout the day-by-day work of the school in all subjects, I should be more impressed by this emotional appeal than I am.
> I see at bottom but two alternatives between which education must choose if it is not to drift aimlessly.

Of the two, our top educators chose the wrong alternative. Education has drifted aimlessly from one fad to another—from one untested program to the next untested one. First, Dewey describes the wrong alternative:

> One of them is expressed by the attempt to induce educators to return to the intellectual methods and ideals that arose

centuries before the scientific method was developed. The appeal may be temporarily successful in a period when general insecurity, emotional and intellectual as well as economic, is rife. For under these conditions the desire to lean on fixed authority is active. Nevertheless, it is so out of touch with all the conditions of modern life that I believe it is folly to seek salvation in this direction.

Dewey was wrong about "the appeal may be temporarily successful." The return to the subject-centered curriculum occurred following Sputnik I. From 1957 to 2005 is more than temporary. It has been a long, long time that our top educators have blundered about the scientific method.

Dewey again:

The other alternative is systematic utilization of scientific method as the pattern and ideal of intelligent exploration and exploitation of the potentialities inherent in experience.

In Chapter 6 I point out that, because of the claims of the Harvard/Conant group and misguided followers (or whoever they are) that the scientific method does not exist, the three basic reasons for the ills of education programs resulted:

A Killed—the widespread teaching of the scientific method

B Killed—the proper use of the scientific method by top education leaders, educational researchers, and others in the field of education

C Killed—the development of a science of education

Dewey warned us in 1938 about all these things, but he was belittled and not listened to by many of our top educational leaders. Some of what Dewey advocated does not sound practical. However, it does not mean that we should not listen to him. Testing is always available to test practicability.

Other Writing by Dewey about the Scientific Method

Here are a few selected quotations from Dewey's famous book *How We Think*, first published in 1910, with a revised second edition in 1933. From the 1910 edition:

We may recapitulate by saying that the origin of thinking is some perplexity, confusion, or doubt. Thinking is not a case of spontaneous combustion; it does not occur just on "general principles." There is something that occasions and evokes it. General appeals to a child (or to a grown-up) to think, irrespective of the existence in his own experience of some difficulty that troubles him and disturbs his equilibrium, are as futile as advice to lift himself by his bootstraps.

From the 1933 edition:

Method of a systematic sort is required in order to safeguard the operations by which we move from one to the other, from facts to ideas, and back again from ideas to the facts that will test them. Without adequate method a person grabs, as it were, at the first facts that offer themselves; he does not examine them to see whether they are truly facts or whether, even though they be real facts, they are relevant to the inference that needs to be made.

Scientific Method Employs Analysis

In contrast with the empirical method stands the scientific. Scientific method replaces the repeated conjunction or coincidence of separate facts by discovery of a single comprehensive fact, effecting this replacement by breaking up the coarse or gross facts of observation into a number of minuter processes not directly accessible to perception.

From the 1933 edition:

Scientific method includes, in short, all the process by which the observing and amassing of data are regulated with a view to facilitating the formation of explanatory conceptions and theories.

Conant Ignored Dewey's Concept of the Scientific Method

Although Conant belittled Karl Pearson's book *The Grammar of Science* (1892) in his *On Understanding Science*, he made no reference to Dewey's ideas on scientific method. Why didn't he evaluate Dewey's position on the scientific method? He was familiar with Dewey, for in *The Child, the Parent and the State* (1960) he mentions Dewey's "proposed radical reforms of education."

I claim that

◆ While many authors followed Dewey's concepts, it was a major blunder that his works on thinking and the scientific method were not more greatly revised, extended, and applied.

◆ Conant should not have ignored Dewey's work when he claimed that the scientific method does not exist. When you make extraordinary claims, you must provide extraordinary evidence.

Look at a Few of the Other Things Dewey Recommended

◆ Curiosity

◆ Observation

◆ The need to test hypotheses

◆ That the method of science—problem solving through reflective thinking—should be both the method and valued outcome of science instruction in America's schools

◆ Teaching academic subjects *and* intellectual training

◆ That science and scientific method were important for all aspects of philosophy

◆ A specific investigation of the nature of science—just what I am pushing for—a science of science

◆ The method of intelligence is the scientific method

Another Great Dewey Insight

In *Scientific Discovery* (1980), Thomas Nickles writes:

> Dewey (1929) and elsewhere interestingly elaborated—and softened—Peirce's theory of inquiry into a rather sophisticated conception of science as our most efficient means of solving problems, rather than as a quest for certainty, *i.e.*, Truth.

This supports the concept that the scientific method is the complete method of creative problem solving and decision making for all fields seeking a solution based on the best evidence available today—not on the "truth."

Hands-On, Inquiry, and Discovery Teaching

Dewey was famous for advocating that children should learn from experiences through hands-on activities and discovery.

Ever since its popularization by Dewey and the educational improvement programs in the early 20th century, hands-on learning has slowly gained a great deal of wide acclaim and praise, especially in recent years. Educators have sought to involve it in their instructions and curricula, while students have enjoyed participating in hands-on learning projects. Children love these methods of learning, and most research has shown that they show a greater interest in science and other subjects as a result of being taught in this manner. A growing interest in teaching through inquiry, discovery, and hands-on methods has taken hold in American schools and colleges.

However, despite the positive aspects of the concept, when properly applied, it lacks one very important ingredient when it has been applied: method. Despite one article's claim that "science education reformers say [hands-on learning] more powerfully motivates students and more closely approximates the scientific method" (*Education Week*, May 11, 1994), the scientific method is seldom tied into this valuable type of teaching. Even though the scientific method is the method of inquiry and the method of discovery, it is ignored by hands-on learning curricula because of controversies over its existence or because course and curriculum designers have not been adequately educated about the nature of the scientific method.

Without any method to the process of hands-on learning, educators largely waste transfer of learning, in which students realize that they can transfer their experiences and knowledge to other subjects areas and to everyday life. In *The Teaching of Thinking* (1985), Raymond Nickerson explained that ". . . one needs to have not only the domain-specific knowledge that is essential to skilled performance, but the knowledge of when and how to apply that knowledge in specific contexts." There has been much criticism of the inquiry, discovery, and hands-on methods, as well as the usual laboratory-style courses, because students often merely rediscover rather than participate in real discovery. This fault can be overcome by sometimes allowing students to choose their own problems and always teaching them to follow the stages of the scientific method.

Dewey's Failure

In *John Dewey* (1966) Richard J. Bernstein states:

> Dewey lacked the technical skill and patience to develop
> and establish his insights in systematic detail. Dewey was a
> philosopher who painted with a broad stroke; he was a man
> of vision and fertile imagination. Without these qualities a
> philosophy can become scholastic, academic, and pointless.
> But imagination and insight must be explicated and modi-
> fied in detailed analyses, and this is what Dewey failed to do
> for us.

With his complete act of thought and other formulas, Dewey did provide us with insight and leads. It is the nature of the method of intelligence to build on ideas like these. This is what failed to happen to
an adequate extent. A summary and analysis of the scientific method
such as I compiled in *The Scientific Method Today* should have been
done by someone a long time ago. It would have been done except for
the **BLUNDER**. I have no illusions about the adequacy of my booklet.
It needs to be promptly refined, extended, and applied.

The Tragedy of Dewey and the Victims—Students, Teachers, Parents, and Society

Dewey was a man of ideas. It is true that he could have presented and
explained them better. The tragedy is that his ideas were not evaluated and the good ones not adequately refined, extended, and applied following the scientific method. Instead they were twisted, ignored, and
misapplied. Even today—more than 50 to 100 years later—there are no
reliable conclusions that allow for their universal and practical application. Even though the experiences we have gone through in those 50
to 100 years have provided all the evidence we need to reach the necessary conclusions, our top leaders have not done so. Worse still, the
situation has allowed fads to proliferate.

Fads Proliferate Because of Dewey's Critics

Dewey's critics and even some historians are forever blaming him and
progressive education for the failures of schools, fads, and the aimless
wanderings of our educators.

These critics are usually also people who have helped perpetuate the
killing of the teaching of the scientific method and thus its nonuse in

educational research and planning. So the fault is not Dewey's or progressive educators'. The tragedy lies in their preventing the development of a science of education.

Thus, we have our victims—students, teachers, parents, and society.

Suggestions for Study and Warning

I was puzzled about what to suggest, so I re-read some of Dewey's writings. I found a 1929 warning of his that I had included in *Edmund's Idea and Research Report on the General Pattern of the Scientific Method* in 1994. I repeat it below.

Let's quickly review the greatest educational and intellectual blunder in history and how it matches Dewey's foresight.

In 1947, Conant, a great man and a teacher of unusual power, the most famous and authoritative of his day, claimed that the greatest idea of all ages, the scientific method, does not exist. Harvard professors backed him up, and many other powerful friends and associates joined in the partisanship. Progress in the recognition and development of the scientific method slowed. Since 1992 I have been sending out my booklets, reports, and briefs containing the "truth" that the scientific method does exist. However, the recipients ignore them and are impervious to my research.

In *Sources of a Science of Education* (1929), Dewey warned about avoiding this type of situation. He stated:

> The existence of scientific method protects us also from a danger that attends the operations of men of unusual power; dangers of slavish imitation partisanship, and such jealous devotion to them and their work as to get in the way of further progress. Anybody can notice today that the effect of an original and powerful teacher is not all to the good. Those influenced by him often show a one-sided interest; they tend to form schools, and to become impervious to other problems and truths; they incline to swear by the words of their master and to go on repeating his thoughts after him, and often without the spirit and insight that originally made them significant. Observation also shows that these results happen oftenest in those subjects in which scientific method is least developed.

The scientific method existed in 1947, but its use was not developed adequately in all fields, including education. Thus, it did not protect us from the partisanship of the Harvard/Conant group and misguided followers (or whoever they are) toward Conant's false claims. As an example, the National Academy of Sciences included Conant's false claim in the 1995 science teaching standards despite my reports to them. If the use of the scientific method had been developed properly in the educational field, this would not have happened.

So my suggestion for study and warning is to heed Dewey and study the need to develop a science of education and the teaching and use of the scientific method in all fields.

? ?

The Mysteries

The more time that passes, the more evidence indicates that many of Dewey's ideas that were rejected, ignored, or twisted into something impractical were indeed practical. Why did so many in the past and even today misrepresent, belittle, ignore, and make erroneous claims about his concepts? Was it jealousy? Was it institutional envy? Was it closed-minded traditionalism? Was it arrogance? After 1947, was it also an attempt to help perpetuate Conant's false claims?

? ?

Chapter 50

A Few of the People Who Should Have Been Listened to since the Start of *the* BLUNDER

I place the start of *the* **BLUNDER** with Conant's 1946 speech and the publication of it in his 1947 book *On Understanding Science.*

Were there insightful, brave people who tried to correct or prevent *the* **BLUNDER**? I watched for these people during my research. While I can't cover them all, I call your attention especially to the following.

Jack Easley (1922–1994)

In 1958 (republished in 1969) Easley presented the only detailed challenge of Conant's claims. Here was the system of science working at its best. A serious and frank scholarly rebuttle of Conant's (a famous scientist's) false opinions. See Chapter 4, where I devote two pages to this.

Rudolf Flesch (1911–1986)

In his famous book *The Art of Clear Thinking* (1951), Flesch was one of the first to challenge Conant's extreme views of the scientific method. See also Chapter 9.

Harold Rugg (1886–1960)

The following excerpt is taken from *Foundations of American Education* (1947) by Dr. Harold Rugg, professor at Teachers College, Columbia University.

> *What Is the Scientific Method?*
> We can be equally rigorous in making our yardstick for the scientific method because Western students have devoted lifetimes of study to its analysis. Much of Dewey's writing, for example, and that of his followers, reduces to this.

He went on and listed what he meant by scientific method.

E. Bright Wilson, Jr. (1908–1991)

E. Bright Wilson, Jr., author of *An Introduction to Scientific Research* (1952), also deserves mention. He was Chairman of the Chemistry

Department at Harvard University. In Chapter 3, "Elementary Scientific Method," he explains what he believes this to be. In his notes he says (very diplomatically, since Dr. Conant was his superior), "A very readable book which emphasizes entirely different aspects of scientific method is *On Understanding Science*."

Kenneth B.M. Crooks (1905–1959)

Dr. Kenneth B.M. Crooks' "Suggestions for Teaching the Scientific Method" was published in the March 1961 issue of *American Biology Teacher*, resulting in my eventual researching the scientific method and writing the SM-14 booklet and this book. After 15 years of searching hundreds of old and new books, I found no other formula for the scientific method as clear, concise, or teachable as that of Professor Crooks. His insight into the method (when others were on the wrong path) is impressive. My first SM-14 booklet is dedicated to him and to the many others who have aided in the development of the scientific method over the centuries.

Born May 25, 1905, in Hanover, Jamaica, British West Indies, Dr. Crooks earned his B.A. (1927), M.A. (1928), and Ph.D. (1940) at Harvard (where he studied chemistry under Dr. Conant). He became a full professor at Hampton Institute in Virginia, was elected a Fellow of the American Association for the Advancement of Science, was a member of many professional organizations, and published more than 30 papers.

On June 20, 1933, Dr. Crooks spoke about the scientific method on WGH Radio in Norfolk, Virginia. In December 1958 he presented a paper, "Suggestions for Teaching the Scientific Method," at the joint annual meeting of the National Association of Biology Teachers and the American Association for the Advancement of Science. Even though he became ill a few days before presenting the paper, he insisted on giving his speech. He returned home to Grambling, Louisiana, and died a few days later. Dr. Crooks' career would make an interesting documentary or movie. He should be held up as a role model.

In 1974, his scientific papers and memorabilia were placed by his family in the Armistad Research Center at Tulane University.

I call special attention to the comment in his paper "that the scientific attitude is really a state of mind, with which one faces the world—really a WAY OF LIFE."

Editors of *American Biology Teacher* in 1961

Someone at this magazine had the intuition and foresight to see the need to publish articles on the scientific method. The March 1961 issue (with a circulation of 5,000 copies) opened with an article favorable to Conant's case history method for teaching biology. Deeper in the magazine were several other articles. One of these was Crooks' excellent article, the article that caught my attention.

If this article had never been published in *American Biology Teacher*, I would never have started researching the scientific method. This is an example of the power and influence of our professional press.

Carlo L. Lastrucci (1911–1998)

Dr. Lastrucci was a professor at San Francisco State University. His writing was mainly in the field of social psychology. In 1963 his book, *The Scientific Approach: Basic Principles of the Scientific Method*, was published by Schenkman Publishing Company.

Of all the books published on the scientific method from 1946 on, I rate this the best. Yet it never received much publicity, sales, or credit, probably because *the* **BLUNDER** dulled interest in the subject. I recently purchased the copyright to be sure that this book remains available. In years to come, Lastrucci's work will be better appreciated by students of the scientific method.

James E. McClellan (1923–2001)

James E. McClellan wrote *Toward an Effective Critique of American Education* (1968). McClellan, who approved of Dr. Conant's case history approach but challenged many of his views on education, said, "One may be dubious of the terminology of 'tactics and strategy of science' as descriptive of desired educational content; it seems the military image has all too deeply impressed itself on Conant's mind."

James K. Feibleman (1904–1987)

Feibleman was a professor of philosophy at Tulane University. He wrote *Scientific Method: The Hypothetico-Experimental Laboratory Procedure of the Physical Sciences*, which was published in 1971 in the Netherlands. It is now published by Kluwer Academic Publishers. I rate this the second best book on the scientific method published since 1946.

Not Many Citations of Those Challenging Conant's Views

I found very few instances of authors citing works that specifically expressed views opposed to those of Dr. Conant, but there was widespread quoting of his views of the scientific method.

Textbooks

We should all salute the textbook authors and publishers who have included a formula for the scientific method. During the decades that the controversies have existed, these have been the principal source for any knowledge students have obtained. Formulas that appear in textbooks vary a great deal but still get across the idea that the scientific method exists.

There are far too many other books to compile and list. However, they have made a great contribution to keeping the idea of the scientific method alive despite its exclusion from national education reform programs. In my Report #5, which was sent to many of our top educators, I list 55 authors whose book or article I have in my small library and who discuss and admit that the scientific method exists.

Chapter 51

An Organization That Had the Potential to Prevent the Blunder: The Institute of Experimental Method

This institute, which lasted only a year, from 1945 to 1946, was composed of a small, little-known group that was interested in seeing a science of methodology developed. You will recall that I have pointed out the need to develop the science of science. This is essentially what they were trying to do. If they had only continued, they might have prevented *the* **BLUNDER** from occurring. They first met at Bryn Mawr College in May 1945 and then in May 1946 at the University of Pennsylvania. My guess is that Conant's claims in 1946 and thereafter that the scientific method does not exist prevented their work from continuing for very long.

Here are some excerpts from *The Permanent Revolution in Science* (1954) by Richard Schanck of Bethany College and the Carnegie Institute of Technology. This book describes the activities, hopes, and thinking of the Institute of Experimental Method.

> The final stage of this emergent development seems a logical one. Can philosophy convert the study of scientific method, the philosophy of science, into a science? A science of scientific method that we might call methodology? To this position the students of Singer have said, "Yes, it can be done," and moreover, they have set about to do it by creating an organization called the Institute of Experimental Method...

> Such a cooperating group as this would achieve the integration and unification of science as well as a working out of the science of method because of their highly specialized training in content and then their methodological program.

> Such a conception of methodology sees it not as the queen of the sciences nor the methodologist as king, but rather the cooperating group as service agency ready to give its specialized service, ready to *give a design for the effective realization of a research program.* [Emphasis mine.]

Please read those last lines again. Fate is funny! If they had only continued the project, I believe *the* **BLUNDER** (a trillion dollar plus one) could never have continued. Educational research would have had to be done based on "effective realization of a research program" instead of the uncontrolled way that developed, causing so many disasters.

It is interesting to note that W. Edwards Deming (1900–1993), who went on to great fame in the quality control and management fields and became famous for his theme of "continuous improvement," was a member of this group.

In the book is this interesting comment:

> At this conference Wroe Alderson, a marketing expert, and Edward Deming, a sampling expert, became very interested in the objectives of the Institute of Experimental Method and have made many contributions to its progress since.

There is now a Deming America Society. The Japanese periodically award a Deming Medal. Books have been written about his work, such as *Deming Management Method* (1988) by Mary Walton.

While I don't claim to be as talented as Deming, we both were or are crusaders for quality. He was very successful eventually with the technique of statistical quality control and management, but I am still struggling to get the greatest quality control method of all time, the scientific method, properly understood.

Chapter 52

Some of the Best Formulas Historically
(not always called the scientific method)

1892 Karl Pearson (*The Grammar of Science*)

"The scientific method is marked by the following features:
(a) careful and accurate classification of facts and observation of their correlation and sequence;
(b) the discovery of scientific laws by aid of the creative imagination;
(c) self-criticism and the final touch stone of equal validity for all normally constituted minds."

1895 Conway MacMillan ("The Scientific Method and Modern Intellectual Life," in *Science*, N.S. I:537–542, 1895)

(This is the best one I found published in the 19th century.)

Facts are recognized, accumulated, and arranged
Hypotheses are framed, tested, and exploited
Conclusions are drawn, verified, accepted, and applied

1910 John Dewey (*How We Think*)

Complete Act of Thought [To my knowledge, Dewey never called this the scientific method.]:

1. a felt difficulty
2. its location and definition
3. suggestion of possible solution
4. development by reasoning of the bearings of the suggestion
5. further observation and experiment leading to its acceptance or rejection, that is, the conclusion of belief or disbelief

1926 Graham Wallas (*The Art of Thought*)

preparation	incubation
illumination	verification

1931 Joseph Rossman (*The Psychology of the Inventor*)

The "steps" in inventing (according to his survey of inventors) are amazingly similar to the stages of the scientific method:

1. Observation of need or difficulty
2. Analysis of the need
3. Survey of all available information
4. Formulation of all objective solutions
5. Critical analysis of these solutions for their advantages and disadvantages
6. Birth of the new idea—the invention
7. Experimentation to test the most promising solution; the selection and perfection of the final embodiment by some or all of the previous steps

1950 W.I.B. Beveridge (*The Art of Scientific Investigation*)

"The following is a common sequence in an investigation on a medical or biological problem.
(a) The relevant literature is critically reviewed.
(b) A thorough collection of field data or equivalent observational enquiry is conducted, and is supplemented if necessary by laboratory examination of specimens.
(c) The information obtained is marshalled and correlated and the problem is defined and broken down into specific questions.
(d) Intelligent guesses are made to answer the questions, as many hypotheses as possible being considered.
(e) Experiments are devised to test first the likeliest hypotheses bearing on the most crucial questions."

1958 Dr. Kenneth Crooks ("Suggestions for Teaching the Scientific Method") SM-14 is based on this.

1. curiosity
2. is there a problem?
3. get the evidence
4. attributes needed
5. weigh all evidence
6. make the educated guess (hypothesis)
7. challenge the hypothesis
8. get a conclusion
9. suspend judgment
10. deductive reasoning

1962 John W. Haefele (in *Creativity and Innovation*) reports on General Electric's training course to enhance creative thinking by their employees. A formula (very close to SM-14) is studied and practiced, according to this sequence:

Recognize
Define
Search
Evaluate
Select
Make preliminary design
Test and evaluate
Follow through

1963 Carlo Lastrucci (*The Scientific Approach*)

stage 1 formulation of the problem
stage 2 study of the pertinently related literature
stage 3 construction of a research design
stage 4 determination of the "universe"
stage 5 gathering of the data
stage 6 interpretation of the data
stage 7 verification of the interpretation
stage 8 presentation of the findings in a report

1972 James K. Feibleman (*Scientific Method*)

1. observation
2. induction
3. hypothesis
4. experiment
5. calculation
6. prediction
7. control

1982 Irving Copi (*Introduction to Logic*, 6th edition)

The general pattern of scientific research:

1. the problem
2. preliminary hypotheses
3. collecting additional facts
4. formulating the hypothesis
5. deducing further consequences
6. testing the consequences
7. application

Another "Typical" Formula

From *Science and Common Sense* (James Bryant Conant, 1951)

[Conant, in disclaiming the scientific method, says the following about current definitions of the scientific method] "They run about as follows:
(1) a problem is recognized and an objective formulated;
(2) all the relevant information is collected. . .
(3) a working hypothesis is formulated;
(4) deductions from the hypothesis are drawn;
(5) the deductions are tested by actual trial;
(6) depending on the outcome, the working hypothesis is accepted, modified, or discarded."

In other books published over the years, there are hundreds of various formulas for the scientific method.

A Paradox: A Version of the Scientific Method Taught under the Name of

Creative Problem Solving

The Creative Education Foundation was founded in 1954 by Dr. Alex Osborn, an advertising agency executive. Soon this progressive foundation was teaching the Osborn-Parnes Process shown below. I compare its formula to SM-14 to show that its is a condensed formula for the scientific method, which I also call the complete creative problem solving method, process, or guide.

Osborn-Parnes Process	SM-14 Stages
1. Objective Finding	1. Curious Observation 2. Is There a Problem? 3. Goals and Planning
2. Fact Finding	4. Search, Explore, and Gather the Evidence
3. Idea Finding	5. Generate Creative and Logical Alternative Solutions
4. Solution Finding	6. Evaluate the Evidence 7. Make the Educated Guess 8. Challenge the Hypothesis 9. Reach a Conclusion 10. Suspend Judgment
5. Acceptance Finding	11. Take Action
	Supporting Ingredients 12. Creative, Non-logical, Logical and Technical Methods 13. Procedural Principles and Theories 14. Attributes and Thinking Skills

Since the foundation was founded in 1954, I would guess that more than one million people have been taught this formula through seminars, classes, books, and lectures. They and others claim no rigidity, no fixed sequential phases, or any of the other false claims applied to the scientific method. The foundation and its members have produced a vast amount of knowledge about creativity. Their self-proclaimed mission is to provoke creativity and inspire imaginative change (worldwide).

So there exists the paradox. For about 50 years, the scientific method is taught under another name to about a million people, while the Harvard/Conant group and misguided followers (or whoever they are) claim that it doesn't exist!

This paradox illustrates:

◆ Our top educational leaders do not see the big picture of education.

◆ Even though the 1983 report *A Nation at Risk* points out the need to teach analysis and problem solving, as do numerous other reports, our top educators only stress textbook type problem solving rather than complex problem solving.

◆ Our top educational leaders have largely ignored the urging of the Creative Education Foundation to teach creativity despite its great importance to America's welfare and world competitiveness.

In revising Dr. Crook's formula to arrive at SM-14, I followed the Osborn-Parnes formula and inserted Generate Creative and Logical Alternatives as a separate stage because of its great importance.

Those interested in the large body of knowledge about creativity accumulated by the Creative Education Foundation can contact the organization at 289 Bay Road, Hadley, MA 01035, or visit its website at http://www.cef-cpsi.org.

Don't Forget Another Paradox

When we entered "scientific method" into the search box of the Internet search engine Google on February 20, 2004, it produced 464,000 hits. This is a paradoxical amount for something that is claimed not to exist! Especially as a very small sampling of these shows only a small fraction that deny the existence of the scientific method.

Summary of Part 8

Again I remind my readers that education and training is a 0.5- to 1-trillion-dollar-a-year industry.

In this part I have shown you just a fraction of the evidence available in the literature that explains and substantiates the existence of the scientific method and its great value.

Thus, the Harvard/Conant group and misguided followers (or whoever they are) have

- ◆ ignored a huge mass of contrary evidence to their false claims

- ◆ complained about formulas for the scientific method but never researched for a good one such as Dr. Crooks' 1958 formula and my improved SM-14

- ◆ made numerous false claims about the scientific method, such as those reviewed in Chapter 7, without doing adequate research to determine their accuracy

- ◆ ignored my literature, special reports, and offers of the use of my library and files

? ?

The Mystery

With the vast body of reliable knowledge that exists about the scientific method, how much longer will we be

prevented from correcting the waste of precious taxpayers' educational money as a result of *the* BLUNDER?

? ?

Introduction to Part 9

The Legal Status of the Scientific Method

There have been two gigantic legal blunders about the scientific method:

- It has not been taught in our law schools and then used in legal work and in the courts.

- The legal (and educational fields) have not acknowledged the importance of the 1993 *Daubert* decision, in which the U.S. Supreme Court clearly recognized the scientific method.

A Mistake: Enough was known when Harvard started to teach law by the case history method in 1870 that the method of science should have been included in the training of lawyers.

An Error: By 1900 the method of science was being termed the scientific method. The mistake of 1870 should have been corrected.

Probably a Blunder: In the period between 1900 and 1946, there was an ever-increasing body of knowledge developed about the scientific method that should have gained it legal recognition.

Big Blunder: From 1946 to 1993, so much more was known that the fact that the scientific method had still not gained legal recognition amounts to a clear blunder, not just a mistake or probable blunder.

Partial Correction of Big Blunder Ignored: In the 1993 *Daubert* decision, the U.S. Supreme Court finally recognized the significance of the scientific method. The legal blunder has been further perpetrated by non-recognition or deliberate hiding of the significance of this decision. Even though it is a landmark decision of "supreme importance," it has not been recognized as such in books and websites of landmark decisions. Nor has the legal profession (and educators) paid much attention to the significance of this decision.

The legal situation of the scientific method is so complex that I will only try to highlight a few areas of it. Please remember that I am not an attorney, but I present my opinion of the situation.

Chapter 53

Legal Considerations of the Scientific Method

The History of Teaching Law Does Not Include the Scientific Method (1870–2004)

A Missed Opportunity at Harvard and Other Law Schools

How should law be taught? Since it is largely a problem-solving and decision-making activity, law students should certainly be taught the scientific method—the complete method of creative problem solving and decision making.

In 1870, when Christopher Langdell became Dean of Harvard Law School, he instituted the teaching of law via the case history method of study. He also added the Socratic method of teaching.

In *Thinking in Time* (1986), Neustadt and May state:

> Harvard Law School has dominated American legal education for close to one hundred years by the visibility of its example. So vast an improvement were Langdell's reforms over the earlier Litchfield type of school that early in the twentieth century Harvard emerged as a model for virtually every American law school.

While at other law schools there has been some criticism of the case study method and the Socratic method, Harvard's example has dominated American legal education.

Langdell "regarded the law as a science to be mastered only by investigation of its source—decisions and opinions. . ." [*Three Centuries of Harvard* (1936) by Samuel E. Morison]. When considering how to train lawyers, however, Langdell paid no attention to T.H. Huxley's 1863 comments about the method of scientific investigation (see Chapter 26) and other knowledge known about the method of science in those days. While it is easy to understand why a mistake was made in 1870, it is hard to understand why it was not corrected in later years. It is even harder to understand why it has not been corrected today.

Historically, then, the scientific method has had an undeserved, unappreciated, and tragic past in the legal field also. The only bright spot was the 1993 *Daubert* decision. However, this is not as bright as it should be, as I will explain.

Some History of the U.S. Supreme Court and the Scientific Method

In the course of writing a two-page report in 1996, an eight-page report in 1997, and a four-page report in 1998 on the relationship of the scientific method to the law, I gained a little knowledge of its history. I have not done a complete search.

In addition, an April 2002 search for Supreme Court decisions referencing the scientific method identified only six references for the years 1893 to 1993, and these citations are of such minor importance that they are not worth reviewing here.

The Period between 1900 and 1946

In *Law in a Scientific Age* (1963), Edwin W. Patterson reports that Justices Oliver Wendell Holmes, Jr. and Benjamin Cardozo were influenced by the scientific method. He also reports that the method could be said to have greatly influenced the school of legal scholars known as the American Legal Realists.

Justices Holmes, Cardozo, and Frankfurter were all admirers of Morris R. Cohen. In *An Introduction to Logic and Scientific Method* (1934), Cohen and Nagel review possible ways of banishing doubt and arriving at stable beliefs, such as the method of tenacity, the method of authority, the method of intuition, and the method of science (i.e., the scientific method).

Their review really gets to the heart of the scientific method situation. There is simply no other method of knowledge that has been recognized and developed, even in the 21st century, that equals or even rivals the scientific method.

Cohen and Nagel (1934) describe the scientific method:

> The other methods discussed are all inflexible, that is, none of them can admit that it will lead us to error. Hence none of them can make provision for correcting its own results. What is called *scientific method* differs radically from these by encouraging and developing the utmost possible doubt, so that what is left after such doubt is always supported by the best available evidence. As new evidence or new doubts arise it is the essence of scientific method to incorporate them— to make them an integral part of the body of knowledge so far attained.

There was a great deal of knowledge added to what was known about the scientific method in the first half of the 20th century besides Cohen and Nagel's important contribution. I describe others in the period 1900–1946 who advocated the use of the scientific method (Part 8). I call special attention to John Dewey.

The Scientific Method Is Also the Method of the Chancery Court

In *Teaching of Scientific Method* (1903), Professor H.E. Armstrong stated:

> The method of science, indeed, is the method of Chancery Court—it involves the collection of all available evidence and the subjection of all such evidence to the most searching examination and cross examination. False evidence may be tendered and for the time accepted; but sooner or later the perjury is discovered.

So there also was in the literature a basic understanding that the scientific method was essential to court proceedings. Its use was not limited to Chancery Court.

Science in the Courtroom Prior to 1993

From *Galileo's Revenge* (1991) by Peter W. Huber:

> In 1923, a federal appellate court issued a landmark ruling in *Frye v. United States.* . . Thereafter, federal courts, widely copied by the states, were bound by the *Frye* rule, which allowed experts into court only if their testimony was founded on theories, methods, and procedures "generally accepted" as valid among other scientists in the same field.

This decision and the Federal Rules of Evidence guided our courts prior to 1993.

The Wheels of Justice Are Said to Turn Slowly—Maybe That Was the Reason Edmund Was Asleep in 1993

Finally, in 1993, the U.S. Supreme Court specifically recognized the scientific method as a valuable tool. I goofed in not learning immediately that they had done so. My weak excuse is that the newspapers and professional journals I read in 1993 did not mention the inclusion. I failed to get a copy of the decision until alerted a few years later by an article in *Science* magazine that made a casual mention of it. No one was publicizing the great event. Thus, I missed including it in all the reports and booklets I wrote prior to 1996. I have tried to make up for this goof by spending many hours studying the significance of this event and writing a few special reports about the decision.

At Last the Scientific Method Gains Legal Status

A historical event occurred in 1993. Despite my efforts, this has not yet been recognized to be of landmark importance.

In the *Daubert v. Merrell Dow Pharmaceuticals, Inc.* [(509 U.S. 579 (1993)] decision, the U.S. Supreme Court ruled:

> But, in order to qualify as "scientific knowledge" an inference or assertion must be derived *by the scientific method.* Proposed testimony must be supported by appropriate validation—i.e., *"good grounds,"* based on what is known. [emphasis mine]

Considering that five of the nine justices of the Supreme Court had attended Harvard, it is to their credit that they included the scientific method in the decision. I forecast that it will be recognized eventually as a landmark decision even though it is not presently recognized as such.

What Influenced the U.S. Supreme Court Justices to Specify the Scientific Method?

I did not research this completely. However, in the 1993 *Daubert* case, various organizations and groups submitted briefs. For example, the following is from the October 1992 brief submitted by the American Medical Association et al.:

> B. "Scientific knowledge" is that body of knowledge that has been learned or developed in accordance with rigorous scientific methodology. The scientific method involves replicable, empirical testing of hypotheses. Hypotheses that cannot be corroborated by such testing are discarded. Hypotheses that are repeatedly corroborated are labelled "theories" and generally accepted as valid. Medical knowledge is one kind of scientific knowledge. *It is acquired through the application of the scientific method to questions concerning the effects of various interventions on human health.* [emphasis mine]

This was one important source of advice to the court on the importance of the scientific method. The next one is even more specific advice.

The American Association for the Advancement of Science and the National Academy of Sciences filed a joint brief. These are two of our most prestigious organizations, so it is readily understood why the Court would pay special attention to the brief. The following are some statements from it.

> Science thus involves far more than mere observation. Valid science must also explain and clarify relationships. The key to valid science is a convergence of well reasoned explanation with supporting observations or experimental results. No discrete set of experiments can establish that an hypothesis is true in all situations. Rather, scientists conduct rigorous experimental testing in an attempt to falsify hypotheses. An hypothesis is accepted as generally valid to the extent that it has survived repeated attempts at falsification. "Observation, reason, and experiment make up what we call the scientific method." n8

n8 R. FEYNMAN, R. LEIGHTON & M. SANDS, THE FEYNMAN LECTURES ON PHYSICS 2-1 (1963) (emphasis in original)

In its decision, the U.S. Supreme Court quoted the AAAS/NAS brief:

> Science is not an encyclopedic body of knowledge about the universe. Instead, it represents a process for proposing and refining theoretical explanations about the world that are subject to further testing and refinement. n6

And a direct reference by the court to the scientific method:

> A new theory or explanation must generally survive a period of testing, review, and refinement before achieving scientific acceptance. This process does not merely reflect the scientific method, it is the scientific method. n15

n15 See J ZIMAN, RELIABLE KNOWLEDGE: AN EXPLORATION OF THE GROUNDS FOR BELIEF IN SCIENCE 130-32 (1978); Relman & Angell, How Good is Peer Review?, 321 NEW ENGL. J. MED. 827, 828 (1989).

I would say, then, that these briefs were instrumental in influencing the court to state:

> But, in order to qualify as "scientific knowledge," an inference or assertion must be derived by the scientific method.

The Big Bad BLUNDER Continues

In Chapters 28 and 29 I pointed out that the American Association for the Advancement of Science and the National Academy of Sciences have, in all their educational activities, failed to include the scientific method. NAS had the government contract to study the 1995 National Science Education Standards. Not only do these standards fail to include the scientific method, but they also deny it. This situation is nothing short of tragic. The confusion is hurting justice, for the U.S. Court of Appeals, Ninth Circuit stated in *Daubert v. Merrell Dow Pharmaceuticals, Inc.* (on remand),43 F.3d 1311 (1995):

> **A. Brave New World**
> [4] Federal judges ruling on the admissibility of expert scientific testimony face a far more complex and daunting task in a post-*Daubert* world than before. The judge's task under *Frye* is relatively simple: to determine whether the method employed by the experts is generally accepted in the scientific community. *Solomon*, 753 F.2d at 1526. Under *Daubert*, we must engage in a difficult, two-part analysis. First, we must determine nothing less than whether the experts' testimony reflects "scientific knowledge," whether their findings are "derived by the scientific method," and whether their work product amounts to "good science." ---U.S. at----, ----, 113 S.Ct. at 2795, 2797.

The "brave new world" would not be anywhere near as bad if *the* **BLUNDER** had not occurred. As I show in the tabulation of questions to ask, if everyone had been trained and educated in the scientific method, it would not be so difficult. It is correct that experts are still needed on the technical methods, but how these are actually applied must follow the scientific method. Thus, judges, jurors, and attorneys will be able to render justice much better when *the* **BLUNDER** as to the supremacy of the scientific method in "banishing doubt and arriving at stable beliefs" is corrected.

We are in a period in which the full significance of the *Daubert* decision is not well recognized. I hope that this book will change that.

Misguiding Our Judges about the Scientific Method Does Not Lead to "Justice for All"

We have or have had these projects to aid our courts regarding scientific evidence:

The Carnegie Commission on Science, Technology, and Government. Created by the Carnegie Corporation in 1988 to help government institutions respond to unprecedented advances in science and technology. I wrote to the Carnegie Commission in 1992, but it no longer exists.

Federal Judicial Center. The preparation of a *Reference Manual on Scientific Evidence* for use by judges, funded by the Carnegie Corporation. I sent the Federal Judicial Center my booklets in 1994 and received no response.

Joint Panel of the American Association for the Advancement of Science and the American Bar Association, National Conference of Lawyers and Scientists. For a number of years this group has studied the problem of scientific evidence in the courtroom.

CASE, a Court Appointed Scientific Experts Project. This is an American Association for the Advancement of Science project to provide judges with independent scientists who "would educate the court, testify at trial, assess the litigants' cases and otherwise aid in the process of determining the truth." There will be four subsidiary bodies. I sent them my legal reports #10 and #17 and my booklets in 1999 but received no response.

These efforts are all admirable, *but* the Carnegie Corporation and the American Association for the Advancement of Science both ignored special reports that I sent to them regarding the scientific method.

One current proposed solution is greater use of court-appointed independent experts to aid the judge and jury. While this will help, it is not enough.

In the 1993 *Daubert* decision, the U.S. Supreme Court stated that expert witnesses must use the scientific method! However, they set no standard as to what comprises the scientific method. A practical, or partial, solution is to require expert witnesses to show in writing how they derived their inferences and assertion following the SM-14 version of the scientific method.

The Disastrous Situation of Expert Witnesses

All the confusion that has resulted from not teaching the scientific method has caused a very bad situation, with many injustices. I now explain a big one.

Help in Solving the Problem of Contradictory Expert Witnesses

In recent years we have had billion dollar litigation involving asbestos, breast implants, drugs, etc. where:

Plaintiff presents "expert witnesses" who testify under oath that it is a fact

Defendant presents "expert witnesses" who testify under oath that it is not a fact

Puzzled judges and jurors don't know who to believe to arrive at "justice for all"

In *Science At the Bar* (1995), Sheila Jasanoff explains about expert witnesses. She states:

> For lawyers in routine cases, the search for the right expert witness is increasingly dominated by a variety of middlemen, either witness brokers who specialize in finding experts for particular types of lawsuits, or clearinghouses, such as the Expert Witness Network and the Technical Advisory Service for Attorneys. Despite their obvious advantages, such intermediaries create entry points for unethical or professionally marginal experts, as in the case of a physician who became a legal consultant after serving a prison term and losing his license to practice medicine.

> In the commodity market of expertise, persuasiveness more than raw scientific credentials determines a witness's worth. Experts may seek to establish themselves (often with the help of entrepreneurial lawyers) as specialists in particular types of cases, sometimes appearing categorically as "plaintiff's witnesses" or "defense witnesses."

Presented next is my first effort to create an example of how expert witnesses could show how they followed the scientific method (SM-14). It was published in my Report #10 of 1997, but I never received any comments about the idea.

THE SCIENTIFIC METHOD AND QUESTIONS FOR EXPERT WITNESSES

The ingredients or stages of the scientific method, SM-14 formula	Here are questions that may be asked to determine whether the expert witness has used the scientific method and in a manner based on "good grounds." Questions will vary depending on the problem involved. The bases for other questions can be found in *The Scientific Method Today*.
1. Curious Observation	Have you been curious about all aspects of the problem? Any new ideas?
2. Is There a Problem?	What is your definition of the problem involved? Does this agree with the issues in this matter so your testimony will add to the jury's knowledge? Previous to this matter, how much research have you conducted in the direct area of the problem now in question? Where?
3. Goals and Planning	Note: By verbally asking questions or by reading a written report of the witness' goals and planning and how he researched his testimony, you will get an idea of his professionalism and whether he followed the scientific method.
4. Search, Explore, and Gather the Evidence	Did you, for this matter, improve your knowledge of the subject about which you will testify? Where, when, and to what extent?
5. Generate Creative and Logical Alternative Solutions	Did you generate and consider alternative tentative hypotheses? Did you consider all contrary evidence? Note: The quality of the answer may indicate professionalism or bias.
6. Evaluation	Did you do any testing or experimenting? Can you show in chart form an evaluation of all tentative hypotheses you considered?

7. Make the Educated Guess (Hypothesis)	Were you able to arrive at a working hypothesis? Did you make predictions based on it? Is it in a form that can be tested?
8. Challenge the Hypothesis	What further tests, experiments, or research did you do to test it? Did the predictions work out? Did you attempt to falsify it as well as support it?
9. Reach a Conclusion	Explain your final hypothesis or theory and its value to the jury in reaching a decision.
10. Suspend Judgment	How certain are you that your final hypothesis is correct? What may yet make it wrong?
11. Take Action	Have you ever subjected the theory you are supporting or one very similar to peer review? If so, what support or opposition resulted?

The following supporting ingredients are part of the SM-14 formula to aid in understanding and teaching the scientific method. The addition of these to the SM-14 formula makes it reflect the whole system of science and thus the complete method of creative problem solving. The proper use of these contribute substantially to the "good grounds" and "good science" that the U.S. Supreme Court requires in the use of the scientific method.

12. Creative, Non-Logical, Logical, and Technical Methods	Which main action methods have you applied in this matter in using the scientific method? Are these methods regularly used in your domain? Is there an error rate involved?
13. Procedural Principles	Have you applied the procedural principles, ethics, and theories normally used to produce unbiased research?
14. Attributes and Thinking Skills	Have you used the personal attributes normally used in impartial research? Have you been skeptical in your research and reasoning?

Chapter 54

Legal Accountability at the Top Levels of Education

The public is dissatisfied with education. Reform program after reform program has failed. Current reform movements are demanding accountability from our schools, and scientifically based research and evidence-based practice from our educators. Pressure on schools will help. But it is unfair and a disaster that will give us only "more of the same" if we don't put pressure on our top leaders and educational researchers to do a better job too, and quickly!

In Chapter 27 I pointed out that those in the social sciences, including education, have erroneously not been required to use the scientific method. Years ago I pinned up this sign in my office:

> Change occurs when the status quo
> becomes more painful than
> instituting a change.

Now is the time to change the "status quo." By including the phrase "scientifically based research" in the ESEA, Congress has provided a new tool to effect this change. This book provides the basis for a proper interpretation of "scientifically based research."

Our natural scientists have long been required to adhere to a strict code of performance when performing under government contracts. Now our government officials must do their job and make it painful for those in the educational field who do not also do so.

An Educational Job Is Involved

Our top educational leaders and researchers are really trying to improve education and are dedicated to doing so. However, they have largely not been educated in the scientific method and the ethical standards of conduct of the natural sciences. Even many scientists who step out of the laboratory to assist in education do not remember their training.

A number of terms other than ethics have been used to describe the desired human quality of work of a researcher or problem solver. A few of these are "research integrity," "responsible science," "integrity of research process," and "professional responsibility." It is another field that is growing in complexity.

Ethics Today

Events of the last few years in business, science, publishing, education, and other domains have created more interest in ethics. The U.S. Office of Science and Technology Policy issued *Federal Policy on Research Misconduct* in January 2001. It states that "research misconduct is defined as fabrication, falsification, or plagiarism in proposing, performing, or reviewing research, or in reporting research results." The problem is the interpretation of these words. Researchers have an increasing burden of concern about what they mean. New regulations are now being considered.

Falsification by Omission Is Not Acceptable

In my research, I find numerous definitions of the scientific method. This one impressed me, as it hints at the reason we have had so many disasters in the field of education and other social sciences.

The following, written by Dr. Art Robinson, appeared in the newsletter *Access to Energy* (January 2002):

> Beyond this, the scientific method is very simple: Every hypothesis or theory is meritorious only so far as it passes experimental test; all experimental evidence must be considered without omission; all results—experimental, semi-empirical, and theoretical—must be communicated with complete honesty; falsehoods—including falsehoods of omission—are not acceptable.

In my research and crusade for the scientific method, I have constantly noticed that one of the worst things is the "falsehood of omission." When you examine what has happened in the social sciences, it is usually obvious that the various stages of the scientific method (SM-14) have not been followed either completely or to a proper degree. The falsehood of omission is far too common. In selective reporting, omission, and structured silence, it is often the case that no one has lied, but other researchers and the public have been misled, with possible important consequences.

Ignoring contrary evidence has also been termed "cooking" by Charles Babbage (1791 to 1871), sometimes called the "Father of Computing." He defined "cooking" as retaining only those results that fit the theory and discarding others (from *Honor in Science*, 1986, published by Sigma Xi).

Other Lapses of Ethics Contributing to *the* BLUNDER

These also probably played a part in *the* **BLUNDER**:

- Misplaced institutional loyalties at the expense of science values.
- Yielding to pressures for grants, jobs, papers published, fame, etc.

Many who have participated did not realize what they were doing, hence the need for greater education in ethics and the scientific method. Little is gained by worrying about the past. We need to end *the* **BLUNDER**.

There Is Increased Interest in Ethics in This Knowledge Age

In the first part of the 20th century, we had a relatively small number of scientists, engineers, and other professionals. The pressures on these people were small. Today we have millions and millions of professionals, so instances of ethical misconduct have increased substantially. The interest in ethics is now at an all-time high. Some of the resources we have today are:

Ethics centers
Government ethics boards and controls
Ethics compliance officers
College courses in ethics in many domains
Professors specializing in ethics
Journals devoted to ethics in a number of domains
Numerous books on ethics
Business Roundtable establishing an ethics institute
Many professions establishing codes of ethics
Many ethics websites on the Internet
International and national conferences on ethics

Suggestions about Ethics

The problem of ethics is growing fast in all domains. In the business, industry, and financial fields, recent headlines have shocked America. These fields must pay special attention to teaching ethics. There is a need to try and develop a science of ethics. We need to establish one or more permanent specialized SM-14 type national research centers on ethics to help prevent over-regulation. They must operate very carefully and be practical in their objectives. Whether the existing centers on ethics can be converted or whether new ones should be established needs study.

I claim that *the* BLUNDER would never have occurred if, long ago, we had a permanent specialized SM-14 type national research center on ethics.

Suggestions for Study by Our Legal Community

Because of self-interest and the long years that the mistake and *the* BLUNDER have existed in the legal field, these suggestions may meet with a storm of opposition and attempts to ignore them. If the public wants "justice for all" and real improvement in education, they must insist that these suggestions be studied.

♦ There should be a general review of the impact on the field of law of the requirement that the scientific method be used.

♦ Jurors chosen from the general population and those entering the law profession all need to know the complete method of creative problem solving. The legal community should join others in asking that the scientific method be taught across the curriculum in all grades.

♦ A permanent specialized SM-14 type national research center should be set up to study the relationship of the scientific method to the law.

♦ The teaching of the scientific method and courses on ethics should be incorporated into all law school curricula.

♦ All presently licensed lawyers should be required to take a course on the scientific method, not to learn the numerous scientific techniques, but to better learn the basics of the complete method of creative problem solving and decision making.

♦ The Judicial Center and all other groups presently attempting to aid judges should review their activities for any misunderstandings or bias against the scientific method. They should incorporate the scientific method into their efforts and objectives.

♦ The American Bar Association should aid in the effort to promote the use of the scientific method.

♦ Attorneys in agencies of the Federal and state governments should start to enforce the real meaning of research, which is that done following the scientific method (SM-14 type).

◆ Congress should initiate changes and clarifications in the Federal Rules of Evidence to reflect the scientific method.

Suggestions to the Education Community about the Legal Situation

In an era of knowledge explosion such as we are in now, the two old cultures of the natural sciences and the social sciences should end. There should be just one.

The U.S. Supreme Court has stated that the scientific method exists for everyone; the No Child Left Behind Act has called for "scientifically based research." While I am not an attorney, I have researched and presented what this means for all domains in the next chapter.

◆ There must be a review of the impact on education of these new understandings and requirements.

◆ The National Science Foundation requires contract holders to exercise "prudent management of all expenditures and actions affecting the grant." In my opinion, a court would find that ignoring vital contrary evidence is not "prudent management."

◆ Universities and others holding government educational contracts will leave themselves open to law suits and damages if they allow the inefficient research of the past that has ignored so much contrary evidence. Huge amounts of money are involved, so don't risk ignoring my research or listening to "authoritative experts." Appoint study groups to review the situation.

◆ As part of my crusade, I intend to send a copy of this book to some of the main attorneys responsible for enforcing government educational contracts; again, don't ignore my suggestions.

? ?

The Mystery

In the legal profession, where problem solving and decision making are major activities, why has the complete method of creative problem solving and decision making and the greatest idea of all time—the scientific method—been so ignored?

? ?

Introduction to Part 10

What Is Scientifically Based Research?

The word "research" comes from re-searching or again searching for the truth as nearly as it can be ascertained and understood based on the best available evidence and practical attempts to falsify the concluding hypothesis.

It is quite amazing that in this age of knowledge a word that is used millions of times every day is so little understood. Perhaps I should say, is it fully and accurately understood? This is just another of the millions of harms of *the* **BLUNDER**.

In this part I cover the current situation in which Congress, in its effort to improve education, used the word research in the No Child Left Behind Act. To ensure that the word research would be understood, Congress added descriptive words. Thus, the phrase that appears more than 100 times in the act is "scientifically based research." Humbly, I show that, to be clear, Congress should have specified research following the scientific method (SM-14 type).

Various other phrases being used in educational reform that stress "evidence" are also explained.

Chapter 55

Big Change!
The No Child Left Behind Act (ESEA) of 2001
Uses a Special Term:
"Scientifically Based Research"

My forecast is that the year 2002 will go down in the history of education as the year in which education first began to emerge from the 1950–2002 era of fads, mis-steps, and wild confusion of one wrong or untested program after another. It will take time for this change. There will always be mistakes and some confusion, but not the large number of disasters and wild times of the second half of the 20th century that followed the abandonment of steering education and educational research toward the use of the scientific method.

It took an act of Congress to correct this divergence from the correct path. The new Elementary and Secondary Education Act (ESEA), also known as the No Child Left Behind Act, was signed into law in January 2002 by President George W. Bush. Congratulations to the Republications and Democrats and to the public that it specifically included "scientifically based research" so often.

An article in *Education Week* (January 30, 2002) reported:

Law Mandates
Scientific Base
For Research

Critics See ESEA Edict
As Unrealistic, Political

The phrase pops up over and over, mantra-like, in the new federal education law: "scientifically based research."

Those words, or an approximation, appear more than 100 times in the reauthorization of the Elementary and Secondary Education Act, which requires practices based on research for everything from the provision of technical assistance to schools to the selection of anti-drug-abuse programs.

Reflected in that repetition is a desire by Congress and the Bush administration to base school improvement efforts less on intuition and experience and more on research-based evidence. That desire also mirrors other attempts in the field to set standards of quality for education research and to synthesize what is known, or identify successful programs and practices, based on those standards. . .

Contrary to the headline, I shall show you that it is far from "unrealistic." It is actually a great advance in education. It is only political in the sense that Congress has reflected the peoples' dissatisfaction with education and has taken a step to correct the biggest ill of education.

Who Decides?

The same article has a subheading:

Researchers Wonder: Who Decides If Studies Are Scientifically Based?

My answer is that ultimately the U.S. Supreme Court will decide. It has already stated (in the *Daubert v. Merrell Dow* case of 1993) that the scientific method exists. The existence of the scientific method is the key to the term "scientifically based research."

I Make This Claim (now I'm the one being arrogant):

Norman W. Edmund is the leading authority on the meaning of scientifically based research.

Join me in laughing at the absurdity of this situation.

◆ We have millions of educators, scientists, lawyers, and psychologists, hundreds of historians and of philosophers of science, but none is as qualified as I am to be a good authority and prepared with the evidence of what the term scientifically based research means.

◆ I am neither a scientist nor a professional educator, nor do I have a full college degree.

◆ We have extensive literature on the subjects of "scientific" and "research" that covers the discussion of the matter for centuries. However, there are no good and easily communicated summaries and a formula to answer today's needs other than mine.

Why Does This Absurd Situation Exist?

◆ As explained in this book, *the* **BLUNDER** occurred and has effectively prevented a science of science from being properly summarized. The adequate use, discussion, debate, and development of the scientific method in the field of education, and a science of education, have also been effectively prevented by *the* **BLUNDER**.

◆ The research I have presented since 1992 on the scientific method has been ignored. It has not been built on and expanded by others.

Our Scientists Have Been Showing Us How

This may all seem confusing. However, remember that scientists working on government contracts for research in natural sciences have been operating scientifically for a long time—not perfectly because of human nature, but certainly to a far higher degree than has been done in educational research and other social science domains. In the coming new age of education, there will be less

arrogance
fads and poor programs
untested programs widely installed
haphazard work instead of following method
ignoring contrary evidence

The Importance of Congress' Action

Everyone in the educational field, now, because of the ESEA, more than ever, needs proper guidance about a correct definition of "scientifically based research" to help them conduct their research and select proper programs. It is probable that there will be many court cases involving large amounts of money. These will arise from complaints that research grant holders and receivers of state and local appropriations have not used or done "scientifically based research."

Definition Identification

Because of its importance, and since it is already being discussed in educational circles and will probably be asked in court, I ask questions and give answers as follows. (Remember that what I discuss is old. The ideas I present are abstracted from the literature. I may use others' words, phrases, and sentences at times.)

Q&A One
What Are Considerations in Defining
Scientifically Based Research?

In the No Child Left Behind Act of 2001, signed into law in January 2002, also known as the new ESEA, scientifically based research is defined in greater detail than it was defined in the Reading Excellence Act of October 21, 1998. It is certainly a blunder that we do not have a good definition in the 21st century.

The definition in the ESEA does not mention the scientific method by name, but uses descriptions of some of the principles often described as part of the scientific method in various philosophy and science books. Any accurate interpretation and defining of Congress' term will only lead back to the scientific method.

In *The Scientific Approach—Basic Principles of the Scientific Method* (1967), psychologist Carlo Lastrucci states (and things have not changed since 1967):

> I.1 In spite of the tremendous influence of science upon modern civilization, there exists as yet no standardized definition of science. Laymen, scholars, and scientists themselves define the term in varying ways and employ it in a variety of contexts. . .
> I.2 Checking the definition of the adjective "scientific" does not help very much to determine its essential features. According to a standard source, the word "scientific" is derived from the Latin word *scientia*, meaning knowledge, plus the term *facere*, meaning to make; both terms were originally employed as a translation from the Greek term *episthemonikos*, or making knowledge (from which the modern term *epistemology* is derived, meaning the study or theory of the origin, essence, methods, and limits of knowledge.

Based on my 15 years of specialized research of the scientific method, I will define "scientifically based research." Then I will comment on the definition in the ESEA.

Q&A Two
What Is "Research"?

Since the main subject is "research," I define this first.

The *American Heritage Dictionary* defines the noun research as:

(1) Scholarly or scientific investigation or inquiry. (2) Close, careful study.

Let's examine this dictionary definition.

"Scholarly"—The method of scholars is another name for the scientific method. Time and scholarly study have shown the scientific method to be the best method of obtaining reliable knowledge. Thus, "scholarly" means using the scientific method.

"Scientific investigation"—Way back in 1863, T.H. Huxley told us:

> The method of scientific investigation is nothing but the expression of the necessary mode of working of the human mind. It is simply the mode at which all phenomena are reasoned about, rendered precise and exact.

Please note that Huxley stated "the mode [method] at which all phenomena are reasoned about, rendered precise and exact." Research is far from simply using common sense. It requires disciplined inquiry.

So again, research basically means using the method of investigation, which is the scientific method.

"Inquiry"—Inquiry is necessary in research, but inquiry gets you wandering aimlessly unless you follow the method of inquiry, which is again the scientific method.

"Close, careful study"—To do close, careful study, you must follow in complex matters the method of study, the scientific method. Centuries of research have established this as reliable knowledge.

Conclusion. An accurate interpretation or definition of the word "research" is research based on and following the method of research, also call the scientific method.

The word "research" has been carelessly used and interpreted. An accurate definition has generally not been understood. Thus, Congress added descriptive words to be sure that the "research" called for was the correct type and "scientifically based."

Now let's consider a definition of "based."

Q&A Three
What Is "Based"?

Congress used the word "based." This is generally defined in dictionaries as referring to foundation, fundamental part, main part, base for that on which a thing rests.

As shown throughout this book, science is fundamentally method and also understood to be our body of reliable knowledge.

Conclusion. Research must be based on:

♦ **Its method—the scientific method**
♦ **Our body of knowledge—but viewed skeptically because of its changing nature**

Here is a little review of some of the things science and the scientific method (SM-14) are based on and a comparison with the opposite, unscientific base.

Base of SM-14	Unscientific Base
Eleven stages of mental activity Used in a flexible manner to originate, refine, extend, and apply knowledge	Proceeding haphazardly Going ahead without a guide or following a complete act of thought
Creative, non-logical, logical, and technical methods are applied following the scientific method guide at each stage to accomplish results	Techniques (often called methods) are used but there is no quality control as to how they are used
Procedural principles and theories Provides fundamentals of good and ethical procedures to follow at various stages	No quality or ethics Proceeding unregulated usually produces unreliable results
Attributes and thinking skills Provide quality guidance	No personal quality standards Often results in poor work

Q&A Four
What Is "Scientifically" and What Is Science?

The U.S. Congress used "scientifically," an adverb. It would, I understand, have been grammatically correct to have said "science-based research." However, if that had been done, it might have provoked so much debate that the passage of the act would have been delayed.

I believe it is best to directly define "science." Thus, I have the difficult and controversial job of defining "science" in order to determine what "scientifically" means.

The Term "Science"

While the Arabs, Greeks, Spanish, English, Germans, and others have been mentioned or credited with the method of science, the start of the general development of science as we know it now has usually been credited to Galileo in the 16th century. He is sometimes referred to as the father of scientific method.

Today the term science has come to have three major meanings:

1. The domains of activities termed "sciences"—the term "science" is used to identify the various sciences, or domains of activity. First to be recognized were the natural sciences, such as physics, astronomy, chemistry, geology, and biology. The human and social sciences have also been termed sciences. Some of these are psychology, economics, education, geography, and sociology. But my research raises the question of whether they have yet reached the status of sciences based on a strict interpretation of the world science and as I define it.

2. Science has long been noted as representing bodies of knowledge accumulated in various domains.

3. "Science is its method." "Science is fundamentally method." "Science is a process." "Science is a method of thought." These and similar statements are found throughout the literature describing science, with frequent mention, beginning in the 19th century, that its method is the scientific method or scientific method.

Conclusion. The most significant meaning of the three is that science is fundamentally method, for its method is what produces the body of knowledge in various domains.

Q&A Five
What Is Scientifically Based Research?

ALL THREE WORDS INDICATE THAT IT IS RESEARCH USING THE SCIENTIFIC METHOD

First—the word scientifically (or science)

♦ Practitioners, including teams, doing scientifically based research must then utilize the accumulated body of reliable knowledge, but considering the usual skepticism afforded any knowledge by the procedural principles of the scientific method.

♦ Since science is fundamentally method, its method must be used—the scientific method.

Second—the word based

The foundation must be on science, which is fundamentally method—the scientific method.

Third—the word research

Research in the strict and correct meaning of the word means research following the scientific method.

Conclusion. The total meaning of the phrase "scientifically based research" means and emphasizes

research following the scientific method.

Q&A Six
What Is the Definition of the Scientific Method?

Preliminary Considerations

Before considering a definition of the scientific method consider the following:

♦ In defining the scientific method, you are also defining, to a great extent, science, as science is fundamentally method.

♦ A study of the literature shows that the various claims that the method does not exist and many other derogatory claims about it are false (see Chapter 7).

◆ In a 1993 decision (*Daubert v. Merrell Dow Pharmaceuticals, Inc.*), the U.S. Supreme Court recognized the existence of the scientific method. The Justices set a requirement that expert witnesses must base their testimony on the scientific method.

◆ While recognized and developed mainly by scientists, it is the natural method of problem solving and decision making for all fields.

◆ We need a standard definition suitable for teaching but also suitable to guide all people in all fields. Therefore, it cannot be too complicated and suit every principle, special features, or techniques of various domains.

◆ I make no claim of originality, copyright, etc., of this definition. It represents an abstraction and correlation from the literature of the best thinking about the subject. I recommend that, until an official body establishes a standard, it be used as a standard.

The Scientific Method (SM-14) Is Concisely Defined as:

The basic method, guide, and system by which we originate, refine, extend, and apply knowledge in all fields.

The definition can be extended to include the following:

◆ We do this through three major phases: problem origination, solution, and challenge of solution.

◆ Eleven major stages of mental activity are involved, usually aided by physical activities and used in a flexible manner. (See *The Scientific Method Today*.)

◆ There are three major supporting ingredients of the method used at the various stages:

> (12) Creative, non-logical, logical, and technical methods
> (13) Procedural principles and theories
> (14) Attributes and thinking skills

◆ Stage 11 calls for action in submitting conclusions, theories, etc. to peer review in professional organization journals, trade magazines, books, meetings, etc. when appropriate. In a minor matter, the action can be putting to verification by practical use.

Thus, the SM-14 formula represents the complete system of science.

Q&A Seven
What Is the Peer Review System of Science?

The usual phases of peer review are presented below, but they are often varied by papers presented at scientific meetings, published books, patent applications, and direct use. The Internet is facilitating electronic preprints and journals of various qualities.

A   A researcher or a group of researchers follows the stages of the scientific method, including its self-correction feature and supporting ingredients, to prepare a research report.

B   The researcher(s) submit the paper to a professional journal.

C   If the journal is interested in the paper, the paper is sent to one or more referees.

D   Referees reject it, send it back for revision, or accept it. *Theoretically, the referees follow the scientific method in evaluating the paper.* In practice, because of the limited time available, they usually use personal knowledge of the domain to form a judgment of the adequacy of the paper. They are skeptical and often conservative.

E   If the editors agree with the referees, the paper is accepted.

F   The community of professionals evaluate the published paper. Then a wide range of activity can occur:

   1. The paper excites no interest and is just added to the body of knowledge in the literature.
   2. The paper is cited by others favorably or unfavorably, to various degrees. Letters to the editor may be published.
   3. The paper excites intense interest, and great debate occurs, including efforts of replication and testing of results.

Accumulate a Body of Reliable Knowledge

If the professional communities or some of their members accept the new knowledge, it is applied and may be further refined, extended, and applied. Gradually, there is an accumulated body of knowledge reliable to various degrees. However, it is widely scattered, as there is usually no organization specifically charged with evaluating and communicating this knowledge other than the professional journals.

There are, however, temporary panels, etc. appointed to make special investigations of important matters. There are permanent groups, such as ethics panels in natural sciences, and there are permanent organizations for standards, such as those in the field of engineering.

In Recommendation #2 (Chapter 58) I propose a series of permanent specialized SM-14 type national research centers on education.

Q&A Eight
What Is Scientifically Based Research as Defined in the ESEA of 2001?

The Act states:

"The term 'scientifically based research' (A) means research that involves the application of rigorous, systematic, and objective procedures to obtain reliable and valid knowledge relevant to education activities and programs; and (B) includes research that:

—employs systematic, empirical methods that draw on observation or experiment;

—involves rigorous data analyses that are adequate to test the stated hypothesis and justify the general conclusions drawn;

—relies on measurements or observational methods that provide reliable and valid data across evaluators and observers, across multiple measurements and observations, and across studies by the same or different investigators;

—is evaluated using experimental or quasi-experimental designs in which individuals, entities, programs, or activities are assigned to different conditions and with appropriate controls to evaluate the effects of the condition of interest, with a preference for random-assignment experiments, or other designs to the extent that those designs contain with-in-condition or across-condition controls;

—ensures that experimental studies are presented in suffi-cient detail and clarity to allow for replication or, at a mini-mum, offer the opportunity to build systematically on their findings; and

—has been accepted by a peer-reviewed journal or approved by a panel of independent experts through a comparably rigorous, objective and scientific review."

Congress Had No Proper Guidance on Their Definition

As mentioned earlier, I did make one mailing of a report to Congress about the scientific method situation. No action resulted. Thus, it was probably not available to or ignored by those who advised on or wrote the legislative bill.

There has existed, to the best of my knowledge, no authoritative definition of "scientifically based research" in our general literature that they could have used, and therefore they assembled a partial one from various sources.

While this description covers many good points, it is difficult for people to understand and follow. It would also be difficult to administer and enforce. It would be much more practical to specify that the scientific method (SM-14 type) be followed.

In our cumulative body of knowledge, we have a large amount on scientific method. The correlation of the information into a specific communicated and practical summary has been lacking due to **the BLUNDER**. To have a good definition requires a thorough knowledge of the scientific method and a practical formula for it. I believe that this chapter and this book mark the first step in having such a definition. While even more detailed, my pamphlet *The Scientific Method Today* is only a beginning in understanding the scientific method. Nevertheless, if we are to improve and have "scientifically based research," we must have an official permanent specialized SM-14 type national research center on the scientific method and the science of science.

Education Department Leaders and the Public Are Misled about "Scientifically Based Research"

From a report of the U.S. Department of Education (February 6, 2002):

The No Child Left Behind Act of 2001, which reauthorized the Elementary and Secondary Education Act, calls for the use of "scientifically based research" as the foundation for many education programs and for classroom instruction.

On February 6, 2002, Assistant Secretary for Elementary and Secondary Education Susan Neuman hosted a seminar where leading experts in the fields of education and science discussed the meaning of scientifically based research and its status across various disciplines. Below is the transcript of the seminar.

I give the grade of F to the transcript of this seminar for clarifying what scientifically based research really is for our top leaders and our state educators.

One paper was from the Department's Office of Educational Research and Improvement and was of little value in clarifying scientifically based research.

The National Academy of Sciences' National Research Council Fails Again to Define "Science"

As official advisor on science to Congress and government agencies, NAS had been invited to the conference and should have provided authoritative advice and guidance of high quality and accuracy. You will recall (Chapter 28) that in June 1999 I sent them a report "Shame on the National Academy of Sciences." Again I say "shame on the National Academy of Sciences" for the guidance it gave at this very important conference. We also have a problem with the term "evidence-based educational practice," as discussed in the next chapter.

Suggestion

A study should be made as to whether it should be understood administratively or specifically enacted by Congress that the definition for scientifically based research should be research following the scientific method (SM-14 type).
Why should government research funds be spent in any domain other than on scientifically based research? A standard summary is needed for all domains, not only education. It would be an administrative and legal nightmare for each domain to have its own definition of scientifically based research.

A New Era Is Here for the Scientific Method with Great Opportunities

This book and the development of the SM-14 formula for the scientific method will end the gray era of the second half of the 20th century. In this past era, the scientific method was recognized and written about by many. But the Harvard/Conant group and misguided followers (or whoever they are) prevailed at the national governmental level and the non-inclusion of the scientific method in national and state educational programs. I have exposed this blunder about the idea that has most changed the world. Because of *the* **BLUNDER**, the terms "research" and "scientifically" have been loosely and often inaccurately used in all domains. Now they can be more precisely understood and even standardized. The opportunities this opens are tremendous. Teams of researchers will be aided by the unity of the scientific method (SM-14).

This book covers only a small part of the changes that will occur in our lives. Again, I claim that trillions of dollars will be better spent in a short number of years.

? ?

The Mysteries

Here we have two words, "scientifically" and "research," used millions of times each week. We all know what they mean in general. But why, since they are so important, haven't we pinpointed their meaning more exactly?

In all the published material I have read on "scientifically based research," mentioned so frequently in the NCLB Act, there has been no reference to the scientific method. Professor Mouly's quote in Chapter 6 reveals that educational research textbooks in the 1970s included the scientific method. Why this silence and lack of mention of the scientific method?

? ?

Chapter 56

Evidence-Based Educational Practice
Evidence-Based Education Policy
Evidence-Based Education Field
Evidence-Driven Educational Progress
Follow the Medical Model

Education Week (April 10, 2002) reports "the Bush administration is stepping up its commitment to what it calls 'evidence-based educational practice.'" The Coalition for Evidence-Based Policy, under the sponsorship of the Council for Excellence in Government, recommended to the U.S. Department of Education and Congress evidence-based education policy in a November 2002 report. The U.S. Department of Education's Strategic Plan 2002–2007 contains Goal Four—Transform Education into an Evidence-Based Field.

On the Positive Side—A Step in the Right Direction

The recent efforts of the Bush administration and Congress to require "scientifically based research" and now "evidence-based educational practice" are great advances. I have reported to you on the many past fads and disasters in the educational field that resulted from untested programs that ignore contrary evidence.

But—the Commitment Should Be for
"The Scientific Method Education Practice"

Here is what is wrong with "evidence based":

◆ It is a vague standard. It leaves everyone wondering what is meant. The scientific method has a more complete existing base.

◆ The program for which evidence is provided may not be the best. It may not have gone through all the stages of the scientific method and thus could be defective in many ways, even if there is evidence to support it. For example, in the past fad after fad has been promoted. The promoters provide "evidence" to support their program but also ignore a lot of contrary evience. In addition, no falsification attempt may have been made.

◆ I remind you that, of all the quality control methods ever recognized and developed, the scientific method has been found to be the best. It is a method, a guide, and a system.

U.S. Department of Education Strategic Plan Goal 4

The plan's goal to "transform education into an evidence-based field" is a great improvement, but again it should be changed to the scientific method-based field. This section of the report even mentions the scientific method.

A User Friendly Guide—Or Is It?

Here is an announcement from the U.S. Department of Education's *The Achiever* (February 1, 2004):

> The federal K-12 grant programs under the *No Child Left Behind Act* require state and local education officials to use scientifically based research to guide their decisions about which programs and strategies to implement. However, they must sort through a myriad of claims to decide which interventions merit consideration for their schools and classrooms.

My comment is that here is proof that the main troubles of education lie at the top. Unfortunate state and local education officials must try to identify which programs to use from a variety of good and bad ones, all the product of our top educators. It is terrible burden on them, but at least they have a "friendly guide" to help them. That is, if they are real experts at determining which are good or bad. In most cases, this will not be so.

The announcement continues:

> To assist educators in finding and using strategies that have been validated in rigorous studies, the Department of Education's Institute of Education Sciences (IES) recently released the user-friendly guide *Identifying and Implementing Education Practices Supported by Rigorous Evidence*. The 19-page publication offers evaluation factors to help determine the effectiveness of an educational intervention—such as a reading or mathematics curriculum, schoolwide reform programs, after-school programs and new educational technologies—that claim to be able to improve educational outcomes and be supported by evidence.

> This guide supports the Department's goal of transforming education into an evidence-based field. It was developed for

IES by the Coalition for Evidence-Based Policy, a nonprofit, nonpartisan organization, sponsored by the Council for Excellence in Government, with the mission to advance government policy based on rigorous evidence of program effectiveness.

An online copy is available at www.ed.gov/about/offices/list /ies/news.html#guide.

The Coalition for Evidence-Based Policy

The website of the Council for Excellence in Government (www.excelgov.org) contains information about the Coalition for Evidence-Based Policy. It explains their work, objectives, and advisors. Their advisors are very intelligent, authoritative people. However, because of *the* BLUNDER, they appear not to be familiar with the scientific method. They place a great deal of emphasis on one of its logical methods—randomized controlled trials.

There is no question that application of randomized controlled trials following the scientific method will improve results. However, the programs that reach this stage must first have been designed following the beginning stages of the scientific method.

The website and objectives are very impressive. Here is an organization that should really be pushing for the full use of the scientific method. It will be interesting to see if this book convinces it to do this. I suggest that it appoint a study group to review the matter. Among its advisors, I see one name I easily identify as one I consider to be a member of the Harvard/Conant group and misguided followers (or whoever they are).

While this December 2003 guide is "friendly" and has a lot of good information, the report places a burden on state and local educators. Rather than a burden, I would say that it is one so complex our state and local officials are not qualified to apply it very efficiently.

National Academy of Sciences and Presentation of "Science As a Culture"

In Chapter 28, The Contribution of the National Academies of Science to *the* BLUNDER, I offered some critical and constructive comments on a report by their operating unit, the National Research Council. The report, *Scientific Research in Education* (2002), is supposed to aid in the evidence-based educational policy movement and discusses how to support high-quality science in a federal education research agency. I was critical of their misrepresentation, inferring that there is no scientific method.

The report further fails to guide all those in federal agencies and the public trying to interpret scientifically based research and evidence-based policy.

The report contains this statement:

> Based on the information gathered at the workshop and through subsequent data collection, our guiding principles of science, the features of education that influence the conduct of research, and the nature of scientific progression, we develop six design principles around the notion of creating a *scientific culture*. We argue throughout this report that science itself is supported through the norms and mores of the scientific community, and we believe that cultivating these values within a research agency is the key to its success. We also note that decades of organizational fixes at the current agency have arguably not done much to improve its culture and, consequently, its reputation.

I reviewed the "six design principles." These are impractical to try to teach and enforce and are incomplete as far as research is concerned. In general, the report gave me the impression of a lot of ivory tower comments of little practical value. The presentation of science as just a culture is just another false presentation of the total big picture of the system of science—the scientific method and its supporting ingredients, such as SM-14 or comparable.

The report calls for constructive discourse. I offer the very constructive suggestion that they seriously review the scientific method situation and the need for the scientific method in educational research. They should withdraw this report and issue a corrected one.

My Analysis of "Educational Research Should Follow the Medical Model"

Hippocrates Gave This Famous Advice: First Do No Harm
So "Doc" Edmund Comes to the Rescue to Prevent Harm!

Lately there have been hundreds (or so it seems to me) of comments that education should follow the medical model. These really upset me! So "Doc" Edmund will try to help the poor patient, educational research.

What is this medical model?

If you analyze the medical field, you quickly find that this field never made much progress until its practitioners and researchers began to follow our natural scientists and use the scientific method. Two influential and well-known books in the medical field are *An Introduction to the Study of Experimental Medicine* (1865) by Dr. Claude Bernard and *The Way of an Investigator—A Scientist's Experience in Medical Research* (1945) by Dr. Walter B. Cannon.

Here is what Dr. Bernard said way back in 1865:

> Reasoning is always the same, whether in the sciences that study living beings or in those concerned with inorganic bodies. But each kind of science presents different phenomena and complexities and difficulties of investigation peculiarly its own.

Here is what Dr. Cannon, a famous Harvard professor, had to say in 1945, just a year before the president of Harvard claimed that the scientific method does not exist:

> The chief grievance which the popularizer expresses is that the teaching of science in grade schools, high schools, and even colleges does not result in a public with a sufficient background of knowledge to allow understanding of the simplest account of new advances. This is a deplorable situation. For a hundred years scientific investigators have been transforming the civilized world. The progress of knowledge in recent times is **chiefly progress in knowledge of science and the scientific method**. The investigators in physics, in chemistry, and in the medical sciences have brought about conditions, within the life span of many now living, that would seem to their fathers nothing short of miraculous. [emphasis mine]

So please—do no harm. The real story is that education should be following the natural sciences model—the scientific method, not the so-called medical model, which is really the scientific model. It is amazing that so many people do not know that our medical progress came from following natural scientists' method.

It is true that some of the creative, non-logical, logical, and technical methods used in medicine can also be used in education, but education must follow the scientific method in order to "do no harm."

It is correct that one of these methods being widely promoted—randomized control trials—is an excellent technique when applied following the scientific method. However, before programs reach this testing stage, they should have gone through the prior stages of the scientific method to prevent trouble and wasted effort.

By the way, I won't make the claim that the Harvard/Conant group and misguided followers (or whoever they are) are using the "medical model" term because they know that if they use "the science model," it will lead to the scientific method that they claim does not exist! The story probably is that there are just too many "misguided members" in this group who have not been taught the scientific method and don't know its true nature and history.

Conclusion

It is a ring around the rosy! Scientifically based research, evidence-based educational practice, randomized controlled trials, follow the medical model—all sorts of claims except the correct one: follow the scientific method!

Suggestion

Evidence is important. But you must see the big picture of a problem to determine what evidence is most valuable. Falsification must also be used to be sure that the evidence cannot be easily disproved.

Restudy the claims for evidence-based education and for following the medical model. In view of all the evidence I show in this book, it is clear that the correct procedure favors the scientific method.

? ?

The Mystery

Will people realize that "evidence based" is a good idea, but it is only one quality feature of the scientific method? To get the best quality control, you must follow all the stages of the scientific method and its supporting ingredients.

? ?

Introduction to Part 11

Recommendations

Throughout this book I have made many "suggestions for study."
I purposely did not call them recommendations so as not to divert
attention from my two major recommendations. Of course, my two
major recommendations need study. They require your greatest attention as soon as possible.

I have mentioned these recommendations many times throughout
this book. In this chapter I cover them more completely.

These two major recommendations are very basic—so much that
there will be no major and continuing improvement in education
until they are adopted.

◆ Edmund Recommendation #1—The Scientific Method
Should Be Extensively Taught, Learned, and Applied
By People in All Domains

In education, this includes

All our educators, including top leaders in all domains
who advise on education
Teaching it across the curriculum in all grades K-12
Teaching it in all subject areas in colleges and universities, and adult schools

---

◆ Edmund Recommendation #2—Establish a System of
Permanent Specialized SM-14 Type National Research
Centers on Education

Chapter 57

Edmund Recommendation #1

◆ Edmund Recommendation #1—The Scientific Method
Should Be Extensively Taught, Learned, and Applied
by People in All Domains

In education, this includes

All our educators, including top leaders in all domains
who advise on education
Teaching it across the curriculum in all grades K-12
Teaching it in all subject areas in colleges and universities, and adult schools

---

In this book I have:

◆ provided plenty of evidence that the scientific method exists and falsified claims that it does not exist

◆ provided evidence that the scientific method is recognized in the literature as the best method ever developed for originating, refining,
extending, and applying knowledge

◆ provided an up-to-date formula for the stages of the method

◆ emphasized that these stages represent a general pattern or guide
that may be followed in a flexible manner

◆ differentiated the stages of mental activity of the method from the
actual techniques or creative, non-logical, logical, and technical
methods used at the stages to produce actual results

◆ identified the supporting ingredients used at the various stages of
mental activity so the method is easier to teach

◆ showed that the scientific method is basically a general problem-
solving and decision-making method for all fields

◆ showed that the scientific method is a basic, natural problem-solving method that even babies use to some degree in the early months
and years of their lives

◆ showed that the deep philosophical disputes about science and the scientific method should not interfere with teaching a practical formula such as SM-14 that represents the scientific method

◆ the base for the unity of education is the scientific method

◆ the scientific method is required for

> science of science
> science of education
> science of teaching
> and for any other field to be a science

Throughout this book I have shown the need and value of teaching problem solving, decision making, the scientific method, and the associated thinking skills. I will not repeat them all here.

Suggestions That Accompany This Recommendation

Adopt the SM-14 Formula Immediately as a Standard

I claim no rights or copyright, etc. to SM-14. It can be freely used. Don't change the wording of the stages. If you want to add subdivisions to reflect your own views, that is OK. There are those teaching the scientific method, authors writing textbooks, and others who need a good standard formula NOW. Eventually, an official study group can determine whether any change is advisable. A standard formula for the stages will greatly facilitate the teaching, use, team work, and better attainment of the benefits of the scientific method.

The Need for Teaching Material on the Scientific Method

While *The Scientific Method Today* provides a good base, we need much more detailed material to properly teach the scientific method (SM-14).

Educational Standards of 1995 and Subsequent Years
Need Correction

All the educational standards must be changed to include teaching the scientific method. It may appear odd at first to suggest teaching the scientific method in many different subject areas, but it becomes plain after study that every domain can benefit from being taught the idea that has so changed the world for the better.

SAT, ACT, and Other Tests Must Include the Scientific Method

Since there is so much pressure on teachers today, "teaching to the test" has increased. Therefore, the SAT, ACT, and other tests should be changed and improved to include questions about the scientific method (SM-14 type).

Teach the Scientific Method across the Curriculum

I explained in Chapter 2 the importance of teaching problem solving and decision making. The old saying should be "Teach reading, writing, arithmetic, and problem solving." Problem solving should be taught from the very beginning of schooling and across the curriculum.

Requirement for College Degrees and Professional Licenses

Anyone earning an educational or other degree in class or on line should be required to meet a set standard of knowledge of the scientific method. The higher the degree, the more comprehensive the standard. Many earning various professional licenses should also be required to meet a standard of knowledge of the scientific method. It should become a custom not to call anyone an "expert" who is not thoroughly knowledgeable about the scientific method and uses it in his or her area of expertise.

When Requiring Essays for Student Evaluation

This ancient practice must be updated to require, instead of just an essay, a report on problem solving or decision making following the SM-14 formula. In an article in the *Chronicle of Higher Education* (January 3, 2003), entitled "Why Johnny Can't Write Even Though He Went to Princeton," Thomas Bartlett reports on the poor job colleges in general are doing in teaching writing.

We Must Teach the Supporting Ingredients of SM-14

Teaching the details of the formula for the scientific method is only part of teaching the scientific method. In addition, we must teach in varying degrees the supporting ingredients of SM-14, stressing that they must also be applied at the various stages of the scientific method in complex situations.

Chapter 58

Edmund Recommendation #2

Edmund Recommendation #2—Establish a System of Permanent Specialized SM-14 Type National Research Centers on Education

Purpose: The accumulation, evaluation, origination, refinement, extension, and dissemination of reliable knowledge about education

---

Top educators mean well by their own standards and are trying hard, but education has just grown haphazardly in all directions. However, all we do is continue getting wrong changes, ineffective changes, or those which do not accomplish what needs to be done. They produce bad new problems, so we have a disillusioned public. They will become unwilling to continue pouring new money into education. Because of the recent decline in tax revenues and requirements for expenditures in other areas, it is also necessary to use educational funds more efficiently. The need to use educational funds efficiently increases as our society becomes more complex.

It is necessary for real educational progress that

♦ we recognize the ever-increasing rate of growth in knowledge
♦ we utilize specialization and team work
♦ we organize and evaluate education knowledge systematically
♦ the educational field become scientific by SM-14 standards

The Size and Importance of Education

Knowledge is said to be our biggest industry, and this is probably correct. The U.S. Department of Education says that the United States spends more than $700 billion per year on education. Peter F. Drucker, the famous management expert, stated in a *Forbes Global* article (March 5, 2000): "I believe that the U.S. now spends around $1 trillion on education and training."

Whether we spend more than $700 billion or $1 trillion when training is included, it is a *huge amount*.

Proposed Idea for a System of Permanent Specialized SM-14 Type National Research Centers

These would be accumulators, evaluators, originators, refiners, extenders, and disseminators of reliable knowledge. They would earn the reputation for being the recognized authority in their specialty. They would usually be located at our colleges and universities, and permanently financed by government, foundations, etc.

Throughout this book, I have pointed out the need for a wide variety of these centers. In the educational field, there has been a tremendous increase since 1950 in data, information, and "knowledge" about education. The basic problems about this are:

♦ Because the scientific method was not required to be used by those researchers producing the information and "knowledge," the big question now is which is reliable and to what degree of reliability.

♦ Many researchers are only writing for other researchers. There is often little utilization and questionable reliability of the research. Thus, a tremendous amount of taxpayers' funds are being wasted.

♦ The data, information, and "knowledge" are widely scattered. We are in an age that requires specialization. Many existing "research centers" cover too broad an area.

♦ There have been few, if any, permanent *specialized SM-14 type* national research centers that have constantly sorted through available "research" and evaluated and accumulated organized bodies of knowledge in specialized fields.

♦ We have organizations at present in the educational field that claim to be "research centers." I have made no detailed analysis of these, but from my limited observation and experience with them, they do not meet the requirement for being *SM-14 type centers*. Some are biased advocacy groups parading as "research organizations." However, some seem to be doing a good job and are not receiving the credit and acknowledgment they deserve.

♦ The Institute of Education Sciences (IES, formerly the Office of educational Research and Improvement, OERI) is an improvement but does not meet the specifications for a permanent specialized SM-14 type research center. It has too broad a responsibility. We live in an era that requires specialization.

◆ Many top educators don't know all that is going on in education.

Fewer Grants—Big Change in Financing Educational Research

At the present time educational researchers have the heavy burden of having to search for and depend on grants from the National Science Foundation, the U.S. Department of Education, other government agencies, foundations, etc. This is not a productive or efficient method of doing educational research or a productive or efficient use of researchers' time and effort.

Under my plan, appropriations would go directly to numerous small permanent centers, which would also have a small budget for grants. Traditionally, educational research has been done at our colleges and universities. Therefore, these institutions should probably be considered first for location.

This system would greatly diminish the size of National Science Foundation and U.S. Department of Education appropriations for educational grants. It is my opinion that the Harvard/Conant group and misguided followers (or whoever they are) have used their influence with these organizations to perpetuate *the* **BLUNDER**. It would also result in less personal and political influence on what is determined to be reliable knowledge.

Unstudied Ideas and a Drastic Change

I am proposing an idea that I have not studied in great detail, but I think that it has more possibilities than anything yet proposed. Here are more thoughts about it.

What Are the Features of a Body of Evaluated, Accumulated, Organized Knowledge?

Based on my research on features of a body of accumulated knowledge mentioned in the literature and on my experience in establishing my own specialized SM-14 type research center on the scientific method, I believe that an accumulated, evaluated, organized body of knowledge in an SM-14 type research center and the center itself will have the following characteristics.

◆ It will be specialized in one particular area and will accumulate an ever-changing and expanding body of knowledge. Those who operate the center aggressively seek additions to its body of knowledge from everywhere. Professional jealousy, arrogance, and "not invented here" practice will not be tolerated.

- Its main activities will be accumulation, evaluation, and suggested developmental programs rather than new complex research that the center does itself. It will be the recognized authority of its specialty.

- The center has a **vision statement and a code of team work and ethics** for its personnel to help in trying to obtain impartiality. For example, no outside fees are allowed; "publish or perish" is not an issue; files and copyrights are in the public domain; etc. The staff will include an internal ethics and vision compliance officer.

- The center has an extensive **reading program** covering all educational publications and various other publications pertaining to its specialty.

- The center **analyzes all reports** issued on education, and a representative attends all educational meetings affecting its specialty.

- The center maintains **extensive subject files** and files on people and organizations in its area of specialization.

- The center will have its own specialized library.

- There will be specialists in various subjects within the center.

- The center has a **standard publication format** (with no outside advertisers) that can be easily utilized by others. It also has a format for those wishing to submit information to the center.

- All sources of information will be sought out, including books on educational reform, toy manufacturers' products, unions, educational organizations, business, industry, consultants, think tanks, foundations, all textbook publishers, etc.

- The center will have frequent direct contacts with schools and teachers as to the practicality of any programs they recommend.

The Centers as Evaluators of Knowledge

A tremendous amount of information and knowledge already exist in most areas of education. A big job of the centers I propose is to impartially accumulate this information and knowledge, also considering evidence for and against various views and theories. In practice, they cannot closely explore whether every book, article, or claim has "scientifically based evidence" behind it. This can be done for very important studies, but not for everything that comes in. The evaluators, as permanent specialists, soon learn how to distinguish important information or knowledge from junk or something of little value. Information and knowledge often come in bits, pieces, and chunks that must be pulled together to be of value. Thus, a specialized library and subject matter files that are always current are essential to the operation of the centers. Good logical thinking, good judgment, creativity, and analytical skills will play a big role.

To produce *The Scientific Method Today*, I had to spend years of extensive reading, file and library building, and abstraction of general principles of many, many authors. This enabled me to build a clearer picture of the scientific method than had previously been presented.

The Centers as Disseminators of Ideas

Another of the jobs of the centers is idea accumulation and dissemination without extensive study of their value for everyone. Various teachers, units, and organizations are always trying programs and ideas. I visualize a system of one or two loose-leaf page descriptions of these programs and ideas being offered, with supplemental information available.

Other Features of the Research Center

- **Financing of center**: It would be highly desirable if the center were permanently financed by the U.S. government, states, or foundations, with assurance of no interference on policy matters. This is hard to achieve when financing is provided by a political body. However, government assistance is needed because of the expense.

- The **pay scale** of the center is adequate to attract the best-qualified people.

- **All employees** must be students of the scientific method (SM-14 type) and endorse the mission statement of the center.

- They represent a more reliable storehouse of specialized knowledge, as opposed to relying on so-called "experts," biased think tanks, outdated reports, scattered knowledge, advocacy groups, etc.

One of the First Centers Needed Is a Permanent "Big Picture" SM-14 Type National Research Center

Previously I pointed out that we don't know the big picture of education to any reasonable degree of accuracy. Now that I have provided evidence of the supremacy of the scientific method for reliable knowledge, we can learn the "big picture" by setting up a permanent specialized research center for this purpose.

Financing

Ideally, this should be financed by the U.S. government and should be the top research center to which other research centers report. However, if political interference cannot be prevented, then it could be financed by a foundation or foundations, with assurance of no interference on policy matters.

Design

I visualize a preliminary design as follows.

Administrative, Personnel, Financial, Ethics, Planning		Technical Director and Speciality Assistants and Contact Office with U.S. President and Congress
Internal Ethics Compliance Officer		
Publication Office	Lecture Room Own Library and Reading Room	Coordinator with Other National Research Centers
International Idea Researcher	Large General Filing Area *(extensive—books are not enough)* Internet Search Department	Visiting Researchers' Work Room
Teachers' Ideas Representative	Representatives of Major Domains Inside and Outside Education	Information Office to Answer Queries from Outside

This center would also have many of the features I suggested for a center earlier in this chapter.

Since this is more an idea than a plan, I will not go into more detail here.

Power Struggle

Many people will not like my Recommendation #2, for it alters the current power status of those who make and receive grants. Those who seek to mold education to their personal opinions and desires will not like it either. Some of our current so-called experts will become less authoritative figures. Thus, you can expect a lot of opposition and belittling of the idea.

The existing system has produced one disaster after another. For example, in an article "Winning Greater Influence for Science" (*Issues in Science and Technology*, Summer 2003), Daniel Yankelovich, chairman of Viewpoint Learning, Public Agenda, and DYG, Inc., states:

> The nonscientific world of everyday life in the United States marches to a different drummer. Public life is shot through and through with irrationality, discontinuity, and disorder. Decisionmakers rarely have the luxury of waiting for verifiable answers to their questions, and when they do, almost never go to the trouble and cost of developing them.

The public will get more of the same unless my recommendations are studied, tested, and implemented. The above description of everyday life should be an incentive for people to really demand that the scientific method be taught and used in every domain.

I again point out that my own little permanent specialized SM-14 type research center on the scientific method has resulted, at the "cost" of a few million dollars, in the discovery, recognition, and exposure of a gigantic blunder, but more likely

The biggest educational and intellectual blunder in history

To close this chapter and to reinforce the need for my recommendations, I call your attention again to the monetary cost of *the* **BLUNDER**.

Consider the Significance of Our Spending $1 Trillion a Year on Education and Training

This book has provided evidence and the reasons why our top educational leaders have, in the past 50 years, been unable to properly analyze and adequately improve education.

It is my claim that ending *the* **BLUNDER** could eventually improve the efficiency of our spending on education by:

20 to 50 percent—let's take 33.33 percent of $1 trillion

This is $333,333,333,333 per year

However, I believe that 50 percent is a more realistic figure. In a 1997 report on the 50th anniversary conference of the American Institute for Research, Nobel Laureate Herbert Simon states:

There is reason to believe that, in applying even today's knowledge of the learning process, we can accomplish twice as much in school as we usually do. That is a goal worth aiming for in a society where so many of the financial and human resources are invested in education.

Now also look to the future in a world where graduates are better creative problem solvers and decision makers. And where adults quickly learn the scientific method to some extent and apply the knowledge to their careers and personal lives.

Is it not then likely that correction of *the* **BLUNDER** in all domains— not just education— is in the area of $1 trillion or more per year?

This book will affect the lives and careers of almost everyone. Therefore it should

◆ be widely reviewed and read

◆ be the subject of news stories, feature articles, debate, study, and documentary films

Introduction to Part 12

Ending *the* BLUNDER

A Big Challenge to Many of Our Intellectuals

It will be interesting and an historical event to see whether this book is accepted and studied by our intellectual community. Since Conant's day, other proponents of the scientific method have been largely ignored, as have my past efforts to correct *the* **BLUNDER**.

The Ideal Way to End *the* BLUNDER

While I have done a lot of finger-pointing at organizations and a little at individuals in this book, it has been done only to get *the* **BLUNDER** corrected. If everyone would only study the matter, I believe that I have presented plenty of evidence to support the fact that a blunder has occurred. Then, rather than worrying about whose fault it was, we should all get going on correcting it. So many are at fault that identifying them does not mean much. Let's give credit to those in positions of leadership and responsibility who now aggressively study the matter and correct *the* **BLUNDER**. They are the ones who will be doing a great public service, according to my research.

Organizations and periodicals that rate colleges and universities and their programs can help by including in their ratings how well these institutions teach the scientific method.

In this part I present some ideas on the acceptance of this book. I also present my concluding messages to

> the public
> the Harvard/Conant group and misguided followers
> (or whoever they are)
> college and university presidents, professors, students,
> and the intellectual community in general
> business and industry

I hope that they will all listen. I am going to rely especially on the public to study what I have presented and for the public to ask for study by those who guide us in important matters.

And finally, after all these years of crusading, I present my conclusion.

Chapter 59

Acceptance of This Book

I Goof—You Goof—We All Goof

I goof, you goof, we all goof. It is the nature of science or the advancement of knowledge that there is a lot of trial and error and success. Einstein himself stated, "I think and think, for months, for years, ninety-nine times the conclusion is false."

Don't be a goofer who

- is too arrogant or too proud to believe he/she could make a mistake
- always blames the other person, never him/herself
- lies, is biased, or twists the "facts" to justify their denial
- never tries anything for fear of being blamed for failure and thus lets profitable opportunities pass by

To make the world a better place to live, to improve the ills of education, and to help our teachers and students, we need people who can say:

- It was my responsibility and I goofed!
- I have excuses for this blunder but none good enough to excuse me.
- I failed this time, but I will learn from my mistake and do better in the future.
- Trial and error is still a basic way of making progress, and fear of failure will not stop me from testing innovative and creative activities.
- For complex problems and decisions, I will learn and follow the complete method of creative problem solving (SM-14) to help reduce my failures and make greater progress.

(I hope the above will be widely quoted.)

In the 1992 and 1994 editions of my little booklet *The General Pattern of the Scientific Method*, I admit on page 47 that I goofed in 1961 in not following my inspiration to write a booklet on the scientific method then. Now I also admit that I goofed in 1975 when I retired and had plenty of time to write. Instead, I went boating and fishing. I waited until 1989, when I was 73, to start the project. So, if I admit that I goofed badly on the scientific method, I can ask others to do the same. *The* **BLUNDER** will be corrected much sooner and the public will be impressed if we all acknowledge that we have goofed!

Acceptance

"Bad" schools and teachers are repeatedly accused of not changing for the better. With this book, I am asking for some major changes by our top educational leaders. Will they accept this book and investigate my claims? Here are some interesting quotes on admission of error.

Sir Peter Medawar in *Advice to Young Scientists* (1979):

> The important thing is not to try to lay down some voluminous smoke screen to conceal a blunder.

In an article in the October 2001 issue of *Scientific American*, Michael Shermer, founding publisher of *Skeptic* magazine, states:

> Critical feedback is the lifeblood of healthy science, as is the willingness (however begrudgingly) to say "I was wrong" when faced with persuasive evidence. It does not matter who you are or how important you think your idea is—if it is contradicted by the evidence, it is wrong.

Admitting errors and blunders is not always easy, but it is acceptable today, as Dr. Henry Ellington states in his essay *The Nature of the Scientific Method* (1983):

> The ideas first presented in Logic der Forschung have influenced a whole generation of scientists, affecting not only the way in which they carry out their work, but also their entire attitude towards science. Before Popper, the ultimate sin in science was to be proved wrong—to publish work that was subsequently discredited. This attitude stemmed from the mistaken notion that science advances by the systematic erection of a body of firmly-established facts. Anyone who published a theory that was later shown to be incompatible with experimental results thus felt that he had been a failure, and that his reputation (and probably also his career prospects) would suffer as a result. This had an inhibiting effect on the work of scientists, and undoubtedly slowed down many important scientific developments.

> After Popper, it was realized that being shown to have been mistaken is not something to be ashamed of, for it is only when ideas are subjected to stringent testing and possible falsification that science can advance at all.

Will I Be Lucky to Get out with My Life?

In my research I read an immense amount of interesting material. Here is part of an essay that tickled my sense of humor, although it does include a lot of "reality." It is "Isaiah's Job" from *Free Speech and Plain Language* (1937) by Albert J. Nock, currently republished as a four-page reprint by the Foundation for Economic Education, Inc.

> In the year of Uzziah's death, the Lord commissioned the prophet [Isaiah] to go out and warn the people of the wrath to come. "Tell them what a worthless lot they are," He said. "Tell them what is wrong, and why, and what is going to happen unless they have a change of heart and straighten up. Don't mince matters. Make it clear that they are positively down to their last chance. Give it to them good and strong and keep on giving it to them. I suppose perhaps I ought to tell you," He added, "that it won't do any good. The official class and their intelligentsia will turn up their noses at you, and the masses will not even listen. They will all keep on in their own ways until they carry everything down to destruction, and you will probably be lucky if you get out with your life."

? ?

The Mystery

In this book Prophet Edmund has called attention to a large number of things and important people that are wrong. I've even told you a number of times that you'll get even "more of the same" if **the BLUNDER** is not corrected. I haven't minced matters. I don't claim that it's your last chance, but now is the time for a change.

The mystery is: Will I be lucky and get out with my life?

It really doesn't matter much, as I've already told you that it is only because I'm so old that I've had the nerve to write this book!

? ?

Chapter 60

Will the Educators and the Educational Journals Goof Again?

In Chapter 9, I explain the disaster of the teaching of reading and about Dr. Rudolf Flesch's fight for phonics. In 2000, the congressionally mandated *Report of the National Reading Panel* said, basically, that phonics had to be included in the teaching of reading. It made no reference to a similar conclusion In Dr. Flesch's 1955 and 1981 books and Dr. Chall's 1967 book.

Here is what Flesch reported in *Why Johnny Still Can't Read* (1981) about what happened after his first book about phonics appeared:

> Let's go on to another major event in the Great Coverup. In 1955 my book *Why Johnny Can't Read* became a national best-seller. The educational journals answered in full cry, attacking me as an ignoramus, a propagandist—they never said for whom or what—a crank, a menace to the cause of good education. In December 1955, half a year after the publication of my book, *The Reading Teacher* came out with a special issue on phonics. It was filled with anti-Flesch outbursts, including a lengthy piece elaborately analyzing the propaganda techniques I had supposedly used in my book.

Subsequently, Dr. Jeanne Chall of Harvard University published a book favoring phonics. Here is what Flesch reports (in his 1981 book) happened:

> When the book *Learning to Read: The Great Debate* by Dr. Jeanne Chall came out in 1967, it couldn't be dealt with as easily. The research evidence was too massive and too detailed. So the look-and-say educators did the next best thing: they reviewed the book to death. There was an orgy of nitpicking, making it seem that Dr. Chall's monumental work was flawed, partly wrong, still controversial and unproven.

> I checked through most of the two dozen reading-instruction textbooks—the books used in teachers' college courses to teach future reading teachers how to do their job. Typically, they mentioned Dr. Chall's book, but immediately proceeded to put it in a dubious light.

Things did not improve for Dr. Flesch even after Dr. Chall's book appeared. He reports in *Why Johnny Still Can't Read* (1981):

> The first chapter of this book [*Why Johnny Still Can't Read*] was published, slightly cut, as an article in *Family Circle* magazine (November 1, 1979). It brought thousands of letters.
>
> Most of them were from mothers, thanking me for writing the piece and telling tales of woe of how their children were miseducated at school and how they were given the brushoff when they complained.
>
> The letters from educators were sharply different. They were full of personal abuse. They called me "a liar," "grossly misinformed," "dastardly," "criminal," "libelous," "alarmist," a "demagogue," a user of "scare tactics" and "half-truths." They said the magazine was doing a great disservice to its readers by printing the article. They said I knew nothing about children, about education, about the English language. They said I was "simplistic" and "absurd."

Flesch was vindicated by the *Report of the National Reading Panel* in 2000. However, it gave him no credit for the battle he fought.

The *Report of the National Reading Panel* says that phonics must be part of the teaching of reading. Since the publication of the report in 2000, there have been a few books and a number of articles denouncing it.

This supports my contention that temporary panels are a poor solution to problems. If we had a permanent specialized SM-14 type national research center on reading, it would be obliged to immediately study and report on any valid claims about the proper teaching of reading, a matter of great national importance. I believe that most public schools are finally using phonics in teaching reading.

When you hear of the poor reading abilities of middle school and high school students today, you hear no comments that they were, in most cases, improperly taught by the whole language method, with little or no inclusion of phonics. Is this another case of top leaders not acknowledging or accepting blame? It is difficult for a top leader to admit to a goof, but there have been so many poor fads in the educational field that it is obvious that many have goofed.

Another Instance

In 1976, Professor Michael J. Mahoney of Pennsylvania State University published *Scientist as a Subject: The Psychological Imperative*. He reports:

> In the writing of this book and the conduct of the research it reports, I have learned to appreciate the need for some degree of autonomy in scientific endeavors. The person who takes an unconventional path is often faced with isolation, and occasionally with persecution. This was underscored by repeated signs of disapproval from my colleagues—three indictments to the American Psychological Association, two attempts to have me fired, and eighteen rejections from journals and publishing companies.

Will Organizations Acknowledge *the* BLUNDER?

In *The Big Test—The Secret History of American Meritocracy* (1999), Nicholas Leman reports that when Chauncey and the College Board were forming ETS, one of Chauncey's lieutenants wrote to him:

> When an organization of this sort becomes big and powerful, it cannot admit itself in error. So much money and so many reputations are involved that if the tests turn out to be no good, evidence of the fact is almost certain to be suppressed, or else the criteria of goodness are themselves called in question.

Regardless of size, power, or reputations, for the good of American and worldwide society, organizations must acknowledge *the* BLUNDER.

I hope everyone will remember what happened with phonics and to Dr. Mahoney. I hope that I will not be treated similarly. I hope that my claims will be honestly investigated in a scholarly and objective manner. However, since I have criticized so much in this book and covered so many fields, it is natural that people will in turn find fault with my work. Undoubtedly, I have made some errors that will need correction. But don't lose sight of the big picture!

Setting the Record Straight by Gerald W. Bracey (2004)

Those educators and members of the public who think that I have exaggerated the disasters in the education field should read *Setting the*

Record Straight by Professor Gerald Bracey. The misconceptions described in this book exist, in my opinion, because we do not require our educational researchers and top leaders to use the scientific method. The misconceptions continue year after year because we do not have a permanent specialized SM-14 type national research center to supply more reliable knowledge about educational problems.

Your Comments on My Work Are Welcomed

I have forecast that thousands of books will be written about *the* **BLUNDER**. If so, researchers will want to examine my files. If you write to me, anticipate that your letter may be subject to review by others and possible publication sometime in the future.

Chapter 61

My Concluding Message to the Public

Let's consider again Rudolf Flesch's campaign for teaching reading by phonics. Flesch published his first famous bestselling book in 1955: *Why Johnny Can't Read*. It was subtitled *"And What You Can Do About It."* The public was interested enough to make this book a bestseller, but educators didn't really research Flesch's findings. He published a second warning in 1981: *Why Johnny Still Can't Read*. The public did not insist on investigation. In 2001 Congress mandated that reading be taught in a way indicated by scientifically based research. This mandate resulted in the recognition of phonics as a correct part of the way to teach reading. The use of phonics in teaching reading became accepted public knowledge by a majority of educators.

Teaching reading is extremely important, but so is teaching the scientific method. You don't want more of the disasters I have told you about in this book.

Here are some of the things you can do:

♦ Request educators, political leaders, and media to study the scientific method situation.

♦ Request the leaders of your professional, educational, business, and other domain organizations to review their positions on the scientific method.

♦ Tell and email your friends and associates about *the* **BLUNDER**.

♦ Organize discussion groups to review *the* **BLUNDER**.

♦ Request that all U.S. government organizations require that research grants for education and the social sciences be held to the same standards as those of the natural sciences.

♦ Study and use the scientific method yourself. Watch the acceptance of this book and progress in correcting *the* **BLUNDER** on my new website www.theblunder.com

♦ If you would like to receive a free email newsletter about developments in the correction of *the* **BLUNDER**, send your email address to edmund@theblunder.com

Chapter 62

My Concluding Message to the Harvard/Conant Group and Misguided Followers (or Whoever They Are)

I apologize for being so tough on you in this book. I fully realize that you are hard-working educators devoted to improving education.

It was unfortunate that a series of events precipitated *the* **BLUNDER**. Sure, the words "no one method" sound logical, and the other false claims seem plausible on the surface. If you will only take the time, your research will show, as mine has, that these claims are false.

The events of the last few years

◆ the U.S. Supreme Court recognizing the scientific method
◆ the U.S. Congress specifying "scientifically based research"
◆ my booklets and now this book

have introduced new factors into the picture. Thus, the old misunderstandings and series of events that got you on the wrong path cannot survive the greater evidence and legal clarifications. Today's fast pace of knowledge growth and the ever-increasing complexity of life require correction of *the* **BLUNDER**.

So protect your reputations and your institutions and join in on really studying the scientific method. If you don't like the word "goof," use "misunderstand."

I quote Dr. Gold again that there is "no gentle way":

> Once a herd has been established in a subject, it can only be broken by the most *crass* confrontation with opposing evidence. There is no gentle way that I have ever seen in the history of science where a herd once established has been broken up.

It is not pleasant for me to have to be so crass in my confrontation with opposing evidence, but my more pleasant well-documented early efforts with many of you did not succeed.

Other Events for You to Consider

◆ Historians are waking up. Read Bruce Mazlish's *Uncertain Sciences* (1998). Even philosopher Steve Fuller is brave enough to report on the false claims of Kuhn, Conant, and others. Read Fuller's *Thomas Kuhn, A Philosophical History for Our Times* (2000).

♦ Some of the theories of Sir Karl Popper, philosopher of science, that contributed to *the* **BLUNDER** are being increasingly discredited. Read Martin Gardner's article "A Skeptical Look at Karl Popper" in the July/August 2001 issue of *Skeptical Inquirer.*

♦ The public is really upset about education, and education cannot be fixed without applying the scientific method everywhere, especially at the TOP.

♦ The Internet is spreading the knowledge about the scientific method. On May 27, 2004, the search engine Google, in response to "scientific method," showed 440,000 hits. A sampling of the first 300 results shows that more than 95 percent of the sites are favorable to the scientific method.

♦ The world has more and more problems, and they are becoming more and more complex. The only solution is better problem solving. The complete method of creative problem solving and decision making is the scientific method.

♦ My Chapter 53, Legal Considerations of the Scientific Method, is going to be called to the attention of government attorneys. This should bring a new era into the way in which social science research is considered.

So if my so-called Harvard/Conant group and misguided followers (or whoever they are) will study the matter, I believe you will join me in saying we all goofed, misunderstood, or did not realize what was happening about the scientific method, and now is the time to correct the mistake. Remember, I am forecasting that thousands of books and some films will be produced about *the* **BLUNDER**. Don't go down in history as one who, even in the face of all the evidence I present, fought the correction of *the* **BLUNDER**.

However, if you still do not agree with me on the major issue, then accept my $100,000 challenge so the matter will be studied.

Chapter 63

My Concluding Message to College and University Presidents, Professors, and Students, and the Intellectual Community in General

The literature is quite clear that the United States has the best college and university system in the world and that it has been a major contributor to making us the greatest nation in the world. Yet, that it produced the biggest educational and intellectual blunder in history, as I claim, is a strange paradox. What has limited its harm is that our natural scientists, engineers, medical researchers, and some others have not participated fully in it.

As a crusader for the scientific method, I must still keep an open mind about *the* BLUNDER. Because of my educational background, I must exhibit some humility in making the claim that, even though by accident, I discovered, recognized, or join others who recognized that a big misunderstanding developed about the scientific method. However, I have done so much research of the literature that I am quite confident that an impartial detailed study will show that my claim of a gigantic educational and intellectual blunder will be upheld—whether it is the biggest in history, I can't be so sure.

College and University Presidents

I know of no college or university president who challenged the position of the Harvard/Conant group and misguided followers (or whoever they are) and took active opposition by offering a curriculum that included teaching the scientific method and a formula for it. However, I made no actual search. I rely only on what I read during my research.

My message to college and university presidents is: you, as leaders of your institutions, should read this book thoroughly and institute an academic audit of *the* BLUNDER and its effect on your curriculum, your students, and your grant holders.

College and University Professors

Even while *the* BLUNDER has been going on, textbooks on various subjects written by professors for colleges, universities, and grade schools often include a mention and a description of the scientific method. Usually, this covers only a few pages, but sometimes more. A very, very rough estimate is that 65 percent of science textbooks and 10 percent of textbooks in other subjects cover the scientific method. In addition, hundreds or thousands who wrote general books on science or other subjects included the scientific method.

Those who have included it and the many who have taught it deserve praise for not allowing *the* **BLUNDER** to prevent them from acknowledging the scientific method in their works and teaching. If it had not been for their effort, very few people would have heard of the scientific method during their schooling.

Considering the highly intellectual nature of our college and university presidents and professors, it is surprising that others did not follow Professor Jack Easley (Chapter 4) in directly challenging Conant's claims. It is also surprising that my literature—sent to a number of them—did not stir up a discussion and debate of the issue. It takes a lot of nerve and sacrifice to be the first one to correct a gigantic blunder, so I suppose it is understandable they have not responded.

My message to college and university professors is to study this book as to how it affects your domain and your individual programs. If I am correct, you need your individual plan of action about what to do. There are also numerous opportunities resulting from *the* **BLUNDER**. Consider them. It is my claim that many books you recommend to students are going to have to be identified as:

Pre- or not affected by *the* **BLUNDER**
partly unreliable because of *the* **BLUNDER**
post-**BLUNDER** correction

College Students

Every college student should read this book. They were not taught much about the scientific method or complex problem solving in high school. In college, depending on their courses and their professors, they may be taught some of it under various names, or they are taught some of the creative, non-logical, logical, and technical methods used at various stages. However, there is a very good chance they have not received a really good education in the scientific method.

College Students Face Great Changes

From "A Battle Plan for Professors to Recapture the Curriculum" by Frank H.T. Rhodes (*Chronicle of Higher Education*, September 14, 2001):

Yet to develop a new curriculum, one has to agree on a few essentials: Should all students share a common body of knowledge, skills, and values? If so, what should that be? How should universities best prepare graduates for a future in which the average American will change jobs, and even careers, six times; in which specialized knowledge has a half-life as short as five years; in which societal and ethical questions are deeply entwined with technical ones; and in which relentless learning over a lifetime is a prerequisite for professional and personal success?

Based on my experience over 50 years in five universities as a student, professor, dean, provost, and president, I believe that the best way to respond to such questions is to consider not what courses universities should require, but what qualities they should seek to nurture in their students.

My Message to College Students

Faced with the changing world you are soon going out into, knowledge is important, as is how to look up knowledge. Learning and practicing the use of the complete method of creative problem solving and decision making—the scientific method—is of great personal importance to you. I have covered this need throughout the book.

Request that you be taught the scientific method now! Otherwise, you will be out of date, for *the* BLUNDER will end soon, and those who follow you will be taught the scientific method. Employers are asking for good problem solvers and decision makers. It is important for your personal life as well as your career.

Your debating societies should debate "resolved that the complete method of creative problem solving and decision making should be taught across the curriculum" or other issues covered in this book.

My Message to Organizations and Foundations

My hope is that you will review your operations and policies. The application of the scientific method will, in many cases, enable you to do a better job. This book reveals a fresh look at education and the scientific method. Please get behind the movement for its greater acceptance and use. We need one or more of you to become its vocal advocate, as at present we have none with this objective.

My Message to the Intellectual Community in General

For many of you who believe in the scientific method and didn't realize there was a question of its existence, this book will just confirm your belief in the method. For others, this book represents a challenge to what you have been taught and come to believe. There is great intellectual enjoyment in the subject of the scientific method.

I would like to call to the attention of all intellectuals a statement by Chester I. Barnard in *The Functions of the Executive* (1938). The anniversary (1968) edition of this book is still available from Harvard University Press.

> The most interesting and astounding contradiction in life is to me the constant insistence by nearly all people upon "logic," "logical reasoning," "sound reasoning" on the one hand, and on the other their inability to display it, and their unwillingness to accept it when displayed by others. Where the higher intellects, especially those engaged in the more exact sciences, are involved, this contradiction is of course on a higher plane and more subtle than among ordinary folk who are not trained reasoners; but the difference seems one of degree. The correctness of reasoning is the issue in violent differences of opinion in every subject.

My message to every intellectual is to use your mental skills to study this book before jumping to any conclusions. Otherwise you may, if I am right, go down in history as still participating in *the* **BLUNDER**.

? ?

The Mystery

This book calls attention to a blunder of historic importance on the part of many in our intellectual community. How will they respond?

In a *Science* magazine editorial (April 9, 2004) entitled "A Welcome Retreat at Treasury," the editor-in-chief stated, "The real story here is that this reversal sets an example for an administration that is notoriously reluctant to admit error. Perhaps we can hope for more of the same." I am hoping that our intellectual community will set an example on willingness to admit error and respond promptly after this book is published.

? ?

Conclusion

When I was about 14 years old, I read an article in *Readers Digest* that urged you to adopt the goal in life of making the world a better place to live. It impressed me, and I have always kept it in mind over the years. However, never did I imagine that one day I would be crusading for the better acceptance of the greatest idea of all ages for making the world a better place to live—the scientific method.

Research the literature and you find that the end of the dark ages, the beginning of the age of enlightenment, and our present age of knowledge all resulted from the recognition and development of the scientific method. So again I repeat—the false claim that the scientific method does not exist by many of our top educational leaders is

The Biggest Educational and Intellectual Blunder in History

One piece of advice given on how to write a successful book is to start with a hard luck story and end with success.

Well, I've given you, from the beginning, the hard luck story about my difficulties promoting the scientific method. I was 73 when I started researching the scientific method, and now, after 15 years of research and writing, as I finish this book, I am 89.

I can report success in my research and a good formula for the scientific method, but I'm sorry that that there is no successful ending with regard to its recognition. I can only report hard luck, as you have read, for recognition by our top educational leaders of the scientific method.

On the dust jacket of this book I make a prediction that the book will prove to be of great importance to America—but I'm depending on you to make this prediction come true. I'm sure you want a better world and a better education that comes from the scientific method for our kids—including those rascals who don't study hard enough!

How Much Better a World Will We Have?

After all students have been taught the scientific method all through their schooling, how will things be? We have to be careful about making this future projection. It has been estimated that students forget 90 percent of what they are taught. However, remember that "practice makes perfect."

In teaching the scientific method across the curriculum through all grades, it will be used and used all through their schooling by students and thus retained, as practice impresses it on memory. Thus, the potential for its application in their careers in the future is great.

Development of the Scientific Method by Our Intellectuals

Once our intellectual elite realize what has happened on the scientific method and are relieved of the restraints I have told you about, they will turn their thoughts, research, and efforts to the development of the scientific method. A tremendous amount of information already lies in the literature. It will be abstracted, refined, extended, and applied in all domains, and turned into numerous books, courses, lectures, computer programs, etc. Each individual stage of the method and the supporting ingredients will generate numerous books about the various features of that stage or ingredient. So there will be plenty of information available for our students and adults who were never adequately taught the greatest idea of all time and all ages.

While my little booklet, *The Scientific Method Today*, is the best abstraction of the information at the very beginning of the 21st century, it will, after the developmental movement has progressed, become an antique and a collector's item.

The Human Factor Remains in the Better World To Come

It will be a far from perfect world, even though the scientific method is the most reliable problem solving and decision making method ever recognized and developed. The human factor in its use is the major factor that retards perfection.

Helping the human factor to be more efficient is Supporting Ingredient #14, which calls for teaching personal attributes. This feature of the SM-14 formula holds great promise to help in the overall success of the scientific method (SM-14) in the years to come.

Goodbye and a Better World for You

Because of my age, I won't be around to see much of the better world I am forecasting, but I hope my readers will live to enjoy this better world. However, "struggle is the essence of life," so there is a price you must pay—study and promote the use of the scientific method (SM-14 type).

Norman W. Edmund
Fort Lauderdale, Florida
2005

Introduction to the Appendix

The Scientific Method Today
Year 2000 Edition

In May 1992 I published a small 48-page booklet (First Student Edition):

The General Pattern of the Scientific Method (SM-14)

ISBN 0-9632866-0-9 (paperback)
0-9632866-2-5 (hardcover)

In 1994 a slightly revised 2nd Student Edition of 48 pages was published:

The General Pattern of the Scientific Method (SM-14)

ISBN 0-9632866-3-3 (paperback)

In 2000 this booklet was greatly revised and published in 48 pages as

The Scientific Method Today

ISBN 0-963286-5x (paperback)

This is presented in the appendix. It gives a more complete picture of the stages of the scientific method and its supporting ingredients.

Tell your friends, students, and others that *The Scientific Method Today* can be viewed at my website www.scientificmethod.com

YEAR 2000 EDITION

The Scientific Method Today

Your Guide to the Complete Method of Creative Problem Solving and Decision Making

SM-14

Compiled and Written by
Norman W. Edmund

Table of Contents

Introduction to
"The Greatest Idea of All Times"

Dear Knowledge Seeker,

The scientific method has earned the title of "The Greatest Idea of All Times." Put this idea to work for you in your problem solving and decision making.

This booklet contains today's most up-to-date, clear, concise and reliable information about the scientific method that has ever been offered.

Applied My Past Experience in Abstracting Basic Principles.
In my 35-year career of starting and expanding Edmund Scientific Company, my big job was abstracting basic principles of operation and of new products. In the past ten years I've zeroed in on the scientific method; purchased over 3,000 books; read professional journals, Internet web sites and reports; and set up extensive files. I've investigated the subject day and night, and considered all claims for and against the scientific method.

You Get the Benefit of All This Research.
You should take advantage of all the reliable knowledge presented here. Unfortunately the scientific method has not been adequately taught in our schools. I explain why in my other reports.Just as the scientific method has brought such great benefits to society, it can do great things for you too. — Good Luck — Get started today.

Norman W. Edmund

This Is The Scientific Method

A Well-researched Description of the Problem Solving & Research Process

The SM-14 Formula for the General Pattern of the Scientific Method

Major Stages

PART I — *Observation through Hypothesis*
1. Curious Observation
2. Is There a Problem?
3. Goals and Planning
4. Search, Explore, and Gather the Evidence
5. Generate Creative and Logical Alternatives
6. Evaluate the Evidence
7. Make the Educated Guess (Hypothesis)

PART II — *Challenge through Suspend Judgment*
8. Challenge the Hypothesis
9. Reach a Conclusion
10. Suspend Judgment

PART III — *Implementation, Peer Review*
11. Take Action

SUPPORTING INGREDIENTS

PART IV — *Supporting or Operating Ingredients*
12. Creative, Non-Logical, Logical, and Technical Methods
13. Procedural Principles and Theories
14. Attributes and Thinking Skills

The research process is not just a collection of miscellaneous "scientific methods." Scientists and other researchers do not proceed in a haphazard fashion. Centuries of trial and error, research, discussions and debates have led to a realization of the general pattern of the scientific method. The pattern represents the major stages of how we obtain, refine and apply knowledge in all fields. The method of science has been called by many names, most commonly the scientific method. It is also a complete method of creative problem solving and decision making for all fields.

There are Eleven Major Stages (1-11) to The Scientific Method

Each stage (1-11) represents a different type of mental activity (usually aided by physical actions). The method is subject neutral.

Flexible Order of Use — While the stages are listed in the usual order of use, in actual practice they will be utilized in a very flexible manner as progress on complex problems is seldom smooth. In using the stages there will be: backtracking, skipping, false starts, looping, sub-problems, and other diversions.

The Supporting Ingredients (12-14) of The Scientific Method

These are included in the SM-14 formula as ingredients rather than stages to help people understand "the method" and as an aid to teaching it to students and others. Presenting only the stages doesn't give you a complete picture of the overall system. The scientific method is the master method of all methods. The word "method" in the term, "the scientific method," is a collective term for the stages. "Scientific" qualifies how scientists and others have historically utilized the stages of the method to accomplish results. Their methods, procedures and human activities are ingredients 12-14: Creative, Non-Logical, Logical, and Technical Methods; Procedural Principles and Theories; and Attributes and Thinking Skills.

The Complete System of Science and Problem Solving

The SM-14 formula embodies the complete method of science — its stages, techniques used, procedural principles and theories, attributes and skills needed and submission to the process of peer review at Stage 11.

3

The Scientific Method is a Complete Act of Thought

With knowledge doubling at a faster rate than ever, it would greatly help everyone if they were taught a clear and simple guide for a complete act of thought.

From my research, I believe that such a guide is most commonly called "The Scientific Method" (also called the general pattern of the scientific method). It was developed by many, but most accurately by scientists (an example is SM-14).

The literature contains many formulas for problem solving, creative problem solving, decision making, and other similar terms. While these are "acts of thought," they usually are not complete acts of thought, because the formulas do not usually cover problem origination, challenge of solution, or suspend judgment. They all contain just parts of SM-14.

Wallas, in the *Art of Thought* (1926), gives a formula for the "Art of Thought:" (1) preparation, (2) incubation, (3) illumination, and (4) verification. This has been widely quoted but is too short for a complete act-of-thought formula for teaching purposes.

Dewey's guide to his "analysis of a complete act of thought" has been widely cited. Professor T.L. Kelley of Harvard, in *Scientific Method: Its Function in Research and in Education* (1932), abstracts Dewey's guide in a little different way than most authors, listing the "steps" shown below (he added #8, feeling it was needed). Also shown is a comparison of these "steps" to the stages of SM-14.

Dewey's Complete Act of Thought as Abstracted by Kelley	Compare To The SM-14 Formula
1. A felt difficulty.	1. Curious Observation
2. A definition of the difficulty.	2. The Problem
3. A tentative solution.	3. Goals, Planning
4. A mental elaboration of the solution, leading to additional tentative solutions and elaboration, if felt necessary, finally leading to #5.	4. Search — Explore 5. Alternate Solutions 6. Evaluate Evidence
5. The belief that the solution is all right	7. Guess — Hypothesis
6. An experimental verification	8. Challenge Hypothesis
7. An appraisal of the experimental findings leading to acceptance of mental solution and a decision for immediate conductor to rejection and a reinstatement of a felt difficulty, The process is continued until a verified solution which is immediately serviceable is obtained.	9. Reach Conclusion 10. Suspend Judgment
8. A forward look to, or mental picturing of, future situations to which the present solution is pertinent	11. Take Action
NOTE: "A Tentative Solution" was not included as a separate stage in SM-14 as it may occur at #1, in between 1 & 2, at 2 or 3, and normally one or more at 4 & 5.	12. Action Methods 13. Procedural Principles 14. Attributes — Thinking

The Master Method of Knowledge Is: The Scientific Method

Characteristics of The Scientific Method

- **Name**—Denotes stages, procedural theories and the system of science.
- **Purpose and Objective**—To obtain, refine, extend and apply knowledge through problem origination, prevention, solution and challenge of solution. Curiosity, a healthy skepticism, etc. finds the problem.
- **Division of Method**—The master method of all human knowledge methods.
- **Stages**—The general pattern of the major types of mental activity usually aided by physical actions.
- **Sequential**—There are 11 major stages that are sequential and progressive. These stages are arranged in order of usual use but may be followed with flexibly.
- **Repeatable**—Stages are so basic and repeatable that they are not likely to change.
- **Range**—Universal to all nature and human activity.
- **Reliability Factor**—Most reliable of all knowledge methods.
- **Application**—Usually follow techniques, procedural principles and theories, high personal attributes and thinking skills of the research communities. Flexibility or "anything goes" is often essential.

The Value of Method

In the *Concept of Method*, Justus Buchler (1985) refers to the common expression "the power of a method." Every day you constantly use methods and this report will help you better use the power of a method to improve your problem solving ability.

Without method, we are left with chance. Chance is the opposite of method and we would have a very disorganized world without methods and techniques. But, what is "Method"? Unfortunately method is a very ambiguous word. It's so ambiguous that it has been widely misused and misinterpreted in the fields of science and knowledge.

There is no better example of the power of a method than the results produced by the scientific method throughout the development of modern civilization. I did a search of the literature on the value of method. This is what various authors emphasize:

The Advantages of Method

- Organizes our thoughts
- Clarifies our thoughts
- Ends aimless wandering
- Helps ideas gather shape
- Guides us to new knowledge
- Is a repeatable procedure
- Aids in transfer of learning
- Trains for change and innovation
- Uses human potential
- Encourages thinking

The Opposite of Method is Chance

- Haphazard guesses
- Wrong analysis
- Wasted time
- No Solutions
- Confusion
- Wasted energy
- Quick fixes
- Wandering aimlessly
- Misdirection
- Mistakes and errors

5

The Scientific Method Is
A Universal Method for All Domains

It is the master method from which sprang many other methods that were given other names but the stages of these methods are the same. These other methods may have special characteristics, such as being aimed at a certain domain or special purpose. They also may use special, creative, non-logical, logical and technical methods as well as the general ones, but the stages to reliable knowledge are the same. Some authors may name different terms for the stages and present a shorter formula.

Just a few of the other methods that are the same, are the methods of:

- Problem solving
- Creative problem solving
- Scientific management
- Investigation
- Medical diagnostics

- Decision making
- Invention
- Design & Engineering
- Change
- Technological design

- Inquiry
- Research
- Planning
- Scholars
- Operation research

Learn SM-14 and you learn the formula for all of the methods listed above.

This is the Golden Age of Knowledge

Estimated years it took for knowledge to double*
1750-1900: 150 yrs 1900-1950: 50 yrs
1950-1960: 10 yrs Since 1960: Every 5 yrs

Projection! By the Year 2020, knowledge will double every 73 days!

We need to study and standardize on the basic method by which we obtain, refine, extend and apply knowledge . . . which is, SM-14.

*Reported at the Teacher Education for 21st Century Conference (1992)

This Is An Age of Technology Growth

| Robots | Space | Automated Tellers | Miniaturization | Talking Computers | Multi-media Communication |

High-paying unskilled jobs are disappearing — skilled, innovative, creative, problem solving, adaptable workers are needed!

SM-14 Formula

Pages 8 thru 35 describe the 11 Stages of The Scientific Method and the 3 Supporting Ingredients that comprise the SM-14 Formula.

Help for Originating Ideas for You to Submit to Your Company's Suggestion System

Many companies have suggestion systems, employee involvement programs, quality initiatives and similar programs. Many of these offer monetary rewards.

> **REMEMBER**—even if your company doesn't have a formal plan, submit ideas anyway. Idea originators, problem solvers, good decision makers and those with the entrepreneurial spirit receive promotions, salary increases and become managers or executives.

Suggestions and Ideas to Help You Use SM-14 to Earn More Money:

1. Study this booklet and reflect on its application to your company and to your job.

2. Review the pages on curious observation (Stage #1) and pages 38, 39 and 40 on creativity carefully. These will be of special help in originating ideas that will save your company money or increase sales.

3. Redesign certain pages or add pages to this booklet to make it a tool tailored to your organization's needs.

4. Pages 44 and 45 show a condensed version of "Your Guide and Worksheet for Applying the Complete Method of Creative Problem Solving and Decision Making (SM-14)." You should get my full size pages on this and develop ideas on how and where your company can use these worksheets. For example:
   - Use the worksheets at meetings, training sessions and/or company wide
   - Change the worksheet's format to suit your company's special needs.

5. Recommend use of the rating scale on page 41.

6. Suggest this booklet's use in training courses and general operations as:
   - The most effective and cost-saving habit anyone can have is using the scientific method.
   - It has the most up-to-date explanation of the scientific method available.
   - *Complex Problem Solving* (1991), reports that most managers do not use rational approaches to managerial problem solving.
   - Today, modern management passes the responsibility of decision making further down the ranks. Because of this, the lower ranks need training in decision making skills to handle this new responsibility.
   - World competition requires more innovation and creativity.
   - A company's intellectual capital is just static assets until its knowledge is invested efficiently using the scientific method.

(Stage #1)
Curious Observation

Curious observation is the start of the inductive process. Discovery of new problems, ideas, theories, decisions needed, and problem prevention usually begin with curious observation using the five senses: smelling, tasting, hearing, feeling, and seeing. Instruments and tools can be used to help extend these senses. Use your sense perceptions and projections — visually and mentally. Turn thoughts over and over in your mind. Use reasoning, your imagination, and introspection. Being in the right mood, being motivated and sensitive helps! Train your mind to interpret what you see.

Where Does Problem Origination or Discovery Begin?

The answer is "no particular place." Some of the more typical instances are:
- **Things you feel might fill a need** — or that irritate or perplex you.
- **Previous experience** — You have some question or theory to investigate.
- **Need project** — Looking or brainstorming for problems or fields to investigate.
- **Triggered interest** — You decide to investigate as a result of surprise, chance, accidental discovery, observation, illumination, serendipity, reading, experimenting, reflective thinking, or clue. It may also result from a combination of events and things.
- **Assigned, suggested, or thrust** — A specific problem or field to pursue.
- **Recognition of potential trouble** — Preventive investigation required.
- **Solution of one problem** — This often reveals other problems.

What Should You Be Seeking and Be Sensitive To?

- Any of the above. Stay alert. Develop recognition skills. Be persistent.
- Problems worthy of solution, practical to investigate, new fertile fields.
- Ordinary things to be examined in a new way and with new meaning.
- Outside stimulation such as:

Curiosities	Relationships	Experiments needed	Leads
Differences	Disturbances	Unexpected failures	Challenges
Similarities	Intimations	Problematic situations	Surprises
Patterns	Unusual results	"Thorns in flesh"	Opportunities
Obstacles	Comparisons	Listen to others	Suppositions

Curious Observation Also Involves Other Thinking Skills

Evaluating	Visualizing	Imagining	Classifying	Abstracting
Planning	Describing	Questioning	Computing	Judging
Communicating	Interpreting	Conjecturing	Inferring	Measuring

Develop the Attribute of Curiosity

You use it throughout SM-14.
- **Constantly observe** — Ask questions: What, Why, Which, Where, When, Who, How, and If. Visualize what might be. Accept nothing as "fact."
- **Be an innovator** — Cultivate curiosity to find and develop new ideas.
- **Read, skip, and skim** publications and internet for data, and triggers for ideas.

Having found something, continue on now and define the problem. If necessary, gather more information before trying to define the problem. Any solutions you derive, no matter how good, should be considered tentative.

Famous Examples of Curious Observation

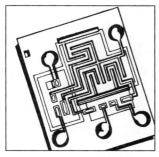

In 1969, Ted Hoff revolutionized the microelectronics industry by inventing the microprocessor — the computer-on-a-chip. This made it possible to computerize ordinary tools and appliances. Hoff believes that successful inventors are curious and are always asking questions.

Aristotle's influence and importance as a great scientist was possible because he had the attributes needed. He saw an "order" to the world and applied scientific method to his environment by being curious and making astute observations. He made the statement, "All men by nature desire to know."

The Thinking Skills Associated With Curious Observation and the Scientific Method

The successful use of the scientific method requires the use of numerous thinking skills. On the opposite page and on the other pages of this book, many of these skills are listed. In recent years the term "critical thinking skills" and "higher order thinking skills" have been extensively used. People defining these terms use a wide variety of definitions — some simple, others are very complicated. This creates many teaching problems. It is really an impossible job to say which are simple ones, which are critical and which are higher order.

Also, the word "critical" is associated with criticizing and this causes misunderstanding and scares students.

Many people point out the principal use for thinking is to solve problems and make decisions. Thus, I recommend the use of the terms "thinking skills" and "problem solving thinking skills," rather than "critical thinking skills" or "higher order thinking skills."

Any time thinking skills are taught you should also teach the stages and supporting ingredients of the Master Method of Problem Solving — The Scientific Method.

Students will be much more motivated to learn problem solving thinking skills than "critical thinking skills."

"You cannot find a solution to a problem until you find a problem."

9

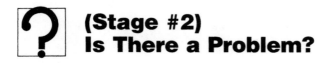

(Stage #2)
Is There a Problem?

An idea, problem, decision or tentative theory should be presented in the form of a question because:
- It encourages you to keep an open mind, and thus seek the "truth"and not to prove a statement
- A question is a tool and a guide for productive thinking about problem solving and investigation of a new subject.

Look at Problems as Challenges and Opportunities

Develop a passion to solve! Define the problem carefully so you know what direction to take.
- It prevents you from wasting time and may indicate whether it is solvable.
- A wide enough (but not too wide) definition allows for alternate solutions.
- "A problem properly defined is often half-solved."

Things to Help You Define and Understand the Problem Properly

- Consider purpose, goals, criteria, and significance.
- Ask: What? Why? Which? Where? When? Who? How? If?
- Know the domain in which the problem falls.
- If you don't know enough about the subject, you may have to loop ahead to Stage #4 and search for information to help define the problem.
- If problem was assigned to you, review its origin. Read and reread it.
- Define the problem's deep (or basic) structure. Juggle the elements.
- End with a question that is brief, clear, purposeful, and thought-provoking.
- Plan to revise the definition as your research proceeds. Read and reread it.
- Things to write down, consider, or do about the problem:

Characteristics	Unknowns	Make concept map
Attributes	Symbols	Draw pictures
Critical issues	Concepts involved	Use models
Analogies	Separate elements	Quantitative aspects
Use imagery	Make idea tree	Other representations
Challenge assumptions	State problem another way	

Tentative Solutions — Keep an Open Mind

Be alert for any possible solutions. Even if enthused with any solutions that arise, consider them tentative until you use Stages #4 through #6.

These Basic Principles Still Hold in Problem Solving

Rene Descartes in *A Discourse on Method* (1637) advised:
- Never accept anything for true which you do not clearly know to be such.
- Divide each difficulty into as many parts as possible for it's adequate solution
- Commence with the simplest and easiest to know
- Do a complete review so nothing is omitted

Famous Examples of
Is There a Problem?

Thomas J. Watson recognized a "felt difficulty" and developed IBM into a leader in the field of computer technology. This is an example of how the innovative and creative efforts of one man, his organization, and related industries have added trillions of dollars to our gross national product.

What? Why? Which? Where? When? Who? How? If? Thomas Edison was constantly on the alert to find and solve problems. He held more than 1,000 patents, including famous ones for the electric light, phonograph, movie projector — adding trillions of dollars to our gross national product.

What Are The Sciences Today? This Is a Problem that Needs Defining

A good example of a need to define is determining "What is a science?"

Years ago when the sciences were referred to, it was understood that people were referring to the domains in the natural sciences such as: physics, chemistry, astronomy, geology and biology.

Nowadays, you read about social sciences, engineering sciences, decision sciences, management sciences and others. Because we are now learning in all domains more intensively and at a faster pace, the 21st century will produce other areas developing into "sciences." The natural sciences have led the way and set the standards.

To really be a "science" there must be:

- A group of practitioners in a domain or sub-domain with relevant professional organizations and publications and following the scientific method in their research and when peer reviewing.

- At the action stage, peer review for their research. The phenomenal results of scientists in the natural sciences has been greatly aided by their peer reviewed publication system. Articles based on use of the scientific method are first screened for accuracy by reviewers. After, corrections and final approval, articles are published for fellow practitioners to challenge, test, approve, use, etc.

- As a group, an attempt must be made to build up a reliable organized body of knowledge in their area of specialization.

"You stop being good when you stop getting better."

11

(Stage #3)
Goals And Planning

GOALS — End results you want to achieve in solving a problem

- Goals must be realistic, flexible, and subject to change.
- Put goals in writing. This helps analyze priorities and avoid carelessness.
- Consider methods, processes, technologies, systems, strategies, and formulas needed.
- Set target dates for stages and completion.
- Learn to process information efficiently.

In considering goals, think about:

Real purpose involved	Sub-goals	Perfection not always needed
Where goal is leading	Criteria to use	Revising as required
Your basic needs	Values to use	Long & short term goals
Future consequences	Time/budget	Measurability/specific end

PLANNING — How to reach your goals.
Always think and plan ahead.

- Planning speeds solution — Avoids wasted time and effort. Put plans in writing.
- Develop plan to use today's huge computer databases of information.
- Abstract and outline theories & basic principles involved in the problem.
- Plan must be flexible — When working on complex, ill-structured problems, things will change frequently. Thus, don't start with too detailed a plan.
- Plan for overall solution — Preliminary program for each ingredient of SM-14.
- At start of work on each ingredient, prepare revised program for this ingredient.
- Compile tentative solutions — Know the scope of areas you are going to search.
- Experiment and test — Watch for methods to test tentative solutions.
- Similar problems solved before — Review records to benefit from experiences.
- Intuition and insight — Use to save you time and aid direction.
- Build your team — Involve them in goals and planning.
- When solving ill-structured problems you must tolerate ambiguities.
- Plan how to control constants and variables.

A few other things to consider in your planning:

Keep log book	Start with easiest sub-problems	Algorithms
Time, budget, priorities	Utilize sketches and diagrams	Alternate plans
Methods, strategies	List factors contributing to solution	Thinking aloud
Resources available	Criteria to meet or establish	Models, analogies
Checking feedback	Supplies, facilities, instruments	Trial and error
Challenge assumptions	Build up your library and files	Watch for clues
Impact on society	Approvals and decisions of others	Emotions, stress
"Anything goes" theory	Laws, licenses, legalities,	Anticipate troubles
Apply innovations and creativity	patent search	
	Assignment of responsibilities	

Sub-Problems

An experienced problem solver soon learns that you should break any complex problem down, separate and solve the sub-problems and sub-sub-problems before attacking the main problem.

Famous Examples of Goals and Planning

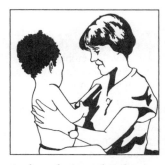

Anthropologist and author Margaret Mead had a lifetime goal to learn about human nature. Her research answered basic questions about human personality. Her plan of action included college study, specialized training, and living with primitive societies.

It was due to careful planning that Gregor Mendel was successful in his experiments with pea plants which provided new insight into the laws of heredity. His goal was to find out how characteristics of parents are passed on to offspring.

Problem-based Learning — Great Goal, But Poor Planning

There is a growing movement to teach law, medicine, engineering, business and other subjects by Problem-based Learning. In many instances those sponsoring this type of learning fail to:

- Include any formula for the stages and ingredients of the scientific method, which is the master method of problem solving.
- Or use inadequate formulas—such as offering one that is too short.

This situation is an example of the excellent goal of teaching problem solving, but poor planning and analysis of what is needed to accomplish the goal.

If you do not teach any formula when using problem-based learning programs, you fail to a great extent getting transfer of learning. Centuries of use of the scientific method have shown there are basic stages to reliable problem solving. SM-14 is a well-researched formula. After reviewing hundreds of other formulas, I have found SM-14 to be the best suited for problem solving.

SM-14 becomes a strategy that guides you in solving complex, ill-structured, real world problems. It has evolved over the centuries since Galileo's time. Another basic principle is that one learns to become an expert by solving a large number of problems, following a formula such as SM-14.

"Defective problem solving is the cause of all disorders in the world."

13

(Stage #4)
Search, Explore and Gather
The Evidence

This is the heart of problem solving. You start to search everywhere, explore all angles, leads, clues, and sources of information. Pick out the basic principles of the material you read, see, or hear. Gather all the evidence that will help you solve the problem, always trying to use innovation and creativity, thus building your list of possible tentative solutions. Learn how to process information productively. Put your thoughts in writing.

Search Your Mind for Tentative Solutions

Before loading your mind with data, other people's opinions, and so-called "facts," list all possible tentative solutions you can think of for your main problem and any sub-problems. Reasons: (1) Provides you with direction and scope in your search.(2) Enables you to utilize imagination before being influenced by prevailing thoughts and theories.

Review Plans and Prepare Your Program

- Keep log
- Build files — use all resources
- Enlist team of advisors
- Prepare broad literature search
- List any known sub-problems
- Read about How-To-Research

Possible Methods, Processes, Strategies, Technologies, and Systems

- Redefine problem as needed
- Draw inferences
- Watch for patterns
- Classify
- Make associations
- Discard the irrelevant
- Find inter-relationships
- Simulate or improvise
- Anticipate the unexpected
- Sampling and statistics
- Measurements
- Work backwards
- Algorithms
- List attributes of subject
- Utilize routines
- Group brainstorm
- Imitate nature
- Utilize computers
- Spot key factors
- Solve sub-problems first
- State problem another way
- Compare to other problems
- Abstract basic principles
- Be flexible — vary your attack
- Watch for leads, clues, hints
- Control variables — causes and effects
- Watch for surprise discoveries
- Plan experiments — be curious
- Interpret data — use all data
- Trial and error
- Look for similarities and differences
- Visualize — watch for "oddities"
- Logical reasoning and speculation
- Use checklists, models and analogies
- Use qualitative and quantitative analysis
- Use sketches, trees, concept maps
- Use flow charts, spreadsheets, symbols
- Look at problems from a different angle

Develop Your Reflective-Directed, Speculative Thinking

Talk to yourself in both language and images . . . silently or aloud. Daydream with your thoughts directed to thinking about the data you reviewed. Think reflectively while searching and while doing routine things such as exercising. Jump back and forth among logical, critical, imaginative, and wild thinking.

14

Famous Examples of Search, Explore and Gather The Evidence

Because of searching, exploration, and information gathering, the teams of NASA scientists, engineers, technicians, and astronauts solved the complex problem of landing man on the moon. The dream became a reality on July 20, 1969, when Neil Armstrong took man's first step on the moon. A triump for the scientific method.

In searching for information to include in this booklet, I used over 15,000 Post-it Notes™ to mark helpful pages. Dr. Art Fry invented 3M's Post-it Notes™ to satisfy a felt need to efficiently mark pages. Experimenting with a special adhesive developed by 3M's Dr. Silver, Dr. Fry developed his idea into a successful product.

The Internet Facilitates Gathering The Evidence

The Internet has caused a boom in the availability of data, information, and knowledge and has already changed our lives in many ways and will continue to do so. Remember that computers and the "Web" resulted from scientists and technologists, following the scientific method.

Users of the internet are going to have to know how to use the scientific method for these reasons:

- The flood of available data, information and knowledge frequently requires evaluation of its reliability—the method to verify reliable knowledge is the scientific method.

- It is the method of change—therefore will be needed more than ever.

- The method of applying all this knowledge is again the scientific method.

- For the sake of your reputation and the good of society, knowledge you put on your "Web" site should have the reliability of having been gained by the scientific method.

- Improvements to computers, the web, software etc., will require the use of the method of invention—that is the scientific method.

"Be sure to double-check everything you read on the Internet."

(Stage #5)
Generate Creative and Logical Alternative Solutions

Logical Solutions (or Trial and Error)

You can solve many problems the same way many great discoveries have been made-by trial and error or by using gradual, systematic, steady, analytical, judicial reasoning and logic. You gather the data and fit it together. What was a puzzle falls into a logical order. Aha! You have a discovery or solution to your problem. Most importantly, however, problems are solved by the leap of the imagination, as often the solutions are infinite.

Innovative Solutions

Search out other people's ideas. Use as they are or adapt for your particular problem by combining reflective thinking and your creative abilities.

Creative Solutions — Use of Imagination

Creativity is usually described as taking two existing ideas and combining them into a new and better idea. It is also termed divergent thinking, lateral thinking, insight, intuition, flash of inspiration, innovation, ideation, guided design, generative thinking, productive thinking, etc. Successful people have also found imaginative thinking helpful in deciding what ideas or directions **not** to use or consider in detail. *There is not enough space to discuss all the ways to generate alternative solutions. Below are what I consider to be the most important methods (see pages 38 to 40).*

- **Reflective Thinking** — You search, explore, follow leads, gather pertinent data, information, basic principles, concepts and use reflective thinking. You can also use rest-illumination or rest-insight. You load your mind with subject data — then rest — then **start** thinking about your problem again in a relaxed manner.

- **Triggers** — Things that stimulate your mind's store of stocked memories and cause recall and new train of thought. It's best to load your mind with data pertinent to your current problem. It is the prepared or loaded mind that can best be triggered. At that point, you then:

Experiment or visualize	Brainstorm
Have discussions-pick minds	Browse through a store
Attend conferences and exhibits	Search your files or periodicals
Use a computer program	Trial and error procedures

While you are doing all these things, you are reflecting on your problem as you acquire more information. Then, EUREKA — suddenly ILLUMINATION comes — or more gradual insight climaxes! Something has triggered your mind and you have an idea, lead, discovery, or a tentative solution. This may be a small or very big idea.

Most Productive of All

Read, skip, and skim through a wide variety of Internet sites, magazines, newspapers, and books. These are the nation's idea banks which are filled with things to trigger your mind. Visit your library where there are hundreds of magazines on display. Books on creativity and school courses usually fail to emphasize the value and importance of using triggers.

Famous Examples of Generate Creative and Logical Alternative Solutions

Karl Pearson, in his famous book, *The Grammar of Science*, published in 1892, stressed creativity as a separate feature of "the scientific method." His exact words were "the discovery of scientific laws by aid of the creative imagination." He also advocated the scientific habit of mind for solving all problems of life.

Alex F. Osborne, author of *Applied Imagination* and founder of the Creative Education Foundation, and Dr. J.P. Guilford made a tremendous contribution to the popularization of interest in and development of the techniques of creative thinking—urging generating alternatives. These efforts spawned many books and seminars.

Logic and Creativity vs. Exercise Problems

Exercise problems, textbook problems, puzzle problems, and game problems are used extensively in schoolwork and tests. While usually referred to as "problems," they really should be called what they are—one of the above names. Schools are teaching the methods, techniques, formulas, strategies and domain-specific information needed to solve them.

While they serve a useful purpose, they are not sufficient preparation for the everyday, real-world problems that we must face.

Real World Problem Solving and Decision Making

These require more real world logical reasoning and the use of creative thinking and methods. The teaching of these in our schools needs to be increased.

Paul D. Hurd, in an article in AAAS's book, *Scientific Literacy* (1989), reports that, since 1983, over 300 reports on the condition of education in the United States have been issued. He states:

Consensus also exists among the reports' goal for science education. The goals are to develop the abilities to (a) solve problems encountered in the workplace and in the conduct of personal life and civic responsibility. . .

"More use of the scientific method will benefit everyone—spread the word."

(Stage #6)
Evaluate The Evidence

By now you should have a list of tentative solutions that are candidates for your educated guess or hypothesis. It is also the stage for experimenting and testing. The final choice is often called your working hypothesis and will be your Stage #7.

Starting guides to consider before working on each ingredient
- **Problem** — Should it be redefined or reframed?
- **Goals and planning** — Any changes? Any new leads or clues? Planning ahead?
- **Goal referencing approach** — Where you started, are now and still need to go.
- **Looking back** — Have you been using the right attributes, methods, strategies, technologies, plus curious observation? Have you consulted your advisor? Have you had a team meeting? Are you keeping your log up-to-date? Being on the right path is important!
- **Are you using innovation, creativity, watching for surprises?** Are you alert to clues and leads?
- **Are you putting thoughts and ideas into writing?** Using all available resources?

Evaluating Your Tentative Hypotheses
- If data on any of these hypotheses is insufficient, gather additional information.
- Check against any list of criteria, formulas, and routines you have established.
- It may be helpful to read the information on Stage #7 to familiarize yourself with the characteristics and traits your working hypothesis must have.

Also, read Stage #8 to alert you as to how it will have to be challenged.

Tests, Experiments and Other Methods, Strategies, and Techniques of Evaluating

Logical reasoning	Measuring	Mathematical solution
Consult literature	Surveys	Independent lab test
Collaborators	Interviews	Expert opinions
Controlled experiments	Modeling	Concepts correct?
Dis-confirming test	Graphs	Improvisation
Data base reliable?	Sampling	Disqualifying
Consider consequences	Speculation	Make predictions
Statistical analysis	Simulations	Challenge assumptions
Design special instruments	"Live It"	Computer testing
"Anything goes" theory	Visualizing	Need to ripen more?

Chart Your Solutions to Weigh the Evidence
Be more careful and make your choice. Criteria can be graded by as many facets, characteristics or angles, as you desire. You can have individual charts or a joint one. Tailor headings to fit your problem.

Possible Comparison Chart								
Tentative	Test Results		Suitability		Feasibility		Acceptability	
Choices	#1	#2	#1	#2	#1	#2	#1	#2
Solution A	Against	For	30%	Okay	60%	Okay	50%	90%
Solution B	For	Against	50%	No	80%	No	90%	20%

Famous Examples of Evaluate the Evidence

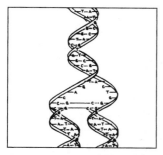

After evaluating all the evidence, biologist James Watson and biophysicist Francis Crick solved one of nature's greatest puzzles — the structure of the DNA molecule the genetic "blueprint" that dictates the traits which living things inherit. They earned a Nobel prize for this discovery in 1962.

Herbert A. Simon, Nobel Laureate, and his associates researched the human problem-solving process. Through evaluation of the evidence, they arrived at the hypothesis that a great variety of problems could be solved by use of a computer. Dr. Simon's books contain a wealth of evidence on problem solving and artificial intelligence.

Evaluate Carefully, But Remember — Perfection Is Not Always Possible

Time, money, emergencies, importance, practicability and constraints on human thinking often mean we can't be thorough, even though we would like to be.

Thus we must often settle for "good enough." Similar descriptions are tolerance of ambiguity, aspiration level, most optimum not needed, satisfactory versus optional standards, adequate for problem, risk within reason, bounded rationality. The general principles in considering all your efforts:

Accept uncertainty of solution
Perfectionism is not always affordable
"Truth" may not exist
Rate: Good — Better — Good enough
Consider community "standards"
Precision — important in science
Waste no time on little differences
No excuse for sloppy work
No single best solution may exist
No better action to take

A good intuitive base of actual experience or reading of other peoples experience will be of great value in making a quick decision on matters of minor importance, but remember if you make decision on wrong "facts," what follows are wrong solutions.

Learn to evaluate as— good, better, good enough, or not good enough — and search for further data keeping in mind costs *vs.* benefits.

"Struggle is the essence of life — true happiness comes from being useful."

(Stage #7)
Make the Educated Guess
(Hypothesis)

Review the starting guides at top of Stage #6 on Page 19. Your educated guess—technically, the hypothesis—is a proposed solution to the most recent definition of your problem. It is your choice of the most-likely-to-be-successful solution from the list of contending ones, which you evaluated.

Terminology, Definitions, and Descriptions:

- **The hypothesis is often called "the educated guess,"** because scientists have long recognized the difficulty of arriving at the real "truth."
- **Working hypothesis** is a term used to describe this proposed solution. It is only a "candidate for truth," as it must be challenged under Stage #8.
- **A hypothesis** would be a theory of nature in the natural sciences. In other fields, it could be a decision, plan, diagnosed illness, idea, design, invention, etc.
- **More than one hypothesis (hypotheses)**—you might propose more than one solution. Problems in the social sciences often require several hypotheses.
- **A perfect solution is seldom obtained** in solving complex problems.
- **Inductive reasoning** has helped reach your hypothesis. See Ingredient #14.
- **Valuable even if proven false**—a hypothesis will often be wrong but may lead to a discovery, a new field to explore, or a modification of the hypothesis

The Characteristics or Traits of a Hypothesis

These are desirable but not always essential or possible;

Relevant and adequate	Adds to existing knowledge
Verifiable or falsifiable	Consistent with existing knowledge
Logically possible	In simplest terms possible
Conducive to further inquiry	Answers defined problem

Predict Consequences

Now that you have chosen a hypothesis, you must make predictions of why and how something will occur, based on the accuracy of your hypothesis. Testing these predictions helps you challenge, justify, or falsify your hypothesis in Stage #8. Then others can try to do so—after, you take action and communicate at Stage #11.

Types of consequences and predictions:

- If change is made, consequences will be . . .
- If experiment is made, it will show . . .
- If reasoned out, results will be . . .
- If cost and benefits are computed, they will show . . .
- If survey or interview is conducted, it will show . . .
- If mathematical computation is made using certain data, it will show . . .
- If a model is made, this will happen . . .
- If a computer simulation is programmed, it will show . . .
- If a scenario is prepared, enumerating all possible results, it will be . . .

Famous Examples of Make the Educated Guess (Hypothesis)

Simon Bolivar — Five republics of South America term him father of their independence. He faced the problem of how to free his country (Venezuela) from colonial oppression. When one hypothesis failed, he generated another and another until he finally succeeded.

Benjamin Franklin is well known for his famous kite experiment in which he explored the nature of lightning. He formed a hypothesis, and in 1749 performed his dangerous kite experiment. Franklin concluded that lightning is an electric charge.

This Technology Era Requires Technical Working Hypotheses

You often hear the term "Science & Technology" but often Technology is lumped under "Science." Regardless, the method of technology is the same as the method of science. You use the scientific method in originating, arriving at a working hypothesis, and finally in solving technology problems as well as when applying technology.

The Technology Panel of AAAS' Project 2061, in their 1989 — Phase I Report, states:

Technology education should emphasize problem solving. The posing and solving of problems, increasingly complex as students move from kindergarten through the twelfth grade, will enable students to develop techniques that are vital to living in a technical world of diverse cultures and technical status. The problems and their solutions may be technical experimental, mathematical technical-social, or value-laden. Designing alternatives to circumvent problems and learning to deal with options are also important techniques . . . Observation, measurement, and analysis are universal tools of technology. . . Intelligent observation is crucial to invention. . . .

"The law that only problem-solvers survive is as inflexibly relentless as the law of gravity."

(Stage #8)
Challenge the Hypothesis

Usually the stage for final experimentation and testing.

Review the starting guides listed at the top of Stage #6 on Page 19.

- **The degree of challenge** to your hypothesis will depend on the type of problem and its importance. It can range from just seeking "a good enough" solution (but not a haphazard or lazy one) to a much more rigorous challenge.
- **To accommodate a broad range**, Dr. Crooks used the term "Challenge." Most formulas for the scientific method use the terms verification, justification, refutability, validity, falsification, testing the theories, experimentation to test and many similar terms indicating that the hypothesis should be challenged.

Experimenting, Testing, and Challenging the Hypothesis

- **Falsification:** Sir Karl Popper advocates trying to prove a hypothesis to be false rather than trying to prove it right. This may save time and avoid bias.
- **Verification:** Many disagree with his falsification theory and believe various methods should be used to verify the hypothesis.
- **Who Is Right?:** This is an extremely controversial and difficult question to answer. Try both approaches. Gather evidence for and against your hypothesis.
- **Predictions:** Use to challenge your hypothesis. Under Stage #7, you made certain predictions that resulted from your hypothesis. The way to challenge your hypothesis is to try to prove these false, probably true, or supported.
- **Modify Your Hypothesis:** In testing your predictions, if you find something wrong, backtrack to Stage #7, modify your hypothesis, and change your predictions. If it fails completely, backtrack to Stage #4 or #5. We learn from failures.
- **Control Variables:** Vary one thing at a time—make notes on each.

Repeatability of Your Tests and Experiments

For your hypothesis to be accepted by others, your testing results must be able to be repeated by you and those who will want to verify your theory.

Log all tests	Results must fit known "facts"	Be accurate
Report unknowns	Experiments must be complete enough	Review data
Control stress	Results must be consistent	Be honest
Try for simplicity	Watch for "bugs" that spoil tests	Get advice
Use sampling	Use statistical verification	Use math

Other Suggestions

- **Fault Tree**—Prepare one on how your hypothesis or tests can possibly fail.
- **Alternate Hypothesis**—Be curious, observant and alert for a better hypothesis.
- **Dis-Confirming Evidence**—Don't ignore, follow up. Be critical.
- **Competing Hypotheses**—Verify by eliminating these, but remain flexible.
- **Some Hypotheses Not Verifiable**—When in social sciences, geological fields, etc.
- **Consequences and Contingencies**—What results from your hypothesis?

Famous Examples of Challenge the Hypothesis

While working as a patent attorney, Chester F. Carlson decided to design a fast, easy, and inexpensive way to make copies of text and tine drawings. After challenging several hypotheses, he successfully produced the first xerographic copy in 1937. This invention added billions of dollars to gross national product.

Dr. Percey L. Julian, by synthesis of the drug physostigmine, brought the healing drug cortisone within the reach of millions. He defeated the challenge of a British rival and proved his theory. Dr. Julian's appointment to head The Glidden Company's research marked the turning point in acceptance of black scientists in the United States.

Predicting and Prevention

Prediction has always been a big feature of the scientific method, whenever it is used. Once a working hypothesis is arrived at, you make predictions to challenge what will happen if they are correct. From them, you can do tests and experiments to determine whether these are correct or false.

Forecasting the Future

Forecasting the future is extremely difficult. Plain guesses and gut intuition are often used but not very reliable. Actually there is no reliable method. But, of all the methods the most reliable one is to follow the stages of the scientific method.

Prevention

While the scientific method is famous for its use in discoveries, it is also the method of prevention.

It is not logical to wait till problems develop or till decisions have to be made after trouble occurs. Therefore, the use of curious observation (stage #1 of SM-14) must also be used to look for things that may happen and that need to be prevented.

The importance of prevention and forecasting are more reasons why every one should learn and be taught the scientific method.

"The solutions of today will be out-of-date tomorrow."

(Stage #9)
Reach a Conclusion

Begin by reviewing the starting guides listed at the top of Page 19. You have challenged your working hypothesis. Now comes the conclusion. If your hypothesis is partially wrong, backtrack, modify, and then challenge again. If completely wrong, you backtrack and take another path.

We learn from our failures. Do not become discouraged! Even great men and women are frequently wrong. If your hypothesis passes the important tests—**you have reached your conclusion!**

Your Conclusion Should Be (Among Other Things):

- broad enough to fit all acceptable data;
- limited enough to meet special exceptions,
- consistent when tested by you (and others) again and again,
- seldom extended beyond the evidence,
- suitable to base a report on, if one is scheduled; and
- an answer to the problem, as you have finally defined it.

Take a Good "Look Back" to Re-evaluate Your Investigation

Gathered all the evidence?   Ethical considerations?
Experiments properly performed?   Overall accuracy good?
No fraud by teammates?   No bias has crept in?
Variables properly controlled?   No wrong assumptions?
Any other possible goofs or errors?   Anything overlooked?
All consequences considered?   Feedback?
Any conceptual blocks?   Environment considered?

Things to Do Now (Preparation for Stage #11—Take Action)

While everything is fresh in your memory, think about and prepare notes on:

- **Limitations.** If there were any limitations on your efforts or results in defining the problem, the search for evidence, or the challenge phase, include them in preparation for reporting under Stage #11.
- **Speculations and Looking Forward.** If you were doing a project that advances the knowledge in your field, you might want to prepare some speculations or predictions even beyond what the evidence supports. Label as speculations.
- **Research Method Recommendations.** Based on your experience, make recommendations, give warnings, hints, and references to those who may try to challenge, verify, or falsify your conclusions.
- **Conclusion Recommendations and Presentation.** If you work on a decision problem, plan, management problem, etc., you may want to prepare recommendations based on your conclusions to submit to authorities.

Intelligent Compromise: In problem-solving or decision-making, in the "inexact" social sciences, etc., your conclusions may have to be an intelligent compromise. The solution of any problem (and its acceptance) depends on good human relations. Consult those who will be affected by your conclusions.

Famous Examples of Reach a Conclusion

Curious to know what ingredient made uranium ore so powerfully radioactive, Marie Curie gathered the evidence. In her search and exploration, she tested all known chemical bodies, discovering two new elements: radium and polonium. For these discoveries, she was awarded the Nobel Prize in Chemistry, 1911.

Albert Einstein's conclusion about the theory of relativity has been tested and has never been disproved. Two famous quotes of his: "Imagination is more important than knowledge, for knowledge is limited." "The formulation of a problem is far more often essential than its solution, which may be merely a matter of mathematical or experimental skill."

US Supreme Court's Conclusion About The Scientific Method

In the 1993 US Supreme Court decision, *Daubert v Merrill Dow Pharmaceuticals Inc.*, the court reviewed the definitions of scientific evidence, scientific knowledge, scientific validity and good science. As part of this case, the American Medical Association, et al, filed an Amicus brief in support of the respondent and stated:

"Scientific Knowledge" within the meaning of Rule 702 is knowledge derived from the application of the scientific method.

As part of its decision, the Supreme Court declared:

"But in order to qualify as "scientific knowledge" an inference or assertion must be derived by the scientific method. Proposed testimony must be supported by appropriate validation — i.e., "good grounds," based on what is known."

Therefore, the official position of the US government is that the scientific method exists. This decision clearly indicates to all agencies of the United States that the scientific method exists. For proper justice to be rendered, our attorneys, judges and the general public, from whom jurors are chosen, should be familiar with the scientific method. It should be thoroughly taught in all our schools.

"Skills are more widely applicable than knowledge and information."

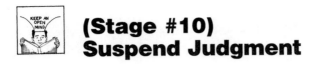

(Stage #10)
Suspend Judgment

Throughout a project, a good researcher has an open mind and a skeptical, but practical, attitude, always suspending judgment to some degree.

You have spent a lot of time and effort to reach a final conclusion, but now you must change your attitude and suspend judgment. Do not "fall in love" with your final hypothesis. Watch for other concepts or trains of thought.

An excellent description of this stage was given by Dr. Crooks in his 1958 paper (mentioned on page 28). Discussing the ingredient of "Suspended Judgment," he stated:

"The investigator must stick to his conclusion until it is proved wrong, but he must keep an open mind and be ready to accept new evidence or speculations if sufficiently convincing. He is therefore ready to adjust his own views if they are untenable.

This is the crux of the scientific attitude: an abiding faith in some view or opinion allied to a healthy skepticism; a questioning challenging doubt of new ideas; but a mind definitely open to new ideas.

This sounds conflicting, but it is not. The true scientist or the citizen with a scientific attitude is no bigoted stand-patter, but he is no wishy-washy turn-coat either; he does not go chasing after strange idols just because they are new, nor does he condemn another idea just because it is old.

He realizes that truth is not simple, that knowledge is forever growing, and that opinions thought correct today in the light of present knowledge may be thought incorrect tomorrow because of new discoveries or the projection of new ideas."

IMPORTANT!

There can be great flexibility in the order in which SM-14 stages are utilized. Stages are numbered and in their **usual order of use**. Utilizing the stages in solving a problem, you may often:

1. Skip ahead
2. Backtrack
3. Stall
4. Loop ahead or back
5. Combine two or more ingredients
6. Use various combinations

Never refer to the stages as steps or rules! However, in many of the methods used under the stages, there may be steps or rules to follow.

Develop Your Communication Skills

Educators and employers increasingly stress the importance of verbal and written communication skills. There is a movement to teach writing across the curricula. Develop proficiency in the following:

How to write a report	Spelling and punctuation	Public speaking
English grammar	Subject terminology	Vocabulary
English composition	Communication Knowledge	Self confidence

Famous Examples of Suspend Judgment

In December 1967, Christian Barnard performed the world's first human heart transplant in Cape Town, South Africa. Before reaching a conclusion that the operation was successful, Dr. Barnard suspended judgment in order to observe and gather more information.

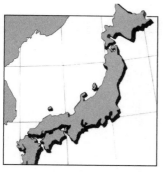

Suspend judgment if you think the Japanese are only imitators. Japan made great strides by just being innovative. Learning to be a good innovator is the first step on the road to creativity. Today, Japan is quickly becoming more creative.

Keep Your Mental Process Open

Even after reaching your conclusion, keep your mind open and thinking. Charles R. Foster, in *Psychology for Life Today* (1966, 16th Printing) describes our thinking process:

"In psychology the term thinking is usually applied to that type of mental process which we identify as problem solving. There are, however, a number of kinds of mental activity, which are sometimes referred to as thinking.

There is a general "stream of consciousness" of which we are aware during all or most of our waking movements. A succession of ideas, images, reveries, and associations streams through the mind, and we are aware, if we stop to contemplate it, of this activity of ours. In most present-day psychology, however, when the subject of thinking is under consideration, the phase of it which has to do with reasoning or problem solving is of chief concern. Hence, in this chapter we are confining our discussion to the psychology of thinking as problem solving.

We are omitting any consideration of thinking as reverie, or as daydreaming in the usual sense of the term — we are thinking mainly of what occurs, in our mental processes as we deal with the everyday problems of life."

The Fuzzy Principle:
"Everything is a matter of degree."

27

(Stage #11)
Take Action

Prepare for Action!

This is often called the "gaining acceptance stage."

- Review your plans and goals. Have the courage to act now.
- Innovation and creativity can help immensely. Read how to present, sell, and gain acceptance of your concluding hypothesis. Get other opinions.
- Give proper credit to your team, reference sources, and associates.
- Report the social and ecological effects of your hypothesis.
- Look ahead—mention possibilities that others may not see.

The Action You Take Depends on the Nature of Your Investigation:

- **Scientific theory, process, discovery**—You will usually prepare a report using the IMRAD format of *Introduction, Method, Results, and Discussion.* This can be submitted to a scientific journal for peer review and possible publication. Other possibilities:

Publish book	Report to superiors	Report to project sponsors
Apply for patent	Sabbatical leave	Enter in Science Fair
Publish pre-prints	Summer school	Present paper at meeting
Press release	Inform colleagues	Commercialize process

- **Invention, technological design, new product idea**—Do any of the above; make a model, apply for a patent, do market research, make an effort to gain acceptance, and sell or merchandise the product.
- **Decision, plan, dispute, social science problem, geography or history research, the arts**—Do any of the above. Implement a solution, if possible. Prevent future problems.
- **Recommendations**—If submitted to authoritative body, wait for review. If modified, rejected, or partially accepted, you will have to coil back to one of the earlier ingredients and work ahead again.
- **New problems**—Solving one problem often leads to new problems. Maybe you made some surprise discoveries or saw opportunities for research in new areas. Consider all consequences—make predictions. Offer clues and leads. Mention in your report.
- **Obstacles to acceptance**—Many eventually highly-successful hypotheses have had a very rough road to acceptance. Others have won immediate popularity. Thus, your action may have to include overcoming these obstacles that cause people to reject new things:

Jealousy	Resistance to change	Organized skepticism
Bias	Loss of prestige	Wrong assumptions
Financial loss	Not enough proof	Poor reasoning
No market	Authoritarianism	Won't admit wrong

- **Aids to acceptance**—All through your problem solving you must think of ways to gain acceptance. Review these and investigate any other ideas. Now develop and apply them. Use your communication skills. From start to finish, we use curiosity. You must also evaluate your action—look back! Are results as expected? Must you modify anything? Use retrospect.

Always the Inquiring Mind

Examples of Take Action

Tribute to All Our Scientists

This booklet is dedicated to Dr. Kenneth B. M. Crooks (1905-1959) whose article "Suggestions for Teaching the Scientific Method" inspired me to write it. It is also dedicated to the past and present members of the intellectual community from whose books and publications I have compiled most of the information in this pamphlet. So many works have been reviewed, it is not possible to credit individuals. They used their many personal attributes productively. Thanks to them all!

Let us also remember the millions of scientists, researchers, inventors, and other problem solvers who have displayed curiosity, persistence, creativity, and honesty in their work. We need to thank them for their contributions to world knowledge and for trying to make this world a better place in which to live.

Action Is Needed to Standardize on A Formula for The Scientific Method Such as SM-14

To the extent that the scientific method is taught in our schools, numerous formulas are used. While many are reasonably good, most are too short. This variety is very confusing to students and teachers.

I recommend that a well-researched formula that has been put through all the stages of the scientific method such as SM-14 be officially adopted as the standard one. This formula, in addition to covering the method of science, is also the same for general problem solving, decision making, operation research, method of inquiry, invention, medical diagnostic and many others. Thus, it would be of a wide benefit to every one who learns it.

This is especially important as all signs indicate the scientific method will, in the future, be extensively taught in all grades and across the curricula.

The US Supreme Court should adopt a standard formula also, to aid in identifying how expert witnesses are using the scientific method in their testimony.

Until such time as an official body adopts a formula, I recommend that all authors, teachers, etc., use the SM-14 formula—it is not copyrighted.

"Chaos is ended only by methods—use SM-14."

29

Supporting Ingredients to The Scientific Method (SM-14)

Supporting Ingredients:

The scientific method is often said to represent the system of science. Frequently formulas for the scientific method are condensed versions of the method. In the SM-14 formula, a more complete formula is presented. To make the formula more suitable for teaching purposes and people to understand the method of science, supporting ingredients have been included in the SM-14 formula. They are:

- #12 — Creative, Non-logical, Logical and Technical Methods
- #13 — Procedural Principles and Theories
- #14 — Attributes and Thinking Skills.

These are explained on the next few pages.

Scientific Methods vs The Scientific Method

(See page 37 for the characteristics of each of these.)

The term, scientific methods, had real meaning in prior centuries when scientists were our principal problem solvers. Today, it would be more precise to use a collective term such as "problem solving methods" for the creative, non-logical, logical and technical methods used in science and general problem solving under the stages of the scientific method. In science literature, the most common alternate word for "scientific methods" is "techniques."

Proceeding Scientifically

This is explained in *Introduction to Logic* (1982) by Irving M. Copi (1917 -) — philosopher, educator, author of books on logic:

"As the term "scientific" is generally used today, it refers to any reasoning which attempts to proceed from observable facts of experience to reasonable (that is, relevant and testable) explanations for those facts. The scientific method is not confined to professional scientists; anyone can be said to be proceeding scientifically who follows the general pattern of reasoning from evidence to conclusions that can be tested by experience. The skilled detective is a scientist in this sense, as are most of us — in our more rational moments, at least."

"Serendipity, the accidental discovery of something valuable is vital to scientific progress. Invention favors the prepared mind."

(Ingredient #12)
Creative, Non-logical, Logical and Technical Methods

NOTE. By including these supporting ingredients, the SM-14 formula now (revised 1997), reflects the whole system of science and the system of the complete method of creative problem solving and decision making.

For teaching students and for general understanding of the scientific method we need to properly identify the *working, action, effective, and applied methods* that *produce actual results*. These are used under the first eleven stages of SM-14. "Methods" as used here include such elements and auxiliary actions as:

Processes	Tactics	Approaches	Operations	Programs
Procedures	Techniques	Systems	Strategies	Criteria

There is no exact line dividing types of methods, as one type often blends into another.

Creative Methods

Creativity often involves change, inspiration, or a combination of old ideas to produce a new idea or solution. A body of methods has developed for improving creativity.Four important creative methods are reflective thinking, rest illumination, triggers, and brainstorming.

Non-logical Methods

While it may not be "scientific" to use non-logical methods, nevertheless, in actual practice, scientists and all problem solvers are always using them. Time is often the main reason these are used. Some non-logical methods used result from habits, emotions, trial and error, arbitrariness, haste, frustration, closed mindedness, experimenting, unreasoned opinions, risk taking, intuitive pure guess, etc. Be alert to whether they affect your results favorably or unfavorably. Chance, accidental discovery, fortunate occurrences, unanticipated novelty, effective surprise, and serendipity probably are non-logical methods or ways.

Logical Methods (in the broadest sense)

Any method based on sound reasoning is classified here as logical. Some researchers may apply logical methods based on accepted rules of reasoning standardized by logicians. Usually, though, people use "semi-intuitive" logic resulting from their base of experiences, thinking skills, and knowledge. Examples of well-known logical methods based on reasoning and experience are methods of:

controlled variations	pattern identification	trial and error	falsification
reviewing the literature	artificial intelligence	classification	surveying

Technical Methods

No standard exists to determine what methods to term "technical." A method involving measuring, mathematics, use of tools, instruments, and apparatus can be termed "technical." Since most others are general methods used in all fields and for all types of problems, some authors point out that these technical methods are really the only ones that can accurately be called the methods of science or scientific methods.

(Ingredient #13) Procedural Principles and Theories

Since Galileo's time, basic principles, guides, objectives, and thoughts about "the scientific method" and its use have been discussed and debated. There are no established standards concerning these procedural principles and theories. Controversy exists about some, if not all, of them. Because these do not always apply to every circumstance, they must be considered and applied with an open mind as you pursue problem solving.

The Organized Sciences

The organized sciences have their peer review systems, professional organizations, customs, consensuses of opinion, ethical standards (I recommend NAS's *Responsible Science: Ensuring the Integrity of the Research Process*, Vol. I & II, 1993), and constant debates about theories, methods, what is the structure of science, and what is our "organized body of knowledge." Look to them for leadership in procedural principles and theories, as they have been responsible for these. A few major ones are listed below.

The Objective of The Scientific Method

The basic purpose is to obtain, refine, extend, and apply knowledge, and to seek the "truth," although the "truth" can probably never be determined. Results must always be held open to extension, modification, and even possible replacement.

- **Experimentation** — Testing and experimentation, whether on a blackboard or computer, or in the lab, are usually essential activities in the use of the scientific method. Government standards must be observed in experiments involving people, animals, and the environment.

- **Replicable** — Results must usually be reproducible.

- **A Skeptical Attitude** — A skeptical attitude toward authoritative statements is required in seeking the truth. Data used in your thinking must be "true" insofar as it is possible to determine "truth." It may be useful to define key terminology.

- **Values and Ethics** — As much as humanly possible, researchers should strive to be free of prejudice and bias that often creep into human judgment and action. They must give due credit to their team or collaborators.

- **Infallibility** — No claims should be made that the scientific method produces infallible solutions. State, rather: "On the evidence available today the balance of probability favors the view . . ."

- **Gather All Evidence** — If bias or inadequate effort causes you to ignore or fail to find available contrary evidence, you will not arrive at the "truth."

- **Mathematics** — Quantitative methods should be used whenever possible.

- **Society** — There is a growing interest in the concept that science is a social activity.

- **All Stages of The Scientific Method** — Have various procedural principles and theories peculiar to them. See the Stages 1 to 11.

The Value of the Scientific Endeavor — Procedural Principles and Theories

Dr. Vannevar Bush stated:

Advances in science when put to practical use mean:

- more jobs
- higher wages
- shorter hours
- more abundant crops
- more leisure for recreation, for study and for learning how to live without the deadening drudgery which has been the burden of the common man for ages past

Advances in science will also:

- bring higher standards of living
- lead to the prevention or cure of diseases
- promote conservation of our limited national resources
- assure means of defense against aggression

The flow of new scientific knowledge must be both continuous and substantial

But to achieve these objectives — to secure a high level of employment, to maintain a position of world leadership — the flow of new scientific knowledge must be both continuous and substantial.

Science Has Done Wonders for All of Us Through Its Method

Dr. Vannevar Bush, one of our foremost scientists and who aided the WWII effort and the establishment of the National Science Foundation after the war, aptly described the value of scientific endeavor when he stated in 1945:

> *"Advances in science when put to practical use mean more jobs, higher wages, shorter hours, more abundant crops, more leisure for recreation, for study, for learning how to live without the deadening drudgery which has been the burden of the common man for ages past. Advances in science will also bring higher standards of living, will lead to the prevention or cure of diseases, will promote conservation of our limited national resources, and will assure means of defense against aggression. But to achieve these objectives — to secure a high level of employment, to maintain a position of world leadership — the flow of new scientific knowledge must be both continuous and substantial."*

It is this "flow of new scientific knowledge" from the scientific method that has earned it these well deserved praises:

- "the greatest discovery of science" and
- "the greatest idea of all times."

"Science is an imperfect but phenomenally successful process."

33

(Ingredient #14)
Attributes and Thinking Skills

The quality of human activity applied to the various stages and action methods involved in the scientific method determines the quality of results achieved. The fame of the scientific method results from the high degree of development of personal attributes and thinking skills that scientists have used in the scientific method. There is some overlap between attributes and thinking skills. Scientists are human and therefore not perfect, but their overall accomplishments have achieved phenomenal benefits for society. The use of their method spread to all domains.

Personal Attributes

A definition of personal attributes also includes character traits, aptitudes, skills, values, attitudes, etc. The number of desirable attributes mentioned in the problem-solving literature is great. Those most frequently mentioned include:

Honesty	Flexible	Logical Reasoner	Attitude
Sensitivity	Skeptical	Suspend Judgment	Open Minded
Motivated	Communicator	Team Worker	Curiosity
Organized	Seek Truth	Passion for Subject	Courage
Creative	Emotional Stability	Knowledgeable	Experimenter

There is no standard combination that is "best." Your success in life depends on developing desirable personal attributes and improving your undesirable ones.

Thinking Skills

In this limited space, I can only impress on you the need to develop your ability to learn and use the thinking skills necessary to adjust to the many changes in our fast-developing world. We will consider the two primary thinking skills which are always used in problem origination, solving, and challenge of solution. They are basic ways of thinking and are termed induction and deduction.

Induction

This is another controversial subject. Some philosophers have advanced theories that claim there is no such thing. For you and me, however, the standard textbook definition is understandable. Professor Huxley gave this example many years ago:

Suppose you bit these small, hard, green apples. Each one tasted very sour.

You then make a generalization that all small, hard, green apples are probably sour. This is inductive reasoning (i.e., *from the specific or particular to the general*).

Deduction

Then you picked up this small, hard, green apple:

By deductive reasoning (i.e., *from the general to the specific*), you decide it must be sour, too. Many of the thinking skills you need, are mentioned in this booklet.

Famous Examples of Attributes and Thinking Skills

John Dewey (1859-1952), educator-philosopher, wrote many books. The most famous is *How To Think*. He was a great advocate of reflective thinking. He asserted that "the method of science-problem solving through reflective thinking should be both the method and valued outcome of science instruction in America's schools."

Thomas H. Huxley, a famous 19th-century English philosopher, claimed, *"We are all scientists."* He reasoned that "the method of scientific investigation is nothing but the necessary mode of working of the human mind." This is what makes SM-14 such a fundamental formula.

Motivation and Self-discovery Hold the Key to Success and Improve the Quality of Human Activity

You can set standards to force people to learn and thus accomplish a little more. But real and continued results depend on proper motivation. With our explosion of knowledge, students and adults must improve their learning to learn skills. One of the basic ways to do this is to use The Scientific Method.

Many studies have shown that students are bored with the usual subject-oriented curricula. They welcome curriculum where inquiry, discovery, methods and self-selection of real life problem solving are included. But it is essential they be taught a formula for the stages of mental activity of the problem solving process.

"Man" is claimed to be a problem solving, skill using, social animal. Allowing self-selection of problems to solve and, a formula to follow such as SM-14, prompt self-discovery of peoples talents, potentials, weaknesses and the motivation of:

Curiosity	Recognition of peers
Thrill of discovery	Mental challenges
Personal well being	Job well done
Social contacts	Desire to know
Competition	Enjoyment of work
Personal values	Love

Finally, no results can be obtained without effort and motivation is the fuel that ignites energy.

"Be endlessly curious — watch for surprises."

Practical Help With Everyday Problems & Decisions

The full SM-14 formula, which you have just read, is usually for complex, ill-structured problems that require research and study. However, problems come in a variety of complexities. Here is a shortened formula:

SM-7 For Intermediate-Type Problems and Decisions

(Can also be used as a preliminary or introduction to teaching the full SM-14 formula)

Stage No.	SM-14 No.	SHORT NAME: SM-7 Short Scientific Method — 7 Stages, Labeled A to G
A	1	*Curious Observation*. Find a problem.
B	2	*Is There A Problem?* Consider purpose, define problem, and estimate requirements to solve problem, all in relation to the time available.
C	4	*Search - Explore*. Review and reflect mentally for solutions. If important enough and time is available, gather evidence as described on Pages 15. Your intuitive base may supply you with answers.
D	5	*Alternative Solutions*. Be sure to devote enough time to generating logical or creative alternative solutions. See pages 17, 38 and 39.
E	6	*Evaluate*. If it is an important problem or decision, you must evaluate, rate, and challenge all possible solutions. Again, memories of past experiences in your intuitive base may be of help.
F	7	*Guess - Hypothesis*. Time may force you to settle for "good enough."
G	11	*Take Action!*

Instantaneous Decisions and Problem Solutions

In the course of a day you make hundreds of simple decisions and problem solutions, usually based on your intuition. They are called by such names as:

Snap judgment	Quick guess	Habit decision
Intuitive decision	Trial and error solution	Instantaneous decision
Leap of understanding	Good enough	Shoot from the hip
Emotional decision	Off the top of your head	Arbitrary guess
Immediate apprehension	Jumping to a conclusion	Hasty decision

Many of these solutions and decisions are really simple, unimportant, and in the habit-type class. Others are of varied importance that you make instantly because of time frames, a good-enough answer will suffice, or you have self-confidence in your intuition. Since some may be important, too many errors can hurt your success, relationships, or reputation. Therefore, it is important to develop your intuition.

"Man is a problem-solving, skill-using, social animal."

Scientific Methods vs.
The Scientific Method

Characteristics	Scientific Methods	The Scientific Method
Name	All problem solving process methods or technical methods	The system of science and the problem solving process in all fields
Purpose	Methods and Techniques for use at the stages of the problem solving process	Guide and system to reliable knowledge in all subject matter areas
Division of Method	Sub-Master, Auxiliary and Action	The Master Method
Stages or Steps	Will vary with specific method	Eleven major stages
Sequential	Yes — some may be rigid	Yes — but highly flexible in use
Repeatable	Yes — but many changing at all times	Yes — Stages unlikely to change
Range	Specific to subject areas	Universal to nature and humans — is subject neutral
Reliability	Depends on method, reliability of some can be expressed as percentage	Best of all knowledge methods or guides
Application & Human Activity	Since specified as "scientific," must be to "standards" of scientific and research communities when applied	Since specified as "scientific," must be to "standards" of scientific and research communities when applied

Scientific Methods

The words "scientific methods," as used today, refer to the creative, non-logical, logical or technical methods or techniques used in the problem solving process such as during the stages of the scientific method. In a strict sense, there are no scientific methods (Popper 1983). In a narrow sense, the only scientific methods are the technical ones that usually involve the use of tools, instruments and apparatus (Wolf 1930). In a wide sense, scientific methods are any type of method used according to the usual high quality of application by scientists. Thus, most problem solving methods used "scientifically" can be called a scientific method (Copi 1982).

The Scientific Method

The term "the scientific method" represents the general pattern of the types of mental activity stages (usually aided by physical activities) that occur in the master method, which we use to obtain, refine, extend and apply knowledge in all fields. Over all, it represents the system of science and the complete problem solving process.

Innovation and Creativity are very important — study the next two pages carefully!

Some Ways to Be Innovative and Creative

The Thinker

Just reflective thinking
8 hours produce 2 good ideas
(1 for each 4 hours)

Group Brainstorming

In a 2-hour session with
4 people, 8 good ideas are produced
(4 for each 4 hours)

SEAGEE

Search
Explore
Alternative Ideas
Gather Evidence
Evaluate
Educated Guess

8 hours produce
16 good ideas
(8 for each 4 hours)

Be More Productive — Trigger Your Mind

- Read, skip and skim publications, search the internet to find existing ideas that can be used "as is" or can be adapted to your needs.
- Find articles, opinions, news and advertisements that stimulate or trigger reflective thinking, imagination, illumination, gradual insight or long-term memory as well as working memory. This produces new ideas, concepts, leads or clues.
- Use library, subject files, telephone, fax machine, computer and discussions with others. Have a continuous learning program.

"You learn to solve problems by solving a large number of problems."

Norm Edmund's Advice on How to
Be More Innovative and Creative

1 **Be a perpetual innovator** — someone who seeks out, adapts and implements ideas — new or old. Actively look for ideas by reading, skipping, skimming through many periodicals, books, reports, catalogs, the internet, etc. Also:

Experiment	Brainstorm	Attend conferences and exhibits
Search files	Have discussions	Use computer idea programs
Travel	Sense felt needs	Browse through stores, etc.

2 **Change your behavior and self-image.** Be progressive, develop necessary attributes and motivation. Develop a love for new ideas, new things, new ways, new technologies, new systems. Put your ideas in writing.

3 **Take action!** Have the courage and self-confidence to be an innovator. Dare to be different! Failure will occur — but we learn from our mistakes. Emotions can aid creativity — control stress. Be persistent.

4 **Welcome change and challenge of problems** — be open-minded, flexible.

5 **Apply ideas** to every facet of your life — in your personal affairs, career, school, business — everywhere. Always ask: In what alternative and better ways can it be done? Generate innovative and creative solutions, ideas, concepts, and theories. Develop a sense of humor. Be sensitive to opportunities. Use checklists.

6 **Study innovation, change and creativity** as well as how to win idea acceptance. Educate yourself. Take any courses available. Develop a passion for your problem. Learn to be a good team member, leader, and perpetual innovator.

7 **Be curious and observant.** Develop a spirit of inquiry. This is the way to originate problems. Practice using the complete method of creative problem solving. Avoid constraints on your thinking. Spot key factors.

8 **Ask What? Why? Which? Where? When? Who? How? If?** Constantly reflect on all aspects of your problems. Don't pre-judge ideas too soon. Don't let your ego stop you from saying, "I goofed!"

9 **Develop your reflective thinking ability and thinking skills.** Daydream about your problem. Jump back and forth among logical, critical, judicial, imaginative, and wild thinking. Improve through study and practice.

10 **Build your knowledge and intuition base** through reading and other activities. Keep neat files. Learn how to research, to visualize.

11 **With a loaded mind, use triggers** to stimulate ideas, insight, and illumination. Utilize activities listed in #1 above to trigger your storehouse of memories and connect with what you read, hear, see, or think, thereby producing ideas by gradual insight or illumination. Be sensitive to opportunities.

12 **Load your mind** with data, basic principles, theories, and concepts about your problem — REST — then be sure to start thinking of your problem again. Gradual insight or a leap of the imagination may occur.

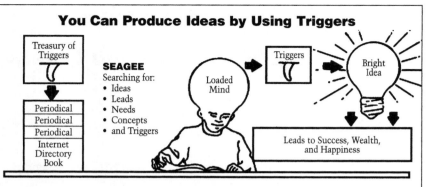

You Can Produce Ideas by Using Triggers

Treasury of Triggers

SEAGEE
Searching for:
• Ideas
• Leads
• Needs
• Concepts
• and Triggers

Periodical
Periodical
Periodical
Internet
Directory
Book

Loaded Mind

Triggers

Bright Idea

Leads to Success, Wealth, and Happiness

(A) Watch for ideas which you can use "as is," or adapt to suit your own needs.

(B) Load your mind with data, principles and concepts related to your problem. Then watch for articles and advertisements containing triggers to set off:
   1. Flash of illumination (leap of imagination).
   2. Reflective thinking leading to gradual insight.

(C) Record idea immediately.

(D) Triggers bring out of long-term memory things not always in working memory.

Try It . . . It Works!

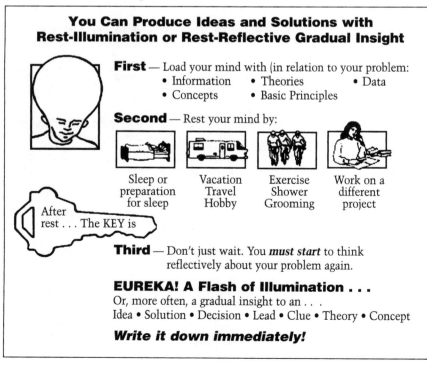

You Can Produce Ideas and Solutions with Rest-Illumination or Rest-Reflective Gradual Insight

First — Load your mind with (in relation to your problem:
   • Information   • Theories   • Data
   • Concepts   • Basic Principles

Second — Rest your mind by:

| Sleep or preparation for sleep | Vacation Travel Hobby | Exercise Shower Grooming | Work on a different project |

After rest . . . The KEY is

Third — Don't just wait. You **must start** to think reflectively about your problem again.

EUREKA! A Flash of Illumination . . .

Or, more often, a gradual insight to an . . .
Idea • Solution • Decision • Lead • Clue • Theory • Concept

Write it down immediately!

Decision Making Is Problem Solving

The stages of decision making and problem solving are the same.

- A decision is basically a problem, so, the stages of decision making are the same as those for problem solving.
- In all stages of problem solving there are constant decisions to be made. Some are so important they become a sub-problem of the main problem.
- Today, the trend in business and industry is to push decision making further down in the organizational chart.
- A leaders job is not only making decisions and solving problems but also seeing that subordinates make correct decisions and solve problems.

Here is a rating scale for problem solvers, decision makers and others. You can make as many copies as you want. Larger size one is available from us.

THE EDMUND RELIABILITY SCALE

Our society is becoming increasingly more complex, team-oriented and adversarial each day. A rating scale such as the one shown below may be of some use. Here is my version of a scale that can be used by a person evaluating his own opinion or conclusion. The scale could also be used by a team leader, scientist, businessman, attorney, judge, juror, etc. to evaluate someone's opinion, testimony, or conclusion hopefully reached by following the stages of the scientific method. By multiplying the raters' own degree of experience in a given subject with the score he/she assesses to an individual's opinion, testimony, conclusion, etc., we can arrive at a total score helpful in determining reliability. You can develop variations of the suggested way to use this scale (shown in reduced size here) or a similar one. **Example:** The numerical units could be interpreted to represent money, time, sales, profit or plans and more. The objective of the scale is to bring method and criteria, hence obtaining reliable ratings.

Rating Scale for:			
Knowledge reliability	Decisions	Theories	Plans
Problem solutions	Testimonies	Criteria	Ideas, etc.

Rater's name and title	Rater's level of experience (CIRCLE)
	LOW 0 1 2 3 4 5 HIGH

WORST   FOR RATING SUBJECT: Circle number you believe applicable   BEST

-10 -9 -8 -7 -6 -5 -4 -3 -2 -1   0 +1 +2 +3 +4 +5 +6 +7 +8 +9 +10

If you rated a 0 please check reason:

❏ Not Sure   ❏ Don't Know   ❏ Neutral   ❏ No Effect

Subject	Date	Score
		_____ X _____ = _____
		Rater's level of experience $\times$ subject's rating = overall score

Establish your own criteria to Overall Score — for example:

Plus Scores: 1 to 16 = C (Average)   17 to 32 = B (Above Average)   33 to 50 = A (Excellent)

0 Scores: Not Sure, Don't Know, Neutral, No Effect

Minus Scores: Indicate degree of failure, unreliability, inaccuracy, disaster, etc.

SM-14 Is Also The Method of Invention and Creativity

While researching, I found only one large survey pertaining to the method of inquiry, discovery, invention, and creativity—which was in Joseph Rossman's excellent book, *Industrial Creativity* (1930). While the survey is an old one, the basics have remained the same. This survey questioned 710 inventors (inventing is, after all, one of the many forms of use of SM-14), asking them to state what methods they followed while inventing. Rossman's careful analysis reduced their inventing procedures to the list in the left-hand column below. The right-hand column contains the SM-14 stages and ingredients. Note the similarities!

Rossman's Survey — Method of Invention (1930)	Compare to the SM-14 Formula
1. Observation of need or difficulty	1. Curious Observation
2. Analysis of the need	2. The Problem 3. Goals, Planning
3. Survey of all available information	4. Search — Explore
4. Formulation of all objective solutions	5. Alternate Solutions
5. Critical analysis of these solutions for their advantages and disadvantages	6. Evaluate Evidence
6. Birth of the new idea-the invention	7. Guess — Hypothesis
7. Experimentation to test the most promising solution; the selection and perfection of the final embodiment by some or all of the previous steps	8. Challenge Hypothesis 9. Reach Conclusion 10. Suspend Judgment
Inventors left "Take Action" as understood.	11. Take Action
SM-14 includes these as important supporting ingredients, especially valuable for teaching ⟶	12. Methods 13. Procedural Principles 14. Attributes — Thinking

Current Osborn-Parnes Process

Objective Finding
Fact Finding
Problem Finding
Idea Finding
Solution Finding
Acceptance Finding

Creative Problem-Solving Process Sponsored by Creative Education Foundation

The formula to the left evolved from the one that Osborn originated and included in the first edition of *Applied Imagination* in 1953. A revised edition of this excellent book is still in print (available from CEF). All problem-solving methods are just variations of the centuries old scientific method. This variation is better than most, as it stresses both finding problems and creative idea finding. As a result of the Creative Education Foundation's efforts, it has been used in thousands of seminars and classes and has been included in hundreds of books. If you will compare this formula to SM-14 (above right column), you will note that SM-14 is more complete and the terminology is more explanatory. As part of standardization, I recommend that everyone interested in creative problem solving use the SM-14 terminology.

Scientific Management

There has been a great deal of misunderstanding about what scientific management and the management sciences really are. These two concepts depend upon the proper use of the scientific method (SM-14), which is basically a complete method of creative problem solving and decision making.

Taylorism is not scientific management!

Frederick W. Taylor pioneered and introduced many management concepts. He is credited with being "The Father of Scientific Management" for his work started in the late 1800's. Many believe that Scientific Management consists of the concepts about time and motion study, he introduced. Study has proven, though, that he merely applied his version of the scientific method for originating problems and for solutions, thus arriving at his conclusions or hypotheses. Scientific Management should not be restricted to any one person's concept or approach to it, or to any one phase of management. It depends on the proper use of the scientific method.

Imperfect, But Still A "Phenomenally Successful Process"

Applying the scientific method (SM-14) to management is imperfect because the human element is always present and because things in the social sciences are less exact than in the natural sciences but is far superior to such ways and processes as:

Hunch or gut instinct	Seat of pants	Doing your "thing"
Haphazard guess	Uneducated guess	Applying existing knowledge
Common sense	Rule of thumb	Outdated intuition
Superficial analysis	Trial and error	Pig in the poke
Management by exception	Chaos	"We always do it that way"
Walk-around management	Fad of the day	Quick fix

While the application of SM-14 is far superior to the above, there are times when some of these serve a useful purpose (trial and error is always a basic way to progress). Proper use of SM-14, however, should prevent many failures due to poor hunches and guesses, quick fixes, and applying the fad of the day.

Management Science

To have a "science," you must basically have a domain or sub-domain with a group of practitioners applying the scientific method to their research to obtain, refine, extend and apply knowledge. The conclusions reached must be communicated, published in professional journals thus being subjected to peer review with the aim of providing a systematic organized reliable body of knowledge.

Summary

Thus, the basic principle is that to manage scientifically, you must:
- be familiar with the management sciences,
- apply these to your work, and
- to follow the stages of the scientific method and its supporting ingredients on complex problems and decisions.

Your Guide and Worksheet for Applying The Complete Method of Creative Problem Solving and Decision Making (SM-14)

Stages or Ingredients of SM-14*	Space for Comments and Notes Provided Below Method or guide keeps our thoughts en route to new reliable knowledge.
1. Curious Observation 	Be alert—What is needed? Be skeptical—Prevent trouble. Discover problems. Ask why?
2. Is There a Problem? Present in form of question	Analyze problem carefully, as Einstein stated: "A problem properly defined is often half-solved."
3. Goals and Planning 	Break problem down into sub-problems. Consider any solutions as tentative till complete Stage 6.
4. Search, Explore, and Gather the Evidence 	Search Internet, books, and other sources. Follow leads. Explore all angles. Build files.
5. Generate Creative and Logical Alternative Solutions 	Search for ideas, read publications to trigger your imagination. Think reflectively.
6. Evaluate the Evidence 	If possible, chart evaluations of your tentative solutions or theories. Compare and test.

*Use shaded stages for less complex and less important problems and decisions.

(Continued)

44

7. Make the Educated Guess (Hypothesis) $Y = x^2 \div 2$ $E = mc^2$	
	State your working hypothesis explicitly. Make predictions for testing.
8. Challenge the Hypothesis	
	Test. Experiment. Control variables. Attempt to falsify.
9. Reach a Conclusion	
	Can others test and confirm your conclusions?
10. Suspend Judgment KEEP AN OPEN MIND	
	Keep an open mind and be ready to accept new evidence. Knowledge is forever changing.
11. Take Action REPORT	
	Submit your theory to peer review or take other appropriate action.

Below are the Supporting Ingredients used at all the preceeding stages of SM-14

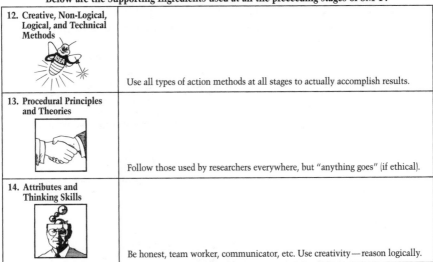

12. Creative, Non-Logical, Logical, and Technical Methods IDEA	
	Use all types of action methods at all stages to actually accomplish results.
13. Procedural Principles and Theories	
	Follow those used by researchers everywhere, but "anything goes" (if ethical).
14. Attributes and Thinking Skills	
	Be honest, team worker, communicator, etc. Use creativity — reason logically.

*Use shaded stages for less complex and less important problems and decisions. 1998 Norman W. Edmund

Pricing and Ordering Information

Quanity	Price	S&H	Total Cost	Stock #

The Scientific Method Today.
2000 edition. Size 5½" x 8½". 48 pages. ISBN 0-9632866-5-X

Quanity	Price	S&H	Total Cost	Stock #
1 to 5	$3.00 each	$1.00	$4.00 each	Stock #5
10	$24.00 pkg.	$3.85	$27.85 pkg.	Stock #6
25 to 100	$2.00 each	You pay	100 or more, call for price	

Spanish and French Editions Available September 2000. Translate TSM into your language. Contact us.

Student Edition: The General Pattern of The Scientific Method,
1994 edition. Size 5½" x 8½". 48 pages. ISBN 0-9632866-3-3

Quanity	Price	S&H	Total Cost	Stock #
1	$3.00 each	Postpaid	$3.00 each	Stock #1

Edmund's Ideas and Research Report on The General Pattern of The Scientific Method. 1994 edition. Size 8½" x 11". 48 pages. ISBN 0-9632866-4-1

For Educators, Researchers, etc.— Important information about the need, advantages and uses for the scientific method; pages on scientific management, thinking and thinking skills, need to teach method and misunderstanding about the method.

Quanity	Price	S&H	Total Cost	Stock #
1 to 3	$5.00 each	$1.45	$6.45 each	Stock #8
5	$22.50 pkg.	$3.85	$26.35 pkg.	Stock #9
25 to 100	$3.33 each	You pay	100 or more, call for price	

Your Guide and Worksheet for Applying The Complete Method of Creative Problem Solving and Decision Making (SM-14).
Size 8½" x 11" double sided. Package of 100.

Quanity	Price	S&H	Total Cost	Stock #
1	$8.00 pkg.	$3.85	$11.85 pkg.	Stock #10

Save on Combination Package
- One copy of **The Scientific Method Today**, 2000 edition
- One copy of **Edmund's Ideas and Research Report on The General Pattern of the Scientific Method**
- Five copies of **Your Guide and Worksheet for Applying The Complete Method of Creative Problem Solving and Decision Making (SM-14)**
- PLUS . . . One full size printed evaluation scale for duplication purposes

Quanity	Price	S&H	Total Cost	Stock #
1	$7.20 pkg.	$1.80	$9.00 pkg.	Stock #11

Other Reports on The Scientific Method are available. For inquires write or call.

Fast Delivery: Orders Shipped 1st Class Mail. Shipment outside USA requires additional postage. Florida residents add sales tax.

How to Order: Send check or purchase order (in US funds only) to Publisher:
Norman W. Edmund
407 Northeast 3rd Avenue
Fort Lauderdale, FL 33301-3233

Telephone: 954-525-7327 • Fax: 954-525-7459
Email: nwe@scientificmethod.com

About the Author

Edmund has not made an original discovery but only has re-discovered an old tried and workable one. He has been able to do what no one else has done—make a better evaluation and condensation of what the scientific method really is and then present it in a more comprehensive form that's easier to learn and teach.

Professor Ritchie Calder in *Science in our Lives* (1962) states: "A great discovery depends on three things—The Method—The Man—The Moment."

The Moment

Today we are in the "Age of Knowledge." Now is the moment to bring rationality to our understanding of the method of knowledge—The Scientific Method.

The Man

Norman Wilson Edmund was born in Boston, Massachusetts in 1916 and moved to Camden, NJ, in 1920 As a boy Edmund was an avid reader, newspaper boy, and Boy Scout. He studied self-improvement and was voted "most studious" in junior and high school. Upon graduation from high school in 1935, during the depression, he enrolled in evening course at the Wharton School at the University of Pennsylvania. Graduating in 1939, he won the same award he had received at high school graduation—"Most Outstanding for the Combination of Scholarship and Extra-curricular Activities."

Immediately after graduation, a serious illness forced him to spend two years in the hospital. Back to health at the age of 25, he was again living with his parents when his creativity and entrepreneurial spirit surfaced. In March of 1942, he started a mail order business selling kits of lenses. His office was a card table in his bedroom. He added prisms, war surplus optical items, telescopes and scientific items. Soon, thousands of experimentally inclined individuals and all the major research labs and universities were buying his products. Each month, he read 200 periodicals looking for ideas.

Upon retirement in 1975, his bedroom office was now a 68,000 square-foot plant.

Years followed with leisurely life in Florida, where he spent his days yachting and fishing. Then in 1989 he gave it all up to research The Scientific Method.

The Method

In researching the nature of The Scientific Method, Edmund's high degree of creativity was now self serving. He used the scientific method process to explore what the method was—i.e. the science of science, sometimes called methodology, philosophy of science or epistemology. The thinking skills he had acquired from being an avid reader, perpetual student, and the experience from his 35-year career of being the top problem-solver at Edmund Scientific, had prepared him for this quest.

Therefore, without any hesitation, I highly recommend that you seize this unique opportunity to acquaint yourself with The Scientific Method (SM-14) formula as expounded in this booklet.

J. Raymond Parent, *past vice-president,*
André-Laurendeau College, Lasalle. Québec, Canada

Praise of SM-14 Formula . . .

"Your proposal to teach SM-14 not only to young scientists but also as part of general education is excellent, and I wish you success."

— Dr. W.I.B. Beveridge, author of the famous and often cited books, *The Art of Scientific Investigation* (1957) and *Seeds of Discovery* (1980)

Praise earned by The Scientific Method . . .

"It has often been said that the greatest discovery in science was the discovery of the scientific method of discovery." — Dr. James K. Feibleman, author of *Scientific Method* (1972)

"The greatest invention of the nineteenth century was the invention of the method of invention."

— A.N. Whitehead (1926)

The Greatest Idea of All Times . . . *A Historic Presentation—*

From Bacon and Descartes in the 17th century, and from numerous other great minds of the 18th, 19th, and 20th centuries, The Scientific Method Today brings you the most reliable knowledge of the scientific method ever summarized in one publication.

Norman W. Edmund
407 Northeast 3rd Avenue
Fort Lauderdale, FL 33301-3233

Price $3.00 (U.S. funds)
ISBN 0-9632866-5-X
Printed in United States of America

Index